Slavery and the Culture of Taste

Slavery *and the*
Culture *of* Taste

Simon Gikandi

PRINCETON UNIVERSITY PRESS   PRINCETON AND OXFORD

Copyright © 2011 by Princeton University Press

Published by Princeton University Press, 41 William Street, Princeton, New Jersey 08540

In the United Kingdom: Princeton University Press, 6 Oxford Street,
Woodstock, Oxfordshire OX20 1TW

press.princeton.edu

Library of Congress Cataloging-in-Publication Data

Gikandi, Simon.
Slavery and the culture of taste / Simon Gikandi.
  p. cm.
Includes bibliographical references and index.
ISBN 978-0-691-14066-7 (hardcover : acid-free paper) 1. Slavery in literature.
2. Slavery—Moral and ethical aspects. I. Title.
PN56.S5765G55 2011
306.3'6209033–dc22   2011007380

British Library Cataloging-in-Publication Data is available

This book has been composed in Sabon and Pelican

Printed on acid-free paper. ∞

Printed in the United States of America

10 9 8 7 6 5 4 3 2

For my beloved children:

Samani Gakure Gikandi,
Ajami-Halisi Simon Gikandi,
Halima-Rakiya Wanjiku Gikandi

Contents

Preface

Epigraphs

Where are your monuments, your battles, martyrs?
Where is your tribal memory? Sirs,
In that gray vault. The sea. The sea
Has locked them up. The sea is History.
  —Derek Walcott, "The Sea Is History"

I start with Derek Walcott's poem because there is a sense in which this book is about the interlaced experiences of the enslaved—those people without monumental histories, battles, martyrs, or tribal memories—and those others, the cultured subjects of modernity, whose lives are available to us through the monuments and institutions of European civilization—what I call the culture of taste.[1] This book is about the encounter between these two groups of modern subjects across the Atlantic, the sea that in our modern times connected the enslaved and their enslavers. But although the book spends considerable time sketching both the visible and invisible connections of two social practices or realms of experience that have been kept apart so that they can continue to do their cultural work, separately and unequally, it started as an almost casual reflection on the gray vault in which common histories are encrypted.

The informing epigraph, or even epitaph, to this project came from an idea, or at least the fragment of a thought, once encountered in the middle of Nicolas Abraham and Maria Torok's "Mourning and Melancholia": What are we to make of those experiences and losses that cannot be acknowledged because they seem to be at odds with the narrative of modern identity and must hence be encased in an "interpsychic tomb"?[2] What are we to make of those events that cannot be visibly celebrated as part of our Western identity, because they seem to be at odds with its informing categories, and yet cannot be mourned, because to do so would contaminate the modes of our self-understanding as civilized subjects? This book is not about celebration or mourning; rather, it is an allegorical reading of spaces of repression in the making of the visible or invisible world. I seek to recover transatlantic slavery, often confined to the margins of the modern world picture, as one of the informing conditions of civilized culture; my goal is to find a language for reading what lies buried in the crypt, what survives in the "secret tomb" of modern subjectivity. In the crypt, note Abraham and Torok, "A whole world of unconscious fantasy is created, one that leads its own separate and concealed existence. Sometimes in the dead of the night, when libidinal fulfillments have their way, the ghost of the crypt comes back to haunt the cemetery guard, giving him strange and incomprehensible signals, making him perform bizarre acts, or subjecting him to unexpected sensations."[3]

Working through the crypt of empire, this book was generated by the need to understand the ghosts lying in the crypts of the black and white Atlantic and the desire to fashion a method for reading the ghostly inside the symbolic economy of civility and civilization. Indeed, the genealogy of this project can be traced to an encounter I had with an early 1700 painting of James Drummond, famous Jacobite and presumptuous Earl of Perth, by the Flemish Scottish painter Sir John Baptiste de Medina (fig. 0.1). James Drummond was recognized as a leading figure in the Scottish Jacobite court in exile in France; he was closely associated with the rebellion to secure the throne for James Stewart, the pretender. Drummond, who became the Duke of Perth in 1716, did not captivate me because of any desire to understand the politics of the English succession or the Jacobite movement in Scotland, which I discovered from the novels of Sir Walter Scott as a student at the University of Edinburgh. What fascinated me about Medina's portrait was, first, Drummond's grandiose pose and, second, what appeared to be its dark counterpoint. In Medina's painting, the sharp colors associated with the Baroque (and a palpable sense of and theatricality) present the viewer with the portrait of the Jacobite as a young man—tall, well shaped, and dressed in armor. This was the pose of power.

In itself, this pose was not unusual. The use of armor as an insignia for the warrior king or prince, or the deployment of bright colors to depict the grandiose nature of the powerful can be detected in paintings of the British court since the early modern period. Famous examples of this pose of power include Sir Anthony van Dyck's portraits of Charles I on horseback. What was different in Medina's portrait of Drummond was

0.1 Sir John Baptiste de Medina, *James Drummond, 2nd titular Duke of Perth, 1673–1720*. Jacobite, about 1700. National Galleries of Scotland, Edinburgh.

the addition of a black boy, a slave with the collar of bondage around his neck, as a supplement to the sign of power and prestige. The inclusion of the slave in the portrait of the Jacobite as a young man raised some disturbing questions: Why would Drummond, a symbol of the Catholic insurrection against the Protestant establishment, seek to inscribe an enslaved boy in his family portrait? What aura did this figure, undoubtedly the quintessential sign of blackness in bondage, add to the symbolism of white power? What libidinal desires did the black slave represent? What was the relation of this blackness, confined to the margin of the modern world picture and placed in a state of subjection, to the man of power with his hand on his hip? And how were we to read this diminished, yet not unattractive, blackness in relation to the center embodied by the wig and armor? And where was one to draw the line between the gesture of incorporation and dissociation?

Walking through the archive of empire and the colonial library, I discovered, as have other scholars before me, that the juxtaposition of such scenes—and the interpretative questions that they raise—was not unusual. Indeed, as I worked on this project, trying to make connections that I initially thought existed on an experiential level and were simply denied or repressed by the institutions of interpretation, it occurred to me that the strange and incomprehensible signs of a black presence in the making of high culture often tended to slip away, not because of the invisibility of the enslaved but because the construction of the ideals of modern civilization demanded the repression of what it had introjected—the experience or phenomenon that it had unconsciously assimilated. I was thus drawn to the meaning of those imaginative figures that were essential to modern self-understanding yet needed to be quarantined from the culture of modernity so that the civilizing process could continue. Cultural or conceptual quarantines seemed to be necessitated by the common belief that the black, as unmodern, was either a source of shame or a toxin that threatened the well-being of civilization. What surprised me in the end, however, was the discovery that the world of the enslaved was not simply the submerged and concealed counterpoint of modern civilization; rather, what made the body of the slave repellant—its ugliness and dirt—was also what provided the sensations and the guilty pleasures of modern life.

Hypothesis and Premises

My basic hypothesis in this book is that both the institution of slavery and the culture of taste were fundamental in the shaping of modern identity, and that they did so not apart but as nonidentical twins, similar yet different. I will show how, in this dialectic of identity and difference, slavery and taste came to be intimately connected even when they were structurally construed to be radical opposites; they would function as what Mary Douglas would call "rituals of purity and impurity" that nevertheless create "unity in experience."[4] For Douglas, reflections on dirt and impurity are also commentaries "on the relation of order to disorder, being to nonbeing, form to formlessness, life to death."[5] Often posited as a moral stain on modern identity, slavery could inform and haunt almost all attempts to construct a transcendental set of categories in areas as diverse as moral philosophy, law, aesthetics, and political economy. But for reasons that I explain in the first two chapters, my focus will be on the introjection of slavery into the realm of manners, civility, sense and sensibility.

The central arguments I present in each of the chapters—and their mode of presentation—will constantly call attention to both the structural connection and disconnection of slavery and the culture of taste. A central thesis of this book is that slavery and the culture of taste were connected by the theories and practices that emerged in the modern period; but I will not argue that they expressively enabled each other in a synchronic structure. On the contrary, I intend to show that these two experiences, though occupying opposite ends of the cultural spectrum, were, in their functions and affect, processes that took place at the same time in the same space and hence need to be studied in what Edward Said has called a "contrapuntal manner" and considered within the economy of what Fredric Jameson terms "expressive causality," the process by which "two distinct regions of social life," even when structurally unconnected, can still be considered to be part of "some general identity" especially at the phenomenological level.[6]

My goal in this book is not to show that the culture of taste and African slavery enabled each other or that enslavement and the ideals of high culture existed in binary opposition. Where evidence warrants it, as in the case studies I provide in the middle chapters, slavery and taste will be shown to have had an undeniable causal relation. In other instances, this relation will be much more discreet and indirect, hence demanding an analogical rather than historical approach. There will be moments of this book when the link between slavery and taste will inevitably appear tenuous; this is especially the case in the first two parts of the book, where I do not seek to establish direct or self-evident connections. What I set out to provide is not evidence from the archives but an allegory of reading, an exploration of the tropes and figures that often point, or lead, to sublimated connections. There are, however, key instances when slavery and taste existed as clear and undeniable binary oppositions. In the American and West Indian colonies, for example, ideals of taste could not be imagined or be secured except in opposition to a negative sensorium associated with slavery. In these cases, my interest is in how this relationship was structured and in the cultural politics that this binary demanded or generated.

Each of the six chapters in this book is informed by an interplay of slavery and the culture of taste as domains of difference and identity. The first chapter serves as an overture to the whole project, reflecting on the character and shape of sensibility in the age of slavery. Here, I explore how ideas and ideals about taste and beauty demanded powerful counterpoints built around notions of black difference. Focusing on British debates on the question of taste and the role of culture in the shaping of

modern identity and the reality of enslavement and its objects, I use this
chapter to reflect on how some of the most important ideas of bourgeois
culture—namely, art and freedom—were mapped and haunted by their
contaminating danger, manifestly represented by the racialized black
body. I also use this chapter to locate my work within changing debates
on empire and the symbolic economy of slavery.

Chapter 2 moves beyond the critical debates raised in chapter 1 to
provide a more concrete narrative of the coexistence of taste and slavery
as aesthetic objects and products of everyday life in the modern world.
Here, I explore the link between slavery, consumption, and the culture of
taste, all-important conduits for understanding modern identity. With a
particular emphasis on changing theories of taste in eighteenth-century
Britain, I provide an analysis or reading of the troubled relation between
race, ideologies of taste, and the culture of consumption. I explore how
slavery enabled the moment of taste; led to fundamental transformations
in the self-understanding of modern subjects; and, consequently, resulted
in a redefinition of notions of freedom, selfhood, and representation.

Having made the case that slavery informed key ideas on what it meant
to be a man or woman of taste in the eighteenth century, I use the middle
chapters of the book to make a more explicit link between the concept
and practice of taste, within the British tradition, and the political economy of West Indian and American slavery. In chapter 3 I present two
instances of how slave money shaped the moment of taste in both pragmatic and conceptual terms. I provide a substantive exploration of the
cultural traffic between Britain and its colonial outposts in order to show
how the experience of slavery was turned into an aesthetic object that
was woven into the fabric of everyday life. I then seek to connect slave
money and the power and prestige of art by focusing on the aesthetic
lives of William Beckford and Christopher Codrington, famous heirs to
slave fortunes, who sought to remake their social standing through the
patronage of art and the mastery of taste.

In Chapter 4, I turn to the relationship between the violence of slavery
and the culture of conduct within the geography of enslavement itself.
Here, I reflect on the status of art and taste in the heart of American
slavery. I argue that although members of the American plantocracy in
Virginia (William Byrd and Thomas Jefferson, for example) sought to
fashion their lives after those of British gentry, they could not separate
themselves from the concrete materiality of plantation slavery. How,
then, could a culture of taste be cultivated in the presence of a thriving
slave economy? At the center of this chapter is the inescapable relation
between the planters' striving for high culture and the deployment of
violence as a mode of containing what was considered to be the danger
of Africa. Africa and Africans enabled the wealth of the planter, but they

needed to be exorcized so that white civilization could take hold in the new world.

Slavery simultaneously challenged and informed some of the central tenets of modern life; it presented a fundamental challenge to the redemptive capacity of art and taste; yet, as I show in chapters 5 and 6, African slaves in the Americas recognized the extent to which their own sense of selfhood depended on the cultivation of cultural spaces outside the regimen of enforced work and truncated leisure. The last two chapters of the book provide a study of the slaves' own response to their evacuation from the realm of taste and modern identity. Some famous former slaves like Olaudah Equiano and Phillis Wheatley sought to master and appropriate the culture of taste itself, but the slaves who interest me in these two chapters are those who sought to develop what I call a counterculture of taste—those subjects who rejected the notions of order, rationality, and proper conduct that appealed to their masters—and created a cultural underground in what Frantz Fanon was later to term "the zone of occult instability" (*déséquilibre occulte*).[7]

A Note on Method

While this work draws on various disciplines—history, philosophy, art history, aesthetics, and literary criticism—and has arguments with scholars in all of them, it is essentially a work of cultural criticism. It is not intended to be a monograph on eighteenth-century social history, the history of modern art, or aesthetic theory. From a historical perspective, my point of reference is the eighteenth century, because that is the age in which slavery and the culture of taste emerged and transformed the cultural landscape of Britain and the Americas. I spend considerable time in the archive of empire in the eighteenth century, because it was in that period when broad questions about taste and slavery became issues for intellectual debate. It was in the age of Enlightenment that slavery appeared to be anachronistic to how modern Europeans imagined themselves and their society. It is in the archive of the period that one could come across figures such as William Beckford regarded as elevated men of taste and patrons of the culture of consumption in England and then read about major slave revolts—for the planter class, the ultimate expression of African barbarism—taking place in their Jamaican plantations.

If the structure of this book appears bifurcated, it is because it is addressed to two audiences, both focused on the same object of analysis—cultures of empire—yet with divergent goals, terms of reference, and methodologies. For students of modern British culture, especially those invested powerfully in the aesthetic and the literary as the mark of cultural achievement, I think there is something useful to be learned about the cultural traffic between the plantations of Jamaica or the antebellum South and the emergence of forms of cultural expressions such as the Gothic. Was it incidental that the authors of two of the most important English Gothic novels, William Beckford (*Vathek*) and Matthew Gregory Lewis (*The Monk*), were both heirs to West Indian plantations and absentee slave masters? Even when the nature of the exact link between West Indian slavery and forms of Englishness might be debatable and should be debated, it is still important to know that the Coromantee rebellion that started in Ballard Beckford's frontier plantation in St. Mary's County, Jamaica, in 1760, transformed the language of Gothic. How colonial events entered the idiom of ordinary Englishness is one of the many concepts this book seeks to understand.

For students of slave culture and the black Atlantic, already the subject of an immense archive, my goal was to cross the historical and social boundaries that have come to characterize studies of the enslaved. Indeed one of the virtues of the broadly cultural-studies approach I adopt here is that it provides me with the freedom to move across the vast landscape of slavery at a time when the immensity of the archive of enslavement has forced scholars to specialize in even narrower regions and periods. My book moves from the West African coast to Scotland, from the West Indies to the antebellum South and, occasionally, to Brazil and Argentina. I adopt this wide-angled approach both to underscore the existence of African slavery as a perversely unique global phenomenon and to provide a thick description for what was supposed to be absent in its theaters of action: an aesthetic experience among the enslaved.

Finally, let me note that the style of this book and the mode of presentation I adopt are as important as the argument that I present. As my first two chapters indicate, I want to tell stories about two traditions that are often kept apart, and in order to do so, I interpolate and juxtapose experiences, eschewing linear structures and chronologies. Quite often, I dislocate categories and experiences in order to defamiliarize our understanding of modern culture. In other cases, I recover older terminologies, such as phenomenology, in order to redirect attention to experiences that are easily elided in the name of antiessentialism. Above all, I read slavery not simply as a shameful episode in modern culture and a sign of moral failure, but as a caesura, a point of division in the narrative of modernity, not a break from it. Here, slavery will be explored in its powerful and painful materiality, but it will also be read, in its figural or semiotic sense, as the sign of the social and moral boundaries that made modern culture possible, signaling who belonged and who was excluded, yet pointing to the ways in which inclusion and exclusion informed each other.

Acknowledgments

This book took a long time to write and, given its historical and geographic reach, depended on the expertise of both friends and strangers. An invitation by Linda Gregerson to give a talk at the Early Modern Seminar at the University of Michigan in 1997 gave rise to my initial thoughts on the relation between the institution of slavery and the culture of taste. I would like to thank Linda for inviting me to think of difference outside my period, and Valerie Traub, who wanted me to go even further back in time. My former colleagues at the University of Michigan created the interdisciplinary conditions in which this project was conceived. The late Lemuel Johnson was perhaps my most important interlocutor, and his resistance to my ideas often led me in productive directions. Larry Goldstein published an early version of what became chapter 2 in the *Michigan Quarterly Review*, and I thank him for his enthusiastic support. Ifeoma Nwankwo invited me back to Michigan to continue conversations about slavery and the making of modern culture with members of the Atlantic Studies Program and was instrumental in a later invitation to Vanderbilt University. I would like to take this opportunity to thank her for her collegiality and friendship.

Early fragments of the book were presented as lectures or seminar papers at the University of Wisconsin–Madison, at the invitation of Susan Stanford Friedman and Neil Whitehead, and at the University of London, where my friend Mpalive Msiska provided me with a forum for enlightened conversations. The middle (American) sections of the book were written during my membership in a working group on slavery and representation at Yale University's Gilder Lehrman Center for the Study of Slavery, Resistance, and Abolition. I am grateful to Deborah McDowell, John Stauffer, and David Blight for convening the working group. At the

Yale workshop and later at Rutgers, Mia Bay provided me with important guidance in the area of historical investigation.

Versions of the last part of the book benefited from the intervention of individuals and groups at several institutions where I was invited to share my research. Members of the postcolonial working group at Royal Holloway College nudged me to think about the meaning of slavery in the culture of the present, and I would like to thank Helen Gilbert and Elleke Boehmer for their hospitality and David Lambert for directing me to new work in the geography of the Atlantic world. At the University of Rostock, at a conference convened under the auspices of the Institute for English and American Studies, Gesa Makenthun and Raphael Hörmann provided me with an opportunity to rethink the relation between the aesthetic and forms of bonded labor. Jay Clayton invited me to Vanderbilt University, where conversations with Ifeoma Nwankwo, Colin Dayan, Houston Baker, and Hortense Spillers pushed me in new directions. At the University of Minnesota, I had the privilege to present a version of the last chapter of the moment thanks to the efforts of Jani Scandura and her colleagues.

The careful, sustained, and substantive reading of three tough anonymous readers immensely enriched this book. While I may have disagreed with some of their responses, I benefited from all of their criticism and thank them profusely for the energies they put into the book. At Princeton University, my chairs, Michael Wood and Claudia Johnson, created the ideal conditions for writing this kind of book, and their generosity and support enabled me to complete the work in a time of change and transition.

At Princeton University Press, Hanne Winasky, with the able assistance of Adithi Kasturirangan and Christopher Chung, nurtured the book through what appeared to be a long process, and I thank her for her professionalism and friendship. Kathleen Cioffi guided the book through the production process with professionalism and care. Many thanks to Jill R. Hughes for copyediting the manuscript meticulously and for respecting my style. Sonya Posmentier was an invaluable research assistant. Valerie Smith and Abiola Irele provided me with unconditional friendship and intellectual mentorship, and my debts to both are immeasurable. My family lived with this book for so long that they cannot imagine a time when it didn't exist. Juandamarie Gikandi provided me with the comforts of home that made it all possible. I thank my children, Samani, Ajami, and Halima Gikandi, for bearing life under the shadow of the book, and I dedicate this work to them with love and devotion.

Slavery and the Culture of Taste

1.1 Harmenszoon van Rijn Rembrandt, *Two Negroes.* 1661.

Overture:
Sensibility in the Age of Slavery

Sometime around 1659, the Dutch painter Harmenszoon van Rijn Rembrandt sat in his studio in Amsterdam and commenced work on *Two Negroes* (fig. 1.1), considered one of the most compelling paintings of the last phase of his illustrious career. Working with African models and operating within a Dutch culture whose domestic economy was driven by the slave trade, Rembrandt sought to turn his black figures, people who most probably had arrived in the European Low Countries as slaves or servants, into elevated subjects through art. This gesture—the transformation of the most marginal figures in society into elevated works of art—was most evident in Rembrandt's keen sense of the contrast between the two African models. This difference was crucial because it implicitly questioned the undifferentiated image of the black as fetish or stereotype that was dominant in the records of Dutch travelers at the end of the seventeenth century and the beginning of the eighteenth century. Rembrandt's Africans were certainly not the generalized villains that agents of the Dutch slave interests were observing on the West African coast—"all without exception, Crafty, Villainous, and Fraudulent," according to William Bosman.[1] On the contrary, these portraits were elevated to a position, common in the early modern period, in which blackness was associated with dignity, decency, and virtue, if not equality.[2] We don't, of course, actually know who the men in the picture were, nor where they came from, but for students of the African image in the European imagination, *Two Negroes* had fulfilled a key tenet in theories of the aesthetic: the painter had used his genius to reclaim the human from the detritus of enslavement. Art had "ennobled this humanity."[3]

In the same year that Rembrandt was ennobling the black in the aesthetic sphere, affirming the humanity of the African in unmistakable and unequivocal terms, the Dutch merchant Pedro Diez Troxxilla wrote a receipt for the slaves he had received from Matthias Beck, governor of Curaçao:

> I, underwritten, hereby acknowledge to have received from the Hon'ble Matthias Beck, governor over the Curaçao Islands, sixty two slaves, old and young, in fulfillment and performance of the contract concluded on the 26th June, A'o 1659, by Messrs. Hector Pieters and Guillaume Momma, with the Lords Directors at the Chamber at Amsterdam; and as the negroes by the ship *Coninck Salomon* were disposed of, long before the arrival of the undersigned, and the ship *Eyckenboom*, mentioned in the aforesaid contract, has not arrived at this date, the said governor has accommodated me, the undersigned, to the best of his ability with the abovementioned sixty two slaves, and on account of the old and young which are among the aforesaid negroes, has allowed a deduction of two negroes, so that there remain sixty head in the clear, for which I, the undersigned, have here according to contract paid to the governor aforesaid for forty six head, at one hundred and twenty pieces of eight, amounting to five thousand five hundred and twenty pieces of eight. Wherefore, fourteen negroes remain still to be paid for, according to contract in Holland by Messrs. Hector Pieters and Guillaume Momma in Amsterdam, to Messrs. the directors aforesaid, on presentation of this my receipt, to which end three of the same tenor are executed and signed in the presence of two undersigned trustworthy witnesses, whereof the one being satisfied the others are to be void. Curaçao in Fort Amsterdam, the 11th January, A'o 1660. It being understood that the above fourteen negroes, to be paid for in Amsterdam, shall not be charged higher than according to contract at two hundred and eighty guilders each, amounting together to three thousand nine hundred and twenty Carolus guilders.[4]

The receipt was more than the customary acknowledgment of goods received; it was also a detailed inventory of objects of trade and the geography in which they were exchanged. And this correspondence, dated June 1659, can be read as a sample of the functional idiom of what would come to be known, in the verbal trickery of euphemism and understatement, as "The African Trade," a triangular commerce joining the industrial centers of Europe, Africa, and the Americas. What made this trade unique in the history of the modern world was that its primary commodity was black bodies, sold and bought to provide free labor to the plantation complexes of the new world, whose primary products— coffee, sugar, tobacco—were needed to satiate the culture of taste and the civilizing process.[5] In this triangle, African bodies mediated the complex relations between slave traders like Troxxilla, colonial governors such as Beck, and the unnamed but powerful directors of the Amsterdam Chamber of Commerce.

Here, then, are the startling contrasts that will initiate my meditation on the relation between slavery and the culture of taste: on one hand, we have the work of art endowing aura to some of the humblest subjects in a modern polity; on the other hand, we have these same people reduced to mere objects of trade. Like the other great works of the major Baroque painters of the period—Diego Velasquez and Peter Paul Rubens, for example—Rembrandt's painting was unique for placing Africans at the center of the frame of the picture and not confining them to borders as was the case in the worlds of an earlier generation of European court painters, including Anthony van Dyck's portrait paintings.[6] But the recognition of the African as a figure worthy of representation in painting was often at odds with the perception of Africans as objects of trade, the primary conception that was making its way into the prosaic discourse of the time, often in the form of official correspondence, decrees, or so-called accurate accounts of Guinea. In the prose of the period, the slaves who had become the cog around which trade and social relationships revolved were conceived as mute and invisible objects, available to their interlocutors only as synecdoche, parts standing for the whole, subject to monetary additions and deductions, valued solely in terms of guilders, or, in the English case, guineas.

On the surface, Troxxilla and the members of the Amsterdam Chamber of Commerce may not seem to have anything to do with the works of one of the most distinguished painters from the Low Countries in the Baroque period. And for modern connoisseurs of art, Troxxilla's almost impersonal and quotidian prose of trade, notaries, and contracts seems so far removed from Rembrandt's painting that it is hard to believe that the two were produced in the same culture, in the same city, in the same year. And yet, in spite of the powerful moral geography that separates them, these cultural texts were united by their physical and cultural proximity. They represent the two sides of our modern identity. Indeed, the now barely visible connection between matters of art and taste and the political economy of slavery generates the questions that inform this chapter and this book as a whole: What was the relation between aesthetic objects and the political economy of slavery? How could such elevated images of art exist in the same realm as the harsh world of enslavement and the slave trade? How could the figure of the black simultaneously be the source of what Walter Benjamin aptly called "aura" and a prosaic object in a discourse of commodity fetishism?[7] And how do we read these two spheres of social life—one rooted in the realm of the aesthetic, civility, and taste, and the other in the political economy of slavery—in the same register? This introductory chapter explores the cultural, historical, and aesthetic context in which these questions emerged and why they continue to haunt the narrative of modern identity.

2

Within the culture of modernity, slavery always appears to be anachronistic. This anachronism arises from the fact that the terms in which the culture of modernity defined itself—and has hence been defined—seemed at odds with all that enslavement entails. Modern identity was premised on the supremacy of a self functioning within a social sphere defined by humane values; indeed, the distinctiveness of this moment in the history of the Western world has been predicated on the existence of free and self-reflective subjects, not bodies in bondage. And while there are disagreements on what constituted modernity and what its key integers were, and while there are still unresolved disputes about the origins, history, and consequences of a modern identity, all major documents on the Enlightenment and its aftermath have been premised on the idea of what Marcel Mauss and others have termed "the category of the person."[8] Whether we approach the issue from the perspective of the German Enlightenment (Moses Mendelssohn and Immanuel Kant) or the British tradition associated with the Scottish Enlightenment (David Hume, Lord Kames, and Adam Smith), the culture of modernity was envisioned across Europe as the moment of liberation of the subject from the dictates of tradition, religion, and old rules of conduct.[9] In its simplest form, the project of Enlightenment, considered to be the high point of modernity, was conceived as the production and valorization of the subject as autonomous, self-reflective, and unencumbered by immediate experience.

Within the European continental tradition, the production of a unique and self-reflective human subject was closely aligned with the project of rationality and the autonomy of aesthetic judgment. Modern subjects were those individuals who were capable of using their faculties of reason and judgment in the conduct of human affairs; the individual was the sole arbiter of meaning and identity, not a cog in a system of institutional and institutionalized rules and behaviors. This, of course, was the claim made at the beginning of Immanuel Kant's 1784 essay, "An Answer to the Question: What is Enlightenment?"

> Enlightenment is man's emergence from his self-incurred immaturity. Immaturity is the inability to use one's own understanding without the guidance of another. This immaturity is self-incurred if its cause is not lack of understanding, but lack of resolution and courage to use it without the guidance of another. The motto of enlightenment is therefore: Sapere aude! Have courage to use your own understanding! For enlightenment of this kind, all that is needed is freedom. And the freedom in question is the most innocuous form of all—freedom to make public use of one's reason in all matters.[10]

Within the series of debates and disputes that came to define the European Enlightenment, reason and the subject's capacity for rationality

were paramount. The idea of Enlightenment was premised on a fundamental belief "in the power of human reason to change society and liber-
ate the individual from the restraints of custom or arbitrary authority; all
backed up by a world view increasingly validated by science rather than
by religion or tradition."[11] The ambition of the Enlightenment, then, was
to understand human life through what Kant considered to be a priori
principles or ideas of reason, now separated from the event as a sensual
or phenomenological experience. All that was needed for enlightened
self-understanding was the most innocuous form of freedom: the "freedom to make *public use* of one's reason in all matters."[12] And if Kant's
little document is considered to represent a major milestone in the story
of European modernity, it is because of its precise isolation of the two issues that would provide the fulcrum for a modern identity—the question
of freedom and rationality.

That the mass of African slaves who drove the European economies of
the time were not free was not a matter that bothered Kant or his British
interlocutors, such as David Hume, because the black was excluded from
the domain of modern reason, aesthetic judgment, and the culture of
taste. Kant and Hume, often considered to be rivals in the battle to define
the contours of reason and taste, would still find concurrence when it
came to the question of an alleged black inferiority, either in morals or rationality. Kant asserted this concurrence of opinion in his complimentary
use of Hume as a source in *Observations on the Feeling of the Beautiful
and the Sublime*:

> The Negroes of Africa have by nature no feeling that arises above the trifling.
> Mr. Hume challenges anyone to cite a single example in which a Negro has
> shown talents and asserts that among the hundreds of thousands of blacks
> who are transported elsewhere from their countries, although many of them
> have even been set free, still not a single one was ever found who presented
> anything great in art or science or any other praiseworthy quality, even though
> some continually rise aloft from the lowest rabble, and through special gifts
> earn respect in the world. So fundamental is the difference between these two
> races of man, and it appears to be as great in regard to mental capacities as
> in color.[13]

This view was a common one in the highest European intellectual circles. In fact, the specter of blackness haunted all attempts to elaborate
and valorize the discourse of modern freedom, and by the middle of the
eighteenth century, when the order of slavery came to be seen as the
central cog in the machinery of commerce and the wealth of nations,
blackness—once exalted as a symbol of sanctity in the last great cycle of
paintings of the Adoration of Christ at the end of the sixteenth century
and the Baroque painters mentioned above—had come to represent what

Peter Stallybrass and Allon White, writing in a different context, have called "the rock bottom of symbolic form."[14]

The "rock bottom" of black representation can even be found in the most unexpected places, such as the *Encyclopédie ou Dictionnaire raisonné des sciences, des arts, et des métiers*, edited by Denis Diderot and Jean Le Rond d'Alembert, published in Paris between 1751 and 1772. Here, under the entry "Nègre," written by M. le Romain, the language and authority of natural science were deployed to set the black apart from the rest of humanity. The African, defined as a "Man who inhabits different parts of the earth, from the Tropic of Cancer to the Tropic of Capricorn," was identified as the figure of radical difference: "Africa has no other inhabitants but the blacks. Not only the color, but also the facial traits distinguish them from other men: large and flat noses, thick lips, and wool instead of hair. They appear to constitute a new species of mankind."[15] The 1798 American edition of the *Encyclopedia Britannica* went a step further, exiling the African from the human community in rabid and libelous terms:

> NEGRO, Homo pelli nigra, a name given to a variety of the human species, who are entirely black, and are found in the Torrid zone, especially in that part of Africa which lies within the tropics. In the complexion of negroes we meet with various shades; but they likewise differ far from other men in all the features of their face. Round cheeks, high cheek-bones, a forehead somewhat elevated, a short, broad, flat nose, thick lips, small ears, ugliness, and irregularity of shape, characterize their external appearance. The negro women have the loins greatly depressed, and very large buttocks, which give the back the shape of a saddle. Vices the most notorious seem to be the portion of this unhappy race: idleness, treachery, revenge, cruelty, impudence, stealing, lying, profanity, debauchery, nastiness and intemperance, are said to have extinguished the principles of natural law, and to have silenced the reproofs of conscience. They are strangers to every sentiment of compassion, and are an awful example of the corruption of man when left to himself.[16]

While it is true that the most powerful arguments against slavery were made by the philosophers of the Enlightenment, it is hard to find a more virulent description of the black than this one authorized by the institutions of modern knowledge, built on scientific explanation, geographical difference, and physiology.

But my main concern here is not why the great philosophers of freedom sought to exclude the black from the narrative of universal reason. Rather, I am interested in the emergence and shaping of a discourse predicated on the need or desire to quarantine one aspect of social life—the tasteful, the beautiful, and the civil—from a public domain saturated by diverse forms of commerce, including the sale of black bodies in the modern marketplace. For if one were looking for a methodological link among a group of philosophers as diverse as the German idealists, the thinkers of the Scottish Enlightenment and the English Whigs, it is perhaps to be found in the articulation of a discourse of social life in which the qualities that distinguished the modern self were transcendental of the "array of cultural materials" that actually constituted the modern self.[17] For Kant, to use a common example, the issue of transcendentalism was simple: in order to have a proper understanding of moral behavior, the age needed "to discover rules or principles of conduct which are logically independent of experience and which are capable of contradiction."[18] Even Adam Smith, who was much more concerned with questions of utility and the production of goods to satisfy immediate desires, was keen to separate the means of wealth from its ends: from "a certain love of art and contrivance," Smith noted, "we sometimes seem to value the means more than the end, and to be eager to promote the happiness of our fellow-creatures, rather from a view to perfect and improve a certain beautiful and orderly system, than from any immediate sense or feeling of what they either suffer or enjoy."[19]

In the new value system rooted in rationality, the analytic spirit would march triumphantly "to conquer reality" and accomplish "its great task of reducing the multiplicity of natural phenomena to a single universal rule."[20] Thus, whether we are dealing with the rule of reason or matters of taste, the project of modernity was premised on the search for rules in which the larger concerns of the world, including the slavery that reached its zenith in the period of Enlightenment, would be sublimated to an idealistic structure. Considered to be a detritus that came between the modern mind and pure concepts, experience had to be processed through higher forms such as reason and the aesthetic. In fact, the turn to a systematic aesthetic theory, one of the major features of the age of Enlightenment, was premised on the belief that it was in the field of art and its judgment that the traditional opposition between reason and imagination could be reconciled. However, the ideology of the aesthetic was predicated on the capacity of the aesthetic or the sensual to be posited as analogical to reason. This is considered to be the achievement of German aesthetic theory from Alexander Gottlieb Baumgarten's *Reflections on Poetry*, first published in 1735, to Immanuel Kant's *Critique of the Power of Judgment*.[21] Here, in the transcendental project of aesthetic practice and judgment, materials that were considered anterior to the process of European self-fashioning, such as slaves, Indians, and the poor, were confined to notational margins and footnotes; the Enlightenment's world picture was adumbrated by "a geographical consciousness based on the distinctiveness of the part of the world that came to be called 'Europe.'"[22]

Europe could not function as an idea or structure of identity without its real or imagined others, who, since the beginnings of modernity at the end of the sixteenth century, were increasingly being incorporated into the modern world picture. Of course, people considered to be others had been central to the emergence and consolidation of a European identity since the Middle Ages, but in the modern period, alterity had become more than a simple inscription of the differences of other peoples, other cultures, other histories; it had now assumed a structural function: the designator of what enabled Europe, or whatever geographical area took that name, to assume a position of cultural superiority and supremacy. This new sense of European superiority was reflected in the new maps placing Northern Europe at the center of the world, or in monumental works of art, such as Giovanni Batista Tiepolo's frescoes at the palace of the prince-bishop of Würzburg, which place the allegories of Asia, Africa, and America alongside a domineering Europe.[23] And as slavery was consolidated and later challenged in the course of the eighteenth century, there was a significant shift: from earlier European views of Africans as agents who could be considered, even tentatively, to belong to the human community to their reduction to objects of trade or figures in the shadows of modernity.

The contrast between Rembrandt's painting and Troxxilla's inventory discussed at the beginning of this chapter was certainly not unusual, but it signifies a more complex shift in the imagination of African others under the pressures of slavery and the slave trade. Indeed, one of the central arguments I will make in this book is that slavery—and especially the powerful moral, visual, and economic claims associated with it—had a salient effect on what one may call the interiorized realm of the European experience—namely, the space of sense and sensibility. These shifts were reflected in the histories, discourses, and images in which African difference and its attendant barbarism were invoked as the counterpoint to modern civilization or civility.

As always, it was the visible and iconographic view that represented these shifts. Consider this example: In 1643 the Christian king of the kingdom of the Congo, Dom Garcia II, sent one of his ambassadors to Recife to see Johan Maurits, the Dutch governor of the Netherlands' possessions in Brazil. In a painting of the ambassador, often attributed to Albert Eckhout (fig. 1.2), the Congolese envoy is represented wearing a broad hat with feathers, a black velvet coat with gold and silver trimmings, and a sash of the same colors, all symbolizing power, prestige, and presence. At a time when the Congolese were considered by Europeans to be equal partners in global trade and cultural exchange, the location of their ambassador at the center of a European portrait was not unusual or extraordinary.

1.2 Albert Eckhout, *Congolese Envoy to Recife in Dutch Brazil*. From Allison Blakely, *Blacks in the Dutch World*, 122.

In contrast, Frans van der Mijn's 1742 painting of the Dutch governor of the slave fort of Elmina (fig. 1.3) indicates the increasing diminishment of black figures in the European imagination and the domination of the slave interest in the construct of the modern social imaginary. Here we have the portrait of the European man at the top of the world, the agent of a Dutch empire that by 1700 had "extended trade and established outposts in western and southern Africa, Asia, and the Americas."[24] By the time the Dutch established their hegemony on the West African coast, slavery had replaced gold as the major commodity of trade, a fact that led to a new addition—the figure of the slave—to the iconography of power and prestige. It is not accidental, then, argues Alison Blakely in *Blacks in the Dutch World,* that the period in which the slave trade accounted for most of Dutch wealth and power also led to the production of the largest category of paintings with blacks as adjuncts to the portraits of "Dutch burgher families, groups, and individuals."[25] According to Blakely, this kind of art, in which the portrait of an aristocratic was framed by a black shadow, was produced in the Low Countries more than anywhere else in the world. These portraits were intended primarily to project the power and prestige brought on by the new trade, "to celebrate achievement and to leave a lasting record for posterity."[26] Confronted with the diversity of the human world, the modern spirit seemed unable to incorporate the difference that it nevertheless needed to imagine its modernity, and hence authorized itself by inventing a hierarchical structure in which the whiteness of Europe would be refracted by the shadows cast by others.

3

My goal in this book is not to recover the figure of the black from the margins of the modern world picture and to restore it to an imaginary or nonexistent center; rather, I have set out to recognize this marginalized figure, often denied even the status of the human, as occupying an essential and constitutive role in the construct of the interiority of modernity itself. I aim to read this figure and the project of modernity—especially its economy of sense and sensibility or taste—contrapuntally, thus, to give slavery, the great unspeakable of our age, an obtrusive identity and to bring it "into active contact with current theoretical concerns."[27] This contrapuntal reading provokes several intractable questions: How do we reconcile the world that Rembrandt imagined when he was painting *Two Negroes* and his careful and calculated focus on the distinctiveness of his two models, their human qualities and individual differences, with Troxxilla's receipt for African bodies crossing the Atlantic Ocean to enrich the coffers of the Dutch golden age? How does one explain the transformation of the African from the center of Rembrandt's portrait to a mere shadow on the margins of Van der Mijn's man of trade?

There are two ways of going about this task, and they are both valid, although they present us with a different set of problems: one concerns the role of the modern system of art in the fashioning of a European identity; the other relates to specific British conceptual and discursive

1.3 Frans van der Mijn, *Jan Pranger, Director General of the Gold Coast (1730–1734)*. 1742.

attempts to reconcile commerce and taste. I will sketch both sides of this narrative of modernity because I want to trouble the boundaries that divide continental European debates on aesthetic judgment from the British culture of taste and also question the conceptual boundaries that have hitherto separated the political economy of slavery from the institution of high culture.

Let me start with the idea and institution of art, without doubt one of the key pillars of both modernity and the culture of taste. Modernity and the idea of the aesthetic constitute a powerful dialectic in Europe in the eighteenth century, and they inform each other in remarkable ways. As Paul Oskar Kristeller observed in a seminal survey of the emergence of the modern system of the arts, the dawn of modernity made the idea of art possible; in turn, the institutionalization of modernity made the emergence and consolidation of some dominant ideas about the aesthetic— "taste and sentiment, genius, originality and creative imagination"— central to modern conversations about the self.[28] A key component of the modernizing gesture of European culture in the eighteenth century was the location of art at the center of systems of knowledge and its wide acceptance, among elites and courtiers alike, as a key cognate in the definition of what constituted a modern social life. In the eighteenth century, perhaps for the first time in European history, "the various arts were compared with each other and discussed on the basis of common principles."[29] And if the role of art in society dominated intellectual debates in almost every major European country, it was because of a certain modern craving for a second order of representation in which the sensuousness of human life could be realized and private desire and public duty, already separated in the categorical imperative of rationality, would be reconciled. But perhaps one of the most important developments in the history of art in the eighteenth century was its democratization, or, more appropriately, its shift from being a preoccupation of elites and their academies, or courts and their courtiers, to "an amateur public."[30] The gist of this transformation was caught by Joseph Addison in a memorable hyperbole in *Spectator* 10: "It was said of Socrates that he brought Philosophy down from Heaven, to inhabit among Men; and I shall be ambitious to have it said of me, that I have brought philosophy out of the Closets and Libraries, Schools and Colleges, to dwell in the Clubs and Assemblies, at Tea-Tables and Coffee-Houses."[31]

The process of democratizing the arts, however, was delimited by the transcendental claims associated with the aesthetic realm. For precisely at the point when it was given special value in the social sphere, art was also asked to stand apart from other domains of lived experience. Indeed, one of the most persistent claims made about art in Europe, at least since the eighteenth century, is what has come to be known as its "ephemerality"— its existence "outside the framework of use and purpose which defines human life."[32] Criticism or judgment of art, even when it was by amateurs, was necessitated by a persistent and widespread desire to establish a fundamental division between art and life. Here, as in the discussions surrounding reason and rationality, the ideology of the aesthetic would become the product of a process of purification, the purging of those categories that seemed to interfere with the drive toward autonomy and disinterested judgment.

Looking back on this tradition of aesthetic judgment, Ernst Cassirer would go on to argue that it was in aesthetic theory that "the pure necessity of philosophic thought" would come to fruition, even claiming it was in the sphere of the aesthetic that a synthesis of the critical and productive functions of thought would be achieved.[33] Before this period, Cassirer claimed, thought had been defined by a struggle between nature and culture, or between scientific and artistic ideals; theories of art struggled to justify themselves in the court of reason and always seemed to fall short. But with the foundation of a systematic aesthetics, a process associated with Alexander Baumgarten, "a new intellectual synthesis opens up."[34] Whereas the criticism of art previously had been predicated on concepts outside the aesthetic domain, now art would become the source of the categories that judged it. Aesthetics—the system of judging art—would thus become a science.[35]

The project of turning the aesthetic into a science, however, was bedeviled by problems from the start; although some advocates of an autonomous aesthetic continued to hold out the possibility that it might provide a higher order of truth, debates about the role of art in the social order were dominated by a recognition of the gap between works of art as material objects and the idealistic or transcendental goals that informed them.[36] It now seems apparent that an aesthetic project that was understood to be "the culmination of Idealist philosophy, or perhaps even Western metaphysics as a whole" would sooner or later come up against its limits.[37] Indeed, if the aesthetic seemed to have fallen out of favor for most of the twentieth century (that is, until its supposed return in the 1990s), it was because when explored from the end or limit of modernity, the work of art seemed to perform, as Max Horkheimer and Theodor Adorno posited it, the same function as enchantment or magic, to serve as a form of deception: "The work of art still has something in common with enchantment: it posits its own, self-enclosed area, which is withdrawn from the context of profane existence, and in which special laws apply."[38]

My position in relation to these debates will become clearer by the end of this chapter, but I hesitate to condemn the ideology of the aesthetic as a form of mystification or alienation, or to endorse the idealistic claims made for art as a form of cognition outside the mechanization of social life. In response to the claims made on behalf of the aesthetic, I want to hold on to the possibility that the realm of the sensuous could simultaneously function as the site in which the black body was imprisoned but also as the conduit for its liberation. Whether we are dealing with questions of aesthetic judgment or the realm of taste, the compulsion for a redemptive hermeneutics through an appeal to sensuousness cannot be dismissed out of hand. As the last two chapters of this book will show, for those who were trapped in the political and moral economy of slavery, the presentation of the self through the work of art or an engagement with culture as a weapon against commodification had the capacity to salvage the human identity of Africans in their sites of repression and denial.

Consider the example of Ignatius Sancho. In both his self-representation as a man of letters and in the historic painting by Thomas Gainsborough, Sancho, born a slave in the middle passage, could become a compelling, indeed, a model, modern subject (fig. 1.4). Here we have an unquestionable affirmation of the intimate relation between subjectivity and representation and of the prism of the aesthetic as an "exemplary form of modern reflection."[39] Sancho's correspondence and transactions with other subjects of taste—people such as John Meheux, member of the Indian Board of Trade in London, or Lawrence Sterne, famous novelist—were the means through which this former slave could reflect on his human identity and emplace himself in the modern public sphere.[40]

Here is Sancho writing to Meheux:

I am uneasy about your health—I do not like your silence—let some good body or other give me a line, just to say how you are—I will, if I can, see you on Sunday.... Now, my dear M[eheux], I know you have a persuasive eloquence among the women—try your oratorical powers.—You have many women—and I am sure there must be a great deal of charity amongst them—Mind, we ask no money—only rags—mere literal rags—patience is a ragged virtue—therefore strip the girls, dear M[eheux], strip them of what they can spare—a few superfluous worn-out garments—but leave them pity benevolence—the charities—goodness of heart—love——and the blessings of yours truly with affection, or something very like it,

I. SANCHO[41]

In an epistolary transaction like this one covering the pleasurable habits of the London metropolitan culture in the middle of the eighteenth century, it was difficult to detect any distinction between Sancho, the former slave, the child of the middle passage, and Meheux, a distinguished English gentleman working for the board that oversaw the governance of India. Sancho was effectively performing the culture of taste as a gesture of affiliation; in the realm of art the former slave could reimagine himself as a human subject.[42]

It is now taken for granted by scholars, ranging from the Frankfurt School and neo-Marxism to poststructuralists of various kinds, that the failure of the aesthetic was inherent in its self-positioning as the fulfillment of reason rather than its opposite. No one can write about the redemptive claims of art, especially in the context of slavery and the Holocaust, without confronting Adorno's admonition that "To write poetry after Auschwitz is barbaric." But Adorno also recognized that the task

1.4 Thomas Gainsborough, *Ignatius Sancho*. 1768. Oil on canvas.

facing cultural criticism was how to develop a method for understanding "the dialectic of culture and barbarism" at its limits, outside the concepts that had enabled it.[43] In *Negative Dialectics* Adorno argued that he had set out "to free dialectics from . . . affirmative traits without reducing its determinacy," and this implied "a critique of the foundation concept as well as the primacy of substantive thought."[44]

One way of troubling the relation between the ideology of the aesthetic and the political economy of modernity, then, is to shift focus from continental European debates on the aesthetic as an epistemological or metaphysical category to British discourses on taste, which emerged under the pressure of the expanding horizons of commercial life in the middle of the eighteenth century. Kant, as is well known, denied the British tradition of taste any claims to philosophical reflection because, as Howard Caygill has noted, "it did not properly account for the universality and necessity of its judgements," and it tended to confuse sensibility and rationality or to endow the former with "the properties of rational law."[45] Kant's complaint was that the British aesthetic tradition was not transcendental or universal enough to claim the status of philosophical reflection: "To make psychological observations, as Burke did in his treatise on the beautiful and sublime, thus to assemble material for the systematic connection of empirical rules in the future without aiming to understand them, is probably the sole duty of empirical psychology, which can hardly even aspire to rank as a philosophical science."[46]

One could, of course, argue that what brought British theorists of taste closer to adjudicating the relation between the realm of art and conduct and the experiences of everyday life was precisely their inability to differentiate sense and sensibility from the properties of rationality and, by extension, their substitution of psychology for empirical rules. Keenly attuned to the daily tensions between commerce and sensibility, British writers on taste were able to generate a set of discourses in which the subjects' phenomenal or sensuous experience could be brought face-to-face with the materiality of modern society. Here, a concern with matters aesthetic was not considered part of an attempt to transcend the world of commerce, but to develop rules and standards that would enable the modern subject to reconcile the opposing demands of the production of goods and civic responsibility. This was the point affirmed by Edmund Burke in the last paragraph of *A Philosophical Enquiry into the Origin of Our Ideas of the Sublime and Beautiful*, where he asserted that his design had not been "to enter into the criticism of the sublime and beautiful in any art, but to attempt to lay down such principles as may tend to ascertain, to distinguish, and to form a sort of standard for them; which purposes I thought might be best effected by an enquiry into the properties of such things in nature as raise love and astonishment in us; and by shewing in what manner they operated to produce these passions."[47]

It is instructive that in key sections of his *Enquiry*, Burke would give "the properties of things" precedence over the ideas or feelings that they generated, for as was true for the writings of many of his contemporaries in the crucial 1750s and 1760s, a turn to matters of taste was also an attempt to account for the meaning and nature of trade or the production of wealth. Indeed, for theorists such Adam Smith, there was an intractable bond between utility and pleasure. A concern with beauty and taste, Smith noted in his *Theory of Moral Sentiments*, was "often the secret motive of the most serious and important pursuits of both private and public life."[48] And it is not incidental that the theories of taste propounded by Burke and Smith, powerful men with vested interests in matters of empire and governmentality, were haunted by the materiality of social life, especially the excessive values generated by luxurious living. Taste was not the path to transcendence, but a centrifugal force that enabled subjects to confront a world of social energies and desires. Taste, and the realm of the senses in general, would become "active, energetic, almost carnal; a matter of immediate sensation, whether culinary or sexual."[49]

What I will be calling the culture of taste in this book, then, is a general reference to a set of practices and ideas that are now considered central to British society in the eighteenth century but are particularly associated with the middle decades of the period. The literature on the emergence of taste as a cultural category and the theories informing it is now extensive, and my goal is to pinpoint those aspects that would ultimately make the category of taste a key mediator between British modernity and what I will call its repressive tendencies—namely, the attempt to use culture to conceal the intimate connection between modern subjectivity and the political economy of slavery.[50]

Briefly, the project of taste was intended to overcome the traditional dissociation of culture, considered to be an object of "aesthetic veneration," from the "profane commodity" that was its condition of possibility.[51] The reconciliation of these two spheres of social life—that of culture and the commodity—was necessitated by the radical commercialization of British society in the eighteenth century and the transformation of consumption into a distinctive social value. The expansion of empire and trade led to consumer revolution in Britain in the eighteenth century as "more men and women than ever before in human history enjoyed the experience of acquiring material possessions."[52] What was new was not just the individual's desire to consume expensive goods, but also his or her ability to have access to new objects of consumption, many of them produced in the empire. The massive expansion of trade triggered what Neil McKendrick has described as "such a convulsion of getting and spending, such an eruption of new prosperity, and such an explosion of new production and marketing techniques, that a greater proportion of the population than in any previous society in human history was able to enjoy the pleasures of buying consumer goods." No longer limited to the purchase of basic necessities but also "decencies and luxuries," consumption would generate a radical transformation in behavior and social attitudes.[53]

But the new structure of consumption would provoke an even more important transformation in the domain of what would later come to be known as high culture. For where one would have expected culture to be denied its claim to exclusiveness by its ties to commerce, especially in an age when aesthetic debates revolved around the autonomy of art, the commercialization of culture actually led to its revaluation. Paradoxically, culture acquired new value because it was now considered to be a commodity. At the same time, as diverse forms of entertainment became available and accessible to the public, the sphere of culture was expanded across class and gender lines. Previously considered antithetical, commerce and culture began to be reconciled, or to maintain the illusion of comity.[54] By 1753, when William Hogarth published his *Analysis of Beauty*, "written with a view of fixing the fluctuating ideas of taste," a new idiom, one revolving around ideas of civility and manners, now occupied the center of debates about British identity.[55]

There were two salient indicators of the ascendance of a culture of taste and its irruption into the public domain: one was the saturation of the common culture by discourses about taste and ancillary categories such as beauty and manners; the other was the expression, and later overcoming, of the traditional opposition between commerce and virtue. From the publication of Lord Shaftesbury's *Characteristics of Men, Manners, Opinions, Times* (1711), continuing with Francis Hutcheson's *Inquiry into the Originals of Our Ideas of Beauty and Virtue* (1725), and ending with Archibald Alison's *Essay on the Nature and Principles of Taste* (1790), a primary, though not exclusive, concern of British intellectuals was the invocation of taste as a cognate for a set of cultural practices that were expected to provide stability in an age of change and crisis. A culture of taste, it was assumed, would serve as what Robert W. Jones has aptly called a "discursive counter."[56] In effect, taste was elevated into a political discourse through which other concerns of the age, including its anxiety about commerce, could be processed, mediated, and regulated.[57] The entry of the category of taste into the domain of politics—and of politics in the field of manners—signaled a larger transformation of British society during this period, one that cut across genders, social classes, and even regions, informing and ultimately transforming all of them.[58] By the end of the seventeenth century and the beginning of the eighteenth, for example, birthright and rank were no longer considered to be the golden standards in determining modes of behavior or social relationships. Where before social rank had been the determinant of one's position in society, the consumption of culture now determined the character and quality of the self.[59]

As most of the major novels of the eighteenth century illustrate vividly, money, rather than rank, had become the major mediator of social relationships, the authorized agent of regulating behavior.[60] Rather than serving as the immutable marker of class boundaries, taste had become an agent for prying the old class system; the upper ranks now seemed open to people with money and education; the availability of imports, such as East Indian textiles, provided greater choices of dress and furnishings; and, of course, colonial wealth reinvented the category of the gentleman.[61] The disappearance of sumptuary laws during this period was a visible indicator of how far-reaching and deep these changes were, for when consumption, which was tied to the ability to pay for goods and services, was accepted as the arbiter of social standing, there was no longer an impetus to maintain hierarchy by statute. Indeed, sumptuary laws, which had instituted dress to denote social station, were now considered an affront to liberty.[62]

But the process of reconciling commerce and taste also created deep anxieties. For one, it generated an "orgy of spending," and this came to be presented as a sign of the excesses associated with new money. The general feeling was that the radical transformations in private behavior triggered by consumption had the potential to disrupt the social order.[63] It seemed as if there was no longer a common standard by which to judge behavior; the age of politeness lived under the shadow of excess, leading Sir Richard Steele to worry that "the most polite Age" was "in danger of being the most vicious."[64] Commerce and commercialization, figures of aggressive acquisitiveness and free spending, seemed to be at odds with the doctrine of politeness and regulated behavior that was at the core of the culture of taste. Moreover, there was a suspicion that commerce, lacking an inherent moral value in itself, needed a set of principles to regulate it, to ameliorate its roughness, and to harmonize it with the ideals of virtue that were central to how the culture imagined itself. This is why debates about art, culture, the aesthetic, or taste in the early eighteenth century seemed constantly driven by a torsion of anxiety created by the drive for consumption, expanding trade, and the need to regulate behavior. There was a need for a new cultural space where these two components would overcome their dialectical and diametrical nature and become part of a totality in which the ideals of a modern identity would be rehearsed, replayed, and affirmed. But where would this space be located, and what would be its nature?

In 1675 King Charles had forbidden the operation of coffeehouses in England, arguing that these houses of leisure, later to emerge as the new centers of the new culture of taste, were distracting tradespeople from their businesses, leading to indolence, and spreading malicious and scandalous reports that led "to the defamation of his Majesty's government and to the disturbance of the peace and quiet of the realm."[65] By the beginning of the eighteenth century, however, coffeehouses and other places of leisure, including operas and luxury gardens, were being recognized not as dens of sedition but as regulatory forums.

Coffeehouses, however, were just the outward symbol of a larger revolution in the British public sphere. From the end of the seventeenth century onward, the project of British political and aesthetic philosophy was primarily the search for, and development of, discursive practices and principles that would be able to govern conduct in an age when old standards were out of joint with the new order of commerce. This was a time when what had been assumed to be Augustan order barely concealed often bitter and confused debates "over the relations between reason, virtue, and passion."[66] Within the confusions and debates that underlay the surface equanimity of the Augustan order, discourses about taste became "part of the search for new social standards and new forms of regulating behavior."[67] Concerned that indulgence, the inevitable consequence of unregulated consumption, was fatal to the body and mind and that "luxury, riot, and debauch" were "contrary to the true enjoyment of life," the Earl of Shaftesbury would embark on an aesthetic project in which the principle of private pleasure would be subordinated to and enhanced by social good or public virtue.[68]

But the acceptance of taste as a regulatory mechanism had not come about without doubt. For most of the 1750s, writers on taste had been preoccupied with the amorphousness of the concept itself: how could a category such as taste, or even ancillary ones such as civility and beauty, be asked to perform such important cultural work and yet be surrounded by "great inconsistence and contrariety"?[69] That was the question posed by David Hume in 1757 as he tried to figure out whether such a subjective category as beauty could be judged on the basis of unanimous rules:

> The sentiments of men often differ with regard to beauty and deformity of all kinds, even while their general discourse is the same. There are certain terms in every language, which import blame, and others praise; and all men, who use the same tongue, must agree in the application of them. Every voice is raised in applauding elegance, propriety, simplicity, spirit in writing; and in blaming fustian, affectation, coldness, and a false brilliancy: But when critics come to particulars, this seeming unanimity vanishes, and it is found, that they have affixed a very different meaning to their expression.[70]

The problem that was bothering Hume in "Of the Standard of Taste"—how to establish standards of taste in the face of subjective responses to phenomena—seemed to trouble a significant number of British philosophers and literary critics in the middle of the eighteenth century. This problem had bothered Samuel Johnson in 1751 as he reflected on the vagueness and undifferentiated nature of beauty, "different in different minds and diversified by time or place."[71] And in his *Enquiry*, Burke constantly worried about the lack of "concurrence in any uniform or settled principals which relate to taste"; concerned that "the term taste like all figurative terms" was not "extremely accurate," he thought it was "liable to uncertainty and confusion."[72] Concerned that the word *beauty* was surrounded by "a confusion of ideas" that made "our reasonings upon subjects of this kind "extremely inaccurate and inconclusive," Burke, like Hogarth, wanted to fix the standards of taste. This could be done, he averred, "from a diligent examination of our passions in our own breasts; from a careful survey of the properties of things which we find by experience to influence those passions; and from a sober and attentive investigation of the laws of nature, by which those properties are capable of affecting the body, and thus of exciting our passions. If this could be done, it was imagined that the rules deducible from such an enquiry might be applied to the imitative arts, and to whatever else they concerned, without much difficulty."[73]

But by the end of the eighteenth century, a consensus seemed to emerge on the role of manners, taste, beauty, and sensibility in the making of the new social order. At this time, Burke would confidently declare that manners were not only of more importance than laws but were also its foundation: "Manners are what vex or soothe, corrupt or purify, exalt or debase, barbarize or refine us, by a constant, steady, uniform, insensible operation, like that of the air we breathe in. They give their whole form and colour to our lives. According to their quality, they aid morals, they supply them, or they totally destroy them."[74] A free market economy, it was assumed, enhanced freedom "by deepening consumption down through the social spectrum."[75]

4

The march of the culture of taste toward clarity, unanimity, and utility had to overcome significant roadblocks that constitute an important context for my discussion. The most obvious roadblock to the project of reconciling commerce and taste was that in order for high culture to have value as an exclusive category, it needed to draw and maintain distinct symbolic boundaries. These boundaries were of two kinds. The first one was structural: as Michèle Lamont and Marcel Fournier have noted, the very idea of high culture as the preserve of elites has often depended on its mobilization "to evaluate or signal status or to create status groups and monopolize privileges."[76] The second roadblock was symbolic and conceptual: high culture was enabled by the expansion of trade and the rise of industrialization, but in order to come into being as a separate sphere it had to negate its connection to the competitive and often ruthless world of commerce.[77] Still, attempts to delink culture from its deep roots in commerce were constantly thwarted by groups whose relationship to the reigning doctrines was considered marginal or tangential. Women, for example, served as "a persistent reminder of the libidinal energies which the culture could unleash and which were so difficult to control."[78] My book will add slaves to the calibration of repression and denial.

A first step in this direction is to recognize the dialectical relationship between culture and commerce, to underscore the fact that in the long eighteenth century, culture had come to be valued because it was a commodity, and commodities had became treasured as cultural objects. The most prominent case of the mutual enhancement of commodity and culture was the pottery business associated with Josiah Wedgwood, based at Stoke-on-Trent. Wedgwood's success arose from both his technical mastery of porcelain and his sense of the market. He realized that pottery had acquired aesthetic value and was treasured for its fashionability rather than its innate merit; he also understood that irrespective of their utility and function, his products would be valued because of the economic power and prestige of the class that consumed them—"the monarchy, the nobility, and the art connoisseurs."[79] Firmly established within the domain of commerce, Wedgwood set out to expand the horizon of art, to reconcile utility and aesthetic value. Through his close collaboration with Joseph Wright of Derby, for example, Wedgwood would "secure royal and aristocratic patronage to secure the social cachet of his wares" and then hire artists like Wright to embody his enterprise in art.[80] While other artists of the age, most prominently William Hogarth and Sir Joshua Reynolds, needed to produce treatises in order to justify the place of art in a commercial culture, Wedgwood and Wright seemed almost oblivious to the inherited assumption that art and commerce were mutually exclusive.[81]

And Wedgwood did not just have a cunning sense of the interlock of the work of art and commerce; he also had a proper understanding of fashionable markets wherever he could find them—in the dining rooms of the wealthy as well as in the hearts of abolitionists—and it is this keen sense of the market of objects and feelings that assured the success of both his china and antislavery emblems.[82] Wedgwood understood how sensibility itself could emerge from the intersection of art, commerce, and social protest and how feelings themselves could be presented in the marketplace. Nowhere is this linkage between the work of art, sensibility, and the market more apparent than in the medallion Wedgwood produced for the Quaker-led Society for the Abolition of Slavery in 1788 (fig. 1.5). To the extent that the medallion was not intended for monetary gain, it is not accurate to say that Wedgwood had tailored the feelings evoked by this piece for the marketplace; and yet there is clear evidence that, as with his famous porcelain, he had cast this work to reach the largest

1.5 Josiah Wedgwood and Sons, jasper
medallion decorated with a slave in chains
and inscribed with "Am I not a Man and a
Brother." 1790s. Ceramic. English School
(eighteenth century).

audience possible. When he sent the medallion to Benjamin Franklin in
Philadelphia in February 1788, Wedgwood expressed the hope that it
would lead to the final completion of the cause against slavery and usher
in "an epoch before unknown to the World," giving relief to millions of
slaves, who were its immediate objects of representation, so that "the
subject of freedom [would] be more canvassed and better understood in
the enlightened nations."[83] The medallion, Franklin was to note, had an
effect "equal to that of the best written Pamphlet, in procuring favour to
those oppressed People."[84]

But in this interplay of culture and commodities, much more was at
stake than the incorporation of the lived experience of slavery into the
sphere of art. As I have already noted, the overwhelming desire for refinement in the eighteenth century signified the emergence of new kinds
of British subjectivities and modes of regulating the social order. When
Archibald Alison argued, in an essay published in 1790, that the fine arts
produced "the emotions of taste," a set of feelings and a form of propriety
that could be distinguished from more unruly passions such as sexual
desire and materialism, he was endorsing a view shared by the major
artists, writers, and intellectuals of the period.[85] From Edmund Burke to
Oliver Goldsmith, the work of art, rather than systems of logic or rationality (the other major categories and concerns of the age), was placed
at the center of all social relations and became the key to understanding
human nature. Now it was assumed that culture and commerce were
twinned in the process of producing new subjects: commerce enabled
culture, art, and taste, which were, in turn, deployed as modes of cultivation and politeness, differentiating the subject of taste from the savagery

and barbarism of a previous time and of other cultures and experiences. This differentiation would be achieved through a process of repression and denial in which those who didn't fit into the structures of feelings and institutional practices associated with taste were left out of its domain altogether.

Throughout the eighteenth century, the most prominent advocates of a culture of taste posited their task as, first and foremost, the promotion of sensibility and politeness as the counterpoint to the uncouthness of trade, and the presentation of the former as the determinative value. In other words, rather than providing the impetus for the destructiveness of body and mind that worried Shaftesbury, commerce and consumption would be chaperoned by politeness, a set of expectations in which individuals would be enjoined to control their passions. Consequently, politeness would become a social mandate, the demand that individuals give up excessive or unruly desires, the libidinal forms of acquisitiveness and competition, and establish "harmony with a properted society."[86] It is this quest for harmony that led Adam Smith to conclude that the end of pleasure and happiness was not simply utilitarian, as his fellow Scot David Hume had argued, but was "the regular and harmonious movement of the system": "The pleasures of wealth and greatness, when considered in this complex view, strike the imagination as something grand and beautiful and noble, of which the attainment is well worth all the toil and anxiety which we are so apt to bestow upon it."[87] Smith's goal was to bring the pleasure principle, the police, and the extension of trade and manufacture into one social whole; in the regime of sense and sensibility, means and ends would be synchronized. His observations here are worth quoting in detail:

> The same principle, the same love of system, the same regard to the beauty of order, of art and contrivance, frequently serves to recommend those institutions which tend to promote the public welfare. When a patriot exerts himself for the improvement of any part of the public police, his conduct does not always arise from pure sympathy with the happiness of those who are to reap the benefit of it. It is not commonly from a fellow-feeling with carriers and waggoners that a public-spirited man encourages the mending of high roads. When the legislature establishes premiums and other encouragements to advance the linen or woollen manufactures, its conduct seldom proceeds from pure sympathy with the wearer of cheap or fine cloth, and much less from that with the manufacturer or merchant. The perfection of police, the extension of trade and manufactures, are noble and magnificent objects. The contemplation of them pleases us, and we are interested in whatever can tend to advance them. They make part of the great system of government, and the wheels of the political machine seem to move with more harmony and ease by means of

them. We take pleasure in beholding the perfection of so beautiful and grand a
system, and we are uneasy till we remove any obstruction that can in the least
disturb or encumber the regularity of its motions. All constitutions of government, however, are valued only in proportion as they tend to promote the
happiness of those who live under them. This is their sole use and end. From
a certain spirit of system, however, from a certain love of art and contrivance,
we sometimes seem to value the means more than the end, and to be eager to
promote the happiness of our fellow-creatures, rather from a view to perfect
and improve a certain beautiful and orderly system, than from any immediate
sense or feeling of what they either suffer or enjoy.[88]

Central to Smith's project, then, was the belief that what lay at the heart
of the civilizing process—and modern identity in general—was the recognition that commercial activities (the means) were not anterior to cultural
refinement (the ends) but were indeed constitutive of it. In this context,
even Hume's utilitarianism seemed appropriate, because it recognized
that the effectuation of the arts and a flourishing of commerce enabled
each other, that the existence of a thriving marketplace made cultural
refinement possible. More specifically, Hume recognized that commercial work, represented by the industrial and mechanical arts, produced
the refined liberal self: "Industry and refinement in the mechanical arts
generally produce some refinements in the liberal; nor can one be carried to perfection, without being accompanied, in some degree, with the
other. The same age, which produces great philosophers and politicians,
renowned generals and poets, usually abounds with skilful weavers, and
ship-carpenters. . . . The spirit of the age affects all the arts; and the minds
of men, being once roused from their lethargy and put into fermentation,
turn themselves on all sides, and carry improvements into every art and
science."[89] Here we can witness the consolidation of a discourse in which
art and its appreciation would provide a mode of managing the world
engendered by commerce. My focus is on what was excluded from the
discourse of taste and the series of omissions, repressions, and conceptual
failures that were its condition of possibility.

5

Leading scholars of consumption and culture in Britain, from John Plumb
and Neil McKendrick to Ann Bermingham and John Brewer, have noted
how significant acts of denial or negation came to function as the raison
d'être for the emergence of culture or leisure as social categories.[90] Moreover, discursive and philosophical debates on the period have tended to
uphold Howard Caygill's argument that British writers, having accepted

taste as a faculty of judgment, came to be caught between the tensions that informed rationality and sensibility as conceptual categories; the discourse on the nature and function of taste ended up turning it into "an intangible medium of exchange between the rational will of providence and the irrational individual sentiment."[91] A culture of taste informed by denial became disembodied. The study of gender and race has been one important site in which these acts of denial and disembodiment have been confronted and exposed. Brewer has noted, for example, how women functioned as "a persistent reminder of the libidinal energies which the culture could unleash and which were difficult to control."[92] New and revisionist historians of the eighteenth century have rediscovered "after decades of comparative neglect, the imperial dimensions of British domestic culture, politics, and social relations are starting to come into focus, significantly revising our conceptualization of Englishness and Britishness and the categories through which 'colonizers' and 'colonized' are understood."[93] Drawing on both poststructuralist and postcolonial theory, the "new" eighteenth-century studies has led to "the revision or problematization of period, canon, tradition, and genre in eighteenth-century studies."[94]

My book continues but also revises the terms of this questioning of repressed others in the making of modernity and the culture of taste. Indeed, a central argument in this chapter and the rest of this book will be that while a grammar of restitution—that is, the recovery of what has previously been neglected or elided in previous discourses—has made imperial margins indispensable to our understanding of Britishness, it has not fully accounted for the specific role of slavery and blackness in the shaping of the ideas and ideals of taste. For when we focus on questions of taste in relation to slavery, what we encounter is not simply the denial of a specific mode of commerce that was necessary for the consumption of culture, or even the censoring of others out of the new order of civility and virtue, but their careful orchestration as part of this order, in absentia, on the margins, but still part of a presence, what Derrida would call a trace, both inside and outside the system, a residue of what exists but cannot be acknowledged.[95] The trace is the signifier of at least four paradoxes that are crucial to understanding the relation between the presence of taste and the absence of slavery in the manifest discourse of modern subjectivity.

Paradox 1: Presence/Absence

Others—women, slaves, and the poor—were not totally excluded from the discourse of modern identity; rather, they were deployed in a subliminal, subordinate, or suppressed relation to the culture of taste. Consider, for example, the Earl of Shaftesbury's discourse on the aesthetic: it promoted the cult of the gentleman as the custodian of taste and in the process seemed to exclude the lower classes from the elevated culture of sensibility. And yet the lower classes were not entirely excluded from the moral geography of civility, for Shaftesbury recognized that the poor constituted a crucial counterpoint for the ideal gentleman. A gentleman, he contended, was a person who held values at odds with the "the vulgar habits of the people as well as the luxurious living identified with the court."[96] Similarly, although there were many aesthetic and moral constraints on how the poor could be represented in English landscape paintings in the eighteenth century, the rural poor could not be totally excluded from the domain of art; indeed, as John Barrell has noted in *The Dark Side of the Landscape*, they became essential to the decor "of the drawing rooms of the polite."[97] Here, the very social classes that were considered to be outside the domain of taste functioned as counterpoints to the ideals of polite behavior or even as figures of desire; that which was outside the manifest framework of the dominant cultural signifiers was essential to their meaning.

Paradox 2: Pain and Beauty

This paradox, which has been discussed at length by Marcus Wood in his study of the iconography of slavery, is related to the larger relationship between art and the regime of punishment and pain: "How can aesthetic criteria be applied to describe the torture and mass destruction of our own kind? How is it possible to make something beautiful out of, and to perceive beauty within, something which has contaminated human values to such a degree as to be beyond the assumed idealisations of truth and art, beyond the known facts and beyond the manipulations of rhetoric?"[98] Slaves could occupy important symbolic roles in English portraiture as figures of status; erotic black figures would be part of massive projects commissioned by colonial governors, such as Sir William Young of the Windward Islands; and supporters of abolitionism, most notably Wedgwood and William Blake, would deploy the figure of the suffering black in support of their cause, but the question of how the enslaved could be represented in images whose goal was to elicit pleasure would continue to persist.[99]

Paradox 3: Slavery in Absentia

Slavery was referred to as the "peculiar institution," but nowhere was this peculiarity more obvious than in Britain itself. Were there slaves in Britain? The question might appear misplaced given the active role of Britain in the purchase, transportation, and sale of African slaves from the 1560s

to 1807, but within the domestic English space itself, the presence of slavery and the kind of moral demands it made on subjects of taste is more
complicated than one might first assume. Now, it is true that slavery was
woven into the British social fabric in diverse ways: British subjects and
agents were actively involved in the slave trade, in the settlement and development of the slave colonies, and later played an influential role in the
abolition of the slave trade and the development of a powerful antislavery discourse. In short, slavery was preponderant abroad, in the British
colonies, and clearly evident at home. In fact, the question of slavery was
central to British domestic politics and the shaping of the identity of the
United Kingdom.

But as James Walvin has noted, black slaves in Britain "did not occupy
the crucial economic role created for them in the slave colonies" and they
were not subject to the regimes of brutality and terror that created the
chasm between art and enslavement that was a marked feature of the
American colonies.[100] From a visual and existential perspective, this situation would be startling. Where one would expect slaves to be subjects
in chains or bolts, under spatial constraint, or even functioning under a
brutal regimen of labor, slaves in England were often considered to be "a
popular and prestigious acquisition as domestic servants," often working
in households at the highest levels of society, including that of Lord Chief
Justice Mansfield.[101] The existence of slavery in absentia would make it
difficult to conceptualize or represent slaves as a visual and palpable ingredient of British society, but as I will show in subsequent chapters,
slavery was part of the political unconscious of Britishness.[102]

Paradox 4: African Slavery and English Freedom

There is, of course, a glaring gap between the reality of slavery and the
ideals of English freedom, and the fact that they were products of the
same moment is one of the initial questions that prompted this study.
For it is indeed ironic that the growth of the African slave trade was
taking place at a time when "the institutions of bondage" had all but
disappeared from English society; slavery became part of the economic
mandate of Englishness in a period when the unique identity of England
was premised on ideals of unquestioned freedom and an assumption,
shared even by slave traders themselves, that "slavery was the worst of
human conditions."[103] As Walvin has observed, the West Indian empires,
the source of much of the wealth and prestige that was concordant with
the culture of taste, were established in the period that "saw the assertion
of important political and human rights" in England:

> As more and more Englishmen came to pride themselves on their newly won
> rights, at precisely that time Englishmen constructed a fabric of colonial slave

society which was specifically designed to relegate the black below the level of humanity. Furthermore, because of the economic and political ties between metropolis and colonies, the two systems of law—English and colonial—often overlapped and frequently clashed. Nowhere was this more apparent than on the question of slavery. On the face of it the chattel status of imported slaves was at variance with the spirit and even the letter of English law. It was this problem which was to tax English courts until the early nineteenth century.[104]

6

My overall approach to the subject of slavery in a culture of taste will revolve around these four paradoxes. One of the arguments that I will be developing in this book, especially in the first half, is that although African slavery was rarely taken up as a central issue in the discourse of taste, it did not constitute what Michel Foucault would call "a fundamental prohibition"; on the contrary, enslavement was the "disquieting enigma" in the culture of sensibility.[105] Conversely, as I argue in the second half of the book, although slaves rarely engaged directly with the debates and practices about sense and sensibility and appear impervious to the questions about taste taking place in British drawing rooms, their modes of cultural behavior were crafted and elaborated under the shadow of the domain of taste, from which they had been excluded. Like women and the poor in England, the slave—and slavery itself—was confined to a shadow existence on the margins of the discourse of cultured subjects, but it is within these margins that we must recover the power of negativity.

In fact, it is when we think about the power of negativity that we can properly recognize the interstices in which the discourse of modern identity itself emerged. A culture of taste had no choice but to acknowledge the powerful, inevitable, and inescapable connection between culture and commerce, but it also needed to hold on to an idea of culture that was not subordinated to the forces of production. To use Marx's parlance, advocates of taste wanted culture to be both a base and a superstructure, to connect with existing forms of social production but also maintain their idealism.[106] But the high priests of taste ended up with a floating signifier—a "middle term whose status is indeterminate and difficult to define."[107] For in the double interstices, or the dialect of commerce and taste, the idea of culture first had to be extricated from commerce, be purified of its social residues, and then be reinstituted as the informing value.

My goal in this book is not to rewrite the cultural history of modern Europe or even to reconfigure the relation between centers and margins; rather, I am trying to make the case, in a narrower but specific sense, for slavery as one of the informing conditions of modern identity. But I also want to call attention to what it meant for slavery itself to be transformed into a modern category. And in order to sustain this argument, I need to establish the structural relationship between enslavement and forms of social identity, both ancient and modern. A good starting point here is to acknowledge that slavery was not a new development in the European imagination, or human society for that matter, nor was it an anachronistic development in the so-called civilizing process. As Christopher Miller has observed in his study of the literature and culture of the slave trade in the Francophone world, slavery and the slave trade are not synonymous, but they are part of a powerful dialectic: "There could be no slave trade without slavery, yet slavery continued after the slave trade . . . the two institutions were inseparable, since each fed and perpetuated the other."[108]

For cultural purists, a concern with slavery and taste would appear to be far-fetched since, as I will show in the next chapter, the abjection of the former always appeared to negate the ideals and claims of the latter. Indeed, given the investment modern society has made in the ideal of cultural purity, slavery could appear to be the greatest danger and threat to the self-understanding of the modern subject as civil and virtuous.[109] This explains why in what were considered to be isolated centers of white civilization, such as the cities of the antebellum South, culture needed to be symbolically quarantined from African slaves, who were associated with dirt and defilement. Here, slaves were considered to be categories of persons who embodied abstract ideas about impurity and contamination; in the slave plantations of the Americas, slaves were associated with a noxious order, one that had the capacity to defile civilized subjects.[110]

But to understand ritual contamination, it is important to probe the sources and uses of this terminology. We need to know, in the words of Mary Douglas, "who is issuing accusations of defilement and who is the accused," for unless "we can trace which categories of social life are being kept apart, how they are ranked and who is being excluded, the usual analysis of defilement is blocked."[111] In this instance, we must remember that although slavery and the civilizing process were separated on the symbolic level, they were powerfully connected in the everyday world of modern life. Furthermore, as an institution, slavery had always been part of how cultures understood and defined their understanding and conceptualization of civilization. In fact, it is not an exaggeration to say that in many human societies, in all geographical areas of the world, there has been an intimate connection between a sense of cultural achievement and superiority and the practice of domination.

As an institution, slavery has often been associated with cultural capital. Moses Finley, the distinguished classicist, once noted that "there was no action or belief or institution in Graeco-Roman antiquity that was not one way or other affected by the possibility that someone involved *might* be a slave."[112] And in his exploration of ideas of slavery from Aristotle to Augustine, Peter Garnsey observed that although slavery was perhaps not a "universal or typical labor system" in the Mediterranean world, "it can hardly be dismissed as marginal, if it was embedded in the society and economy of Athens, the creator of a rich and advanced political culture, and of Rome, the most successful empire-builder the world had thus far known."[113] The West Indian and antebellum aristocracy invested heavily in developing fences to quarantine white civilization from what was considered African barbarism, but they could not avoid rehearsing and reaffirming the claim that there was an innate connection between slaveholding and cultural achievement. Often the cultural status and intellectual lineage of the British and American planter classes depended on their claim that the enslavement of Africans gave slaveholders the authority and gravitas of antiquity. For example, George Frederick Holmes, the son of a British planter and official in Demerara, educated at England's Durham University, was considered "the most brilliant and creative of the proslavery school," and, like his peers, he drew on Aristotle's ideas on natural slavery to justify the institution of bondage in the American South.[114] The people whom Garnsey has described as "the proslave theorists of the old south" embraced ancient Athens and Rome "as the standard-bearers of classical civilization and understandably called them up in support of their cause, along with the Biblical slaveowning societies of ancient Israel and early Christianity."[115] In his *Sociology for the South*, first published in 1854, George Fitzhugh would claim that domestic slavery had "produced the same results in elevating the character of the master that it did in Greece and Rome"; he compared the nobility of leading Southern aristocrats like George Washington and John Calhoun to that of Greek and Roman senators, insisting that both had been ennobled by slaveholdings.[116]

During the debates on the future of slavery in the United States in the 1830s, an anonymous Southern clergyman provided the most succinct connection between slavery and civilization, arguing that the institution of slavery "ever has been and ever will be the only sure foundation of all republican governments."[117] The clergyman had a point: ancient civilizations assumed that slavery was a key fulcrum in communal organization, part of an elaborate political and symbolic economy, and the authorizing agent of claims to cultural superiority. In addition to Greece and Rome, slavery was one of the major sources of political and cultural capital in the Middle East, Africa, India, and China. In sub-Saharan Africa, undoubtedly the major casualty of modern slavery, the rise of the great kingdoms of the Sahel—Mali, Ghana, and Songhai—depended on the control of the lucrative slave routes of the region. Great empire builders and cultural heroes of African resistance to colonialism, such as Samouri Toure, are still remembered in West Africa as slave raiders.[118]

There were, of course, important differences between ancient and new forms of slavery, both in terms of their organizing principles and the ideas informing them, but modern slavery presented particular difficulties to European society, because it emerged in an age when legal bondage had disappeared in the cultures that were most active in the slave trade. The Atlantic slave trade thrived at a temporal juncture in which modern identity was predicated on the question of freedom and in an era when subjectivity depended on the existence of free and self-reflective subjects. As a modern institution, slavery was anachronistic simply because it seemed to be at odds with the aspirations of the age; however, it provided the economic foundation that enabled modernity.[119] And yet, and perhaps because of this anachronism, slavery informed and haunted the culture of modernity in remarkable ways; its infiltration of the governing categories, from morality and the law, natural history, and even discourses on the nature of the self, was unprecedented.

Slavery constituted the ghost or specter that would "mark the very existence of Europe," informing but also displacing "its great unifying projects."[120] And nowhere was this informing and haunting more dramatic and vivid than in the American colonies, where slavery was so palpable, so visible, and so phenomenal that it could not be buried in an underground economy of representation. Here, where slave owners considered themselves to be subjects of freedom, where migration and settlement had often been generated by the desire for even greater freedom, the existence of others as slaves was always necessary but also disturbing. Quite often, debates on the nature of African slavery in the new world were prefaced by the necessity to affirm the distinctiveness of an English identity that had to account for its presence and prescience in zones of displacement and enslavement.

To put it another way, the greatest anxieties about freedom were often expressed by those invested in the enslavement of others as if they, the free, might fall into the condition that sustained their lives. Thus a Maryland statute of 1639 would define the settlers of the tobacco colony as Christians who were entitled to the liberties, immunities, privileges and customs "as any naturall born subject of England."[121] In a now famous address to Oliver Cromwell, the Assembly of Barbados defined itself as a body of "Englishmen of as clear and pure extract as any" entitled to "liberty and freedom equal with the rest of our countrymen."[122] And in the 1650s, "a number of royalist sympathizers taken by the Protectorate and sold in Barbados described their situation to Parliament as slavery (and therefore, because they were English, unjust) without betraying any awareness of the condition of the Africans with whom they must have worked."[123]

Two ironies mark what I will call the negative dialectic of slavery. The first one is that the existence of slavery clarified the meaning of freedom. As the English exiles in Barbados realized, freedom could best be imagined and desired when slavery was witnessed as its radical other. The second irony was that the most virulent demands for freedom in Europe were taking place at precisely that moment in the eighteenth century when it became "imperative to reconcile the revival of slavery in modern times with various theories of human progress."[124]

7

It is in response to the challenge presented by the cauldron of slavery in an age of freedom that new modes of scholarly interpretation have emerged to excavate forgotten histories and narratives of slavery and empire and to locate them at the center of European life. But what does it mean to recuperate the meaning and value of suppressed groups on the margins of the modern world system? How is the essential condition of marginalization, exclusion, and alienation retained in relation to undiminished centers? How do we read the fragmented, transient, and often deeply elusive presence of the slave, located on the margins of the world picture, acknowledging the enslaved as an indispensible source of labor, as a counterpoint to dominant ideas about society and social organization, yet recognizing that this other of modernity could perform its function only in exclusion, in absentia, and in disavowal?

When I started work on this book, these questions were much easier to address than they are now. Slavery was absent or only minimally present in the monumental works that sought to explore modern culture during a period defined by the so-called aesthetic turn in literary and cultural studies, just as empire was absent from the dominant histories of the period. The revisionary works by Laura Brown, Felicity Nussbaum, Linda Colley, and others mentioned earlier were just entering the mainstream of social history and cultural criticism; empire was making its way into the study of Britishness, but it had not yet come to be recognized as crucial to the formation of the issues that interested historians and cultural scholars of the period, questions about money, state formation, and art. There were still elements of empire that seemed to threaten the core center of modern European identity. Imperial questions could not be avoided, but they needed to be managed, contained, or excluded. At the time, this containment and exclusion took two forms. First, slavery and the imperial condition in which it functioned were considered peripheral in the discourses that concerned themselves with the reconstruction of the moral and cultural geography of modern life. The most notorious example of this exclusion was Simon Schama's monumental book on the Dutch golden age, *The Embarrassment of Riches,* a work in which the most minute aspects of the Batavian temperament were scrutinized and presented without the slightest acknowledgment of how the riches that embarrassed were derived from the slave trade.[125] One was troubled by the fact that neither Schama's book, nor even the great cultural histories of European culture in the modern period, nor the monumental commentaries on the Enlightenment in various parts of Europe, nor the philosophical discourses of modernity, seemed able to incorporate slavery into their grand designs.[126]

There was a second register for excluding slavery and its ugliness from the narrative of modern identity: inherent in the so-called aesthetic turn, often posited as an alternative to cultural criticism, was a desire to recuperate the work of art as a sensual object transcending the violence and ugliness of modern life. This neo-Kantian turn to the aesthetic ideology, evident in Elaine Scarry's *On Beauty and Being Just* and Peter de Bolla's *Art Matters*, were driven by the belief that, faced with the ugliness of modern life, the self needed to turn to the sensual and pleasurable as the source of a redemptive aesthetic if not hermeneutics. In *On Beauty,* to use one prominent example, Scarry would locate the power of beauty in the "realm of sensation" and connect it to the "sacred" and "unprecedented"; the beautiful would thus be endowed with a deep auratic sense and powerful cognitive capacity: "The beautiful, almost without any effort of our own, acquaints us with the mental event of conviction, and so pleasurable a mental state is this that ever afterwards one is willing to labor, struggle, wrestle with the world to locate enduring sources of conviction—to locate what is true. Both in the account that assumes the existence of the immortal realm and in the account that assumes the nonexistence of the immortal realm, beauty is a starting place for education."[127] In *Art Matters*, de Bolla, whose previous book *The Discourse of the Sublime* had been a powerful accounting of the history of the modern subject, would now invoke the power of the aesthetic experience and locate it solidly in what he called a "poetics of wonderment" that was made distinct from "other forms of experience" through its "absolute divorce from the ordinary or everyday."[128] Yet, as my opening juxtaposition of Rembrandt's painting and Pedro Diez Troxxilla's slave receipt illustrates, the modern period was characterized by a tenuous relation between the aesthetic object and lived experience. How could Rembrandt and Troxxilla, living in the same city at the same time, occupying the same habitus, engage in a different set of economies (symbolic and real) and yet not be troubled by each other's presence?

My initial response to this question was to present my project as one of rectification. I would rectify what appeared to be the omissions of slavery and the phenomenology of blackness from the dominant histories and discourses of modernity by bringing the political economy of slavery into a direct confrontation with narratives about aesthetic judgment and taste in philosophy, social history, and cultural criticism. My objective was to locate slavery at the core of Englishness and debates about English identity and thus reconceive what was considered marginal to the project of modern self-making as essential to its identity. But this initial premise was preempted by the emergence of new revisionist studies in eighteenth-century culture and imperial history. Indeed, slightly earlier attempts to rethink the history of empire, most notably Colley's *Britons: Forging the Nation* and Nussbaum and Brown's *The New Eighteenth Century,* had already begun to question traditional assumptions about the historiography of the period. Colley had noted how after 1707 the British came to define themselves as "a single people not because of any political or cultural consensus at home, but rather in reaction to the Other beyond their shores."[129] Others had turned to literary theory to try to pry eighteenth-century studies from what has come to be termed "a Whiggish teleology."[130]

The critique here was directed at the general insistence on a continuous and stable history and culture in the eighteenth century, one in which the relationship between centers and margins was intelligible and unchanging, one driven by what Nussbaum and Brown describe as "a political stability linked to an image of equivalent social and cultural coherence, to a sense of an unchallenged class hierarchy represented and perpetuated in a literary culture where aesthetics, ethics, and politics perfectly mesh."[131] Subsequent new histories of empire sought to undo this ideology of order and coherence to account for what has been described as "non-elite and non-western pasts" and to recognize empire as a site of interconnection and interdependence, and the search was on for a method to "disrupt oppositions between metropolis and colony and allow us to rethink the genealogies and historiographies of national belonging and exclusion."[132]

All of these new histories and studies brought about a significant correction, if not balance, in the study of the European self and its colonial others in several areas, which provides an important backdrop for my project. But they also raised a new set of questions and indeed seemed to redefine the problematic of difference in the culture of modernity in terms I did not always find adequate to the task of accounting for the figure of the slave in modern culture. Three of these problems are crucial to bringing the culture of taste and the political economy of slavery into a productive encounter: the tension between the epistemological framework and logic of the modern and the existential life of the enslaved and colonized; the paradigm of difference in an age of cultural hybridity; and the problematic of race in general and blackness in particular in the elaboration of British theories of taste. Let me take each problem in turn.

The Epistemological Framework of Modernity

As I have already noted, the most compelling scholarly work on the culture of modernity has been driven by the imperative to recover the lives and experiences of subjects outside what has been described as "the political and epistemological models of Enlightenment and modernist Europe."[133] Revisionist histories and studies of modernity have not set out to undo epistemological frameworks as such; they are part of a project whose goal is to dilate their boundaries and terms of reference, to pluralize the range of experiences that are the objects of investigation, stepping out of the universalizing and universalized structures of knowledge to recover the signs of what Dror Warhman aptly calls "the unstructured institutions" that "underlay people's fundamental assumptions about who they were and who they could be."[134] And to the extent that epistemologies imply justified beliefs and knowable categories, they depend on visible experiences and stable entities—they need structured frameworks. Indeed, in Wahrman's *The Making of the Modern Self*, the pasts that are recovered from the margins were those that had left either "unself-conscious *traces*" or "unintended *marks*."[135] And these traces and marks would become historical when they were rewritten within a set of norms, brought under the rule of what Foucault once called a "procedural rationality."[136]

But traces are not enough. As I will show in the second half of this book, slaves left many traces and marks, both conscious and unconscious in form and nature. From birth to death, from occult practices to dance and fashion, there is no aspect of the experiences of African slaves in Europe and the Americas that has not been reconstructed through the traces they left behind and the glimpses of their lives that are available to us in the archive of the masters.[137] At the same time, however, the bodies of slaves, their lives, and their activities were considered to be outside the rationality of modernity and its normative order and thus outside the epistemological framework of the modern. This does not mean that the lives of slaves were not represented in the grid of modern identity. Slaves occupy an important part in the explanatory structures of modernity from natural history to the aesthetic. But they exist in this framework as proof of their incapacity for modern identity. They are, in effect, constituted as unmodern subjects or simply objects of modern trade. Concerning epistemological frameworks, then, the following question remains outstanding and inescapable: What are we to make of the faint traces of the slaves and the marks that are often only available to us through the narratives of their masters? How do we speak of those events and experiences that Toni Morrison identifies as the disturbing element of "black surrogacy"?[138] Or as Joan Dayan asks in *Haiti, History, and the Gods*, how are we to deal with "those reactions that did not get written down?"[139]

These questions have been asked by others in different forms. In *Contradictory Omens* Jamaican poet and historian Kamau Brathwaite was one of the first to raise the question of visibility and invisibility in the slaves' articulation of their existence in relation to the dominant world of masters who had written massive histories with the goal of affirming the inhumanity of the slave within the rational order of the Enlightenment.[140] In her provocative essay "Mama's Baby, Papa's Maybe," Hortense Spillers reflects on the consequences of the slaves' "veritable descent into the loss of communicative force."[141] Who tells the stories of the enslaved and how are they told? That is the question raised by Jenny Sharpe in the *Ghosts of Slavery*?[142] And making her way into the archive of slavery, Saidiya Hartman would discover that nothing in her training had prepared her for the invisible and the phantasmal, "those who had left no record of their lives and whose biography consisted of the terrible things said about them or done to them."[143]

I cite these books on slavery by literary and cultural scholars not to privilege one discipline over another but to call attention to two further points. First, the history or story of slavery that is told and circulated functions under the rubric of a disciplinary order, each part of which has its own claims and counterclaims, openings and closures. Culture and literary scholars like those cited above—and I include myself in this category as well—will not contribute much in terms of epistemology if by this term we mean "the categories that structure our thought, pattern our arguments and proofs, and certify our standards of explanation."[144] The questions that I find compelling will not have answers, evidence, or proof, nor will they satisfy any standard of explanation, because my objects of analysis—slavery and enslavement—are surrounded by silence and are submerged under what Patrick Chamoiseau, the Martinican novelist, has called a "web of memories which scorch us with things forgotten and screaming presences."[145]

Second, it is clear to me that one of the reasons that slavery could not be included in the discourse of taste, even when it pervaded its cultural forms, is because it was not compatible with the epistemological categories that defined high culture. As I will show in several key moments in this book, the establishment of a realm of taste, or even the valorization of ideals of beauty, depended on systematic acts of excluding those considered to be outside the systems of explanation that were being established as social norms. My goal here is not to establish an alternative normativity built around the marginalized, but to understand how the "formation of a vocabulary of the pure and impure" functioned as the linguistic and semantic foundation for modern identity.[146] I will be reading the figure of the slave as the informing yet interdicted symbolic in the representation of the culture of taste, outside or excessive of the epistemological framework of modernity.

But my refusal to privilege an epistemological framework should not be construed as obliviousness to the temporality of empire and its ever-changing boundaries. I recognize that theories and practices of empire changed often during the long history of the modern period, as did the general understanding of the condition of enslavement. Comprehending the plurality of empire is indeed essential to accounting for its omissions. Here I concur with those scholars, most notably Kathleen Wilson, who argue that there were many imperial projects in the Georgian period that were "engaged with by planters, reformers, merchants, explorers, missionaries, settlers, adventurers, indigenes, and the enslaved," and that there was "no universal colonial condition or imperial experience, but discrete practices of power and ways of imagining it in specific historical periods."[147] Within this changing empire, the condition of the slave in the public imagination would depend on shifting interests, ideologies, and practices. The slave who entered the realm of the British empire in the beginning of the eighteenth century, when the trade was very much accepted as a quotidian aspect of imperial trade, was not the figure we would encounter at the end of the century or at the beginning of the nineteenth, when abolitionism transformed the terms of debate and representation. We will see these differences at play in what I have called the changing aura of blackness.

And yet the moral economy of slavery tended to retain some enduring and often singular elements. African slaves, often because of their color or other forms of difference, continued to occupy "a savage slot" in the European imagination.[148] English attitudes toward slavery were changing continuously, and quite often the most pernicious and brutal images of the Africans deployed by agents of the slave trade and its apologists co-existed with some of the most benign representations. At the same time, however, both of these images could be found in earlier periods, existing in an old and enduring archive of Africanism that could be deployed to respond to the contingencies of the moment. The violent images of the Africans in the works of slave agents such as Robert Norris and Archibald Dalzell, published at the end of the eighteenth century to mount a rearguard action against abolitionism, belonged to a specific moment in the 1790s, but they were also rehearsals of earlier portraits by an older generation of slave factors, most notably, William Bosman, whose words opened my reflections in this chapter.

If I seem to prefer working with emaciated temporal frames rather than epistemological frameworks, it is because I believe that working with a weak sense of history or with porous boundaries is one way of liberating the slave not from history but from the hold of historicism. Long ago, the planter class laid claim to historicism as one of its authorizing agents. Similarly, if I locate this book in what might seem to be an amorphous geography, it is not because I am not aware of the differences between the culture of taste in England and Scotland or Virginia, or because I am impervious to the variety of localities in which slavery operated and shaped its landscapes; rather, I want to underscore the large projects that animated both the project of Enlightenment (which posited itself as English, Scottish, and British, but also European) and the almost universal assumption that the enslaved African, whether he or she lived in Bristol, England, or Bristol, Jamaica, was the counterpoint to modernity itself.

The Paradigm of Difference

My project also sets out to rethink the paradigm of difference, without doubt a key concern of the new imperial histories, literary and global studies, and postcolonial theory. Difference has become a key paradigm in the project of rethinking modernity and Enlightenment. In fact, one could argue that nearly all revisionist and postmodern accounts of modern identity have been attempts to wage war against the totalitarianism of modern rationality by activating differences.[149] In literature and cultural studies, it is impossible to escape from the poststructuralist critique of Enlightenment rationality, its universal claims, and its rejection of what Jean-François Lyotard called metanarratives. In fact, Lyotard has defined the postmodern as "incredulity toward metanarratives," insisting, in his famous report to the government of Quebec, that the narrative function has lost its "its functors, its great hero, its great dangers, its great voyages, its great goal."[150] Writing in the same vein and spirit, Michel Foucault would pose the essential question for the West at the end of the colonial era: what right "did its culture, its science, its social organization have to laying claim to a universal validity?"[151] Here, the difference of the "Third World" would be deployed against "Reason—the despotic enlightenment."[152]

As I have already noted, revisionist accounts of modern British identity have sought to recover the repressed and unheroic histories of others, including women, slaves, workers, and to make them alternative factors in what are often presented as small stories. As scholars have sought to question and displace the mythical centers of Britishness and to undo the fulcrum that has sustained the mythology of English identity, cosmopolitanism, and empire, they have turned to the lives of those located on the margins and peripheries of empire for evidence of the instability of the center.[153] A turn to the periphery of the eighteenth century thus becomes part of an attempt "to broaden and sharpen our perspectives on the period and its critical tradition as well" and to supply "a more inclusive view of the period than those which are limited to the dominant culture alone."[154] An axiom of difference reroutes the history of empire in terms best described by Catherine Hall in *Civilising Subjects*:

> The time of empire was the time when anatomies of difference were being elaborated, across the axes of class, race and gender. These elaborations were the work of culture, for the categories were discursive, and their meanings historically contingent. The language of class emerged as a way of making sense of the new industrial society in Britain of the late eighteenth and early nineteenth centuries. The language of "separate spheres" became a common way of talking about and categorising sexual difference in this same period of transition. It was colonial encounters which produced a new category, race, the meanings of which, like those of class and gender, have always shifted and been contested and challenged. The Enlightenment inaugurated a debate about racial types, and natural scientists began to make human races an object of study, labouring to produce a schema out of the immense varieties of human life, within a context of relatively few physical variations.[155]

And a fundamental question remains unanswered here and elsewhere: could this idiom of difference escape the imperial center's capacity to generate and manage categories of alterity?

Empire, of course, produced alterity in order to secure the identity of the domestic self, and the paradigm of difference and hybridity that some critics now seem to endorse as a source of agency and restitution often functioned as a mechanism for consolidating the center in the face of the real or imagined danger posed by the other. We can take it as axiomatic that when the English, at home or abroad, turned to the identity of others, it was to reflect on, or even endorse, their own unique identities, that the space of alterity enabled what Edward Said has termed the "consolidated vision of empire."[156] Fictional accounts of Englishness in the modern period (and the same case could be made for earlier ones) were driven by the need to enhance the nature and meaning of Englishness against the symbolic danger represented by colonial others who, though barely visible, and confined to the margins of the discourse, enabled "those feelings, attitudes, and references" that located the domestic space at the center of an ever expanding global culture.[157] But if empire produced functional differences, how can a discourse of alterity now be deployed to deconstruct the hegemony of the imperial account and thus disperse its authority? And if slavery produced the first hybrid cultures in the modern period, how can this hybridity, one produced through interdiction and violence, now be celebrated as a condition of postcolonial agency? And if the effect of colonial power was the production of hybridization, as Homi Bhabha has claimed, how can this same colonial hybridity have the capacity to unsettle "the demand that figures at the center of the originary myth of colonial power"?[158] And how do we avoid the trap of recuperating others merely as what Srinivas Aravamudan describes "as subordinates in some larger nationalist metanarrative" in which Britain remains central?[159]

On the Question of Blackness

The final critical problem, one that signals my major point of departure from revisionist histories of the modern period, concerns the complex racial markers of difference, the blackness that marked the slave as a slave because of his or her color. How does one write about the other as part of the technology of metropolitan identity and still underscore the fact that people conceived as others functioned as analogical figures of difference because they were considered to be part of the abnormal and pathological? How does one tell stories about an order of blackness that was essential to the maintenance of a modern European identity yet was considered so unruly that it needed to be controlled, displaced, or repressed if the modern self was to come to its own as a self-reflection subject of reason, of morality, and of taste? Clearly, the question of race in general and the problem of blackness in particular have to remain an intellectual site for continuing debates and controversies in the rethinking of modern identity. But in order to have a better understanding of the place and role of racialized bodies in making of the culture of taste, scholars should not lose sight of some difficult yet foundational questions: Was modernity itself a racialized category? Could modern slavery have existed outside a racialized economy?

That a powerful racial ideology was central to the theories and practices of modernity is not in doubt. The journey to modernity, whether from its imagined barbarism in the Middle Ages or to its high point in the eighteenth century, was conceived as the passage from an era that was impervious to difference to one in which difference was essential to the maintenance of identity. From Cervantes's *Don Quixote* to Defoe's *Robinson Crusoe*, the foundational narrative of modernity was the coming into being, or self-awareness, of a European self in relation to the other—the Moor, the Indian, or the savage. Difference was, of course, always an important part of Western identity, but it was in the modern period that it became essential to its core set of values.[160] Even where a moral economy of difference was not dramatized as the condition of possibility of European identity, a sense of separation from other forms of meaning—be they secular or divine—characterized what Louis Dupré has called the passage to modernity, the removal of transcendence from structures of meaning and its replacement by a structure of separation:

> Whereas previously meaning had been established in the very act of creation by a wise God, it now fell upon the human mind to interpret a cosmos, the structure of which had ceased to be given as intelligible. Instead of being an integral part of the cosmos, the person became its source of meaning. Mental life separated from cosmic being: as meaning-giving "subject," the mind became the spiritual substratum of all reality. Only what it objectively constituted would count as real. Thus reality split into two separate spheres: that of the mind, which contained all intellectual determinations, and that of all other being, which received them.[161]

In the cultures of the eighteenth and nineteenth centuries, this split could be secularized and radicalized so that the discourse of Enlightenment, in spite of the universalism that has drawn the ire of philosophers of difference, depended on powerful binary oppositions for its maintenance. During this period, what had started as a system of classifying nature in the works of William Petty and Carl Linnaeus would coalesce into concepts of human difference explained by environmental, evolutionary, and developmental theories. And the need to justify or oppose slavery would lead to the racialization of difference in unprecedented ways. Indeed, one of the great ironies of the age of enlightenment is that it was in the later phase of the eighteenth century, when slavery was under attack by abolitionists and others, that racial economies seemed to circulate with the greatest vigor and venom.[162] But what appears most startling is that the more theories of modernity evolved in order to account for the unique identity of Europe, the more they needed the black to function as the pathological figure that would serve as a counterpoint to beauty, taste, and civic virtue. As Sander Gilman has noted, when writers in the age of Enlightenment turned to "speculations concerning basic principles of art, the function of such figures in theoretical contexts provided a clue to the comprehension of the exotic as well as of the specific role of the Black in eighteenth-century thought."[163]

Nowhere was the necessity of the black as the counterpoint to white visuality more marked than in debates on the physical and physiological nature of perception, a question central to eighteenth-century reflections on the distinction between what Gilman calls "acquired and innate responses to perceptual categories": was our sense of perceptual categories such as size, perspective, and color innate in ourselves as human beings or acquired through our education or formed habits?[164] Responses to and debates about this question came to revolve around the report of an experiment carried out by Dr. William Cheselden, one of the most distinguished anatomists of the age, at St. Thomas's Hospital in London. Cheselden had carried out an operation on a boy with impaired sight and reported the transformations in his patient's conception of colors. Cheselden reported that after the operation the patient was forced to rethink his previously faint notion of colors: "Now Scarlet he thought the most beautiful of all Colours, and the others the most gay were the most pleasing, whereas the first time he saw Black, it gave him Uneasiness, yet after a little Time he was reconcil'd to it; but some Months after, seeing by Accident a Negroe Woman, he was struck with great Horror at the Sight."[165]

Cheselden's conclusion was that that since the boy had never seen a black woman before, and had hence not acquired the ability to associate blackness with ugliness through culture and instruction, his terror was immediate and intuitive; his fear of blackness was physiological, not social. In other words, on their opening, the boy's eyes had made an immediate, unmediated association of blackness with a set of negative values not acquired through social association. Cheselden's experiment had led Burke to conclude that blackness and darkness were made painful by "their natural operation, independent of any associations whatsoever":

> The horror, in this case, can scarcely be supposed to arise from any association. The boy appears by the account to have been particularly observing, and sensible for one of his age: and therefore, it is probable, if the great uneasiness he felt at the first sight of black had arisen from its connexion with any other disagreeable ideas, he would have observed and mentioned it. For an idea, disagreeable only by association, has the cause of its ill effect on the passions evident enough at the first impression; in ordinary cases, it is indeed frequently lost; but this is, because the original association was made very early, and the consequent impression repeated often. In our instance, there was no time for such an habit; and there is no reason to think, that the ill effects of black on his imagination were more owing to its connexion with any disagreeable ideas, than that the good effects of more cheerful colours were derived from their connexion with pleasing ones. They had both probably their effects from their natural operation.[166]

In Burke's view, blackness terrified us not simply because we had been taught to fear it, but because our dread of darkness had a physiological source—it caused tension in the muscles of the eye and this, in turn, generated terror. For Burke and many of his contemporaries, it was precisely because of its innate capacity to produce terror that blackness functioned as the source of the sublime. And the sublime, as is well known, came to occupy a central role in the aesthetic ideology, as it was variously associated with the ethical discourse of the Enlightenment and with revolutionary terror.[167]

Radical theories of racial difference now tend to be adduced to the end of the eighteenth century and the nineteenth century, and economies of difference in the period are posited as diverse and malleable, but the new readings of alterity continuously struggle to reconcile the larger moral economies of differences with the more specific racialized forms that stand out at the end of the century. Roxanna Wheeler, for example, has argued that "throughout the eighteenth century older conceptions of Christianity, civility, and rank were *more explicitly* important to Britons' assessment of themselves and other people than physical attributes such as skin color, shape of the nose, or texture of the hair."[168] She has further asserted that other marks of rank, such as dress, manners, and language, constituted more visible forms of difference and that developmental, so-called four-stage theories of human development, "arguably offered a more significant form of racialization of the body politic than the categories concerning the physical body found in natural history."[169]

But my overall focus on the role of blackness in the negative dialectic of modernity departs from this diffuseness of difference, or, rather, its pluralization. Models developed within philosophy or natural history would, of course, be more nuanced than the images of black difference that circulated in the common culture, but this does not make them more compelling for two particular reasons that are central to my project. First, the power of visual images—what has come to be known as "the scopic regime" of modernity—cannot be underestimated.[170] From early modern notions of perspective to the retinal images that Descartes put at the center of his philosophy of mind, the visual was the dominant model of representation in the reimagination of a modern identity, and this has led scholars of theories of the mind, the imaginary, and epistemology to conclude that modernity was "resolutely ocularcentric" and to identify the "ubiquity of vision as the master sense of the modern era."[171]

Second, explored in purely visual terms, the image of the black would retain surprising consistency, thus challenging the ideas of immutable difference noted earlier. Here, the issue is not whether images of blacks in the European regimen of representation were positive or negative; rather, across the whole spectrum of modernity, from the early modern period to the era of high imperialism, from the European courts to the streets and coffeehouses of the modern period, the black stood out because of his or her color. It was color that made black difference visible, either in a demonic or benign fashion. In fact, in the few instances when they sought to overcome the logic of difference, European commentators and engravers of African scenes strove to find a way around blackness altogether and present the African in a "white face" thereby deploying analogy to efface polarity.[172] The preference of analogy over polarity was particularly marked in the early modern period when Europeans sought to convert

Africans and thus sought paradigms that would efface difference. Many Italian or Portuguese accounts of African social and political institutions from the end of the sixteenth century and throughout the seventeenth assumed that black polities and principalities were not different from European ones and hence did not shy away from the superimposition of African experiences with European ideographs.[173] Looking at Theodore de Bry's illustrations of the dresses of Congo nobleman (fig. 1.6), for example, one can assume that the famous engravers did not make any distinction between Africans and Europeans, that blackness was not a negative or remarked feature in their imagination of the other.[174] Alternatively, one could argue that African subjects, cultures, and customs could only be communicated through European models or masks.

The De Brys did not, of course, set foot in Africa, and their illustrations were based on the accounts of the travelers whose works they were engraving, but one can assume that what was foremost in the minds of both writers and illustrators was the task of assimilating Africa to fit into European ideals of social class, cultural practices, and behavior. Here, the work of conversion or cultural translation was predicated on both the recognition of difference and its transcendence. For, as Vicente Rafael has observed in a different context, translation "involves not simply the ability to speak in a language other than one's own but the capacity to reshape one's thoughts and actions in accordance with accepted forms."[175] Premised on the need "to submit to the conventions of a given social order," translation becomes "a matter of first discerning the differences between and within social codes and then of seeing the possibility of getting across those differences."[176]

Still, the discourse of similitude was always marginal and ephemeral. The causes of this ephemerality were the political, cultural, and legal demands of slavery, especially in the Americas. The political and moral economy of slavery mandated the separation of the black and white, even in similar conditions of servitude, as was the case in colonial Virginia, and the isolation of the African from what was considered human under law and convention. Racial attitudes and imagery may have hardened at the end of the eighteenth century, but no one doubts that they had been there at the beginning of the modern period. Similarly, it is difficult to conceive of modern slavery without its manifest racism. This racism had a paradigmatic, syntagmatic, and pragmatic value. The paradigmatic axis was one of negation and dissociation: blackness served a useful purpose in the modern social imaginary because it represented the spectrum against which whiteness was imagined. Blackness also helped nurture what Winthrop Jordan has called a "novel relativism"; the color of the African "was to remain for centuries what it had been from the first, a standing problem for natural philosophers."[177] The whiteness of Queen

1.6 Johan Theodore and Johan Israel de Bry, *Dress of the Noblemen and Commonalty of Kongo*. From Thomas Astley, ed., *A New General Collection of Voyages and Travels* (London, 1745–1747), vol. 3, plate xv, facing p. 248.

Elizabeth's alabaster bosom was often measured against the color of the "blackmoores," who, though threatening to contaminate the realm, could still find a place as pendants on her earrings and at the top of the family crest of John Hawkins, her slave trader.[178] Whether elevated or demonized in the European imagination, "it was the African's color of skin that became his defining characteristic, and aroused the deepest response in Europeans."[179] Even William Blake, an opponent of slavery in good standing, couldn't imagine Africans having an identity outside their color (fig. 1.7)

The visual visibility of blacks does not imply that they were the only others considered outside the norm of the human and thus essentially fated for slavery. On the contrary, scholars of slavery have noted how, in the Americas especially, Native Americans were imagined and processed to provide the first paradigm for difference as a precondition for domination.[180] From the mines of Peru to the farms of North America, native peoples were the first to be included in the economy of bondage. And yet the enslavement of Native Americans was rarely justified through the invocation of their color, for while Europeans and white Americans held "a deep prejudice against almost all aspects of Indian culture," they did not have a strong bias "against Indian color, shape, or features; the American native was socially deplorable but physically admirable."[181] The distinction between culture and color would have important consequences both for debates about the notions of taste and for the presence of slavery in domains that prided themselves for their innate capacity for freedom.

One way that advocates of the Enlightenment and the culture of taste in the Americas could rationalize slavery, for example, was to insist on the alienness of the African, as denoted by color, in the geography of the new world. Like other members of the Virginia aristocracy, to cite one famous example, Thomas Jefferson considered Native Americans to be similar to whites; they were essentially the same people "and the differences between them were superficial, the effects of environment rather than biology."[182] In contrast, Jefferson would often reflect on the meaning of the black skin and the deficits associated with it, seeking to establish a scientific and rational explanation for the syntagmatic that was also the stigmata:

> The first difference which strikes us is that of colour. Whether the black of the negro resides in the reticular membrane between the skin and scarf-skin, or in the scarf-skin itself; whether it proceeds from the colour of the blood, the colour of the bile, or from that of some other secretion, the difference is fixed in nature, and is as real as if its seat and cause were better known to us. And is this difference of no importance? Is it not the foundation of a greater or less share of beauty in the two races? Are not the fine mixtures of red and white, the expressions of every passion by greater or less suffusions of colour in the one, preferable to that eternal monotony, which reigns in the countenances, that immoveable veil of black which covers all the emotions of the other race?[183]

Jefferson would go on to a make a direct analogy between the civilizational abilities of native Americans, or at least their potential for

1.7 William Blake, *Europe Supported by Africa and America*. 1796. Engraving. From John Gabriel Stedman, *Narrative of a Five Years' Expedition against the Revolted Negroes of Surinam*. Copy in Princeton University Library.

membership in the kingdom of culture and the realm of taste, and black cultural incapacity:

> The Indians, with no advantages of this kind, will often carve figures on their pipes not destitute of design and merit. They will crayon out an animal, a plant, or a country, so as to prove the existence of a germ in their minds which only wants cultivation. They astonish you with strokes of the most sublime oratory; such as prove their reason and sentiment strong, their imagination glowing and elevated. But never yet could I find that a black had uttered a thought above the level of plain narration; never see even an elementary trait of painting or sculpture.[184]

One could argue, of course, that the development of a racial imaginary, especially one predicated on color differences, was driven by the pragmatic need to establish moral and legal boundaries between white servants and black slaves in the American colonies. But as I will show in the next three chapters, even when the political economy of slavery presupposed racism or used it as a form of rationalization, it still demanded a relentless racial logic and a sensorium predicated on blackness as a form of disgust. For some leading cultural citizens of Virginia, blacks as a race were considered to be, in the words of Arthur Lee, "the most detestable and vile that ever the earth produced."[185] This was a view echoed by Edward Long in the *History of Jamaica*, which I will return to in later chapters.[186]

Theories of race and racism were shifting throughout the modern period, and it may well be the case that by the end of the eighteenth century, hard-core racist thinking had moved from the broader cultural sphere to what Wahrman has termed "eccentric outposts."[187] But whether we are dealing with the belated attempt by agents of the slave trade—the Liverpool interest, for example—to deploy the specter of race to justify their profits; or the abolitionists' imposition of a pathos of suffering on the black body, as was evident in Josiah Wedgwood's famous medallion for the committee on the abolition of the slave trade; or Blake's attempts to imagine the African woman in the comity of nations, racialization seems to have increased rather than diminished at the end of the eighteenth century. The aura of blackness seemed inescapable.

Intersections:
Taste, Slavery, and the Modern Self

Judging from the entry she made in her diary, Monday, April 24, 1797, was a very good day for Anna Margaretta Larpent (fig. 2.1), a theater critic and woman of taste. On that particular day, Larpent rose up early and, after prayer, attended to some family business, including hemming and mending a handkerchief for her son George; she then read Claude Carloman de Rulhièr's *Histoire ou Anecdotes sur La Révolution de Russie; en l'Année 1762*. She would spend the rest of the day visiting or corresponding with friends, attending to other domestic matters, and doing some reading. We know that reading was an important part of Larpent's life, because a marked feature of her diary entry for Monday, April 24, 1797, as for other days, was the summary of the texts she had read, often presented as the culminating act of what was supposed to be an ordinary day. Indeed, a good portion of her entry for April 24 was devoted to reflections on Rulhier's book, calling attention to the anecdotes that had bemused her most, including "among others the meeting between Biren and Munich when Peter the Great recalled them and ordered them to drink together."[1]

Read as fragments or glimpses into a day in the life of an English-woman in the second half of the eighteenth century, Larpent's diary entries strike one as quotidian, but considered as a whole, in their entire seventeen volumes, these diaries now stand as some of the most impressive records of the lived experience of the culture of taste in the eighteenth century, a compelling account of what John Brewer has termed the "pleasures of the imagination."[2] Here we have a vivid account of an intellectual, middle-class woman at the end of the long eighteenth century, one whose identity had been enabled by an aesthetic sensibility, cultural uplift, and the careful mastery of the economy of manners and taste. For those looking for the objects and practices that constituted the fabric of

2.1 Entry from *The Diaries of Anna Margaretta Larpent, A Woman's View of Drama*, 1790–1830.

modern, cultured life, Larpent's diaries affirm the principle of the archive as one of "consignation, that is, of gathering together" fragments of the everyday to constitute a social, regulated order of the self.[3] In this record of a life, carefully recorded and choreographed to live up to the ideals of sense and sensibility, commerce and politeness would appear to have been reconciled. Here we have a subject going about the business of consuming culture as the precondition of a modern identity. And for women like Larpent, to be modern was to find a secure space at the intersection of art, civility, and good manners.

◇◆◇

Monday, April 24, 1797, did not go too well for an African woman named Nealee. On that day she was part of a coffle making its way slowly through the Sahel region of West Africa on the way to the Atlantic coast. As a slave, Nealee did not leave a diary or any kind of record about her life or experiences; indeed, had she not been traveling in the company of Mungo Park (fig. 2.2), the Scottish botanist and explorer, she could have been one of the many voices lost in the vault of African slavery. Park was in the final phase of his journey through the unforgiving terrain of the Sahel, and his route had taken him from Jillifree (Juffurreh), on the mouth of the Gambia River, through the Bambara and Wolof countries, and then back to the Atlantic coast. At a place called Kamalia (fig. 2.3) "situated at the bottom of some rocky hills, where the inhabitants collect gold in considerable quantities," Park was the guest of a slave trader called Karfa Taura.[4] During Park's stay in Kamalia, Karfa acquired slaves—presumably bartered for gold dust—from the Bambara country and kept them under fetters and bolts, waiting for the opportune time to transport them to the Gambia, on the Atlantic coast. On April 19, 1797, Karfa and his slaves—and Park, the sole scriptural witness to this event—embarked on their arduous journey in a typical slave coffle consisting of "twenty-seven slaves for sale, the property of Karfa and four other slatees."[5] Several days later, on April 23, the coffle left the Mandingo territories and entered what Park described as the "Jallonka Wilderness," a landscape bearing the scars of war as rival African kingdoms fought to harvest human captives to feed the expanding plantation economies of the Americas.[6]

On April 24, the very day when Anna Margaretta Larpent was going about the ordinary business of consuming culture and consolidating her middle-class identity, reading books on Russian history and holding conversations with her friends, Nealee, one of Karfa's slaves, got "very sulky," refused to eat, and developed an irreversible wish to die.[7] Apparently, Nealee had decided that it was better to die in the Sahel than live under servitude in the alien lands that lay across the unknown ocean. Of course, we don't know the exact reasons for Nealee's desire to die, but from Park's description, it is quite obvious that a certain drive for death had overcome her. Park observed how Nealee lagged behind the coffle and complained "dreadfully of pains in her leg"; he also noted how her laggardness functioned as either as an expression of a death wish or a form of passive resistance:

> Her load was taken from her, and given to another slave, and she was ordered to keep in the front of the coffle. About eleven o'clock, as we were resting by a small rivulet, some of the people discovered a hive of bees in a hollow tree, and they were proceeding to obtain the honey, when the largest swarm I ever beheld, flew out, and attacking the people of the coffle, made us fly in all directions. I took the alarm first, and I believe was the only person who escaped with impunity. When our enemies thought fit to desist from pursuing us, and every person was employed in picking out the stings he had received, it was

2.2 Mungo Park, frontispiece, 1799. From Mungo Park, *Travels in the Interior Districts of Africa*. Copy in Princeton University Library.

2.3 View of Kamalia. 1799. From Mungo Park, *Travels in the Interior Districts of Africa*. Copy in Princeton University Library.

discovered that the poor woman abovementioned, whose name was Nealee, was not come up; and as many of the slaves in their retreat had left their bundles behind them, it became necessary for some persons to return, and bring them. In order to do this with safety, fire was set to the grass, a considerable way to the eastward of the hive, and the wind driving the fire furiously along, the party pushed through the smoke, and recovered the bundles. They likewise

brought with them poor Nealee, whom they found lying by the rivulet. She
was very much exhausted, and had crept to the stream, in hopes to defend
herself from the bees by throwing water over her body; but this proved inef-
fectual; for she was stung in the most dreadful manner.[8]

Apparently, whichever way she looked at it, Nealee's life would end at a
point of death. The only question was how and where this death would
occur.

Here we have one day in April 1797, two cultural geographies, two distinct lives: Anna Margaretta Larpent, icon of social mobility in the culture
of taste, writer of voluminous diaries, a woman attuned to the cultural
sensibilities of her time; and Nealee, a faceless African woman slave in a
coffle, bought for gold dust in an Bambara slave market, destined to die
somewhere between Sego and the Gambia. These two women were in the
crucible of modern culture, invariably separated by race, geography, and
fate, but also conjoined by a new global economy that revolved around
the sale of black bodies on the West African coast, their enforced labor
in the Americas, and their use in the production of the goods—primarily
tobacco, coffee, and sugar—that were to epitomize luxurious living and
the culture of taste. These small stories of two women represent the true
entanglement of modernity, of the unlikely yet inevitable meeting of the
most elevated and the most demeaned subjects of the modern era, the age
of reason, enlightenment, and civility, which was also the time of slavery.
And beyond their individual and asymmetrical experiences in the library
of empire, the stories of these two women raise several issues that go to
the heart of the tenuous relation between slavery and the culture of taste:
How does one tell the stories of lives and experiences that were structurally connected through the political economy of slavery yet conceptu-
ally and symbolically separated? How does one overcome the ostensible
incommensurability between Larpent's highly visible narrative of modern self-fashioning and Nealee's almost invisible story of abjection, her
existence as a thing without a sign, one condemned to "bear the weight
of meaninglessness" and to leave behind a mere trace in the archive of
modern identity?[9] And how does one tell these two stories in the same
register? This chapter will seek to answer these questions in three discursive operations. First, I will sketch out the context in which subjects like
Larpent were transformed through the consumption of culture; then I
will provide a reading of the typical life of a slave like Nealee confronting European modernity for the first time; and, finally, I will explore the
intersections of these two modes of life in the theater of our modern
identity.

2

To examine Larpent's life in the eighteenth century or to consider her mastery of the practices and theories of modern life is an invitation to reflect on the exemplary ways in which culture became the most obvious form of social mobility and self-making in the century that invented the modern individual.[10] Larpent's elaborate diaries contain a tutored insider's view of the culture of taste in the eighteenth century and represent the elegance of a Georgian woman of taste. And in her command of high culture, which involved, among other things, reading radical pamphlets and conduct books, attending plays and art galleries, and socializing with public officials and diplomats, Larpent transformed herself from an ordinary housewife into a lady of taste, a cultured middle-class subject. Married to John Larpent, who was the examiner or censor of plays at the office of the Lord Chamberlain, Anna Margaretta was so deeply involved in the Georgian art scene that she often acted as the unofficial deputy to her husband; in this capacity she had access to some of the most important dramatic works of her age.

Larpent's central location in the geography of English society at the end of the eighteenth century—the period in which the category of culture became central to British self-understanding—has prompted John Brewer to identify her as the quintessential "cultured lady of late eighteenth-century London":

> She was not an aristocrat but neither was she poor. Though she was busy with household duties and the education of her children, like many other moderately prosperous women (the family income was more than £400 a year) she had enough time and leisure to enjoy many of the metropolis's cultural activities. But she did not view her recreations frivolously. She aspired to what she called "a refinement which can only be felt in the pure pleasure of intellectual pursuits." The proof of this quest, the evidence that her frequent play-and concert-going, together with her assiduous reading, were edifying rather than amusing, is to be found in her journal.[11]

Working with the evidence Larpent left behind in her diaries, Brewer notes that she was not only living the cultured life but was also "carefully and repeatedly" representing herself as "a cultured person": "Though she certainly saw herself in other ways—as a Christian, a friend, a mother and a wife—her overriding concern in the diary was with her fashioning of a refined persona. Her version of the good life is one devoted to self-improvement through literature, the arts and learning."[12] Larpent's social mobility, and thus her self-willed movement from the margins of English society to its center, was not enabled solely by money (her means, as Brewer rightly notes, were modest), nor was her rise on the social scale achieved by rank or marriage; rather, her self-fashioning was shaped through the mechanisms of cultural consumption that I discussed in the last chapter.[13]

Larpent had an uncanny ability to overcome the assumed divide between the business of everyday life and the rarified work of culture; in fact, an intriguing aspect of her method as a diarist was the fusion of quotidian matters with what Raymond Williams would call "the general process of intellectual, spiritual and aesthetic development."[14] Her diary entry for Wednesday, April 26, 1797, illustrates how on any given day she would make having breakfast, attending to family matters, and commenting on her readings for the day appear almost seamless: she rose at eight, said her prayers, attended to her journal, had breakfast, settled the last week's bills, dined at five, and then, as if the whole day needed to be laundered through the practice of culture, "read and finished Bertrand de Malleville's memoirs."[15] Larpent's deep sense of culture was crucial to her self-presentation in public space. Although born in Turkey (the daughter of a British diplomat) and orphaned early, she would adroitly use her intimate knowledge of the idiom of taste to enter the public sphere at its moment of emergence and consolidation.[16] She fashioned herself with the best cultural objects available to her—assemblies, balls, plays, concerts, art galleries, and, of course, an engagement with the key texts of her time, including Thomas Paine's *The Rights of Man* and Samuel Richardson's *Clarissa*. All of this locates her at the center of a historical moment in which the rise of a culture of taste as the mediator of social position constituted an important mode of freedom, one as important as the philosophical treatises of the age of Enlightenment. Moreover, culturedness enabled women like Larpent to have access to a set of social privileges that in previous generations had been the preserve of aristocratic men.

The terms in which female subjectivity was constructed at the end of the eighteenth century have been debated and questioned, and there is no doubt that women, even privileged ones, still occupied a subordinate position in relation to aristocratic and middle-class men, but as Ann Bermingham has noted, the "aesthetization of women" signaled a new valuation of the female as—almost—a work of art.[17] Undoubtedly, cultured women like Larpent were presented and valuated through the anxieties and desires of male patrons and spectators (very much like aesthetic objects), but the dominance of the masculine gaze did not preclude a certain degree of freedom in the structure and mode of sensibility. In short, there is no indication that Larpent perceived her place in the family as a form of confinement, nor did she make the analogy between her condition and that of African slaves in the manner of Jane Eyre in Charlotte Brontë's novel of that name.[18] On the contrary, the journeys that Larpent would make on an ordinary day, crisscrossing London's cultural and human geography, suggest great mobility and with it a cherished sense of freedom. Her diary clearly, consistently, and forcefully demonstrates that the domestic scene, often associated with feminine confinement by many critics, overflowed into the public domain.[19] It shows how an engagement with the fine arts and the cultivation of a cultural sense redirected the self toward a new set of privileges and entitlements, so that with "the gradual profusion of Georgian assembly rooms, plays, picture galleries, libraries, museums and pleasure gardens, a full range of cultural resources was now available for those who wished to be refined."[20] Moreover, the tone of her diaries indicates that Larpent felt fortunate to have been born in an age in which the palpable intersection of wealth, consumption, and culture had created a public space for presenting the self as freed by its contact—and contract—with culture.

For Larpent and many of her contemporaries, then, an association with the culture of taste, the self-conscious engagement with cultural matters, located the modern self in a larger moral space. This moral space, as the philosopher Charles Taylor has argued, was one of the preconditions for the emergence of a modern identity.[21] In the domain of cultural consumption and refinement, the private self would become a public subject. Indeed, the presentation of the cultured self in public spaces of entertainment such as luxury gardens, concert halls, and theaters, or even the presentation of what might appear to be private gestures, including reading, as public acts was a prerequisite for what one may call the pose of the self. Even when culture was consumed privately, it needed to be publicized in portraits and conversational pieces. Indeed, paintings such as Sir Joshua Reynolds's *Theophila Palmer Reading "Clarissa Harlowe"* are often cited as prominent examples of the staging of reading as an act of cultural distinction, a fact that Larpent was conscious of, because the longest entries in her diaries are about the books that she read.[22] Similarly, the proliferation of "conversational pieces" was a striking feature of English culture in the eighteenth century. Affirmed and mocked in William Hogarth's best works, such as *The Cholmondeley Family*, these domestic scenes of cultural posturing provided the prism through which the new leisure class wanted to be viewed in the emergent public sphere. In paintings like these, domestic scenes would be conceived as simultaneously private and public spaces, sites of cultural refinement and its possible undoing.[23] Conversation pieces, like diaries, represented the intertwining of the public and private contexts that enabled "the emergence of a new identity as a public person of taste and refinement."[24]

To understand the relationship between slavery and the culture of taste, however, one must question, qualify, and complicate the structural relationship between the private realm, carefully cultivated to represent the ideals of the cultured subject, and the public site of presentation, the scene of the world picture, as it were.[25] This kind of interrogation is necessary because often the form of representing modern life as both private and public, as was the case with diaries, portraits, and conversation pieces, was intended to erase the difference between the picture and its referents or, rather, to make the picture an idealized stand-in for social life. Artists like Hogarth operated under the knowledge that their wealthy patrons wanted them to represent domestic life as orderly and ordered even when it was quite apparent that social life in the modern world was often more disordered than the symmetrical mandate of the portrait or conversation piece suggested. The challenge for artists, then, was to represent this complex and sometimes-chaotic world as a set of stable images of cultural well-being. Inevitably, the resulting images, like the reigning discourses of the age, promoted a set of values that were often at odds with the materiality of modern life. The aesthetic ideology of the eighteenth century emphasized an order of "exacted thoughtful conduct, clear intellect and organised design," one whose correlatives were "political and religious balance instead of frenzy, efficient style and idea instead of complexity, discipline of vision instead of spasmodic tentativeness."[26] But outside this vision of Augustan order was to be found the most aggressive and successful maritime economy of modern times. The consequence of this was that at its center, British identity was characterized and informed by a critical dichotomy between the ideal of commerce as part of the civilizing process and the actual conditions of commercial growth in the imperial zone. More significantly for my discussion here, the projection of an Augustan order based on politeness, good taste, and manners was at odds with the logic of economic development in the reaches of empire, which demanded total control and brutal governance—and slave labor.[27]

Was the coexistence of a culture of order and refinement and an aggressive empire an anomaly? To answer this question, which is one of the objectives of this chapter, it is important to recall the function of the picture (or the aesthetic) in the making of modern identity. Martin Heidegger has argued that one of the essential consequences of the modern age was "the production of objectivism" as a correlative to individualism: at precisely the moment that the human became a subject, freed from the bonds and obligations of tradition, it found itself in a world in which the nonindividual, in the form of the collective, "came to acceptance as having worth."[28] This claim—that the age of the individual was also the moment of emergence of the collective—is essential to understanding the paradoxes of the culture of taste in Britain, for it was in the crucial middle decades of the eighteenth century that a discourse was produced in which the valorization of the autonomous individual was dependent on conformity to a certain set of communal norms.[29] The Kantian idea that taste was "the capacity for judging the conformity of the power of the imagination in its freedom with the legitimacy of the understanding" was not going to get very far in Britain.[30] On the contrary, as Lord Kames argued in *Elements of Criticism* (which he dedicated to George III), the goal of the aesthetic project was to develop a theory of art to serve the social order: "The Fine Arts have ever been encouraged by wise Princes, not simply for private amusement, but for their beneficial influence in society. By uniting different ranks in the same elegant pleasures, they promote benevolence: by cherishing love of order, they enforce submission to government: and by inspiring a delicacy of feeling, they make regular government a double blessing."[31]

If there is one term that runs consistently through British theories of taste, it is regulation—the management of feelings, behavior, and government. Still, as major scholars of the order of art in the eighteenth century have noted, the category of taste and the idea of the aesthetic in general arose as part of a concerted attempt to stabilize the potentially excessive and disruptive aspects of commerce. This has led critics of the so-called ideology of the aesthetic to conclude that the turn to matters of taste was an attempt to force ethics, aesthetics, and politics into a harmonious existence: when the whole of social life is aestheticized, Terry Eagleton concludes, an image of a social order is made "so spontaneously cohesive that its members no longer need to think about it."[32] But as I have already indicated in my brief exploration of Larpent's world, it was precisely because the culture of taste was being asked to perform the task of harmonizing culture at odds with the lived experiences of modern society that it could not exist outside the pressures of everyday life and by extension its materiality. Thus, to talk about the culture of taste as an ideology is to recognize its capacity to mediate what Louis Althusser has called the lived relation between subjects on both the conscious and unconscious levels.[33]

One way of contextualizing the world that produced cultured subjects, then, is to develop a genealogy of the idiom these people deployed in order to make sense of their world. This idiom—made up of terms such as *taste* and *politeness* that might strike us as archaic within the larger philosophical discourse of modern subjection pegged on rationality— was essential to the maintenance of the idea of modernity, or at least its perception. Take, for example, the vocabulary of politeness. On the surface it would appear to be nothing more than the commonsensical dictum that subjects should maintain a certain mode of behavior in public and in relation to one another. But in the middle of the eighteenth century, the notion of politeness would be promoted as the key word in the construction and presentation of British common culture and a potential unifier of private virtue and public commercial activities, the two poles that defined modern society. Indeed, politeness was considered so crucial to the conduct of Englishness that the distinguished jurist Sir William Blackstone would assert, in his influential *Commentaries on the Laws of England*, that the English were "a polite and commercial people."[34] Politeness came to define what the English were, or thought themselves to be; it provided the singular visual aesthetic and discourse through which generations of students have come to see and imagine modern England. The idea of politeness so powerfully defined the aesthetic of the eighteenth century in England that it was "stamped on the country houses and portraits" and inscribed in the "standard texts through which modern readers customarily encounter eighteenth-century literature."[35]

There was, however, another side to the ideal of politeness: it was also intimately connected to commercial activities and the rather impolite business of moneymaking; in an age of unprecedented economic expansion, questions of trade and exchange were considered not anterior to cultural refinement but expressive of it—their condition of possibility. It is thus not paradoxical that, as a social category, politeness came into being as a social norm at a time when the nature and meaning of commerce was being reevaluated. In effect, politeness would come "forever to be associated with the enterprise of an age of extraordinary economic growth, accompanied by the first clear signs of industrialization."[36] The consumer boom in England at the end of the eighteenth century—"the rapid transmission of new wants, for the rapid spread of new fashions, for class competition, social emulation and emulative spending"—demanded a recalibration of social relationships at the most basic level.[37] The commercialization of society in areas as diverse as politics and leisure lay at the heart of the modernizing or, as Norbert Elias called it, "the civilizing process."[38]

Still, the idea of politeness in the age of commerce presents us with a few analytical knots that need to be untied. The most intractable of these was the tenuous idea of politeness as a private category, which was, nevertheless, authorized or legitimized by its perspicuity in the public realm. Here, again, Larpent provides us with an excellent case study. Her diaries showcase a life in which the most private behavior was seamlessly connected to the public life of an intellectual and cultured woman. Her everyday occupations reflect an almost effortless linkage of the mundaneness of domestic life (the mending of her son's handkerchief, for example) and the reading of popular and sometimes canonical texts of her day. Her daily movement from the scene of domesticity to the realm of high culture seems to overcome any assumed difference between these two spheres of social life. The act of keeping a diary—the putting of one's life into writing—was crucial in overcoming the private public dyad, which, according to Jürgen Habermas, was one of the transformative categories of modern culture.[39]

Attempts to blur the distinction between the private and public spheres through regulated modes of conduct concealed both the tensions that informed them and the constraints that persisted even after their enforced reconciliation. To the extent that it could not be legislated, politeness was a mode of private behavior that depended on the desires and choices of individuals. And yet, in order to become a socially acceptable category, politeness had to be presented as a public act for modes of behavior acquired value through their exhibition, where culture was "characterized by an emphasis upon social display" and cultured sites became "places of self-presentation in which audiences made publicly visible their wealth, status, social and sexual charms."[40] Furthermore, where politeness did not come naturally to certain social classes, such as the lower classes, it needed to be regulated by what Lord Shaftesbury called a "sensus communis." [41] Although Shaftesbury considered the ideal of politeness to thrive in conditions of liberty, he believed that its promotion as the reigning code of conduct might need to be enforced through "rigorous Prescription."[42] Within the culture of the aristocracy, where politeness might be assumed to come naturally, reconciling private interiors with the public domain presented its own difficulties of representation—namely, how to achieve a balance between communal duty and personal desire.

The tension between public duty and private desire was evident in the great country houses that came to define refinement and politeness. Monumental buildings, such as Castle Howard, designed for Charles Howard, 3rd Earl of Carlisle, by John Vanbrugh and Nicholas Hawksmoor between 1699 and 1712 (fig. 2.4), were already perceived as visible expressions of a new, stylized way of living and being. In such buildings, commerce had acquired an aesthetic form, one associated with a "civilized if secular outlook" with "its faith in a measured code of manners, its attachment to elegance and stateliness, its oligarchic politics and aristocratic fashions."[43] Conceived and built when the culture of taste was in its infancy but completed when it was at its peak, Castle Howard would come to reflect the tensions between an unregulated private desire and the measured code of manners expected of the leisured class.

More significantly, the evident transformations in the architecture of Castle Howard reflected changing notions of taste in the course of the long eighteenth century. Originally conceived in the Baroque style of the late seventeenth century, the building reflected what one critic has termed a "cumulative symmetry" and "carefully articulated relationships" that were not at odds with the then reigning idea of order and control: "Each element in the composition—the main block, the curved colonnades, and

2.4 The garden front of Castle Howard in Yorkshire, England. Early eighteenth century. From Colen Campbell's *Vitruvius Britannicus.*

the little palaces which form the wings—has its own sufficient life, yet by a skilful transmission of units through the entire design absolute congruity is achieved."[44] Although Castle Howard's exteriors were notable for their ornate façades, elaborately carved coronets, ciphers, and coats of arms, these fit into the dominant idea that ornateness was not in itself inimical to social order. But as the building continued to be constructed through the Palladian period, which is closely associated with the culture of taste, its new wings came to reflect the sober and measured style favored by the Whig aristocracy. In both cases, however, the Baroque and Palladian still invested heavily in the idea of symmetry and control over the extravagance of the neoclassical or Gothic styles that were to supersede them at the end of the century.

The differences that are important to this argument, then, are not those between the Baroque and the Palladian as measures of the way the culture of taste understood the relationship between form and social space, but the distinction between exteriors and interiors. For what is startling about Castle Howard is the radical contrast between its carefully articulated exteriors and the extravagant interior, especially the domed entrance hall and gallery, filled with expensive furniture, statues, and china, and the works of some of the leading European painters, including Peter Paul Rubens, Sir Anthony van Dyck, and Sir Joshua Reynolds. The contrast between a symmetrical exterior and an extravagant interior reflected the bifurcated order in which the culture of taste thrived: on one side, controlled and measured exteriors; on the other, an extravagant display of the best art objects that money could buy. This bifurcated fashioning of cultural life would eventually call attention to the essential interpretative problem that the culture of taste would present to its interlocutors: how could the world of money be reconciled to the sensuousness of culture?

Anna Larpent was obviously not in the same class as Charles How-ard or the colonial barons I discuss in the next chapter, but she stands out for her acute sense of how the exteriors and interiors of modern life could be reconciled. In this sense, middle-class subjects were ahead of their aristocratic contemporaries in understanding how the two spheres of social life could be reconciled. Yet neither in Larpent's diary nor in the refined world of Castle Howard is there a hint of the nature of the political economy of the period, especially the crass commercial activities that had compelled Richard Steele to warn that "the most polite Age" was in "danger of being the most vicious."[45] An aggressive commercial culture rooted in imperial control and expansion had enabled the culture of taste, but it had become its unspoken, almost unspeakable, event. Also unspoken and often unspeakable were the other bodies in this equation— the millions of African slaves, whose bodies were a key ingredient in the production of the wealth that made the culture of consumption possible.

3

And it is precisely at this point when the culture of taste seems most silent about the material conditions that enabled it, that Nealee, the woman in my second story, enters the scene of modern culture and its apparatus of representation. As I have already noted, the colonial library does not contain much information about her existence, and except for snippets about the last years of her life contained in Park's *Travels in the Interior Districts of Africa*, she would be considered absent from the imperial archive. Her truncated presence, however, is crucial to a contrapuntal reading of the colonial library and its texts, for what we glimpse in those few pages devoted to her is a life presented under erasure; in her pres-ence and absence we encounter a repertoire of experience that disturbs the epistemological frame of the imperial archive itself.[46] How do we, then, read Nealee's last days *sous rature* (under erasure) in the narrative of Mungo Park?

Let us start with what we know about her: We know that she was an African from the Sene-Gambia region of West Africa, captured in war and sold into slavery at the end of the eighteenth century. We know that in roughly the same years that Anna Larpent was transforming herself into a subject of politeness and taste, Nealee was being held captive in the Bam-bara kingdom of Segu for three years before she was sold to an African slave trader called Karfa, who put her on a coffle headed for the Atlantic coast on April 24, 1797. We know that Nealee was born in a world where slavery, as a commodity and mode of exchange, was highly treasured, a place where bodies for sale were valued as much as gold dust.[47]

How did this world of commodified black bodies appear to Park, a man born and brought up in the heart of the Scottish Enlightenment, educated as a scientist at the University of Edinburgh, thus feeding from the culture of taste in one of its intellectual centers? As a Calvinist, Park may not have shown much interest in the consumption of culture, but he could not have ignored the codes that regulated behavior in his time, so we can assume that his encounter with the world of African slavery was both strange and eerily familiar. The culture of African slavery perhaps did not present itself as a modernist institution, but because its existence depended on the demands of the modern economies of Europe and the Americas, it was attuned to the rules of *supply and demand*, an economic term first used and popularized by Park's fellow Scots James Denham-Steuart and Adam Smith. Here in the Sahel, as in other world trading centers, the exchange of credit and goods was what made the wheels of time move, and, on the surface, economic transactions would appear to be quite ordinary. This ordinariness is evident in Park's description of the laws of supply and demand that were at work at the slave market of Kamalia: "About a week after the departure of Karfa, three Moors arrived at Kamalia with a considerable quantity of salt, and other merchandize, which they had obtained on credit, from a merchant of Fezzan, who had lately arrived at Kancaba. Their engagement was to pay him his price when the goods were sold, which they expected would be in the course of a month. Being rigid Bushreens, they were accommodated with two of Karfa's huts, and sold their goods to very great advantage."[48] There was no hint that this was anything but an ordinary marketplace.

But beyond the ordinariness of this scene of exchange, there was an added dimension to the system of trade in the Sahel: here, slaves were a prominent part of the commercial nexus, mediating both the exchange of goods and the nature, if not structure, of social relationships. Rather than being a radical deviation from the order of things, Parks noted, slavery mediated both the exchange of goods and private affairs such as marriage: "On the 24th of January, Karfa returned to Kamalia with a number of people, and thirteen prime slaves which he had purchased. He like-wise brought with him a young girl whom he had married at Kancaba, as his fourth wife, and had given her parents three prime slaves for her. She was kindly received at the door of the Baloon by Karfa's other wives, who conducted their new acquaintance and co-partner into one of the best huts, which they had caused to be swept and white-washed, on purpose to receive her."[49] What Park was observing here was not a spectacular event but a casual everyday transaction, one in which the exchange of slaves for valuable goods was not different from the use of gold or even salt in such matters. In fact, slaves were a more common form of exchange than either gold or salt. Here is Park again: "The slaves which Karfa had brought with him were all of them prisoners of war; they had been taken by the Bambarran army in the kingdoms of Wassela and Kaarta, and carried to Sego, where some of them had remained three years in irons. From Sego they were sent, in company with a number of other captives, up the Niger in two large canoes, and offered for sale at Yamina, Bammakoo, and Kancaba; at which places the greater number of the captives were bartered for gold-dust, and the remainder sent forward to Kankaree."[50]

It would appear extraordinary that a bride had been exchanged for slaves, or that bodies were bartered for gold dust, but what is perhaps more interesting about Park's account is the quotidian nature of these transactions and the matter-of-fact tone he adopted in describing enslavement in the political economy of the Sahel. There was no hint that the explorer considered this to be a scene of moral luck.[51] Indeed, morality as a whole seems to be absent from the interrelations between the free and enslaved in the emerging global markets of the eighteenth century. The absence of moral judgment does not, however, preclude conceptual connections. Like Larpent, Nealee was caught in the middle of the political economy of modern life, an experience that, to loop back to Charles Taylor's phrase, was categorized by a sense of ordinariness.[52] But, unlike Larpent, Nealee was not free; she was the enforced object of this ordinariness, not its subject—the consumed, not the consumer. In fact, what would finally force Park's account to break through the quotidian character of slave trading, or rather the use of slaves as objects of trade, were the images of shackled captives, including Nealee, on their long march to the West African coast and its slave ports:

> They are commonly secured, by putting the right leg of one, and the left of another, into the same pair of fetters. By supporting the fetters with a string, they can walk, though very slowly. Every four slaves are likewise fastened together by the necks, with a strong rope of twisted thongs; and in the night, an additional pair of fetters is put on their hands, and sometimes a light iron chain passed round their necks. Such of them as evince marks of discontent, are secured in a different manner. A thick billet of wood is cut about three feet long, and a smooth notch being made upon one side of it, the ankle of the slave is bolted to the smooth part by means of a strong iron staple, one prong of which passes on each side of the ankle. All these fetters and bolts are made from native iron; in the present case they were put on by the blacksmith as soon as the slaves arrived from Kancaba, and were not taken off until the morning on which the coffle departed for Gambia.[53]

Although some of the slaves in Karfa's coffle seemed to bear their hardships stoically, the majority of them "were very much dejected, and would sit all day in a sort of sullen melancholy, with their eyes fixed upon the ground."[54] And Nealee was the most melancholic, refusing even to eat her gruel. She seemed resigned to her physical imprisonment, but she was determined to resist her psychological enslavement by all the means at her disposal. She wanted to die.

Why was death so appealing to Nealee? Park thought that African slaves dreaded the prospect of being sold at the coast because they held a "deeply rooted idea" that "whites purchase Negroes for the purpose of devouring them, or of selling them to others, that they may be devoured hereafter."[55] But there was much more than this fear of real or imagined death. Although Nealee had spent at least three years in the stockades at Sego and endured many of the hardships that characterized the life of a body in bolt and chains, her journey on the slave route to the Atlantic coast represented a radical departure from the life she had known so far, for, as I will show later, there was slavery and the slave trade, and they represented different degrees of bondage and suffering.[56]

For most of April 24, after the bee attack episode described at the beginning of this chapter, Nealee refused to continue with her enforced march to modernity. As Park reports, "the wretched woman obstinately refused to proceed any further; declaring that she would rather die than walk another step."[57] Entreaties and threats were used on her to no avail. The whip was then applied, and this forced her to walk for another five hours; then she made an attempt to escape from the coffle but was too weary to get very far and she fell in the grass. The whip was applied again without effect, at which point Karfa had her put on the donkey that usually carried provisions; but the ass, "being very refractory," could not carry her forward, so she was borne on a litter of bamboo cane, which was carried by other slaves. It was quite apparent that Nealee was slowing the coffle considerably and thus jeopardizing the profits that awaited the slatees, or slave merchants, at the Gambia slave markets. A moment arrived when a decision needed to be made about her fate. Now a cold calculus came into play:

> April 25th. At daybreak poor Nealee was awakened; but her limbs were now become so stiff and painful, that she could neither walk nor stand; she was therefore lifted, like a corpse, upon the back of the ass; and the Slatees endeavoured to secure her in that situation, by fastening her hands together under the ass's neck, and her feet under the belly, with long slips of bark; but the ass was so very unruly, that no sort of treatment could induce him to proceed with his load; and as Nealee made no exertion to prevent herself from falling, she was quickly thrown off, and had one of her legs much bruised. Every attempt to carry her forward being thus found ineffectual, the general cry of the coffle was, *kang-tegi, kang-tegi*, "cut her throat, cut her throat;" an operation I did

not wish to see performed, and therefore marched onwards with the foremost of the coffle.[58]

Here we have the phenomenological situation that scholars of modernity and slavery must inevitably engage. On one hand we have Nealee's desire for death, which emerges from an almost existential recognition of the paradox of freedom; she seemed to realize that it was only through the nonexistence represented by death that she could be liberated from perpetual bondage. On the other hand, from the point of view of the slave traders, cutting Nealee's throat would have been the most pragmatic thing to do, ensuring the successful delivery of the other slaves in the coffle to the Atlantic coast, but this would also mean yielding to her desire to die. So the enslavers came up with an intriguing solution: "I had not walked above a mile, when one of Karfa's domestic slaves came up to me, with poor Nealee's garment upon the end of his bow, and exclaimed *Nealee affeeleeta* (Nealee is lost). I asked him whether the Slatees had given him the garment, as a reward for cutting her throat; he replied that Karfa and the schoolmaster would not consent to that measure, but had left her on the road; where undoubtedly she soon perished, and was probably devoured by wild beasts."[59] Why did Karfa and his associates refuse to consent to the cutting of Nealee's throat? Since they left her to die in the bush, this might seem to be an academic question, but it goes to the heart of a problem that will constantly haunt modernity—namely, the role of the body in the construction of identity.

As is well known, the idea of a modern identity, especially one predicated on the terms of taste that I discussed earlier, was premised on the radical separation of the self from the body. A basic premise of the aesthetic ideology was that art had the capacity to transform or raise the body from its material condition into a transcendental, hence sensuous, subject—a self.[60] Although slaves like Nealee were considered to be objects for sale, they were already directly or surreptitiously disturbing the regimen of modern self-fashioning by blurring the distinction between bodies and selves. Was the slave a human subject or a disposable body? Was her progress in time and space a journey toward the enhancement of the self or a movement toward its dissolution?[61]

Initially, Nealee's desire for freedom through death was matched by the determination of her captors to discipline her using all the technologies of power within what Foucault calls an "'epistemological-juridical' formation."[62] Here, Nealee's treatment by her captors, especially the deployment of numerous disciplinary mechanisms intended to make her submit to the regimen of enslavement, illustrates how the body of the condemned slave was bound up with "complex reciprocal relations" of power and wrapped up with "relations of power and domination" and

also how "a well-regulated system of subjection" would become "a useful force only if it is both a productive body and a subjected body."[63] My
conjecture here is that Karfa could not allow Nealee's throat to be cut,
because killing her would function as a symbolic attainder—it would nullify the condition that made her a valued body, though not a self. It would
effectively put into question the slave's status as a productive body. More
significantly, killing Nealee, thus granting her wish to die and become
free, would take away Karfa's power of subjection.[64]

Left on the road to die, she was, of course, no longer a productive body,
but she was still a subjected one. It is significant, then, that Park's narrative of Nealee's last days, plotted as a movement from one site of subjugation to another, would end with an aporia: she was left on the road,
"where undoubtedly she soon perished, and was probably devoured by
wild beasts."[65] This aporia would serve as a figure of doubt and suspen-
sion in this economy of debate. But given the inevitability of Nealee's
death, we are left wondering what task Park's rhetoric of equivocation
was being asked to perform. Was it intended to secure the humanity and
humanness of Karfa, a slave trader and a perfect host, whose actions Park
resisted judging? Or did it express Park's consistent refusal to be drawn
into making moral judgments about slavery and the slave trade, whose
quotidianness he was willing to accept as a fait accompli? Or did Park,
who had private qualms about slavery, invoke the figure of this aporia as
a way of expressing doubt about enslavement without alienating his British readers, or the majority of his backers, who subscribed to the African
slave trade without question.[66]

Some possible answers to these vexing questions are suggested by the
final scene in Nealee's drama: the effect of her death on the whole coffle:
"The sad fate of this wretched woman, notwithstanding the outcry be-
forementioned, made a strong impression on the minds of the whole
coffle, and the schoolmaster fasted the whole of the ensuing day, in consequence of it. We proceeded in deep silence, and soon afterward crossed
the river Furkoomah, which was about as large as the river Wonda. We
now travelled with great expedition, every one being apprehensive he
might otherwise meet with the fate of poor Nealee."[67] The shift of responsibility for Nealee's death from her captors to unseen and unknown
forces in the wilderness would have two consequences: one was that she
would disappear into the historical record without ostensibly affecting
the identity of her captors, who would continue to live the lives of good
Muslims and traders; the other was that it would appear to be a tangent
in the archive of empire, important here more for what it tells us about
Park the observer than for what it says about the subjected body.

Indeed, it could be said that in representing this and other episodes
involving African women, Park was already constructing a posthumous

identity for himself and his heroic fate in the African wilderness. After reading Park's account of his travels in Africa, mesmerized by a section in which the Scottish traveler found hospitality in the hut of an African woman during a storm, Georgiana Cavendish, Duchess of Devonshire, wrote a poem that was later set to music by G. G. Ferrari. As the first and last stanzas of the poem illustrate, it was an ode to mercy and hospitality rather than a testimony to slavery and suffering:

> THE loud wind roar'd, the rain fell fast;
> The White Man yielded to the blast:
> He sat him down, beneath our tree;
> For weary, sad, and faint was he;
> And ah, no wife, or mother's care,
> For him, the milk or corn prepare:
> . . . .
> The storm is o'er; the tempest past;
> And Mercy's voice has hush'd the blast.
> The wind is heard in whispers low;
> The White Man far away must go;—
> But ever in his heart will bear
> Remembrance of the Negro's care.[68]

Georgiana, who had mastered the idiom of sympathy and sensibility, was keen to direct her readers' sentiments to the white man who had survived the African wilderness rather than the black woman in shackles or the one who had taken him into her care. In a curious way, however, the duchess recognized the surreptitious connection between Park, the Scottish adventurer and modern man of science; the African woman left to a cruel fate in the midst of a brutal trade; and herself, the English beauty who had attracted the attention of distinguished painters, including Joshua Reynolds and Thomas Gainsborough. Like sensibility, beauty existed under the shadow of slavery.

4

What I have provided above is, of course, an allegory of reading rather than a history of two actors and agents in the theater of empire. I have not focused on the authenticity of the experience represented or on the verifiable facts in the lives of Larpent or Nealee, which are available to us only through a set of texts, but on the rhetoric of representation and visible semiotic codes.[69] An emphasis on the rhetoric of presentation, in turn, opens the way for a contrapuntal reading of the distinctive, yet ultimately connected lives of two subjects of modernity located at opposite spectrums, thus ensuring a dialectic between the visible subjects of modernity and its invisible actors. On one hand, we have Anna Larpent, a middle-class British woman whose movement through the time and space of modernity would lead her to new heights of prosperity and subjecthood, to a self-conscious sense of herself as a cultured subject; and on the other hand, we have Nealee, a lonely African slave, in shackles, awaiting death, which she considered the only sensible alternative to an enforced and violent entry into the world of commodities and exchange. As Larpent was securing her identity within the culture of a triumphant middle class, the young African woman was frog-marched into objectification, torn from home, community, and language into what has come to be known as social death.[70]

But what is the usefulness of these contrasts? Were they actually acknowledged in the lived experiences of the subjects themselves, or are they products of the mode of reading hat I have adopted here? Larpent's diary does not record the lives of slaves, although perhaps some of the servants she alludes to regularly were Africans; and apart from Park, her fellow traveler, Nealee's image of white people was that of apparitions and cannibals. Still, although they didn't know this, the two women were operating in the same orbit; they were, as Louis Althusser would say, overdetermined, and the "index of their determination" was slavery and empire.[71] My contention is that the key to understanding the repressed relationship between the subject of modernity and the object of slavery could be found in both their affective and structural relationship. Larpent's happiness and her everyday conviviality must be read against Nealee's melancholy and tragedy.[72] An allegory of reading enables us, then, to see Larpent and Nealee as figures who overflowed the roles assigned to them by history or destiny. In this scenario, Larpent functions as a supplement—a stand-in—for the middle-class subject in Britain at the end of the eighteenth century, just as Nealee is the residual sign of the unremarked slave.

I reduce these two subjects to semiotic terms not to diminish their historicity or negate their identities but to reflect on the inner world of modernity, one that is available to us only through its effects or affects. For if, as it is generally agreed, members of the rising British middle class in the Georgian period became cultured subjects because luxury and refinement were now within the "*reach even of relatively humble families*," then the kinship between Larpent and Nealee, though obviously unacknowledged, was part of the political unconsciousness of the period.[73] And this connection is to be explained not simply through the now obvious fact that slaves were producing the goods that were being consumed by the middle class, but also through the fact that it was precisely the existence of slavery—at odds with the key theories of modernity, yet enabling of it—that prompted the long, complicated, and perhaps unresolved debate on the relation between the rarified objects of culture and the messy world of commercial transactions. Philosophers of taste often agonized on how beauty could coexist with a materiality that seemed to negate its demands, and many of them would strive to separate white beauty from black ugliness, but for ordinary middle-class subjects, such as Larpent, the universe of culture did not seem to have a language of negativity. Since consumption and its display in the public space endowed modern subjects with the psychic energies that countered any sense of loss or displacement, the world of progress and luxuriousness was one of total sensuousness—and happiness.

Culture and luxury were informed by a powerful sense of moral and cultural superiority: the *"alliance of money and gentility was calculated to maintain the morale and sense of superiority of propertied people. Politeness was the mark of an immensely vigorous but also a remorselessly snobbish society."*[74] In contrast, Nealee was available to the culture of modernity only as the object of servitude and abjection. Like other slaves observed in coffles, markets, or the bowels of slave ships, her essential countenance was one of sadness, identified by Julia Kristeva as "the fundamental mood of depression."[75] Sorrow, notes Kristeva, "is the major outward sign that gives away the desperate person"; it is the *"the psychic representation of energy displacement* caused by external or internal traumas."[76] Located against her will in a circuit of power that demanded her submission to servitude as a precondition for survival, Nealee was perhaps using her subjection to counter the poison pill of modernity. Her melancholy, which we can recognize in the eyes of the enslaved women observed by Sir John Willoughby more than a century later in Portuguese East Africa (fig. 2.5), was perhaps the counterpoint to the bargain of the "middle passage," what the poet Robert Hayden has called the "voyage through death / to life upon these shores."[77]

A possible objection to the argument I have presented here is that the opposition I am working with—between Larpent's happiness and Nealee's abjection—emerges out of my allegorical readings rather than their lived experiences. One could then argue that there is no reason to suppose that cultured subjects like Larpent did not have moments of melancholy or that slaves like Nealee did not have bouts of happiness. But the surface discourses, the texts that constitute our only evidence of their lives, suggest otherwise. Larpent's diaries are constant performances of happiness and contentment as a condition of modern, cultured life; Nealee's countenance, as observed by Park, presents nothing other than abjection.

The opposition between Larpent's conviviality and Nealee's melancholy does not, of course, represent the essential opposition between the

2.5 G. Durand, "Under the Portuguese Flag. Slavery in the Portuguese districts of South-east Africa. From a sketch by Sir John Willoughby." *The Graphic: An Illustrated Weekly Newspaper* (London), vol. 45 (1892). Copy in Princeton University Library.

condition of freedom and that of enslavement. One can assume that Larpent had her moments of sadness and that Nealee's enslavement did not exclude moments of happiness. At the same time, it is quite apparent that the condition of happiness was imagined or performed as one of the defining characteristics of the culture of taste as experienced by Larpent and her generation, just as melancholy was a signal for bondage. Simply put, happiness was one of the assumed goals of the logic of consuming culture discussed earlier.[78] In fact, one remarkable feature of the eighteenth century was the emergence of "commercialized leisure" as an essential mechanism in the civilizing process.[79] Leisure was a key component of the sense and sensibility we have come to associate with the modern age; it was associated with the realm of freedom, representing "the liberation of the libido from the past, from tradition, from the judgment of society, elders, family and peers."[80] But leisure was not considered extraneous to morality or political economy. In fact, in order to be considered legitimate, the modern subject's capacity for enjoyment needed "a sound moral excuse."[81] Liberated from Calvinism and its ideas of original sin, modern subjects shifted the moral economy of goodness to that of happiness and thus "opened the gates for a new psychology of personal and social adjustment."[82] From David Hume cloistered in Edinburgh to Samuel Johnson, Joseph Addison, and Richard Steele in London, the work of cultural criticism was premised on the integration of happiness and civic virtue.[83] The leisure palaces of the period, such as Vauxhall Gardens, were in effect functioning as places where happiness could be both performed and consumed. In an age when leisure was supposed to operate under the law of morality, the palace at Vauxhall Gardens appeared to none other than the *Spectator*'s fictional narrator, Mr. Spectator, to be "a kind of *Mahometan* paradise" in need of "more nightingales, and fewer trumpets."[84] Such monuments to leisure however, were far removed from black life. When they appeared at Vauxhall, for example, blacks—even free ones like William Henry Lane, who performed at the garden later in the nineteenth century—did so as minstrels, objects of distorted entertainment (fig. 2.6).

5

Still, one has to account for the relation of the slave to the new edifice of culture even if this involves conjecture and unverified reconstruction, for as I argued in the introduction, the imaginary can help us resuscitate what is but a bare fragment in the archive of empire. Let us assume for a moment that Nealee did not die in the heat of the Sahel. Let us suppose that she survived the West African wilderness on that fateful night

2.6 *William Henry Lane,* a.k.a. "Master Juba," from *The Illustrated London News,* August 5, 1848. From Hans Nathan, *Dan Emmett and the Rise of Early Negro Minstrelsy.*

of April 25, 1797. Let us imagine that she woke up in the morning and was found by another group of slave traders, who nursed her body back to health in the hope of making a good sale on the slave markets of the Atlantic coast. What would the world of Enlightenment, of culture and taste, of freedom and progress mean to her as she stood on the threshold of modernity?

For a start, Nealee would be recruited into another slave coffle and put back in chains and bolts. These metal fetters would be notable for two things: they most probably would have been manufactured in the emerging centers of British industry—at Bristol and Liverpool, for example— and they would have a decorative character that, on the surface, was at odds with their utilitarian function, or rather was one indicator of how enslavement had acquired an aesthetic character. Another instance of how the slave trade had transformed cultural value and semantics was

2.7 The Donkor Nsuo (Slave River) at Assin Manso, Ghana. Photograph by the author.

2.8 The pond at Assin Manso, Ghana. Photograph by the author.

the ironic fact that slave chains and bolts were often cast in the same factories as the manila bars that were used as currency on the West African coast.[85] Still another index of semantic transformations was the use of the word *coffle* to denote a procession of slaves. The word *coffle*, John Thornton informs us, "derives from an Arabic term for caravan."[86] In normal circumstances, trade caravans would constitute communities of traders traveling together for security and support; in the world of slavery, however, this term had come to refer to enforced journeys into bondage.

If she were part of a coffle heading south, Nealee would be marched for days through the elaborate slave routes of West Africa, crossing the desert, into the savanna, and then into the rain forest. After a long journey along the slave routes, the coffle would arrive at a major slave market, such as Salaga in northern Ghana, and then be dispatched on the final voyage to the coast. But before the encounter with the waters that divided Africa from Europe and America, the slaves would make a final stop at Assin Manso in what is now the central region of Ghana. Here, at the Donkor Nsuo (Slave River) and ponds (figs. 2.7 and 2.8), Nealee and other slaves would be allowed to take a final ritual bath before being sold off to another group of native traders, the agents who would escort them to the edge of the ocean deep.

In spite of these long journeys, however, Nealee's entry into modernity proper had not yet begun. So far, the transactions and modes of exchange to which she had been subjected retained a feudal character; her captivity was within the same cultural region, part of what Raymond Williams might call a knowable community.[87] Her captors and sellers were, like her, all black, Muslim, or animist. Neither race nor religion seemed to make much difference as to who was bought or sold, or who did the buying and selling. At the slave markets witnessed by Park, the slave trader could be Wolof, Bambara, or Fulani, and the victims would belong to whatever ethnicity found itself on the losing side of local wars. The modes of slavery that Nealee had known up to this point retained their old, feudal character, regulated by ancient codes of honor, including the ones that determined the disposal of slaves according to social rank, kinship ties, and the mastery of the Koran. The bathing rituals at Assin Manso would suggest that the slavers were still attached to older rituals of purity, which the slave had to pass through before he or she was forced out of the human community and turned into a commodity.

In contrast to the cleansing wells, the slave castles that Nealee would encounter at the slave coast would signify the modernization of slavery itself. Indeed, these castles, which have come to be seen as physical signs of the long European struggle to dominate the West African coast, would have stood out, in those months in the 1790s, as emblems of the modernity of Europe and how it projected itself into the outside world. In other words, the slave enclosures were not just fortifications; like medieval castles, they were valued as much for their utilitarian value—the command of the coast—as for their imposing, symbolic presence. The architecture of the slave castle signaled, for both slavers and enslaved, the shift from the older feudal forms of trade at the slave markets of the African interior, mediated by rituals of barter and its compulsory obligations, to modern slavery, which had reduced the slave into a pure object of exchange. Since slave castles were the visible signs of modernity in the landscape of enslavement, their architecture and semiotics provide a fascinating example of how the culture of taste was entangled in the slave trade.

The architecture of Elmina, the oldest fort on the Gold Coast, is a percipient example of the relationship between slavery, modernity, and the built environment. Originally built by the Portuguese in 1482, Elmina was subsequently captured by the Dutch in August 1637 and by the British in 1872. In an age of European political and economic rivalry, played out against what Christopher Decorse calls "a backdrop of shifting alliances, wars, and political intrigue," whichever nation controlled Elmina was the superpower on the Gold and slave coasts.[88]

And each period of control demanded a different architecture, a new aesthetic, to match the growth of power and the control of trade. For example, in their major rehabilitation of Elmina in the early eighteenth century, the Dutch reconstructed the façade of the main courtyard and added iron balustrades and a "monumental gate" in the wall leading to the drawbridge (fig. 2.9).[89] Albert van Dantzig reports that one of the Dutch governor generals of Elmina had the sundial of Elmina constructed to look "like the one in the Amsterdam Admiralty House."[90] Successive renovations of the castle were prompted by both functional and aesthetic demands. From a functional point of view, the castle needed to be updated to account for the increasing volume of slaves, but the architecture of reconstruction was intended to master and display changing aesthetic forms in Europe.

In his elaborate descriptions of the castle in his account of the Gold Coast, *A New and Accurate Description of Guinea*, William Bosman, the Dutch slave agent at Cape Coast, obviously considered Elmina valuable because of its strategic location and strength, but he also constantly called attention to the beauty of the castle: "It is built square with very high walls, four good batteries within and another on the outwork of the castle; on the side toward the land it is adorned with two canals cut in the rocks on which it stands, which are always furnished with rain and fresh water sufficient for the use of our garrison and ships."[91] Bosman also had a keen sense of the relation between utility and ornamentation. The tower in the middle of the castle, he noted, was not only an adornment to the building, "but from the top affords a most beautiful prospect of the

2.9 Entrance to Elmina Castle, Ghana. Photograph by the author.

circumjacent land and ocean, as well as usefully serves to discover ships seven or eight miles distant at sea."[92]

There is another dimension to the relation between the architecture of the slave castle and the culture of taste: over the long history of the Gold Coast, European governors were attuned to specific national styles in Europe. For example, the rebuilding of Cape Coast Castle between the middle of the seventeenth century and the end of the eighteenth century was carried out according to what was conceived to be the fashionable architectural style in England. In the two decades between the 1770s and 1790s, when the castle was rebuilt several times, it adopted the Palladian architecture that had been popular in England in the first half of the seventeenth century. This explains why the front façade of this infamous dungeon (fig. 2.10) is uncannily similar to the entrances of great English houses such as Houghton Hall, designed by Colen Campbell and James Gibb around 1729 for Sir Horace Walpole, the prime minister (fig. 2.11). What are we to make of this concordance between the architectural taste of slave agents and the Whig aristocracy?

Deep affiliations and anxieties explain aesthetic relations of this kind, but also at play is an ironic mode of recognition, for like their Whig counterparts, slave agents were conscious of the transformations that

2.10 Cape Coast
Castle, Ghana. Photo-
graph by the author.

2.11 Colen Campbell
and James Gibbs,
drawing for the façade
of Houghton Hall.
From Colen Campbell,
Vitruvius Britannicus.

were taking place in European architecture and its informing doctrines
of taste. And in order to understand this relationship, one must reject
the claim that slave agents operated on the margins of their cultures and
insist, as I do in the next two chapters, that slave traders and plantation
masters studiously held on to, and jealously guarded, their identity as
modern European subjects; that they used architecture and art to assert
their location in the mainstream of European fashion; and that the cultivation of taste was an important counterpoint to the barbarism of slavery, which always had the potential to engulf their claims to be modern,
rational subjects.

Arriving at Elmina or Cape Coast, then, a slave like Nealee would be
encountering the insignias of a self-conscious modernity and its institutions for the first time. Deprived of freedom, she would become a mere

object of trade in the first truly global business enterprise.[93] Here Nealee would encounter people who had probably moved in the same circles as Anna Larpent. And this encounter would be a radical transformation of her prior understanding of the integers of time and space, for while they were providing the bodies that were transforming capitalism, the men who had hitherto owned or traded Nealee were not conscious of modernity, its meaning and reach. They belonged to another epoch, an African "middle ages" defined by powerful attachments to religion and the rule of nature; still holding on to ancient notions of space and time located in the realm of tribe or Islam, they had not heard of, nor cared about, Enlightenment.

For a young African like Nealee, enslavement would become the radical gesture of modern identity. At the first site of exchange, the slave would be reduced to an object of barter, but in the process, being sold would forcefully and paradoxically insert her into the domain of the modern. Now her transition would be signaled by the complexity of trade transactions, which had moved from the simple barter that Park had observed at Kamalia to an intricate mode of exchange in which money, the sign of the modern fetish, would be exchanged for the body of the enslaved.

A sense of the complexities of exchange can be gleaned from an entry in a log left by Captain Thomas Phillips, aboard the slaving frigate *Hannibal* in the year 1693, in the early days of the age of Enlightenment:

> The best goods to purchase slaves here are cowries, the smaller the more esteemed; for they pay them all by tale, the smallest being as valuable as the biggest, but take them from us by measure or weight, of which about 100 pounds for a good man-slave. The next in demand are brass neptunes or basons, very large, thin, and flat; for after they have bought them they cut them in pieces to make anilias or bracelets, and collars for their arms, legs and necks. The other preferable goods are blue paper sletias, cambricks or lawns, caddy chints, broad ditto, coral, large, smooth, and of a deep red, rangoes large and red, iron bars, powder and brandy.[94]

In barter the interchangeability of slaves with cowries would seem to nullify any claims to the latter's human identity or any sense of the supremacy of the cultured subject over nature, the claim that was taken for granted by subjects of taste.

6

The intertwined stories of cultured subjects and African slaves that opened my discussion suggest a new way of rethinking the history of centers and margins and the necessity of a contrapuntal reading of slavery and the culture of taste. A contrapuntal analysis will show that even when the lives of enslaved Africans were located at the opposite pole of modern identity and when their objectification was at odds with the triumphant subjectivism of modernity, slaves were intimately connected to the political and moral economy of the modern world. It was difficult to imagine a modern identity that was totally detached from the Africans' subjection. By the same token, the existence of slavery at the center of modern commerce made modern subjectivity valuable. Surrounded by a mass of slaves in ships, markets, and plantations, Europeans involved in various facets of the slave trade were conscious of, and sensitive about, their modern identity as a mark of their distinctiveness. Evidence suggests that the more they became entangled in the business of transforming black bodies into objects of trade, the more the slavers sought to secure or cultivate their own identity as cultured subjects, to affirm their virtue in the midst of a commercial activity whose moral character was rarely settled.

Consider, for example, the now famous case of John Newton, the slave captain later turned abolitionist. In the summer of 1751, aboard his slave ship, the *Duke of Argyle*, on the way to transport his human cargo to Antigua, Newton was preoccupied with the usual, everyday worries of a slave captain: rumors of a plot by slaves to poison the water, weather so humid that not even the slaves could stand to be on deck, and the nasty and hasty business of burying two slaves who had died of flux. Still, in the midst of all these mundane concerns, Newton had the time to catch up on some taste, reading Gilbert Burnet's biography of Sir Matthew Hale, Oliver Cromwell's chief jurist, while wistfully thinking about the London cultural scene, which embodied refinement and taste.[95]

For Newton, the thought of culture contemplated in absentia was a source of both longing and consolation. On July 23 Newton wrote to his wife expressing some thoughts about the music of Handel and on David Garrick playing Hamlet, most likely at the Theater Royal, Drury Lane: "You will perceive by the date that this is one of the days which I pass, as much as I can, in retirement and reflection."[96] Clearly, any thoughts of Garrick playing Hamlet, a cultural event that was worthy of commemoration in a painting by Hogarth, was an important act of affiliation with the culture of taste. In the confused scene of his slave ship, Newton turned to God for guidance but also acted out the role of a man of taste, using his Sundays to reflect, read, and converse through correspondence with learned writers and artists back in London. In the slave ship under his command, Newton could hallow a space of culture and taste identical to that of Anna Larpent back in London.

But did he ever reflect on the disparity between his yearning for the culture of taste and the practice of slavery? Did he wonder how he, a modern subject, could be in the inhumane business of buying, packaging, and retailing other human beings? Newton's reflections on the African slave trade, written after he had renounced slavery and become an ardent abolitionist, were paradoxical:

> During the time I was engaged in the slave trade, I never had the least scruple as to its lawfulness. I was upon the whole satisfied with it, as the appointment Providence had worked out for me; yet it was, in many respects, far from eligible. It is, indeed, accounted a genteel employment and is usually very profitable, though to me it did not prove so, the Lord, seeing that a large increase of wealth would not be good for me. However, I considered myself a sort of goaler or turn-key and I was sometimes shocked with an employment that was perpetually conversant with chains, bolts and shackles.[97]

From a legal, moral, and commercial perspective, Newton had no qualms about the justifiability of the slave trade—it was lawful, providential, and profitable. Even in the midst of slavery, he remained a devout Christian, leading his crew in prayer twice a day; it is reported that he wrote one of his hymns, "Amazing Grace," on the slave coast of Africa as he waited to load human cargo on his ship.[98] Still, Newton did worry that his participation in the slave trade had turned him into a jailer and arrested his development as a modern subject, or at least retarded his aspiration to achieve the ideals of civic virtue that defined the life of a gentleman.

The dilemma for Newton—and for many others engaged in the slave trade in the modern period—was this: slavery was supported by established law, religious beliefs, and established commercial practices, yet it seemed to demand enforcement through acts of violence that challenged the integrity of the disciplining self as much as the disciplined body. Often the main cause of the slavers' scruples was the obvious contradiction between the legality of the slave trade and the need to resort to violence in order to enforce it: if slavery was morally right, why did it demand violent rationalization, and what did the constant use of force do to the slavers' moral character?

On the surface, captains of the slave ships were not perturbed by slavery's effects on their own moral character; they could always resort to other worldly explanations for their involvement in the trade. Captain Hugh Crow, one of the most important slave ship captains to come out of Liverpool, expressed the strong opinion that slavery was "permitted by that Providence that rules over all, as a necessary evil."[99] After all, slavery had made Liverpool one of the major centers of industry and trade, its ships cruising the seas, ferrying the cargo in human trade, its houses of trade proudly named after slave ports. One of its major warehouses was proudly named Goree, after the infamous Senegalese slave port. It made sense for the men who had made fortunes in the slave trade to justify it by invoking providence, but this continuous invocation of a higher power to rationalize slavery seemed driven by the sense that questions of law and profit were not enough justifications for the destruction and death that the slavers had to deal with every day.

It was impossible for slavers to escape the death and violence that was attendant to their trade. To say that violence and death are the primary topics in the logs of slave captains, from William Snelgrave to Samuel Gamble, is not an exaggeration.[100] The vocabulary of providence would thus come to mediate the double demands made on these men of taste: the imperative that that they live their lives according to the rules of civic virtue yet be good agents of commerce; that they affirm their identity as self-reflective modern subjects, yet quarantine or occlude African slaves from the domain of the human. In other words, in order to be a modern subject, the slave trader had to narrow the terms of the human.

Thus, after two voyages in which he had interacted with his slaves at the basic level of the human or bodily, witnessing their agony at sea and handing them over to their new masters in the West Indies, Newton seemed to recognize how slavery made the terms of his own subjectivity fragile. This is Newton writing to Dr. David Jennings a few days after his second voyage:

> I have now by God's helping finished a long, troublesome and precarious voyage, with entire satisfaction to myself, my friends and my employers and am now very busy in preparing for another: for it is not in my power to command any respite. . . . I am more than content, in some degree thankful for my lot, which with all its inconveniences I know preferable to many millions of my fellow creatures: yet I still find myself unequal to this fluctuating way of life, where the scene is continually shifting and I am everyday engaged with some new kind of incumbrance.[101]

Indeed, concerning moral questions, slavery was caught between the torsion of freedom and the necessity of commerce, and nowhere is this contradiction more manifest than in John Locke's *Second Treatise on Government* published in 1690. As is well known, Locke had stated that human beings were born in a state of freedom and equality and had inalienable rights to life and property:

> To understand political power aright, and derive it from its original, we must consider what state all men are naturally in, and that is, a state of perfect freedom to order their actions and dispose of their possessions and persons as they think fit, within the bounds of the law of nature, without asking leave, or depending upon the will of any other man.
>
> A state also of equality, wherein all the power and jurisdiction is reciprocal, no one having more than another; there being nothing more.[102]

If slavery did not exist in the period these words were uttered, there perhaps wouldn't be any apparent contradiction between the right to property and equality. But the existence of slaves as property made Locke's first proclamation—the freedom to action and the right to dispose of one's possessions—at odds with his second claim, the existence of a state of reciprocal equality.

Now there is a continuous debate about Locke's stance on slavery in a culture of freedom and whether he accorded equal rights to African slaves, a fact complicated by his role in the settlement and administration of the American colonies, but as far as the bona fide slaveholding class and their supporters were concerned, the ownership of slaves was part of an undisputed and inalienable right to property supported by tradition and law.[103] This is the position staked out angrily by Edward Long, a Jamaican planter and lawyer, in his response to British debates on the morality of the slave trade and his objection to the Mansfield Decision of 1772:

> As our trade esteemed Negroe labourers merely a commodity, or chose in merchandize, so the parliament of Great Britain has uniformly adhered to the same idea; and hence the planters were naturally induced to frame their colony acts and customs agreeable to this, which may be termed national sense, and declared their Negroes to be fit objects of purchase and sale, transferrable like any other goods or chattels: they conceived their right of property to have and to hold, acquired by purchase, inheritance, or grant, to be as strong, just, legal, indefeasible and compleat, as that of any other British merchant over the goods in his warehouse.[104]

Long's language may have been extreme, but he seemed to recognize that Africans in bondage were mere chattel—goods for sale in the marketplace. What he didn't recognize was the dialectical relationship between these "objects of slave and purchase" and the ideals of selfhood that defined the middle-class subjects of the eighteenth century. If Long had not been disingenuous, he could have acknowledged that transforming the slave into an object of trade was an important part in the process of modern self-fashioning.

7

It is significant that the slave-owning class expended a lot of energy in the process of turning the African into an object. For a woman like Nealee (assuming she survived the caravan route), the process of objectification would start the moment she stepped into the courtyard of the slave castle: she would be branded with the seal of the company that owned her, effectively fixing her fate as a commodity. While Anna Larpent and others were enjoying the expanded spaces of the London theater, concert halls, and Vauxhall Gardens, Nealee would find herself in a dungeon in the

2.12 Cape Coast Castle, Ghana, "Door of No Return." Photograph by the author.

bowels of a slave castle like the female dungeon at Elmina. Here, in the eerie moment of the night, she would await the fateful morning when she would be pushed into the modern world through the infamous door of no return (fig. 2.12).

Slaves, of course, responded to, or imagined, their dislocation in various ways. Olaudah Equiano recalled the first time of enslavement as "painful as it was sudden and unexpected"; he plotted it as the movement from a state of innocence and bliss to "a scene which is inexpressible by me" and inscribed it as the radical separation from a world of "familiar manners, customs and language" to one of nonrecognition.[105] For Quobna Otto-bah Cugoano, the story of enslavement meant radical loss to his "dear indulgent parents and relations," the fall from "a state of innocence and freedom" to a "state of horror and slavery."[106] Even for Phillis Wheatley, who had a more eschatological view of enslavement, the journey from Africa to America denoted temporal dislocation. The movement in one of her most famous poems, "On being brought from *Africa* to *America*," underscored the chasm between the "*Pagan* land" of her birth and the refined and "angelic train" that was her goal and aspiration.[107] Predicated on the slaves' capacity to survive genealogical isolation, the providential design of the slave narrative would come to structure the history of the African self as a struggle with the problem of modern time. Similarly, the transformation of the slave from a figure of bondage to a reading or writing subject would mark the moment of arrival into the kingdom of culture and taste, which was nothing less than coming into selfhood out of bondage. This moment of arrival was marked either by the adoption of the language of sense and sensibility exemplified by the letters of Igna-tius Sancho discussed in the previous chapter; by the presence of former slaves as cultured subjects in paintings by famous artists, such as Thomas Gainsborough, and their imitators; or simply by the presentation of the scene of reading as the triumph over modern time.

Equiano, who imagined the act of reading as the key to understand-ing "how all things had a beginning," was dumbfounded when the book did not talk back to him.[108] And in one of the most famous examples of literacy and subjecthood, Frederick Douglass would assert that his read-ing of the abolitionist newspaper *The Liberator* enabled his coming into being as a free subject: "The paper became my meat and my drink. My soul was set all on fire. Its sympathy for my brethren in bonds—its scath-ing denunciations of slaveholders—its faithful exposures of slavery—and its powerful attacks upon the upholders of the institution—sent a thrill of joy through my soul, such as I had never felt before!"[109] But these majestic claims to a modern identity obscure the extent to which the movement of slaves through time and space was out of joint with the established tem-poral frames of the modern, or at least the philosophical, discourses of modernity. At a time when philosophers of modern culture were celebrating temporal rupture as the enabling condition of modernity, slaves were reacting to their own dislocation with dread. What one group saw as the necessary condition for being modern, the other conceived as a form of distortion or dislocation, the source of moral collapse and cultural terror.

The contrasts here are significant and worthy of close reflection. For philosophers of modernity from Hegel to Habermas, modernity has been conceptualized as an "an epochal concept," one that marks a break with a previous period and thus privileges the future as the site of fulfillment.[110] In his preface to *Phenomenology of the Mind*, for example, Hegel would invoke his readers to see modern time as the "birth and transition to a new period," asserting that the modern spirit had "broken with what was hitherto the world of its existence and imagination and is about to submerge all this in the past; it is at work giving itself a new form."[111] The trajectory of the modern subject, which is exemplified by the life of Anna Larpent, discussed at the opening of this chapter, could hence be read as a strategic deployment of new technologies of culture to subsume the past and create a new temporal frame for social life. Submerged in this movement of the self through time, the past had no value; everything was invested in the future as a horizon of expectations. Indeed, what Habermas has called "the differentness of the future" is what distinguishes the modern from the old world.[112]

However, this was not the story of the African slave's trajectory in the temporality of modernity and the forms of social identity associated with it. On the contrary, the movement of the enslaved spirit was dominated by fear of the future, itself a symptom of an acute sense of regressive time. The slaves' notion of the future, noted an observer on the slave ship *Albion-Frigate*, was that of a space of death and cannibalization: "It has been observed that some slaves fancy they are being carried away to be eaten, which makes them desperate, and others are so on account of their captivity, so that if care be not taken, they will mutiny and destroy the ship's crew in hopes to get away."[113] As the ship in which he was held moved away from the African coast, Cugoano and his fellow slaves concluded that "death was now preferable than life," and they concocted a failed plan to "burn and blow the ship, and to perish all together in the flames."[114]

These competing visions of time would find expression in the mentalities of the slave traders themselves. These were subjects who were not only at the front line of the modernizing enterprise, but those who were also constantly reminded of the arrested nature of modernity itself. Slave traders, as I have already argued, were products of a generation that had been brought up to believe in the inviolability of freedom, the authority of selfhood, and the sanctity of private property, but within the field of slavery the dialectic of freedom came face-to-face with what it thought it had exorcised from European selfhood—namely, bondage. Caught between the abstract idea of freedom and the profitable business of slave trading, slave traders did not have an appropriate grammar for describing the apparent contradiction between their cherished notions of freedom and the claims of captive bodies under law and custom, or even a proper way of accounting for the coexistence of theories of freedom and the profitable business in human chattel. In contrast, slaves did not have difficulties recognizing that the defining characteristic of their altered state was the loss of freedom across time and space.

Consider this example: In 1721, after an aborted slave rebellion on his ship, Captain William Snelgrave demanded to know from his African slaves what had induced them to mutiny. The slaves' response, transmitted through a linguist or translator, goes to the heart of the contradiction of the politics of selfhood in the eighteenth century that concerns me in this section: "They answered, 'I was a great Rogue to buy them, in order to carry them away from their own Country; and that they were resolved to regain their Liberty if possible.' I replied, 'That they had forfeited their Freedom before I bought them, either by Crimes, or by being taken in War, according to the Custom of their Country; and they being now my Property, I was resolved to let them feel my Resentment, if they abused my Kindness.'"[115] The slaves took one fact for granted: that their sense of self depended on their connection to natal spaces, to country, to culture, to custom. Snelgrave, on the other hand, assumed that the Africans had been acquired through a legal or customary transaction and were hence his property, not humans entitled to rights or liberty.

More than semantics was at issue in the standoff between Snelgrave and his slave cargo, for this verbal exchange reflects the paradox of enslavement in the modern age that has been the overt subject of this chapter. In fact, what we have here is the double paradox of having slavery in the midst of a culture of freedom. The first paradox, perhaps the most obvious one, is that Snelgrave, a product of the age of sovereignty, could not recognize the slaves' desire for freedom at the most basic level. He seemed genuinely puzzled that his African captives considered themselves free subjects and put their lives in danger for the sake of a freedom that, in his mind, they had forfeited the moment they were sold. The second paradox is that despite the deployment of powerful instruments of social control and the threat of death, slaves could not be reduced to mere property; their desire for liberty, signified by acts of revolt and the capacity to talk back, was propelled by the need to assert the supremacy of human rights. It is precisely because the slaves were not commodities in the totally objective sense, subject solely to the laws of property, that rituals of punishment would become immanent to the practice of slavery.

Indeed, no sooner had Snelgrave's slaves promised to be obedient than they started planning the next mutiny.

Here we can recognize the centrality of what Kathleen Wilson has called the "ontology of identity as a coercive process" and her claim that in the imperial zones, where slavery was unique and ubiquitous, "identity was structured in part by the epistemic violence attached to the notion of human property."[116] But I want to extend this argument even further in two directions: first, to establish the close relationship between the dialectic of violence and the production of modern subjects, and, second, to explore how the process of culture or taste was underwritten by its own disciplinary, though apparently benign, structures. For if a dialectic of violence was essential to structuring the differential identity between masters as modern subjects and slaves as objects, it was because there were no natural categories defining the terms of identity. Masters and slaves did not have a common language for describing the self. In these circumstances, violence was truly ontological—it was through its bond that selfhood could be defined and redefined. The community of masters as slaves, Frederick Douglass realized on witnessing the beating of his aunt Hester by her owner, was initiated through a "bloody transaction."[117]

Still, it was precisely because of the contingency of the terms of identity that the invention and valorization of visible divisions became necessary. As modern subjects, slave masters understood the threat enslavement posed to their own ideas of selfhood. They thus sought to elevate the act of domination to a symbolic level, often turning punishment into what Foucault has called a "spectacle, sign, and discourse."[118] In slave ships and plantations, so-called medieval forms of punishment that had ostensibly disappeared from European courts were promoted as instruments of exorcizing the idea of freedom out of the slave. On Snelgrave's ship, after yet another failed mutiny, a slave was put through a brutal regimen of punishment for having killed a white man. The resulting scene of punishment reads like a spectacle from Foucault's *Discipline and Punish*:

> The Body being let down upon the Deck, the Head was cut off, and thrown overboard. This last part was done, to let our Negroes see, that all who offended thus, should be served in the same manner. For many of the Blacks believe, that if they are put to death and not dismembered, they shall return again to their own Country, after they are thrown overboard. But neither the Person that was executed, nor his Countrymen of Cormantee (as I understood afterwards), were so weak as to believe any such thing; tho' many I had on board from other Countries had that Opinion.[119]

To understand the power of symbolism in this violent mode of punishment, we need to recall that for slavers, black bodies were more valuable alive than dead; they were part of an expensive cargo, and one could not be disposed of unless the stakes were extremely high. In this particular situation, other traders had reminded Snelgrave that the condemned man would have no value dead, while alive he would fetch a good price on the slave markets of the new world. However, Snelgrave resisted this argument, apparently believing that the destruction of the body of the rebellious slave took precedence over its commodity value. What necessitated this ritualization of violence and death? Why would the spectacle of punishment take precedence over the rule of property?

Judging from his language, Snelgrave understood that the transformation of free persons into slaves depended on the use of ritualized violence; he knew that in order for the ritual of punishment to be effective in separating the slave from the free, it needed, to use Foucault's majestic phrase, to "perform ceremonies, to emit signs."[120] If slave revolts were expressions of the slaves' refusal to be objects, then the slavers needed to counter them in the relentless ritual of punishment and death; for as I suggested in the last chapter, the ideals of cultural purity, whether located in taste or beauty, depend on the existence of "a symbolics of impurity."[121] Turning to the disciplinary structures within the culture of taste is perhaps another way of inverting the relationship between the pure and impure, the high and the low, the relationships described in the previous chapter as the enabling conditions of the culture of taste.

8

The culture of taste contains few overt traces of the violence of slavery, but this absence tells us a lot about the extent to which the agents of modernity and the civilizing process were willing to go to repress or contain what was considered to be unmodern. Consider, for example, the discourse on civic virtue that circulated in the common culture for most of the modern period. In Britain as elsewhere in Europe, the promotion of a culture of sense and sensibility, of politeness and conduct operated as if the problem of enslavement belonged to the distant reaches of empire far away from the domestic scene in which new identities were being constructed. And although perhaps few consumers of culture would deny that slavery underwrote the wealth that made their new lives possible, many would have considered enslavement remote from their everyday preoccupations. As argued previously, slavery and enslavement were considered anachronistic to the modern imagination in general and to Englishness or Britishness in particular. Not only was slavery deemed to be at odds with the theories of liberty that ostensibly separated the moderns from the ancients, but it was also considered antithetical to the moral geography of Englishness. And nowhere was this form of anachronism more marked than in English debates on liberty and the law and the pressures imposed on these categories by the existence of chattel slavery. Could the practice of slavery be reconciled to ideals of English liberty? That was perhaps one of the central questions dominating English jurisprudence in the second half of the eighteenth century.

In reflecting on the centrality of slavery in shaping English laws, it is imperative to note that the tension between property and liberty was confined mostly to the domestic scene, for in the reaches of empire, in those English colonies where slavery was ubiquitous, questions of jurisprudence were not about rights but about the practical business of managing relations in societies in which the denial of liberty to a substantial part of the population because of their race was considered central to the regulation of the social order. For example, a crucial aspect of English slave laws in the West Indies was its dissociation of slave acts from the basic tenets of English common law. Thus the laws the British enacted to regulate slavery in the West Indies were considered to be not a continuation of English legal practices, but a set of new codes to manage slaves. The slave laws of the British colonies, noted the eminent West Indian historian Elsa V. Goveia, "were made directly by the slave-owning class" and were thus "an immediate reflection of what the slave-owner conceived to be the necessities of the slave system."[122]

Goveia notes that a basic conception of English law in relation to the enslaved was not that slaves "were an inferior kind of subject" but that they were "a special kind of property—that is, property in persons": "Thus, the slave was merchandise when bought and sold in the course of the slave trade. Once acquired by a planter, he became his owner's private property—regarded in part as a chattel, in part as real property. As chattels, for instance, slaves could be sold up for debts if other moveable assets were exhausted. But in other cases they were disposed of in accordance with the laws of inheritance of real estate. They could be entailed, they were subject to the widow's right of dower, and they could be mortgaged."[123] Slave laws in the West Indies were not derived from traditional or constitutional ideas on liberty; on the contrary, they were a set of police regulations intended to maintain the slave system. Slaves were property, and the law was there to regulate this principle. There was no ambiguity on this matter. In England, however, the situation was much more complicated: caught between the desire to uphold ideals of liberty and to protect the rule of property, the managers of jurisprudence were not sure what to do with the black slave who happened to make his or her way into the realm. How could the law adjudicate between liberty and property when there were human beings who were considered chattel?

After trying to avoid arbitrating between private liberty and public property, the English courts were finally forced to confront the issue head-on in the case of James Somersett brought before Lord Mansfield, the chief justice in 1771. Somersett, the slave of Charles Steuart, of either Virginia or Boston, was brought by his master to London, where he managed to escape; but he was captured soon after and put on a ship bound for Jamaica, where he was to be sold into slavery. His friends petitioned the court in London on November 28, 1771, and Lord Mansfield issued a writ of habeas corpus. On June 22, 1772, after months of debate, Lord Mansfield issued his famous decision preventing the return of James Somersett to West Indian slavery.[124] The language of his judgment would seem to have removed any doubts that slavery was impermissible under English law: "The state of slavery is of such a nature, that it is incapable of being introduced on any reasons, moral or political, but only by positive law. . . . It is so odious, that nothing can be suffered to support it, but positive law. Whatever inconveniences, therefore, may follow from the decision, I cannot say this case is allowed or approved by the law of England; and therefore the black must be discharged."[125]

Some interpreters of the Mansfield Decision, most prominently Goveia, have questioned the notion that the judgment represented the triumph of the ideal of liberty over the rule of property. Goveia argues that in the absence of police regulations for slaves in England, English jurisprudence had no option but to treat Somersett as a subject:

> Given police regulations, the English law in the West Indies worked against the slave, because he was there reduced to the status of "mere property," or something very near it. In the absence of such regulations, the slave had to be regarded as an ordinary man; and, in that context, respect for the liberty of the subject, which was also a part of the English legal tradition, worked in his favour. Somersett's case illustrates the operation of the principle of liberty of the subject. There was no law against slavery in England. But the absence of laws providing sanctions for the enforcement of slavery enabled Somersett to win his freedom by refusing to serve any longer as a slave.[126]

Goveia's argument, then, is that Somersett could not serve as a slave in England, because there were no laws regulating servitude in the realm. But if Somersett had returned to the slave colonies, then he would find laws that would regulate his life as a person who was also an object of property. This point is highlighted by the case of a slave named Grace who, returning to Antigua after a visit to England, discovered that her status as chattel property had not changed. As Lord Stowell, the judge in the case, reminded her in a judgment made in 1827, the West Indies was a place where "slavery could not be avoided."[127] The Mansfield Decision reflects some of the ways in which English law in the eighteenth century was formulated under the pressures of slavery and serves as an illustration of how the presence of the African in bondage would generate debates and disputes about the content and character of liberty. In this case, slavery raised a question that might otherwise seem innocuous: what was the relationship between the idea of liberty under English law—a law rooted in custom and natural rights—and the rules of property, operating under the rubric of contract? As English jurisprudence tried to untangle this knot, it came up against the power of slavery as a form of property.

The haunting power of slavery can be found more explicitly in Sir William Blackstone's *Commentaries on the Laws of England.* Considered to be one of the most important commentaries on English law, Blackstone's work has been the standard reference for students of jurisprudence in Britain and its former colonies for several centuries; but perhaps few of those who refer to it to settle questions of law recognize the distinguished scholar's reflections of slavery as the fulcrum around which his authoritative commentaries on liberty revolved. Blackstone's work contains two important commentaries that touch on the question of slavery under English law in decisive, though contradictory, terms. In the first chapter of the *Commentaries,* where he dealt with the rights of individuals, Blackstone argued that the spirit of liberty was so implanted in the English constitution, its meaning and character, that "a slave or negro, the moment he lands in England, falls under the protection of the laws, and with regard to all natural rights becomes *eo instanti* a freeman."[128]

The question that Blackstone had to confront, however, was the essential character of the slave caught between two competing ideas. Blackstone's challenge was how to reconcile his categorical claim that slavery was not allowed by English law with the simple fact that slaves constituted significant property in the British empire. Blackstone tried to deal with this cauldron in the fourteenth chapter of his book:

> I have formerly observed that pure and proper slavery does not, nay cannot, subsist in England; such I mean whereby an absolute and unlimited power is given to the master over the life and fortune of the slave. And indeed it is repugnant to reason, and the principles of natural law, that such a state should subsist any where. . . . Upon these principles the law of England abhors, and will not endure the existence of slavery within this nation. . . . And now it is laid down, that a slave or negro, the instant he lands, in England, becomes a freeman; that is, the law will protect him in the enjoyment of his person, his liberty, and his property. Yet with regard to any right which the master may have acquired, by contract or the like, to the perpetual service of John or Thomas, this will remain exactly in the same state as before: for this is no more than the same state of subjection for life, which every apprentice submits to for the space of seven years, or sometimes for a longer term.[129]

Here we can see the difficulties the jurist faced as he tried to reconcile two important principles in English law—the right to absolute freedom and the sanctity of property. Blackstone found slavery repugnant, but he was not willing to go far enough to exclude slaves from the right of contract; on the contrary, he argued that even in England, the slave could still be tied up in the perpetual contractual relationship that he or she had entered with his or her master. This principle—the right to contract—seemed so important to Blackstone that in the second edition of his *Commentaries*, he modified the chapter on absolute rights to reconcile it with his thinking on contract. In the new edition, he argued that slaves who arrived in England still fell under the protection of the law, but with the important qualification that "the master's right to his service may probably still continue."[130]

It should not come as a surprise that many discussions of the place of slavery in Blackstone's *Commentaries* have focused on this shift in emphasis and, more precisely, on his insistence that slaves could enter into any kind of contract with their masters. As early as the nineteenth century, commentators on Blackstone, most notably Edward Christian, Downing Professor of the Laws of England at Cambridge University, were calling attention to the absurdity of any notion that a black person in a state of slavery, one who was not free sui juris, could enter into any enforceable contract. After all, he concluded, a contract of service entered into by a person in a state of slavery "would be absolutely null and void."[131]

But what I find striking in these debates is not the quibbles over matters of law, but the fact that Blackstone was more willing to amend his views on liberty rather than modify the law as it pertained to existing rights of property. Indeed, while those involved in debates about the legality of slavery in the English tradition were keen to secure the ideals of absolute right under custom and nature, the existence of slavery clouded matters in telling ways. In slavery a form of private property existed at odds with the key principle of the law, and not even the most ardent advocates of a culture of taste that might be transcendental of such matters could escape the shadow of slavery.

A dramatic example of how these two ideals—liberty and property—would continue to define the cultural sensibility of Britishness in the eighteenth century can be found in the dispute between Dr. Samuel Johnson and his close associate James Boswell over the case of *Knight v. Wedderburn*. Joseph Knight had been purchased in Jamaica by John Wedderburn and had been brought to Scotland, where he served as a servant for several years before declaring himself free, apparently as a calculated move to test whether the Mansfield Decision applied in Scotland as much as in England. Knight's claim to liberty was affirmed by the local sheriff, citing the Mansfield Decision; but Wedderburn appealed to the Court of Session, Scotland's highest court, claiming that the Mansfield Decision applied only to England.[132] On July 22, 1778, a split court affirmed Knight's claim to liberty: "The dominion assumed over this negro, under the law of Jamaica, being unjust, could not be supported in this country to any extent: that, therefore, the defender had no right to the negro's service for any space of time, nor to send him out of the country against his consent: that the negro was likewise protected under the Act 1701, c. 6, from being sent out of the country without his consent."[133] Among the powerful dissenters was Lord Monboddo, distinguished Scottish jurist and philosopher, man of letters and taste, and a friend of Johnson and Boswell.

There were two varied and memorable reactions to the decision of the Scottish Court of Session, which I see as an example of the tension between the claims of liberty and property in the eighteenth century and thus the ways in which slavery haunted the making of modern culture. On one side of the debate was Dr. Johnson, who, in characteristic fashion, welcomed the court's affirmation of Knight's freedom as the assertion of "moral rights" against "political convenience" and the triumph of "human virtue" over "the temptations of interest":

> The laws of Jamaica afford a negro no redress. His colour is considered as sufficient testimony against him. It is to be lamented that moral right should ever give way to political convenience. But if temptations of interest are sometimes too strong for human virtue, let us at least retain a virtue where there is no temptation to quit it. In the present case there is apparent right on one side, and no convenience on the other. Inhabitants of this island can neither gain riches nor power by taking away the liberty of any part of the human species. The sum of argument is this:—No man is by nature the property of another: The defendant is therefore, by nature free: The rights of nature must be some way forfeited before they can justly be taken away: That the defendant has by any act forfeited the rights of nature we require to be proved; and if no proof of such forfeiture can be given, we doubt not but the justice of the court will declare him free.[134]

For Johnson, slavery in any form was abhorrent. No rules about property would justify the existence of human bondage.

Taking a different perspective on the debate was Boswell, a lawyer wedded to custom and tradition and uncomfortable with what he considered to be Johnson's moral absoluteness and "zeal with knowledge."[135] Siding with the dissenters in the case, Boswell came down on the side of the rule of property. Objecting to the "wild and dangerous attempt" to abolish "so very necessary a branch of Commercial interest" without regard to the interests of planters and merchants, Boswell argued, quoting

Thomas Gray's "Elegy Written in a Country Courtyard," was to "shut the gates of mercy on mankind":

> The encouragement which the attempt has received excites my wonder and indignation: and though some men of superior abilities have supported it; whether from a love of temporary popularity, when prosperous; or a love of general mischief, when desperate, my opinion is unshaken. To abolish a status, which in all ages God has sanctioned, and man has continued, would not only be robbery to an innumerable class of our fellow-subjects; but it would be extreme cruelty to the African Savages, a portion of whom it saves from massacre, or intolerable bondage in their own country, and introduces into a much happier state of life; especially now when their passage to the West Indies and their treatment there is humanely regulated.[136]

Interestingly, neither Johnson nor Boswell seemed startled that there were blacks serving as servants in the prominent estates in Scotland, or that debates about personal and property rights were being transformed by the lives of Africans, who, ostensibly removed from the culture of taste, were familiar sights on the British landscape. Francis Barber, a freed African slave, worked for Dr. Johnson and was probably the model for Sir Joshua Reynolds's *A Young Black*. During their journey through the Scottish Highlands in August 1773, Johnson and Boswell were guided for part of the way by Gory, the black servant of Lord Monboddo, one of the dissenters in the Knight case. On this occasion, Johnson and Boswell were struck by the sight of an African in the North of Scotland "with little or no difference of manners from those of the natives."[137] If they had visited the seats of other important Scottish lairds, such as Lord Drummond, second titular Duke of Perth and famous Jacobite, and looked closely at the paintings on the wall, or the insignias on the servant's collars, Johnson and Boswell would have noticed how slavery had indeed become inscribed into the lives of the powerful and their social imaginaries (see fig. 0.1).

Unspeakable Events:
Slavery and White Self-Fashioning

The year 1763 was a traumatic one for Olaudah Equiano (fig. 3.1), future abolitionist and Anglo-African man of letters. After spending four ostensibly blissful years in England and the high seas living out a meaningful life as a sailor, a profession that often masked his condition of enslavement, Equiano suddenly found himself back in the belly of the beast that was slavery. Without warning or explanation, his master, Michael Henry Pascal, decided to sell Equiano to a Captain James Doran, who planned to take the African back to the West Indies and the accursed life of plantation slavery. This was almost ten years before Lord Mansfield's decision barring the return of James Somersett into bondage and before English jurisprudence settled the vexed question of whether the slave was property or person. Despite all of his protestations against the evils of slavery and the invocations of the law, Equiano had no recourse. He was quickly plunged into what he described as a new form of bondage and bundled onto a ship.

On February 13th, 1763, Equiano found himself on the island of Montserrat in a recursive gesture that appeared to him to be nothing less than the rehearsal of the primal scene of enslavement he first described in the opening two chapters of *The Interesting Narrative*:

> At the sight of this land of bondage, a fresh horror ran through all my frame, and chilled me to the heart. My former slavery now rose in dreadful review to my mind, and displayed nothing but misery, stripes, and chains; and, in the first paroxysm of my grief, I called upon God's thunder, and his avenging power, to direct the stroke of death to me, rather than permit me to become a slave, and to be sold from lord to lord.
>
> In this state of my mind our ship came to an anchor, and soon after discharged her cargo. I now knew what it was to work hard; I was made to help

3.1 Olaudah Equiano or Gustavus Vassa, the African. From Olaudah Equiano, *The Interesting Narrative of the Life of Olaudah Equiano* (London, 1789).

to unload and load the ship. And, to comfort me in my distress in that time, two of the sailors robbed me of all my money, and ran away from the ship. I had been so long used to an European climate that at first I felt the scorching West India sun very painful, while the dashing surf would toss the boat and the people in it frequently above high-water mark. Sometimes our limbs were broken with this, or even attended with instant death, and I was day by day mangled and torn.[1]

For the enslaved African, what had initially appeared to be the narrative of providence and progress, one sustained by the illusion of the life of a global citizen on the open seas, had now become the nightmare of regressive time. Equiano found himself moving from island to island in the West Indies, "daily exposed to new hardships and impositions," and plunged into the midst of the violence and cruelty that governed the lives of the enslaved; he was far from the cosmopolitan centers of Europe in which he had been gallivanting only a few months before.[2] Cosmopolitanism and its ideals of freedom now seemed a distant dream. Savannah, Georgia, rather than London or Paris, seemed to be the natural destiny of the black.[3]

But in 1763 Paris was very much on the mind of David Hume, the Scottish philosopher and man of letters. Hume was considered by many to be the ideal cosmopolitan subject of his age, a man of learning, culture, and taste. In that year, Hume arrived in Paris as acting secretary to the British embassy; for the next three years he captured the attention and the imagination of the Parisian elite not so much for his consular activities, but for his effect on the emerging cosmopolitanism of the age. In fact, Hume's reputation as the representative man of the age of Enlightenment, a subject wedded to the ideals of reason and taste, had preceded him to France. Welcoming Hume in Paris in 1763, Frederick Grimm, the French writer, compared his guest to Denis Diderot: "My dear David, you belong to all the nations of the earth and you never ask a man a place of his birth. I flatter myself that I am like you, a citizen of the great city of the world."[4] In uttering these words, Grimm was probably thinking about Hume's famous description of the cosmopolitan as "a creature" whose thoughts were not limited by what he called "narrow bonds, either of place or time" and a person able to carry researches "into the most distant regions of this globe, and beyond this globe, to the planets and heavenly bodies."[5] And to be visiting Paris in the middle of the eighteenth century was to be in the one place in the world where the ideals of culture and good taste were shepherding modernity. In the salons of the city, such as the one run by Mme Marie Thérèse Rodet Geoffrin, the best minds of the age would meet for enlightened conversation. Cosmopolitanism was the gold standard of good taste, and the salon, the favored site of social interaction, was as far removed from the slave port and markets of Savannah, Georgia, as one could imagine.

The line dividing cosmopolitan culture and the moral geography of slavery was not, however, as wide as the images of the salon and the slave port invoked here might suggest. As I argued in earlier chapters, it was precisely the proximity of these two spheres of social existence—a cosmopolitan culture and the world of bondage—that necessitated their conceptual separation. For if the goal of the project of taste was to quarantine the modern European subject from contaminating forces associated with the political economy of slavery and commerce in general, the desire for cultural purity was continuously haunted by what it excluded or repressed. Here, what Paul Ricoeur has called a "vocabulary of the pure and impure" would come to depend on the ambiguity of the idea of culture itself; aspirations to cultural status would oscillate between the desire for the refined subject or object to exist for itself and the ugly fact that the idea of cleanliness was often driven by a mechanism of exclusion.[6]

Ideals of taste would be adumbrated though the repression of the "symbolic stain" that was slavery.[7] As a consequence, many conceptual attempts to establish the moral boundaries separating the high from the low were under constant pressure from the real or imagined presence of the enslaved. Theorists and practitioners of taste went to great lengths to block the figure of the slave and the drudgery of slavery from entering into the domain of taste, and the claims and counterclaims they made in regard to sense and sensibility would lead to the policing of the invisible line dividing Equiano, aspiring for cultural mastery, and Hume, determined to quarantine cosmopolitan Europe from black dirt.[8] My concern in this chapter, then, is the powerful, visible, and material presence of slavery in the symbolic drawing rooms of modern Britain and the haunting of established ideas of high culture, consumption, and taste by the world of African bondage: why is it that the early generation of African writers in Europe and the Americas, almost without exemption former slaves, came to trouble the men of high culture, often cloistered in universities, coffeehouses, and salons, which seemed so far removed from what Saidiya Hartman has aptly defined as the violent "scene of subjection"?[9]

2

On the surface, Hume's intellectual concerns, the power of which in shaping all facets of modern identity from morals to the law is undisputed, would appear to be remote from such lowly scenes as the slave market and the plantation. As one of the most distinguished cosmopolitan subjects of his generation and a leading figure in the Scottish Enlightenment, Hume was engaged in a universal project whose goal was to chaperone the culture of taste along rational lines and to endow it with a solid philosophical foundation or "reflected utility."[10] In 1757, six years before his arrival in Paris, Hume had published "Of the Standard of Taste," a seminal essay on the nature of aesthetic judgment, where he set out to establish "a rule, by which the various sentiments of men may be reconciled" and to establish a standard of taste for people "of good sense and delicate taste."[11] Like many discussions of taste in the period, Hume's project was surrounded by ambiguity and circularity; but it was also driven by the desire for a resolution to what Preben Mortensen has isolated as one of the central problems of the age: "how do we, in a world where there is no longer a central authority, create new forms of agreement" about taste and social relationships?[12] An overriding goal of Hume's project was to aggregate taste and its subjects; he sought to go beyond the idea that all judgments of taste were equal and to identify subjects who were bestowed with a refined sensibility. In particular, Hume wanted to show that there was a standard of taste that was understood and shared by people of good sense and, equally, that although the principles of taste were universal, only a few were qualified "to give judgment on any work of art, or establish their own sentiment as the standard of beauty."[13] True men of taste were rare, Hume reminded his readers, but they were "easily distinguished in society, by the soundness of their understanding and the superiority of their faculties above the rest of mankind."[14]

Hume recognized that attempts to fix a standard of taste, and thus "reconcile the discordant apprehensions of men," were subject to some variants, notably individual temperament and differing manners, but he was confident that in spite of subjective and temporal differences, the general principles of taste were, in his words, "uniform in human nature."[15] Although he was wedded to an aristocracy of taste, Hume considered prejudice inimical to aesthetic judgment. A judgment of taste, he insisted, depended on the subject's ability to "preserve his mind free from all *prejudice,* and allow nothing to enter into his consideration, but the very object which is submitted to his examination."[16] His belief that prejudice was "destructive of sound judgment, and perverts all operations of the intellectual faculties" was unequivocal; in fact, he deemed "the principles of taste" to be universal "and nearly, if not entirely, the same in all men."[17] But what was included in this category of "all men" or even the universal principle of taste? Could the same general principles of taste apply to colonial subjects, most notably black slaves in the Atlantic world, who had by now become the backbone of the commerce of empire and the most visible insignias of racial difference? Where did the black

3.2 D. George Thompson, *A Literary Party at Sir Joshua Reynolds's*. 1851. Stipple and line engraving. Published by Owen Bailey, after James William Edmund Doyle.

figures who, in a fascinating engraving by George Thompson (after a painting by Sir James Doyle [fig. 3.2]), hovered around the powerful men of culture fit into the discourse and practice of taste?

Such questions were probably not troubling Hume when he turned to the question of taste in 1757, because he had already answered them in a now infamous footnote to the second edition of an essay called "Of National Characters" published in 1742. In this essay, which was to be cited and recited by his contemporaries, Hume declared that "negroes . . . and other species of men" were "naturally inferior to the whites."[18] That Hume could insist on the inferiority of "negroes . . . and other species of men" should not, of course, surprise us given the discourses of denigration that surrounded the figure of the African slave especially in the middle of the eighteenth century. What is surprising is that an intellectual of Hume's caliber and humanistic interests, one whose goal was to establish universal moral and aesthetic judgments, and one who considered prejudice injurious to this endeavor, seemed untroubled by his own sense of prejudice. What was even more startling about this footnote was how Hume proceeded to clarify the terms by which black subjects were excluded from the universe of taste and, more particularly, what was supposed to be its universality.

It is notable that Hume had not taken the easy way out of the apparent contradiction between the universal principle of taste and the inferiority of the black. On the contrary, he had studiously avoided characterizing the "Negro" as nonhuman; he did not categorically state that blacks were naturally inferior—he was expressing a mere suspicion. But even with this tentativeness, Hume seemed too willing to fall back on the grammar of racial difference provided by natural history, which he used to explain black cultural lack; ascribing the characters of human beings to geography—at least "the air and the climate"—not to a simple raciology. When it came to matters of culture and civilization, however, Hume was not so tentative; he had no doubt that the white race was superior in the area of aesthetic genius and cultural achievement: "There never was a civilized nation of any other complexion than white, nor even any individual eminent either in action or speculation." Hume contended that among the "the most rude and barbarous of the whites, such as the ancient GERMANS, the present TARTARS," was to be found "something eminent about them in their valour, form of government, or some other particular," while there were "no ingenious manufactures" and "no arts, no sciences" among nonwhites. His claim was that such "uniform and constant differences" could not happen in so many countries in all ages unless nature had made what he called "an original distinction" between "these breeds of men."[19]

Hume clinched his argument by turning specifically to blacks. There were black slaves dispersed all over Europe "of which none ever discovered any symptoms of ingenuity, tho' low people, without education, will start up amongst us, and distinguish themselves in every profession." For Hume, the most obvious sign of black inferiority was aesthetic lack and a general incapacity in the realm of taste. Casting around for evidence of black aesthetic lack, Hume would inevitably turn to the colonies: "In JAMAICA, indeed, they talk of one negro as a man of pans and learning; but it is likely he is admired for very slender accomplishments, like a parrot, who speaks a few words plainly," Hume concluded his footnote.[20] The "data" provided here was taken up by major philosophers and planter historians alike. The world of the enslavement and the slave, considered far removed from the drawing rooms of the cultured, would become a philosophical point of reference, in absentia, for the rules that governed high culture.[21] In fact, Hume's commentary on the black's lack of inventive genius would became the "authoritative" source for Immanuel Kant's verdict on black cultural and aesthetic inferiority:

> The Negroes of Africa have by nature no feeling that rises above the trifling. Mr. Hume challenges anyone to cite a single example in which a Negro has shown talents, and asserts that among the hundreds of thousands of blacks

who are transported elsewhere from their countries, although many of them have been set free, still not a single one was ever found who presented anything great in art or science or any other praiseworthy quality, even though among the whites some continually rise aloft from the lowest rabble, and through superior gifts earn respect in the world.[22]

Here, again, we have a vivid example of how the culture of taste and its informing concerns was being calibrated against black aesthetic lack, and how artistic criteria and sensibility, or their absence in the other, had now become one of the visible measures of difference.[23]

Of course, neither Hume nor Kant was particularly interested in the lives of black slaves or their place in the sophisticated schemes of freedom that they were elaborating. Yet the black could not be left out of it altogether; blackness was, after all, part of the "fabricated presence" through which ideals such as beauty and genius could be imagined.[24] In this particular case, the fabrication was Francis Williams (fig. 3.3), a free Jamaican black who had been sent to Cambridge under the sponsorship of the Duke of Montagu as part of an experiment to determine whether blacks, "if properly educated," were capable of "the same improvements as whites."[25] At Cambridge, and later as a schoolmaster in Jamaica, Williams had written poetry in Latin and cultivated the life of a gentleman.

Williams's audacious decision to produce poetry had attracted the attention of both pro-slavery and antislavery interests in England. Opponents of slavery, seeking to salvage the humanity of the blacks through the aesthetic, presented Williams as evidence that black subjects had the capacity to produce art, a precondition for a modern identity.[26] For exponents of slavery, however, Williams's Cambridge education and his production of verse in Latin threatened their central claim that the black subject was incapable of artistic genius. They hence set out to prove that the poetry Williams had produced was not original, but a poor imitation of works he had encountered in the course of his education. Transforming Hume's footnote into a memorable chapter in the *History of Jamaica*, for example, Edward Long translated Williams's poetry from Latin in order to expose its derivativeness and, though not stated directly, its mediocrity. To consider the merits of Williams's poetry impartially, Long asserted, "[W]e must endeavor to forget, in the first place, that the writer was a Negroe; for if we regard it as an extraordinary production, merely because it came from a Negroe, we admit at once that inequality of genius which has been supposed, and admire it only as a rare phenomenon."[27]

How, then, was this poetry to be judged? Long had some critical views on the matter: "We are to estimate it as having flowed from the polished pen of one, who received an academic education, under every advantage that able preceptors, and munificent patrons, could furnish; we must

3.3 Anonymous. *Portrait of Francis Williams.* Circa 1745. Oil on canvas.

likewise believe it to be, what it actually was, a piece highly laboured; designed, modeled, and perfected, to the utmost stretch of his invention, imagination, and skill."[28] As far as Long was concerned, Williams's genius was educated, not natural, and a cultivated genius was not a mark of a rational and moral self but the manifestation of the mimicry that Hume had noted in his footnote. Long was not in doubt that the question of artistic production was at the heart of the argument on racial difference and that whichever side prevailed in this dispute would perhaps win the debate on some of the most important questions of the time, including the nature of human character and the immanency of slavery. In this context, it could be argued that the question of Williams's intellect and genius would come to function as the body on which many of the philosophical and cultural issues that dominated the long eighteenth century have been debated; he would come to function either as the symptom of black achievement or of its failure in areas that were considered essential to subjectivity, civility, and taste.[29]

But what is even more intriguing here is that Williams's story, read as a successful or failed experiment in the education of the African, could easily move from the domain of plantation politics to Enlightenment

Scotland and back without being transformed by the modes of intellectual reflection one would expect from the best minds of the time. The involvement of Long, a distinguished member of the slave-owning class in Jamaica, in this debate should not be considered to be a minor episode in the history of the aesthetic ideology. Long is important to the debate on the aesthetic and the ordering of the arts in the modern period because he was forced, often by political expedience, to make a clear connection between questions of morality, artistic genius, and the economic interests of the slave-owning class. It was Long who gave substance to Hume's conjecture, and he did so from the perspective of one who saw black subjects as a phenomenological rather than abstract threat to Western notions of morality and selfhood.

Long's racism was grounded in what he considered to be undisputed facts; this was the basis of his authority and of the shadow he was to cast over the whole project of theorizing difference in the modern period. Far from moving from the mainstream of a "broader cultural milieu" to a "more eccentric outpost," as Warhman has suggested, Long was indeed constituting a new economy of debate in which the debasement of the black was the signal of a particular way of speaking about modern identity.[30] Long's views were certainly extreme even by the standards of the age, but they were part of a calculated phenomenological project: the production of a black specter that would consolidate the vision of the West Indies and the image of the slave-owning class as the custodian of civilization. What Elsa Goveia once called the "pseudo Africa" of the white Creole imagination was intended to conjure up "a country of unspeakable barbarity and terror, by contrast with which the West Indies could be represented as a virtual paradise."[31]

While Hume's racism has been the subject of debate and dispute, my interest here is to restate the enormous influence he had on matters of race and questions of taste in the modern period.[32] His footnote was to influence serious philosophers like Kant just as it was to embolden the philosophical pretensions of West Indian planters like Long in their rearguard attempt to salvage the slaving interests in the age of abolition, or even American "liberals" like Thomas Jefferson as they tried to reconcile the ideology of Enlightenment with the necessity of enslavement. At the center of this racial project was the exclusion of blacks from the domain of art and sensibility, of both a formal and informal aesthetic. This explains why those blacks who aspired to genius and cultural achievement seemed to irritate and even threaten the project of white cultural self-fashioning in the eighteenth century more than other marginalized peoples. This irritation was most apparent in the thinking of Jefferson. John Chester Miller has noted that when Jefferson "heard of a colored person distinguishing himself or herself in the arts, science, or literature, his first question habitually was how much white 'blood' this particular individual possessed."[33] Jefferson considered the letters of Benjamin Banneker, the self-taught black mathematician, "childish and trivial."[34] Phillis Wheatley (fig. 3.4) may well be what Henry Louis Gates has called "the mother of African-American literature," but Jefferson did not consider her to be a true poet, asserting that the "compositions published under her name are below the dignity of criticism."[35]

In his *Notes on the State of Virginia*, Jefferson described the black as a figure of sensation rather than reflection; he conceded that blacks were equal to whites in the area of memory but inferior in the realm of reason; crucially, he argued that "in imagination" they were "dull, tasteless, and anomalous."[36] Jefferson identified areas in which blacks excelled (they were gifted in music, for example), but their failure of imagination was the basis of skepticism, if not censure. Echoing a view expressed by Hume and Kant on the blacks' incapacity to progress even when they had been given a liberal education or "lived in countries where the arts and sciences are cultivated to a considerable degree," Jefferson asserted that he had not found "a black [who] had uttered a thought above the level of plain narration; never saw even an elementary trait of painting or sculpture."[37]

But it is when he turned to the question of the imagination that this lack seemed most glaring:

> In music they are more generally gifted than the whites with accurate ears for tune and time, and they have been found capable of imagining a small catch. Whether they will be equal to the composition of a more extensive run of melody, or of complicated harmony, is yet to be proved. Misery is often the parent of the most affecting touches in poetry. Among the blacks is misery enough, God knows, but no poetry. Love is the peculiar oestrum of the poet. Their love is ardent, but it kindles the senses only, not the imagination. Religion indeed has produced a Phyllis Whately [*sic*]; but it could not produce a poet. . . . Ignatius Sancho has approached nearer to merit in composition; yet his letters do more honor to the heart than the head. They breathe the purest effusions of friendship and general philanthropy, and shew how great a degree of the latter may be compounded with strong religious zeal. He is often happy in the turn of his compliments, and his style is easy and familiar, except when he affects a Shandean fabrication of words. But his imagination is wild and extravagant, escapes incessantly from every restraint of reason and taste, and, in the course of its vagaries, leaves a tract of thought as incoherent and eccentric, as is the course of a meteor through the sky.[38]

Significantly, the terms that Jefferson used to exclude blacks from the realm of the imagination reflected his own mastery of the idiom of the culture of taste and the ideology of the aesthetic. He had a good sense of

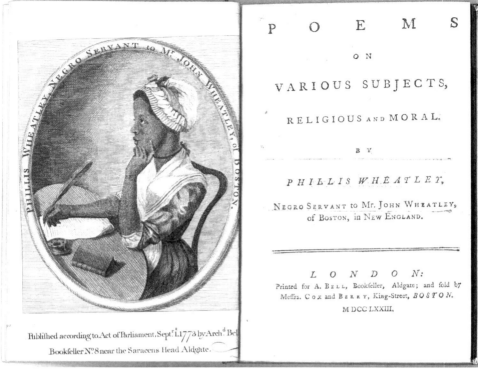

3.4 Phillis Wheatley, Negro Servant to Mr. John Wheatley, of Boston, frontis-piece, Phillis Wheatley, *Poems on Various Subjects, Religious and Moral* (London, 1773).

the distinction between instincts and reflection, of the difference between ability and cultivation in the arts, and of the line that divided the wild and extravagant imagination that he adduced to Sancho and the "restraint of reason and taste." This was the unadulterated vocabulary of the culture of taste.

Why did even the hint that blacks could be active agents in the production of art and consumption rile the enlightened men of taste? In order to answer this question, one needs to try to recover the world in which these men (and occasionally women) operated against the backdrop of the often invisible slavery that enabled the culture of consumption. One needs to provide an allegory of a world in which reason and taste, the indices of civilization and modernity, were intimately connected with the materiality of a slavery that seemed to undermine the moral geography of modern life, including the middle-class desire for cultural purity and subjective freedom. And in order to show how slavery informed and haunted the project of taste, it is necessary to clarify the theoretical categories that will guide my discussion in the rest of this chapter—repression and overdetermination.

J. Laplanche and J.-B. Pontalis have defined repression as "an operation whereby the subject attempts to repel, or to confine to the unconscious, representations (thoughts, images, memories) which are bound to an instinct"; it occurs when "to satisfy an instinct—though likely to be pleasurable in itself—would incur the risk of provoking unpleasure because of other requirements."[39] But repression also has a looser meaning: it serves as a defense, part of a group of operations intended to reduce and eliminate "any change liable to threaten the integrity of the biopsychological individual."[40] Overdetermination is aligned to repression because it refers to the process by which certain formations of the unconscious, such as dreams and symptoms, "can be attributed to a plurality of determining factors"; the formation is shown to result from multiple causes and a "multiplicity of unconscious elements."[41] In this context, slavery and taste, though divorced through a powerful theoretical scheme that assumed that the haunting power of the former threatened the integrity of the latter, need to be recovered in their identity and difference. The rest of this chapter will show how slavery and the culture of taste encountered each other in the social and moral geography of Englishness. More specifically, I will explore how slavery functioned as the great unconscious in the infrastructure of modern identity.

3

Given its overwhelming presence in the British colonies in North America and the Caribbean, the suggestion that slavery was repressed would appear to be anomalous. It was an institution that was visible on the geography of its practice and places of enactment; it was considered to be a source of honor and prestige; but it was often surrounded by a violence and shame that, as I will show later, the masters could not escape. And it was precisely because of its capacity to provoke what was unpleasurable, in both a moral and aesthetic sense, that the link between slavery and the culture of taste needed censoring mechanisms, schemes that would keep apart what was unpleasurable so that it could continue to satisfy instincts and desires that had become integral to modern culture.

Consider, for example, the role of sugar in the making of the culture of taste and economies of pleasure in general. Sugar was the commodity that sweetened the pivot of coffee around which the culture of taste revolved. Without sugar and coffee, the fashioning of categories such as politeness and the overall reconciliation between virtue and conspicuous consumption discussed in the first part of this book would not have been realized. Sugar was one of the many commodities from the reaches of empire that "entered everyday life and changed forever the domestic face of Britain itself."[42] Since the fifteenth century, sugar, as the primary source of sweetness, had come to serve as the link between Europe and its colonies, with "the passage of centuries only underlining its importance even while politics changed."[43] Changing sugar fortunes were intricately connected to the private and public roles of leading men of taste such as Christopher Codrington and William Beckford. Sugar also defined the meaning of taste and consumption; as an object of pleasure it was one visible example of how a colonial economy was built on slaveholding and domestic Englishness. And sugar was not just "the engine for the transformation of British overseas trade," to use James Walvin's term; it was also located at the nexus between private pleasure and public power. Sugar "became established in European taste preferences at a time when European power, military might, and economic initiative were transforming the world."[44]

And since the institution of slavery was shaped by the production of the commodity, sugar provided the vital and inescapable link between white consumption and black labor. The demand for sugar in Britain led to the expansion of West Indian plantations and a rise in imported African labor.[45] Sugar could not be produced without massive imports of cheap labor: "Every stage of the sugar making process required strenuous labor, close supervision, and careful timing."[46] And only the African slave could be conscripted into a regimen that is now remembered for its brutality. In fact, the production of sugar—plus tobacco and cotton in North America—has been identified as the single most important catalyst for the African slave trade. In *Capitalism and Slavery*, Eric Williams, the pioneer Caribbean historian and nationalist, argued that black slavery had nothing to do with race or climate; on the contrary, its existence could be expressed in "three words: in the Caribbean, Sugar; on the mainland, Tobacco and Cotton."[47] By the end of the seventeenth century, notes Angus Calder, "King Sugar would have unchallenged reign over the island colonies."[48] Sugar and slavery developed hand in hand, "two faces of a single phenomenon," adds Dunn.[49] In effect, the counterpoint to the European coffeehouse was the Caribbean sugar complex, the growing, processing, and export of this commodity enabled by African slaves.

But my interest here is not the generalized debate on the connection between the demand for sugar and the rise of West Indian slavery; rather, I am interested in elaborating a direct connection between the slave regime and the construction of a culture of taste in England. As I noted in the introductory chapter, it was difficult for an individual to belong to the culture of taste without money and status. While it is true that the culture of taste could enable social mobility, the production and consumption of beautiful objects needed moneyed patrons. And at a time when the patronage of art and culture had shifted from the courts and aristocracy to the middle classes, the only people with amounts of money large enough to patronize the institutions of cultural production were colonial barons, those who had made their money in slavery and related colonial enterprises. Indeed, from the end of the seventeenth century until the end of the slave trade at the beginning of the nineteenth, the richest members of the British ruling class were those with economic interests in the slave plantations of North America and the Caribbean or economic interests in India and the East. But without question, sugar dominated the political economy of the eighteenth century, prompting Adam Smith to note that the tobacco colonies did not send "such wealthy planters as we see frequently arrive from the sugar islands."[50]

American historian Lowell Joseph Ragatz well described the hegemony of sugar in the opening lines of his classic 1929 study, *The Fall of the Planter Class in the British Caribbean, 1763–1833*: "The sugar planters were the conspicuously rich men of Great Britain in the middle of the seventeen hundreds. 'As wealthy as a West Indian' was proverbial."[51] This point was echoed by Angus Calder almost fifty years later: "The major absentee families—Long, Codrington, Lascelles, above all Beckford—were among the wealthiest in England."[52] The great slaveholding families were not adventurous like early modern buccaneers; on the contrary, they were seen as modernizers who had the capacity to transform the grammar of everyday life, to manipulate markets, to place property at the center of the meaning of value, and often, to shape the nature of the law through their influence in Parliament. Slaveholders were the major patrons of the culture of taste in their times; without the massive profits made in sugar production in the Caribbean, conspicuous consumption could not have been possible.

Such connections were not always visible. Although British consumers certainly knew that sugar was produced by slaves in the West Indies, they operated in a world in which a discursive or conceptual gap separated the leisure of drinking coffee or tea from the brutality of slavery. In this sense slavery enabled the culture of taste because it provided the structures and institutions that made it possible, but its presence was non-visible. To put it another way, it is unlikely that people enjoying a cup of coffee in an English coffeehouse or a cup of tea at home would make a direct link between such pleasurable activities and the suffering of slaves in a West Indian plantation. On the level of culture and consumption, it seemed that slavery functioned as the absent cause of modern Englishness. On the level of trade and politics, however, slavery was the source of power and prestige in the realm, the foundation of new presentations of the self in the public sphere.

We are now so used to thinking about English slavery from the vantage point of its abolition and the humanitarian discourse surrounding it that we have forgotten that at one point to oppose slavery was considered un-English and unpatriotic. As Eric Williams argued powerfully in the second chapter of *Capitalism and Slavery*, from Quakers to cardinals and admirals, supporting the slave trade was at one point expected of every true English man and woman. There was a time when William Wilberforce, the abolitionist, was the most hated man in England, his cause considered to be anti-English. Lord Nelson, the hero of Trafalgar, couched his disdain for the abolitionists in the language of patriotism: "I was bred in the good old school, and taught to appreciate the value of our West Indian possessions, and neither in the field nor the Senate shall their just rights be infringed, while I have an arm to fight in their defence, or a tongue to launch my voice against the damnable doctrine of Wilberforce and his hypocritical allies."[53]

If Nelson was irritated by abolitionists, it is because the true, unsung heroes and patriots of England in the eighteenth century were slave traders, men like Thomas Golightly, owner of a slaving ship and the mayor of Liverpool, a city built on slave money. On February 14, 1788, Golightly and the slaving interest in Liverpool sent a petition to the House of Commons calling attention to the threat that abolitionism posed to British commerce. The petition is worth quoting in detail, because it illustrates how central slave trading had become to the identity of nation and empire:

> To the honourable the House of Commons, the humble petition of the Mayor, showeth that the trade of Liverpool having met with the countenance of this honourable House in many Acts of Parliament, which have been granted at different times during the present century, for the constructing of proper and convenient wet docks for shipping, and more especially for the African ships, which from their form require to be constantly afloat, your Petitioners have been emboldened to lay out considerable sums of money and to pledge their Corporates seal for other sums to a very large amount for effectuating these goods and laudable purposes.
>
> That your petitioners have also been happy to see the great increase and different resources of trade which has flowed in upon their town by the numerous canals and other communications from the interior parts of this kingdom, in which many individuals, as well as public bodies of proprietors are materially interested. And that from these causes, particularly the convenience of the docks, and some other local advantages, added to the enterprising spirit of the people, which has enabled them to carry on the African Slave Trade with vigour, the town of Liverpool has arrived at a pitch of mercantile consequence which cannot but affect and improve the wealth and prosperity of the kingdom at large.

Your Petitioners therefore contemplate with real concern the attempts now making by the petitions lately preferred to your honourable House to obtain a total abolition of the African Slave Trade, which has hitherto received the sanction of Parliament, and for a long series of years has constituted and still continues to form a very extensive branch of the commerce of Liverpool, and in effect gives strength and energy to the whole; but confiding in the wisdom and justice of the British Senate, your Petitioners humbly pray to be heard by their counsel against the abolition of this source of wealth before the Honourable House shall proceed to determine upon a point which so essentially concerns the welfare of the town and port of Liverpool in Particular, and the landed interest of the kingdom in general and which in their judgment must also tend to the prejudice of the British manufacturers, must ruin the property of the English merchants in the West Indies, diminish the public revenue and impair the maritime strength of Great Britain.[54]

What the captains of the slave trade seem to have understood more than their abolitionist opponents was the extent to which slavery permeated the fabric of English life. Coming from Liverpool, Golightly and his associates walked in the streets of a city where wet docks were full of slave clippers, warehouses were proudly named after slave ports such as Goree, and the iconography of the slave trade was to be found on emblems of daily life, including deft bowls, plates, and vases. It is this everyday aspect of slavery that was to be lost in the intellectual debates surrounding the culture of taste and the contaminants it sought to exclude from the domain of beauty.

Moreover, the urgency of tone in the petition reflected the slave interests' fear that the British parliament and public might have forgotten that the slave trade—which was increasingly facing opposition at home and was indeed prohibited from English soil—was still an important fabric of social life. Hence, the petitioners were keen to remind their representatives that far from being an aberration, investments in the slave trade had been undertaken under Acts of Parliament; that slavery had been the engine driving the train of progress; that although the vigor and pitch of the trade was located in Liverpool, the business of selling African bodies had led to the creation of wealth and prosperity in the whole of the United Kingdom. The petitioners also called attention to what was then considered to be the unthinkable consequence of slavery, focusing not on the morality of the debates surrounding enslavement, but the financial aspects of abolition, including its effect on public revenues and the impairment of British naval power.

Facing the challenge of abolitionism at home, the tactic of the slave interest was to recover slavery from the unconscious and mark its manifest presence in the shaping of British public life. In this sense, their attitude was different from that of the intellectual class, which, as I argued in the first chapter, was constantly agonizing over the relationship between art and commerce. The commercial class did not shy away from mapping out the connection between the slave trade and British life; their insistence on the nation's common interest in enslavement was a significant departure from the theories of disinterest that sought to construct the aesthetic subject as what Elizabeth A. Bohls has described as "a process of exclusion" and "a special mode of attention defined as excluding any practical stake in the existence of the object."[55]

Interestingly, colonial planters who on the surface might not have been expected to be troubled by the contradiction between the theory and practice of taste were the first to confront the difficulties of reconciling commerce to an ethics predicated on an ordered moral life. As subjects located on the margins of the British social system, for example, West Indian planters pegged their modern identity on their capacity to consume English goods. From the second half of the seventeenth century onward, ships from England were bringing in luxury goods for the West Indian master class—"silks, furniture, expensive groceries, and wines."[56] There was a clear understanding that the consumption of luxury was essential to the maintenance of an English identity in the tropics. Luxury goods, a Port Royal merchant noted in 1674, had to be "fresh and good and fashionable, for there is a proud generation in this Countrey, although people in England thinke any thing will serve here."[57] But living in close proximity to slaves, West Indian planters were also attuned to how conspicuous consumption continuously called the ethical imperative of modern life into question. Planters aspired for a modern identity that depended on active participation in commercial activities, yet they lived in a period when subjective identity depended on one's capacity to examine or interrogate the basis of selfhood itself.[58]

How could planters extol the virtues of commerce without questioning their own participation in the violence attendant to slavery? There were two possible ways around this problem. The first and easiest one was for West Indian planters to "absent" themselves from the complex of sugar and slavery in order to enjoy the luxuries of modern life without the taint of this crass commerce. By the end of the eighteenth century, many West Indian planters were leaving their plantations to "enjoy their wealth in more polished surroundings."[59] But absentation did not in itself resolve the problem of consumption within colonial society. Indeed, while conspicuous consumption was the fulcrum around which theories and practices of taste in Britain revolved, it was often conceived as the major threat to the identity of West Indian planters as modern subjects. A second approach to the problem of reconciling commerce and virtue was for the planter class to transpose the most visible elements of what was conceived as a modern culture over the scarred landscape of enslavement. In both cases, a measure of engagement with slavery would lead to a transformation of the vocabulary of taste.

4

In the West Indian plantation, the tension between virtue and commerce discussed in the previous chapters would become vivid and inescapable. For what often struck observers most about the lives of white planters in the new world was their inability to control the excesses of commerce, to regulate luxury or simply to enable an ordered culture of consumption. While at home a culture of taste was supposed to harmonize commerce and virtue, in the slave colonies the British tended to lead lives at odds with this dictum. Slave masters often seemed caught between the demands of the new polite culture that had evolved in Europe, one that depended on self-restraint and the management of passions as well as the materiality of the plantation system, often driven by greed and opulence and manifested in moral disorder. Observing a typical planter meal during her trip to Antigua and St. Christopher between 1774 and 1776, the Scot Janet Schaw was astounded by its "great extravagance":

> They have various breads, ham, eggs, and indeed what you please, but the best breakfast bread is the Casada cakes, which they send up buttered. These are made from a root which is said to be poison. Before it goes thro' the various operations of drying, pounding and baking, you would think one would not be very clear as to a food that had so lately been of so pernicious a nature, yet such are the effects of Example, that I eat it, not only without fear, but with pleasure. They drink only green Tea and that remarkably fine; their Coffee and chocolate too are uncommonly good; their sugar is monstrously dear, never under three shillings per pound. At this you will not wonder when you are told, they use none but what returns from England double refined, and has gone thro' all the duties. I believe this they are forced to by act of parliament, but am not certain. This however is a piece of great extravagance, because the sugar here can be refined into the most transparent sirup and tastes fully as well as the double refined Sugar and is certainly much more wholesome.[60]

For most of the eighteenth century, planters in the West Indies struggled to construct a new cultural order based on the blueprints of domestic Englishness as if to remind themselves that they were actually English in spite of their distance from the cultural centers of the motherland. In architecture, for example, the planter class was attuned to developments in England, and they often went out of their way to match the designs that were dominant in Britain. Irrespective of their local and peculiar circumstances, planters built houses to reflect what was vaguely described as an "English style" or "English manner."[61] Thus it is not unusual to see houses built by Barbadian planters in the middle of the seventeenth century echoing the Jacobean style that was prominent in England in the second half of the seventeenth century. For example, in its front façade, its ornamental style, and the loggia that defines its entryway, the Principal's Lodge at Codrington College in Barbados (fig. 3.5), built around 1670, echoed, on a smaller scale, the Jacobean house built by Lord Zouche in Bramshill, Northumberland, between 1605 and 1612 (fig. 3.6).[62] These buildings also reflected the planters' deep anxiety about their English identity. Indeed what struck most commentators about the English houses in Jamaica and Barbados was how often their strict emulation of English style negated climatic needs such as cooling and ventilation. The English style "was geared to the English climate, not to the Caribbean."[63]

The association between opulence and excess in the conception and execution of the "English" buildings in the colonies was not incidental. As an icon of Englishness and money, the great house in the tropics represented what Ragatz aptly describes as "an imposing structure": "Whenever possible, it stood in a commanding position, frequently facing the sea. Almost invariably it was set some distance back from the road and was approached by an avenue of cedars, palmettos, or cocoanut trees."[64] Edward Long's description of the house built by his patron Sir Charles Price in St. Mary, Jamaica, captures well the symbolic grandness of the great house:

> The house is of wood but, well finished, and has in front a very fine piece of water, which in winter is commonly flocked with wild-duck and teal. Behind it is a very elegant garden disposed in walks, which are shaded with the cocoanut, cabbage, and sand-box trees. The flower and kitchen-garden are filled with the most beautiful and useful variety which Europe, or this climate, produces. It is decorated, besides, with some pretty buildings; of which the principal is an octagonal saloon, richly ornamented on the inside with lustres, and mirrors empaneled. At the termination of another walk is a grand triumphal arch, from which the prospect extends over the fine cultivated vale of Bagnals quite to the Northside Sea.[65]

In its best form, the Caribbean great house was as distinguished in its appearance on the West Indian landscape as its English counterpart. The owners and builders of these houses had set out to construct monuments for Englishness in the tropics, and the similarity between the West Indian big house and its English counterparts was often startling. For example, the front and portico of Rose Hall, built on the North Coast of Jamaica in the 1770s (fig. 3.7) has a striking resemblance to Parkstead House, Roehampton, designed by Sir William Chambers for Lord Bessborough around 1758 (fig. 3.8).[66]

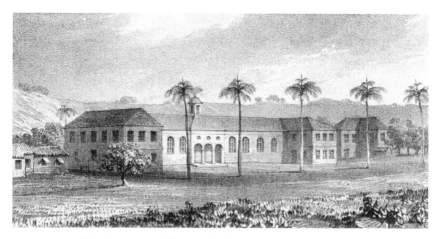

3.5 A View of Codrington College Barbados looking from the Sea (1830). From F.W.N. Bayley, *Four Years' Residence in the West Indies, 1833.*

3.6 Old Bramshill, Hampshire. Photograph by Geoff Cheshire, 2005.

3.7 Rose Hall, Jamaica. Courtesy of Urban Walnut / Wikimedia Commons.

3.8 Sir William Chambers, Parkstead House, Roehampton.

In spite of their grandeur, however, the West Indian great houses often struck observers as out of place in the tropics. There were two reasons for their anomalousness. First, these houses were out of place in a physical sense because even their most appealing designs seemed to defeat the logic of the tropical climate of the colonies. Second, they were out of place in a cultural and moral sense; existing in a social or cultural vacuum (even when they were rehearsing the culture of taste) and surrounded by slaves and sugar, these houses were constant reminders of the unhallowed ground in which wealthy planters were trying to plant the seeds of their imagined Englishness. So, in the end, the alliance between money and taste, or attempts to bring consumption and virtue into some kind of equilibrium, seemed to fail in the face of the materiality of slavery. And there was perhaps no better illustration of this failure than the association in the English mind of the colonial landscape with the very excesses that the culture of taste at home was trying to control or exorcise.

But houses built in the "English manner" in the colonies were not simply representations of imaginary and phantasmal homelands, and it is limiting to suggest that the cultural traffic in art, design, and taste moved in only one direction, from the metropolitan center to the colonial margin. Some of the most significant developments in English architecture, such as the emergence of the Palladian style at the beginning of the seventeenth century, were enabled by the patronage of colonial planters. Indeed, the implosion of Palladianism depended on the convergence of the interests of a new generation of master builders, such as Colen Campbell, and what John Summerson has called "an ascending phase of building activity," a housing boom fueled by colonial money.[67] An example of the creative relationship between colonial money and architectural design can be seen in Wanstead House, Essex, designed by Campbell for Sir Richard Child, the heir to an East Indian fortune. The design of Wanstead House, especially its "size and the lavish splendor of its grounds," was to influence the construction of country houses in Britain for half a century.[68]

The lavish exteriors and opulent interiors of these houses could not have been possible without colonial largesse; their designs fused the aggressiveness of new money with a sense of power and thus called attention to the control and self-fashioning of the nouveau riche who had made it into the aristocracy through the combination of sugar and slavery. In Britain itself, away from the culture and geography of slavery, West Indian planters would turn to the culture of taste and the aesthetic ideology to inscribe their often tenuous English identity and to mediate their deep anxieties brought on by the tar brush of colonial identity. Here, art would become an important conduit for laundering a self produced by slave money into a civic, virtuous subject. It would also provide a site for displacing or repressing the culture of slavery.

5

Consider, for example, the case of Christopher Codrington. The public image we have of him represents the best of the culture of taste as it emerged in Britain in the eighteenth century. As Vincent Harlow noted in a 1928 biography, by the age of thirty, Codrington had it all—"a brilliant record, a high position, vast wealth, and an engaging personality"—and on account of his immense wealth, he was also "one of the most courted men in the literary society of the capital."[69] Codrington was a distinguished statesman and soldier, the man who had commanded the troops that pushed back the French from the Leeward Islands and consolidated the English hold on the eastern Caribbean. He was one of the leading philanthropists of his generation: his bequests include All Souls College, Oxford, which he endowed with books worth six thousand pounds and ten thousand pounds, and the Codrington Library at the college, one of the finest law libraries in the world. More significantly, Codrington was a powerful figure in the shaping of the culture of taste in England. As a scholar he was closely associated with the high culture of All Souls College. He was a close friend of John Locke and Lord Blackstone, an associate of Joseph Addison and Richard Steele, a poet, a dramatist, a wit, and a great patron of the arts.

Codrington assiduously cultivated the image of the well-rounded subject of taste. His public persona was heavily mediated by the idiom of the culture and the aura of classicism. This is evident in existing portraits of him. A statue of him located at Codrington Library, Oxford (fig. 3.9), represents him as a Roman senator; Sir James Thornhill's painting of him on the entry hall of All Souls College presents a rarified posthumous portrait of the philanthropist as a young scholar and lawyer. Other portraits and engravings, including a stipple engraving by R. Clamp at the National Portrait Gallery in London, capture the aura of the classical gentleman scholar.

What is not clear from these representations, however, is whether the image Codrington presented to the English public was intended to enhance his social standing or to camouflage the sources of the wealth that enabled him to befriend and patronize the key architects of taste in his time. For although Codrington's pedigree was beyond reproach, his family fortune was made in Barbados, where he was born and owned sugar estates and many slaves. By the time he succeeded his father as the governor of the Leeward Islands in 1698, Codrington was "the wealthiest English landowner in the West Indies, with holdings on Barbados, Nevis and Antigua."[70] How did this wealth, derived from African bondage, enable Codrington's self-fashioning as a person of taste?

On the surface, Codrington's intimate connection to the complex of sugar and slavery was not repressed. He was proud of his family's involvement in the politics of the Leeward Islands, especially Barbados. When he died in 1710, one of his last gestures, apart from the endowment to All Souls, was the establishment of Codrington College in Barbados, which has been the major center of educating the island's black elite. But the Codrington plantation was a typical West Indian plantation, not a liberal enterprise; it was a place where slaves were driven hard, and some hanged themselves in despair; the cultivation of sugar was as brutal

3.9 Sir Henry Cheere, Statue of Christopher Codrington. 1734. Codrington Library, All Souls College, Oxford. Photograph by Miguel Bernas. This file is licensed under the Creative Commons Attribution-Share Alike 3.0 Unported license and the permission of the photographer.

as in any other plantation on the island of Barbados; slaves were put to work at an early age; and good money was paid for runaway slaves.[71] There were hence two sides to the narrative of Codrington's life: on one side, there was the distinguished English gentleman, the quintessential man of taste; on the other side, there was the seasoned West Indian slave master. These two narratives have not been disputed. What is puzzling and invites further reflection is why cultural historians and biographers have found it difficult to reconcile Codrington's standing as the eighteenth century's ideal man of culture and taste with his role as a slave owner and to discuss the two sides of his personality in the same register. Why has it been necessary to separate Codrington the man of culture and taste from Codrington the slave owner and to treat the two sides of his life as disjunctive?

Two forms of separation or repression are involved here: one is the repression of slavery in the biography of the man of taste; the other is the expurgation of art from the slaveholder's life. In his authoritative biography of Codrington, for example, Harlow solidly locates the man of taste in his milieu but seems unwilling to make an explicit connection between his subject's unmatched ability to sponsor the culture of taste with his control of a West Indian fortune. Any references to West Indian fortunes—the control of slaves and the production of sugar—are attributed to the father, and the moral responsibility of slavery is transferred from successors to progenitors. Thus, in his discussion of Codrington's role as a planter after his return to Barbados in 1700, Harlow would fall back on the now familiar post-abolition claim that although Codrington was "a firm believer in the wisdom and rightness of slavery," he was indeed a reformer of the system.[72] But the claim that Codrington was humane in his treatment of slaves appears tautological given the fact that all planters believed, as their most distinguished historian Edward Long asserted, that slave masters were incapable of cruelty and barbarity, because as gentlemen they were "possessed of more-disinterested charity, philanthropy, and clemency."[73] In contrast to the ostensible repression of the culture of slavery from the man of taste, historians who have undertaken the minutest studies of the Codrington plantations in Barbados barely make any connection between the everyday world of the slave-owning planter and the culture of taste in England. Even those who acknowledge the connection find it more convenient to describe Codrington's philanthropy as "aberrancy" rather than to locate it in the logic of the slave master trying to refashion his identity within the culture of taste.[74]

It is, of course, possible that the connection between Codrington's West Indian fortune and his role in the making of the culture of taste, which appears obvious to us now, was invisible to people in his circle, many of whom invested heavily in the ideal of an autonomous aesthetic, one that derived its authority from an ideology of disinterest. At the heart of this ideology was the belief that the realm of the aesthetic represented an alternative sphere of experience separated from the vulgarity of the everyday. This view was summed up by J. C. Friedrich von Schiller in *On the Aesthetic Education of Man* (1794), where he noted that the problem of politics would be resolved only through the aesthetic, "because it is only through beauty that man makes his way to freedom."[75] A slave owner like Codrington would thus enter the public domain as an aesthetic subject by separating himself from colonial slavery through a kind of *dédoublement*, a gesture of self-conscious alienation.

While it is not clear exactly what his aesthetic objectives were, it is apparent that Codrington's investment in the arts denoted his way toward some calculated measure of autonomy, a way out of the materiality of the life that was his legacy and inheritance. Indeed, until he returned to the Caribbean in triumph as a soldier and governor in 1700, Codrington's connection to the island of Barbados was minimal or minimalized, as he suspended the oppressive materiality of slavery for the rarified life of Oxford and the London coffeehouse. Sent to England to be educated at the onset of adolescence, Codrington's adulthood was defined by his cultivated desire to separate himself from the world of his father: "Whereas the father spent all his days among hard-living planters and negro slaves," notes his biographer, "the younger man grew up among the scholars of Oxford and the literary lights of Paris and London."[76] And if the world of slavery was considered corrupting, then the path to England and Oxford, the sentimental education in the ways of culture, provided Codrington with the characteristic virtues that would make him transcend the world that enabled his being as a modern subject. When he was asked to defend British interests in the West Indies as a soldier and governor, notes Harlow, Codrington "wrote Home discussing Locke's philosophy while leading armies and wrangling with assemblies in the West Indies."[77]

We can now identify the double movement that enabled the man of taste to transcend the culture of slavery that was his condition of possibility: the son of the planter would be sent to the mother country to be isolated from the brutal and uncultured life of the plantation; in turn, an aesthetic education would serve as an antidote to the world of politics and commerce and the moral corruption associated with slavery while providing the financial resources that enabled the patronage of taste. Indeed, Codrington's education in the ways of culture meant occupying, maybe colonizing, all aspects of taste, which would act as his conduit into polite society. Thus, at the age of seventeen, "Christopher Codrington matriculated as a gentleman commoner of Christ Church in the University of Oxford"; at the age of thirty, he had established himself at the center of high society.[78]

It is interesting to note that Codrington did not gain entry into high society by patronizing politicians or using his immense wealth to influence parliamentary debates; rather, he used his money to cultivate the friendship of poets, painters, and philosophers and to pay the bills of scholars such as Thomas Creech, who otherwise would have been indigent. But to argue that Codrington was admitted into polite society and artistic circles because of his talent, as Harlow does, is to miss the role money played in fashioning a public persona. Ignoring the fact that the source of money that made the patronage of art possible was derived from scenes that were far removed from the ideal of an aesthetic education negates the extent to which the planter class used art and culture to launder its dirty wealth. Let us not forget, after all, that even when their descent was unquestionable, as in the case of the Codringtons, to be born in the colonies, to be a white Creole or an Indian nabob, was to exist under the shadow of what I call white anxieties.[79]

And there are some compelling reasons why these anxieties came to function as an important mark of modern identity in the British Isles. For in the second half of the eighteenth century, notes Michael Edwardes in reference to Indian nabobs, the repatriation of colonial money to Britain generated deep anxieties in the social establishment, leading to some kind of moral panic—"the British upper classes felt, and displayed, both publicly and privately, the sort of panic that might have been caused by the arrival in England of the hordes of Genghiz Khan—carrying the plague." The source of this panic was "a comparatively small number of men who had acquired, by various means, usually dubious, large fortunes in India which they intended to spend in ensuring their entry into 'society'." Colonial barons were feared because they were the only ones among the middle classes with enough money and political clout to penetrate "the political, social, and economic preserves of the English landed gentry."[80]

Significantly, colonial barons understood the significance of art and taste as their point of entry into the inner sanctums of Englishness. They often used their money and political influence to control art and taste, commissioning elaborate paintings and building opulent mansions. The typical British response to the panic generated by colonial money was to turn these barons into figures of caricature and mockery. For example, Sir Thomas Rumbold had risen in the ranks of the Indian trade to become a governor of Madras, and, like most wealthy people of his period, he commissioned Gainsborough to produce a massive double portrait of himself and his son in the 1770s. Still, this extravagant reconfiguration of selfhood through art did not salvage Rumbold's image; as a nabob he was subject to ridicule, reduced to a money monger at best and a fraud at worst. This same fate was reserved for most West Indian Creoles, whose origins were often the subject of aspersion and whose manners were constantly derided. The cultural dilemma of white Creoles—and hence the source of the anxiety that was both indispensable and disposable in the making of the culture of taste—was this: they were the only people with enough money to drive the engine of taste, which demanded luxury and consumption, but they were also considered to be the furthest removed from good manners and politeness.

From a genealogical perspective, the Codringtons were lucky to be associated with the pedigree of the English landed gentry before their foray into the West Indian plantation complex, and this seemed to ease their way into English society. In this sense they are atypical of colonial barons, and they seemed to have a free hand in shaping the social and physical landscape of modern Britain. Indeed, for almost two centuries the Codrington family used its immense wealth to transform Dodington Park, a property whose history reflects the changing nature of taste in physical form. When the family first bought the building in the late sixteenth century, it was a typical Elizabethan house with large cables and an adjunct church. When the second Christopher Codrington hired James Wyatt, probably the most important British architect of the late eighteenth century, to construct the new Dodington House (1798–1813), the building reflected the neoclassical revival of the day. Here, as elsewhere, fashionability was enabled by the family's income from its West Indian sugar holdings.[81]

A more complex story is that of colonial planters with enough money to pay for all the objects of taste but not the pedigree that was an essential part of a privileged Englishness or the manners required of people of taste. As people born in the colonies, white Creoles and nabobs were already classified as a distinct social category, and with their white identity often in doubt, they had to work hard to earn the designation of "men of taste," people who, in Hume's words, were "easily distinguished in society, by the soundness of their understanding and the superiority of their faculties above the rest of mankind."[82] In this context, white Creoles, like the Indian nabobs, were located in the space of the repressed in the culture of taste: they were neither black enough to occupy the slot reserved for the African slave nor white enough to be considered English, although they craved for Englishness more than anyone else.

6

In a culture in which, as Peter de Bolla reminds us, "writers held up the man of taste as the exemplar of the highest possible level of cultural and social rank," white Creoles were both outsiders and insiders: money made them belong to the ruling circles; their colonial origins excluded them from the inner sanctum of manners.[83] The culture of taste was predicated on the marriage of money and manners; the white Creole had too much of the former and too little of the latter. As the life of William Beckford illustrates vividly, it was in the figure of the white Creole—"Almost the same but not white," to use Homi Bhabha's apt phrase—that money and taste would come to trouble each other in unprecedented ways.[84]

Some background and context is necessary here. In Britain there was no better representative and practitioner of the ideals of taste and the aesthetic than William Beckford. He had all the necessities on which a modern subjectivity depended—money, rank, and taste. When Lord Byron described him as "England's wealthiest son," he was calling attention to something more than Beckford's immense inheritance; he was perhaps also thinking about how money and culture had come to constitute subjective identity.[85] Beckford's father, popularly known as "the alderman," had inherited a massive fortune from his own father and had used it to climb to some of the highest social and political ranks of English society. He had served as an alderman and sheriff for the city of London and was twice lord mayor of the metropolis before entering the House of Commons. He had fathered at least thirty children, but William was his only legitimate child and his sole heir.

Clearly, young William's life was one of privilege. When he was baptized in the parish church at Fonthill Gifford near the family estate on September 29, 1760, the younger Beckford was surrounded by the best society in England: William Pitt the Elder, a close friend of his father, was the godfather, and William Pitt the Younger, later prime minister and distinguished statesman, was his playmate. And since young William's aunt Effingham was the chambermaid at St. James's palace, the boy had many occasions to meet King George III and to familiarize himself with the inner workings of the court. More significantly, Beckford's education and life experiences were deliberately programmed to actualize many of the theories about manners, culture, and taste that were circulating in Britain at the time. The family estate had a memorable gateway, which was apparently designed by Inigo Jones, one of the most prominent British architects of the period, while Fonthill Splendens, the family home, was described as "one of the most princely edifices in the kingdom" and "a magnificent seat surrounded by an extensive park, landscape gardens, and grottoes."[86]

Young William's first drawing lessons were supposedly conducted by Sir William Chambers, founder of the Royal Society of Architects and drawing master for George III when he was Prince of Wales. It is even said that when a young music genius named Wolfgang Amadeus Mozart passed through England in 1765, William Beckford, then five years old, had a chance to play a tune or two for the child prodigy from Salzburg. Indeed, Beckford would die insisting that he was the one who produced "Non più andrai," the famous aria in *The Marriage of Figaro*. In addition to such encounters, which constituted an important part in his aesthetic education, Beckford's mother had imported a tutor from St. Andrews, a prestigious Scottish university, just to be sure that her son's education in the way of beautiful things was balanced by proper instruction in morals and religion.

A few more details need to be added to this portrait of Beckford as the quintessential eighteenth-century subject of taste before exploring the anxieties that were attendant to white self-fashioning in the age of slavery. As I showed in the last chapter, one's subjectivity during this period was not simply fulfilled by living the life of the aesthete; in the emergent bourgeois culture, the presencing of virtue and rank depended on portraiture, "considered as the public commemoration of greatness" and "the clearest possible indications of rank."[87] Toward this end, the alderman made sure that his son had the best portraiture money could buy: young Beckford's first portrait at the age of six was painted by Andrea Casali, the one at eight or nine was done by either William House or Nathaniel Dance, with further portraits by Sir Joshua Reynolds and George Romney at the ages of twenty-one and twenty-two, and by John Hoppner at forty (fig. 3.10).

As was to be expected of a wealthy gentleman of the time, William Beckford considered the grand European tour to be at the heart of what it meant to be cultured. He seemed to have subscribed to Dr. Samuel Johnson's dictum that "A man who has not been in Italy, is always conscious of an inferiority, from his not having seen what it is expected a

3.10 John Hoppner, *William Beckford, ca. 1800.*

man should see."[88] For Beckford, the grand tour, like many of his other cultural activities, was an indispensable form of self-fashioning as a member of the English cultural elite. Indeed, his encounters with Italy were posited as nothing less than a mark of cultural arrival, part of an elaborate scheme in which the subject would inscribe himself into the center of European social and artistic life. On his second grand tour, in May 1782, for example, Beckford made his way through the Low Countries in such glamour and splendor that he was mistaken for European royalty: "His equipage was so splendid and the speed of his progress so great that many people, including greedy innkeepers, believed he was the Emperor of Austria travelling incognito."[89] And Beckford seemed to have been eager to follow the rituals of the grand tour to the letter. As the diaries he kept and the letters he wrote at the time attest, his journey through the European landscape was seen as a salient way to construct a character and genealogy for himself, settling the questions about cultural pedigree that had plagued his father before him, a man who had been mocked for his Creole identity and Jamaican accent.

In a set of gestures that in retrospect seem far removed from the sugar cane plantations of Jamaica, Beckford adopted the European landscape as purely aesthetic. His stopping points on the grand tours—Italy, Switzerland, France, and Portugal—were often conceived as a way of cultivating the sublime and as "a prerequisite for the development of the aesthetic palette."[90] Beckford's presentation of his arrival in Rome during his tour of 1782 is an example of what he considered to be the sublimity of the European landscape, the terrain of his desire as the modern European subject of culture:

> "When you gain the summit of yonder hill, you will discover Rome," said one of the postillions: up we dragged; no city appeared. "From the next," cried out a second; and so on, from height to height, did they amuse my expectations. I thought Rome fled before us, such was my impatience; till at last we perceived a cluster of hills, with green pastures on their summits, inclosed by thickets, and shaded by flourishing ilex. Here and there, a white house, built in the antique style, with open porticos, that received a faint gleam of the evening sun, just emerged from the clouds and tinting the meads below. Now domes and towers began to discover themselves in the valley, and St. Peter's to rise above the magnificent roofs of the Vatican.[91]

And in order to make a claim to belonging to this Europe of his imagination, Beckford went to great lengths to transform its landscape into a desirable aesthetic object:

> Every step we advanced, the scene extended; till, winding suddenly round the hill, all Rome opened to our view.
>
> A spring flowed opportunely into a marble cistern close by the way; two cypresses and a pine waved over it. I leaped out, poured water upon my hands, and then, lifting them up to the sylvan Genii of the place, implored their protection. I wished to have run wild in the fresh fields and copses above the Vatican, there to have remained till fauns might peep out of their concealments, and satyrs begin to touch their flutes in the twilight; for the place looks still so wondrous classical, that I can never persuade myself, either Constantine, Attila, or the Popes themselves, have chased them all away.[92]

Considered by other aristocrats to be a mere fad, Beckford conceived the grand tour as a forceful presentation of himself in the public sphere. Thus his second grand tour was meticulously plotted to rehearse and fulfill the established rituals of travel in the late eighteenth century, to make certain that the traveler was unquestionably a person of culture and taste and was recognized as such by those who witnessed the procession. Beckford's itinerary, then, was canonical, following on the established routes of continent travel trodden by famous predecessors, but he also ensured that his sojourn through the Low Countries entered the public realm and was perceived as a prelude to his Italian apotheosis.

Beckford's second grand tour was also unique because it enabled him to display his capacity to influence both the production and consumption of art. On this occasion Beckford brought along John Robert Cozens, already an important landscape painter, and tried to use him as a conduit for redirecting the nature of British art. In his partnership with Cozens, Beckford conceived his role not merely as that of a wealthy patron but also as an important theorist of art, one concerned with the history of English painting and its place in the social order. As E. S. Shaffer has noted in a compelling discussion of the relationship between patron and artist, there was what one may call a tripartite structure between Beckford's second grand tour, his aesthetic project, and some of Cozens's most important paintings, such as *Padua after 1782*.[93] Beckford was a wealthy patron for Cozens, providing the artist with the leisure to produce his most important landscape paintings, but he was also an active agent in determining the themes and style of the work of art; the collaboration between patron and artist was intended to transform aesthetic practice in Britain.

If Beckford's aesthetic was impelled by the need to change the conventions of British art, and especially to make the imagination rather than memory the organizing principle of this art, then it is easy to see how being on the road provided him with the license for this kind of project. It was in the process of describing the landscapes he encountered on his tour that Beckford developed his vision for English art, a program in which what was observed and its effects on the sensations were as important as what was imagined or visualized, and one in which natural objects, such as mountains, could be recollected and re-created in the mind independent of their location and temporality. The work that Cozens produced on the grand tour was similar to Beckford's writings done at the same time; both testify to what Shaffer aptly calls "the deepening of the relationship between the traveler and his landscape, and between writing and painting, and marks the conversion of fashionable staging posts in a social ritual into a melding of inner and outer experience in what would later be called by Wordsworth 'spots of time'."[94]

Like Cozens's paintings, Beckford's travel narratives indicate his fondness for ekphrasis, and the many "painterly" scenes in these writings reproduce Cozens's landscapes. And yet the closeness of patron and artist observed here has not gone down well with critics of English art, some of whom have blamed what they consider to be the shortcomings in Cozens's work on Beckford's overwhelming influence. Sir Anthony Blunt, for example, dismissed *Padua after 1782* as the worst example of Beckford's imposition of his "spoilt, whimsical and temperamental" attitude on Cozens's delicate sensibility.[95] Evidence of this imposition, Blunt argued, could be found in the dislocation of the painting from its immediate setting. The painting purports to be the representation of a storm over Padua that Beckford and Cozens witnessed when they were visiting that town during the grand tour of 1782, but there is no mention of such a storm in the letters and diaries Beckford kept during the same period. On the contrary, the painting is a meticulous representation of a storm that Beckford had witnessed in Padua during his first grand tour two years before, a scene vividly represented in the diaries from this period. This discrepancy in time would lead Blunt to conclude that far from being the representation of an immediate and sensuous experience, the painting was a recall of a past scene that the wealthy patron had forced upon Cozens. The implication here was that the painting represented the patron's whimsical vision rather than the artist's power of observation and sensibility.[96]

But this kind of post-romantic reading of *Padua after 1782* misses the point: the fact that the sublimity of the painting depended on the artist's capacity to evoke an emotion independent of its topography and history.[97] Cozens could bring his imagination to bear on the storm over Padua because he hadn't personally witnessed it; the impact of his work would depend not on an observed experience, but on a kind of autonomous imagination, something akin to Wordsworth's definition of poetry as "the spontaneous overflow of powerful feelings," which "takes its origin from emotions recollected in tranquility."[98] In this context, Beckford, who was praised as a collector and vilified as a man of taste, understood the close relation between the grand tour, the narrative of travel, and the romantic imagination. For him, notes Shaffer, "actual travel became the occasion for mental travel in which the well-stocked mind of the traveler constructed his own landscape, sometimes merely whimsically but gradually refashioning the raw materials of familiar Grand-Tour topoi into new modes of visual encounter with inner landscapes."[99] There are, however, good reasons to question Beckford's understanding of the aesthetic. Was his interest in art motivated by reigning theories of beauty or by utilitarian, some might say self-aggrandizing, motives? The case for the latter is supported by Beckford's notorious propensity for collecting beautiful and expensive objects.

As is well known, Beckford was the leading collector of his day, owner of a rich array of precious and magnificent objects on display in today's museums, including works in porcelain, metal, and wood.[100] There is perhaps no single major museum in Europe and North America without a dazzling object from the Beckford collection. The Fonthill Ewer, with its smoky crystal and enameled gold mounts, probably made in the workshop of Ferdinand Eusebio Miseroni in Prague in 1680, can be seen at the Metropolitan Museum of Art in New York City; the Fonthill-Gaignieres Ewer, a Qunbai porcelain jar now at the National Museum of Ireland, dates to the Yuan dynasty (ca. 1300); and some of the best collections of French furniture at leading institutions such as the Wallace Collection and the Victoria and Albert Museum were initially owned by Beckford. For Beckford, collecting art objects and expensive objects had become an obsession. At one point toward the end of the eighteenth century he was in Paris several times, with a cursory interest in the politics of the French Revolution but primarily lured there "by the thought of the spoils he might pick up in the glittering debris left in the wake of revolution."[101] Many of Beckford's precious pieces of art and furniture were bought on the cheap from a fleeing French aristocracy. This art came to be woven into the fabric of Beckford's life; as an 1822 epitaph in the pages of the *Times of London* noted, he was "one of the few possessors of great wealth who have honestly tried to spend it poetically."[102]

But for Beckford and other colonial barons there was something else driving this desire to collect art and to locate the self at the center of the culture of taste, and this had very much to do with the hidden hand of sugar and slavery. In effect, slavery functioned as the hidden cause—the political unconscious, as it were—of Beckford's aesthetic being.[103] And to understand the role this absent cause played in shaping the desires and aesthetic demands of the subject of taste, one needs to highlight two points about Beckford's relationship to the culture of consumption. First, it is evident that most of his artistic endeavors in areas as diverse as design, architecture, travel, and even the writing of his gothic novel, *Vathek*, were driven by deep anxieties about his identity, his genealogy, and his relation to the public culture, where he was both an insider and outsider. Beckford was an insider because his immense wealth had enabled him to live the life of the aesthete; he was an outsider because the Beckfords were deeply involved in West Indian slavery, being major slaveholders on the island of Jamaica. In spite of having been described as "the third generation of the Beckford clan of buccaneering sugar potentates," Beckford's father had risen in the political system to become lord mayor of London, and he had used his immense wealth to secure cultural standing in English high society for strictly utilitarian reasons.[104]

Alderman Beckford did not for once imagine that he could erase his Jamaican identity and the structure of difference associated with it. On the contrary, he used his immense wealth to buy his way into the English ruling class while using his political skills to align himself with the ascendant Whigs. More importantly, he had a keen understanding of the role of the culture of consumption and the organization of the arts in ensuring an individual's social standing. For example, when he married into the aristocracy in 1756, the alderman began "the construction of a building of increased grandeur, more suited to his social standing and political aspirations." The new building, Fonthill House (fig. 3.11), was modeled on Houghton Hall, which Sir Robert Walpole had built "as a monument to political merit."[105] Designed and constructed in the dominant Palladian style that was popular with the English ruling class, Fonthill House reflected the taste of the Whig establishment, of which Alderman Beckford was an important part.

It is important, then, to underscore the alderman's utilitarian view of art as a counterpoint to his son's much more subjective relationship to the aesthetic. Unlike his son, the alderman did not aspire to be more than what he was allowed to be within the culture of Englishness—a Jamaican Creole with a lot of money and the political clout that came with it. In contrast, young Beckford engaged with art at moments of psychological crisis and considered it central to his identity as a modern subject; for him, art was the mediator of a conflicting set of desires and a form of compensation. Thus Beckford valued the landscape and its painting because he saw himself as a "passionate nomad," and he saw collecting as essential to his engagement with Englishness.[106] As a collector, Beckford's only other rival in the kingdom was the prince regent, later George IV. But while the prince and other aristocrats collected objects out of curiosity or fashion, Beckford had what Bet McLeod describes as "a very personal engagement with his collection," which was informed by a "highly individual and romantic streak."[107]

The intensely subjective relationship between Beckford and his collection provides important insights into his overall relationship with the ideology of the aesthetic, and it is perhaps not an exaggeration to say that it was in his acquisition, rather than admiration, of works of art that he sought to transform his "not quite white identity" into the quintessential subject of taste and thus of what was assumed to be true Englishness. In short, Beckford considered the mastery of the culture of taste to be the essence of his being and the conduit to an Englishness that he couldn't take for granted. What were the sources of Beckford's deep anxieties about his cultured self? Why would a subject born into and brought up in the most privileged economic and political circumstances of the eighteenth century live under the shadow of deep anxieties about the self and its place in

3.11 View of the west and north fronts of Fonthill House. 1823. From John Rutter, *Delineations of Fonthill.*

the public sphere while ordinary middle-class people, subjects like Anna Margaret Larpent discussed earlier, could use limited cultural resources to fashion themselves as part of the aristocracy of taste?

There are some obvious and popular explanations for Beckford's cultural anxieties. One is that beneath the mask of taste and civility, Beckford's life was haunted by what one of his biographers has called the absence of "a dazzling descent."[108] Another is that Beckford's homosexuality marked him as an outsider, a fact confirmed by the reaction to his alleged affair with an adolescent boy named William Courtenay, the event used by his enemies to ruin his political and social standing, effectively turning him into the subject of scandal rather than taste.[109] Both of these are valid explanations, but both point to some of the ways in which Beckford's social anxieties were tied up in the knot of colonialism and slavery. Colonial origins aggravated Beckford's sense of cultural isolation and alienation as much as his sexuality and behavior did.

One possible counterpoint is that other colonial barons, like Codrington, had been able to succeed in the aristocracy of taste without the hindrance and taint of their vast slaveholdings. But even before their involvement in the colonial and slaving enterprise, the Codringtons were already part of the English aristocracy. The irony here is that Codrington, who never disavowed his ownership of slaves or concealed close ties to the West Indian plantation system, could be accepted as a founding member of the culture of taste, while Beckford, who had been born in England and whose ties to Jamaica were minimal, couldn't find a similarly secure place in the system of art and culture. The issues here, then, are of social class and colonial disavowal, and they need to be sketched out carefully in order to account for the subject of taste who didn't make it to the inner sanctums of Englishness.

With regard to class, the facts are straightforward. William Beckford's great-grandfather, Peter Beckford, the son of a Clerkenwell cloth worker, migrated to Jamaica in 1643 to join his brother, who was already involved in the slave trade. By taking advantage of the opportunities offered by the colonial space and the revolution that new rules of property had triggered in the British economy, Peter Beckford was able to acquire enough land and slaves to become a member of the white Creole oligarchy in Jamaica, rising to be president of the council under Charles II and lieutenant governor and commander in chief under William III. By the time of his death, Peter Beckford had amassed what was considered to be "one of the greatest fortunes to come out of Jamaica in an age when to have a vast commercial fortune one must either be a Nabob from India or a sugar king from the West Indies."[110] This wealth was passed on to his son, also named Peter, who held it intact for the two William Beckfords, the alderman and his son.

Irrespective of their wealth and power, however, the Beckfords lived under the shadow of a questionable genealogy. As part of the plantocracy in Jamaica, the Beckfords were on top of their world, but in England they were wealthy but without pedigree. Their challenge was how to process this wealth into an elevated standard of social respectability. As we have already seen, Alderman Beckford bought his way into the establishment, marrying into it, becoming lord mayor of London, and controlling the institutions of power as a member of its powerful guilds. However, the alderman's aspirations were limited to the exteriority of power; he did not set out to "pass" into the inner sanctum of Englishness. In fact, he seemed to have found a way of being both Creole and English, emulating whatever was dominant in the cultural geography of Englishness but inflecting it with his Jamaicanness.

The architectural style of Fonthill House was a superb example of this compromise. From one perspective, the house was an outstanding model of the Palladian style favored by the second generation of the Whig aristocracy, and by building a house that closely resembled that of the prime minister, Alderman Beckford had found a way of identifying Whig aristocracy and its fashions. He understood, almost intuitively, the close relation between politics, identity, and architecture in eighteenth-century England. He knew, for example, that after the failed Jacobite uprising in 1715 and the resulting hostility toward Catholicism and things deemed

Catholic, architecture, like other forms of art, came to function as an expression of the idea of Britain as a Protestant nation. As one critic has noted, the "extravagant and exaggerated architecture" associated with Catholicism was now out of fashion, replaced by controlled and proportional systems of design.[111]

Despite its size and majesty, Fonthill House was intended to be a model of proportion and Protestant restraint. From another perspective, however, the interior of the house seemed to qualify, or even defy, Protestant order. The ornate rooms of the house had a distinctively un-Protestant quality to them. A contemporary observer was struck by the extravagance of these interiors, their "touches of vulgarity" and "the appearance of riches almost tawdrily exhibited."[112] This was clearly a house built on Creole money; its penchant for ostentatiousness was a sign of the owner's desire to display new wealth. And thus, standing in juxtaposition to the controlled lineament of the house's exterior was its unabashedly orientalist interior, complete with an entrance known as the Egyptian Hall and a Turkish Room. How do we explain these contrasts?

In his work on Indian nabobs, Edwardes has noted that an owner or heir to a colonial fortune seeking to reposition himself in relation to the conflicting impulses of the eighteenth century would be adept at using the architecture of the ruling class to both inscribe and conceal his own ambiguous identity, putting on "a Classical or, more precisely a neo-Classical front behind which he could display as much or as little Asian luxury as he chose."[113] This was the process at work in Alderman Beckford's buildings. In Fonthill House he had brought together all the key features of the Palladian style of the aristocracy of taste and pollinated them with the alterity of orientalism and the West Indian landscape. The most original aspect of Fonthill was its setting "at the bottom of a wooded valley on the west margin of an artificial lake, complete with bridge, grotto and unique boathouse, apsed and aisled like a rococo basilica in miniature."[114]

In this setting the alderman had simultaneously attempted to capture the ideal of the garden as a sign of what Horace Walpole called "the English Constitution" and to recapture the landscape of the Jamaican great house.[115] Like other wealthy outsiders, Alderman Beckford perceived the country house as both a symbol of social standing and an expression of his claim over the English landscape. The external structure of the country house would mirror the architecture of the ruling class; its interior would be a place where luxuries acquired through colonial enterprises could be simultaneously displayed or concealed. In these circumstances, Palladianism attracted nabobs and West Indian planters because it was a style that enabled both revelation and concealment, representing order and control on the outside but retaining a measure of extravagance within, in its decor and furnishing. Alderman Beckford understood the primacy of display and concealment well. While the façade of his house reflected the architecture of his class, its interior exhibited the magnificent style associated with the colonies, including the Baroque. Indeed, there is a sense in which Fonthill House can be read as an extension of the West Indian Georgian house, including Drax Hall in Jamaica, which Alderman Beckford purchased in 1762.

Alderman Beckford had somehow managed to maintain the relationship of the metropolis and the colonial periphery in equilibrium and to fashion a narrative in which the centers of British life were seamlessly connected to his periphery. In this narrative, the dominant forms of eighteenth-century political culture seemed to be untroubled by the residual forms of colonial slavery.[116] Where colonial money fed political power and social standing there was no need for repressing a colonial background. Oblivious to the oppositional values assigned to metropole and colony in the English imagination, the alderman would not have been troubled by the disjunctive relationship between the two houses he had bought or built—one in Wiltshire, in the heart of Englishness, the other in Jamaica, the biggest sugar and slave colony in the British empire. What about the son? How did he deal with his ambiguous inheritance?

7

If the key to understanding Alderman Beckford was his adoption of the cultural style of the Whig aristocracy, including its preferred mode of building, his son's life can best be understood in relation to the expensive objects he set out to accumulate. For the younger Beckford, collecting would come to reflect deep anxieties about the self and its place in society, and would eventually mark the limits of the culture of consumption itself. In fact, as David Watkin has noted in his insightful discussion on the psychology of collecting in the age of Enlightenment, some of the great British collectors of the eighteenth century—John Soane, Thomas Hope, and William Beckford—were "outsiders in some ways, facing real or imaginary opposition."[117] He also remarks on "the trauma experienced by men of taste at finding themselves at war with France, a country that they regarded as the most civilized in Europe."[118]

Isolated in Britain in the second half of his life because of various scandals, Beckford, who had turned to Paris for solace, was certainly traumatized by the outbreak of hostilities between England with France. There was, however, an even greater source of trauma that has not adequately been accounted for in existing accounts of Beckford's struggle to define himself in relation to the culture of taste: the fact that he was oppressed by the constant reminder that his sense of self as a modern subject was built on fortunes made in the complex of sugar and slaves. Slavery was the greatest repressed force in Beckford's life. He knew that his wealth depended on it, yet he could not acknowledge its presence in his life. The few commentators who have paid attention to Beckford's connection to Jamaican slave life have underscored "his near total detachment from the source of his wealth, his Jamaican plantations, and most certainly his complete disregard for the slave laborers who produced his wealth."[119]

Writing of a period later than the one covered here, Raymond Williams has noted that repression was one of the defining characteristics of the emerging bourgeois in the first half of the nineteenth century. He has further argued that "the repressed culture is that consequence of the bourgeois failure to recognize even the facts of its own experience and above all its sexuality."[120] In this case, Beckford can be seen as the figure of the proto-bourgeois subject emerging out of the culture of taste, driven by the conviction that the self-fashioning was enabled by repression or disavowal. Thus, while Jamaica is rarely mentioned in accounts of Beckford's life, when it is, biographers have been struck by what has appeared to be the dissonance between the man of taste and his colonial possessions. Although Beckford was known to be a generous landlord in Wiltshire, noted one observer, he apparently did not feel any responsibility toward "those laboring to build his fortune, and it is true that he did not in the least concern himself about his Jamaican slaves."[121] Is it possible that Beckford's disregard for his Jamaican slaves was a form of disavowal rather than neglect or disregard? The distinctions here are crucial, for while neglect is self-conscious and deliberate, disavowal is a defense mechanism. Indeed, disavowal in the Freudian sense is a mode of defense "which consists of the subjects refusing to recognize the reality of a traumatic perception."[122]

Jamaica could be absent from Beckford's biography, but this does not mean he was not aware of the extent to which his ability to live the lavish life of an aesthetic subject depended on his slaveholdings. We find acknowledgment of this connection in a letter to Lady Craven in 1790: "One of my new estates in Jamaica brought me home seven thousand pounds last year more than usual. So I am growing rich, and mean to build Towers, and sing hymns to the powers of Heaven on their summits, accompanied by almost as many sacbuts and psalteries as twanged around Nebuchadnezzar's image."[123] But dependence on colonial fortunes could also create deep anxieties. On a grand tour in Portugal in 1794 and 1795, Beckford worried about the effects of sugar prices, slave revolts, and legal challenges to his Jamaican holdings on his ability to maintain Fonthill House, which he had inherited from his father. By 1819 the family's plantation in Jamaica, Drax Hall, was in severe financial crisis, and this was affecting Beckford's standard of living and his precarious position in the culture of taste. Nevertheless, the language used to express these colonial anxieties was one of denial, avoiding the subject at hand, refusing to recognize the source of the trauma, to be drawn close to it, or even to speak its language.

Hiding behind the clichéd language of lawyers and agents, and using citations and indirect discourse, Beckford worked hard to distance himself from the unnamable event that was his legacy. In his correspondence on the political economy of slavery, then, Beckford preferred to recite what he called the "scorpionish" letters from his lawyers rather than to clarify matters himself:

> Since the beginning of the scorpionish letter is in rather ornate style, I'm taking the trouble to copy it down: "My dear Sir, I am sorry to be the herald of bad news but the uncontrollable Elements having occasioned serious mischief upon your Draxhall Estate, I am unwillingly obliged to be so." Poor Besti-fownes will be cruelly afflicted, and rightly so: the merchants, in their fine honeyed tones one knows so well, will doubtless beg me "to be so indulgent to them and to my own affairs as to revert to the £750 instead of £1000 (quarterly) etc. etc. I await a thousand torments reproduced in a thousand forms.[124]

Here, Beckford had sought sanctuary behind the ornate style of his lawyers and avoided the dreadful realization that his holdings were collapsing and he was in deep financial trouble, or that his identity as a man of taste was tied to the changing fortunes of West Indian sugar and slavery.

Denial was Beckford's mode of existence in the numinous zone between English freedom and African bondage, between Britain and Jamaica. He was aware that his success as a collector and man of taste was tied to slavery and sugar, but any direct association with black bondage was injurious to the social standing of a modern subject, especially toward the end of the eighteenth century, when slavery was no longer in vogue. One of the great ironies of Beckford's life was that it was built around powerful, if not radical, notions of freedom. His whole life "was a protest against those inventions of society that made men and women into machines. He had at an early age determined not to sink his individuality, and to the end he preserved his striking personality."[125] In this context, Beckford's role as a collector raises an even more intriguing question: was the collection of expensive aesthetic objects an attempt to assimilate and sublimate the excesses of the material world, to bring some order to the residuality that remained in him, consciously or unconsciously, of that other world—of slaves and imaginary Orientals?

This is not a far-fetched question, for there is an implicit connection between collecting and nervousness about the world. In their classical work on collecting, John Elsner and Roger Cardinal have noted that beneath the "houses and masterpieces" of the collectors, "there is much to be learned by listening in to the quieter, subversive voices rising out of that 'unacceptable' residue lying in culture's shadow." They further observe that at the margins of the social conventions associated with collecting, there lie "urges sublimated in careful arrangements and informative labels: desires for suppression and ownership, fears of death and oblivion, hopes of commemoration and eternity." The compulsion for collecting is the desire for another world, one at odds with the dominant culture system of the collector:

> Collections gesture to nostalgia for previous worlds (worlds whose imagined existence took place prior to their contents being collected) and also to amusement. Across history there have been innumerable "trivial" collections (few of which have survived, for obvious reasons), based on ironic whim, on personal reverie, on casual caprice. Yet even amusement (which hints at the muses and at museums) is in some sense an aesthetic category, so that casual pleasure—no less than social climbing—bears testimony to the standards and rules of the mighty cultural system of which collecting is part.[126]

Collecting is associated with deep cultural fears of the underworld of "the mighty cultural system"—a fear of what is uncultured.

Can we, then, suppose that the devotion to art that marked Beckford's life was indeed a mechanism for dealing with the terror of slavery as much as the probity associated with homosexuality?[127] The enigma of Beckford is that he used his money to amass the most significant collection of art and decorative objects, thus continuing his father's project, but then chose to direct these insignias of civility against the culture of taste itself. Beckford is now remembered for his "social excesses" and for his failure to control the "socially disruptive" forces that threatened his cherished desire to master civic virtue as defined by late eighteenth-century culture. This struggle between passion and virtue is most apparent in his repressed sexuality and his art. Beckford's love for William Courtenay, which began when the former was nineteen and continued into middle age, has come to be seen as the signifier of his romanticism and a certain longing for "freedom from moral responsibility" and an expression of the "wayward passion" that an aesthetic education was intended to contain.[128] Similarly, Beckford's literary works, especially his gothic novel, *Vathek*, have come to be read as a conduit for his social excesses and thus a manifestation of how the ordered life of the aesthete was continuously at odds with disruptive passions.

Undoubtedly, ownership of art located Beckford in the public sphere, but it also enabled him to negotiate those aspects of his life that were excessive of the authorized cultural space. In this sense, he fits the model of the collector, who, in Jean Baudrillard's words, divests the object of its function and makes it relative to his own subjectivity; the system of collection thus becomes "the basis of which the subject seeks to piece together his world, his personal microcosm."[129] One curious aspect of the massive Beckford collection at Fonthill, notes McLeod, is that "there is an obvious discrepancy between the large quantities of objects noted as being housed in the rooms, and the scarcity of objects on view."[130] McLeod goes on to speculate that "showing a massed arrangement of relatively small-scale objects, would have upset the visual harmony and staged setting that work so successfully in portraying the grandeur and scale of the Abbey."[131]

Beckford was not eager to display his collection, because he was actually hoarding it. As a matter of fact, it is possible to argue, following Baudrillard, that in the system of collecting, any given object one has can either be utilized or be possessed, but it cannot serve both functions: "The first function has to do with the subject's project of asserting practical control within the real world, the second with an enterprise of abstract mastery whereby the subject seeks to assert himself as an autonomous totality outside the world."[132] Baudrillard goes on to note how collecting, premised on the divestment of the object of its function, can become a form of fanaticism: "Surrounded by the objects he possesses, the collector is pre-eminently the sultan of a secret seraglio. Ordinary human relationships, which are the site of the unique and the conflictual, never permit such a fusion of absolute singularity and indefinite seriality. This explains why ordinary relationships are such a continual source of anxiety: while the realm of objects, on the other hand, being the realm of successive and homologous terms, offers security."[133]

Beckford's system of collection supports these presuppositions powerfully. As I have already noted, he turned to collecting as a way of dealing with his own insecurities, not least the fact that he, England's wealthiest son, was the owner of slaves in Jamaica. We have also seen that the collection of objects was a form of asserting the autonomy of self against demands of social convention. Through the system of collecting, Beckford could exist inside and outside his culture—inside because he had complete ownership and control over the most valuable objects, and outside because the collection, which was rarely on display, could not connect him to the English public sphere. And if we recall that a crucial aspect of the modern self was its ability to exist as a public self, a point discussed at length in earlier chapters, we can see how Beckford's retreat into the inner sanctum of his imaginary castles and abbeys deprived him of a constitutive element of modern selfhood. Trapped between an elaborate interior and a recalcitrant public sphere, Beckford would turn his collection into the expression or mediator of his own phantasmal relationship to England and its colonial others. This phantasm was to find expression in Fonthill Abbey (fig. 3.12), the Gothic house that Beckford built in rebellion against his father's Whig Palladianism. Judging from his correspondence with his distinguished architect, Sir James Wyatt, Beckford's goal was to build, as an addition to his father's Palladian house at Fonthill, a new dwelling that would call into question the central categories of the culture of taste into which he had born. Variously described as a tabernacle or abbey, the anticipated house would reflect a style that was radically at odds with the sense of order and proportion associated with Palladianism.

On its completion, Fonthill Abbey was to become a living monument to the nature of English Gothic, and it is in its Gothicness that it is now read as an affront to the whole discourse on the ordering of the arts that had dominated the eighteenth century. Defined against the Protestantism associated with English Palladianism, Fonthill Abbey was designed to re-semble what James Lees-Milne has aptly called "a Catholic cathedral in Protestant England."[134] Like the tower rising from its center, Beckford's new house stood out as a sign of defiance and deviancy; it was the angry statement of a person who, having worked so hard to be accepted as a true-born Englishman, a person of good breeding and status, had been rejected by the culture into which he had poured his wealth and fortune. In these circumstances, the journey from the Palladianism of the father to the Gothicism of the son is a symptom of the changes that were tak-ing place as the dominant idea of the aesthetic—good taste, judgment, proportion, and control—began to collapse under its own strains, just as Fonthill Abbey began its slow descent into a ruin, its once opulent and magnificent halls reduced to rumble.

Many critics were to complain that the abbey had no utilitarian func-tion, let alone taste; architectural historians derided "its scale as the vul-gar concept of an eccentric millionaire not quite in his right senses."[135] But these critics were the ones who were still attached to aesthetic ideals that were being called into question by colonial events, most notably the Haitian revolutions. Beckford seemed, in an almost perverse way, to be attuned to the spirit of the times. Confronted with a financial crisis in his Jamaican estates, he had to borrow heavily to complete his building; still, it was his commission, made possible by what remained of colo-nial money, that enabled Wyatt, who was looking for a new architectural style, to explore the possibilities of Gothic buildings on the English land-scape. Those critics who were to deride Fonthill Abbey as Beckford's folly seem to forget that this Gothic structure was also the manifest sign of Wyatt's "genius and his failings."[136] The radical nature of Wyatt's Gothic design for Fonthill Abbey becomes apparent if we compare his design for Beckford's tower to the neoclassical style of Dodington House, the man-sion he had designed and built for Christopher Codrington in Avon. In Dodington House, Wyatt had chosen a symmetrical design dominated by Grecian columns and a staircase that incorporated materials from "old

3.12 John Gleghorn, *Fonthill Abbey: The Grand Drawing Room.* 1823. Engraving. Plate 5. From John Rutter, *Delineations of Fonthill.*

Fonthill."[137] In contrast, the design of Fonthill Abbey sought to emphasize the unevenness of form and display a provocative allegory. The house was planned on an irregular cross with a cluster of turrets and gables and an octagon steeple. Fonthill Abbey wore its religious character defiantly and exhibited its "Catholicism" in the very heart of Anglicanism.

8

To conclude, there are many fronts on which the complex relationship between aesthetic reflection and the political economy of slavery can be explored. One could reflect on the fact that there was an intimate association between the Gothic and the sublime with colonialism; that two of the most important works of Gothic fiction in Britain (Beckford's *Vathek* and Matthew Gregory Lewis's *The Monk*) were written by heirs to West Indian plantations.[138] But the one link I have sought to underscore in this chapter is the relation between the work of art, or rather its collection, and the questions of white identity and self-fashioning.

Consider Beckford's situation in 1799. Despite his education, ownership, and mastery of the economy of taste, he had failed in all of his efforts to be accepted by the English establishment; his greatest desire in life was to become a peer of the realm, but the fact that his childhood friend Pitt the Younger was now prime minister did not make much of a difference. Beckford's homosexuality and his colonial origins were used to frustrate all of his efforts to acquire gentility. At the same time, the plantation economy that had enabled the Beckfords rise to power in the first place was in convulsion, faced by the twin forces of revolution and emancipation.[139] It is at this point of radical insecurity that Beckford built his abbey as a monument to St. Anthony of Padua, the ward against misfortune, and as a mausoleum for expensive objects. In the tower, art was there not so much to be enjoyed, but to be possessed; in this total ownership of valuable objects one could push the logic of aesthetic reflection to its limits. As he sat in his abbey in the last years of the long eighteenth century, lonely and melancholic, Beckford could embrace his pictures as empty signs for the lost slaves, sugar, and elusive gentility. He could content himself with the fact that what he had on his walls was the best collection of art in private hands in the whole of Europe, work by masters such as Giovanni Bellini, Rogier van der Weyden; paintings by Rembrandt and Rubens, Van Dyck and Van Eyck, even Velasquez's portrait of Pope Innocent X. This is what the mixture of slaves and sugar had brought Beckford; a collection of the most expensive and beautiful art objects in the world and social orphanage, complete isolation from the institutions and structures that would have given the self honor and esteem. But if art and taste had been Beckford's way of dealing with what one of his biographers has called his "displaced anxiety" and "sense of inadequacy," then he had failed miserably.[140] Ownership of art, as William Hazlitt observed in a scathing attack on Beckford's taste, did not guarantee its appreciation.[141]

The larger issue here, however, was not simply the relationship between money and good taste; rather, what Beckford's case highlights are the deep anxieties that were driving the culture of taste against the pressures of slavery. The origin of Beckford's anxieties and inadequacies was colonial slavery. His deep connection to the culture of slavery, though unacknowledged, haunted Beckford's aesthetic desires, and this haunting goes a long way to explain the key shifts in his aesthetic sensibility, especially his transformation from the most elegant collector to a hermit hiding in the bowels of a Gothic cathedral. Like other colonial monuments to art, Beckford's abbey marked the white Creole's troubled relationship to England. The form of Gothic registered a relationship of identity and difference. Indeed, in its monumentality and excessiveness, its prominence and weirdness, Fonthill Abbey sought to affirm the identity of its owner as the "controlling and finalizing energy" behind the aesthetic order and his revenge against it.[142]

It is not accidental that Fonthill Abbey seemed constructed as a mausoleum to works of art, a place to hoard and inter the most precious products of European modernity over several centuries and exotic collections from the edges of empire. This interment and hoarding was Beckford's revenge against the ideology of taste, which, as I argued in previous chapters, demanded the public display of beauty. Art had failed to rescue Beckford from the stigma of colonialism, and in this regard he seemed to have rethought its mode of exhibition; instead of being displayed publicly, precious ornaments could be confined in a crypt where they would be adored, like idols, by the sultan in his seraglio. The descriptions that exist of Fonthill Abbey all call attention to Beckford's expansive and expensive collections, but none seem to have attracted interest as works of art; neither pictures nor objects seemed to demand attention to themselves as objects of pleasure; they were either dwarfed by the morbid architecture of Fonthill Abbey or seemed to deepen the gloom of Beckford's later years, when he had been virtually ostracized from society. Once intended to be a mark of arrival into the culture of taste, art had become the colonial baron's revenge against Englishness. By 1817 Beckford was living in a state of solitary confinement, and his rich collection of art and objects could not alleviate his gloom or melancholy. Indeed, objects of taste seemed to act as reminders of his isolation. The only proof that Beckford was a man of taste, noted Hazlitt in his review of the collection at Fonthill Abbey, "*is his getting rid of it.*"[143]

For Beckford, black slavery had enabled the collection of art but apparently also retarded the slave owner's entry into the temple of culture. In 1817 Beckford's various attempts to reenter society collapsed ostensibly because of his bad temperament, but perhaps more so because of financial difficulties: "Affairs in Jamaica" were going "from bad to worse," he noted.[144] By 1822 those affairs might have become extremely worse, because Beckford was forced to sell Fonthill Abbey to an American—"the obscure millionaire Mr. Farquhar."[145] On December 21, 1825, the central tower of Fonthill Abbey "collapsed for the third and final time . . . damaging much of the building and fueling its legendary status."[146] The ruins of the house would come to stand as a prominent example of Beckford's failure to reconcile art and commerce. In fact, it has been my argument in this chapter that when it is analyzed in a contrapuntal relation to the colonial event, the criteria driving the aesthetic ideology in the eighteenth century—disinterest and virtue, among others—had come to be haunted by slavery. As I will show in the next chapter, this haunting would continue in the American colonies.

Close Encounters:
Taste and the Taint of Slavery

In January 24, 1790, Gouverneur Morris, a New York citizen of the new American republic, wrote a letter to George Washington, then the president of the United States, urging him to "fix the taste" of the new country and to become a model of what we may now call the aesthetic self: "It is . . . my wish that everything about you should be substantially good and majestically plain, made to endure."[1]

This was an earnest but unusual request for three reasons. First, it was puzzling because on the surface there was no apparent reason why Morris should have been concerned about Washington's ability to be a person of taste and to serve as a model for his citizenry in matters of deportment and style. After all, Washington came from what Louis Wright once called the "agrarian aristocracy" of the antebellum period, a class of landowners who emulated the lives of English country families, using their ownership and attachment to the land to rehearse gentility, civic virtue, and good taste.[2] For example, in a painting by Thomas Pritchard Rossiter and Louis Remy Mignot depicting a meeting between the president and the Marquis de Lafayette at Mount Vernon in 1784, Washington was presented as the archetypal country gentleman (fig. 4.1). Second, the request was puzzling because it was not clear why now, in the birth throes of the American republic, Morris, writing to his president, would place the question of fixing taste at the center of the national agenda. Third, the man appealing to Washington to set the standard of taste in the new country was neither an ordinary correspondent nor a cultural debutant detached from the pressing matters of the polity. On the contrary, Morris was at the center of the instrumental process in which the United States was created as a nation.

Born into a wealthy landowning family of Welsh and Huguenot descent in Westchester County, New York, Morris was educated at King's

4.1 Thomas Pritchard Rossiter and Louis Remy Mignot, *Washington and Lafayette at Mount Vernon*. 1859.

College, the predecessor to Columbia University, where he obtained an education that was heavily steeped in the ideals of the Enlightenment. Later he represented Pennsylvania at the convention in Philadelphia in 1787 and is generally considered to be the author of the United States Constitution, the document that put the issue of liberty at the center of debates about subjects and their relation to their governments.[3] In other words, Morris was not a cultural debutant; on the contrary, he is perhaps the closest one finds of a natural-born aristocrat in the United States in the eighteenth century.

Why, then, did a man who was so attuned to the whole panorama of colonial life consider issues of taste to be central to American self-fashioning? What was the lack that he was asking Washington to fill? Why would he want to bother General Washington with matters of deportment and self-presentation, in that winter of 1790, as the general contemplated the future of the United States? Why would Morris, a gentleman of the new American republic be anxious about the public behavior of the new nation's aristocracy and its conduct in matters of taste in the first place?

Morris's anxieties probably came from two directions. First, he might have been worried that the colonial American aristocracy was belated, connected to an agrarian tradition that was out of place in the culture of modernity and its social imaginary. Second, and perhaps more importantly, Morris must have been aware, as were many intellectuals of his age, that all questions about freedom and taste in the United States were haunted by the question of slavery. In the culture of slavery there was no guarantee that the natural deportment of the landed gentry or the men of taste could withstand the pressures of the peculiar institution. There is certainly evidence to suggest that slavery was a major issue at the 1787 Constitutional Convention, where Morris had been a major player. We know that he took a middle position between Southern states, eager to continue with the traffic in black bodies, and Northern states, which considered slavery abhorrent to the doctrine of freedom. As John Madison put it aptly in his notes, "Mr. Gouverneur Morris wished the whole subject to be committed including the clauses relating to taxes on exports & to a navigation act. These things may form a bargain among the Northern & Southern States."[4]

Considering the question of slavery essentially one about tariffs and duties rather than morals and rights, Morris may perhaps not have fully understood how the existence of slaves in the heartland of the republic haunted the ideals of deportment and tastes that he wanted Washington to uphold. But Southern gentlemen like Washington could never escape the shadow of slavery and its powerful effect on the self-fashioning of the subject of freedom. Even when the presence of the slave seemed marginal to national debates about American character and destiny, discussions about taste and manners in the antebellum South could not move beyond the institution of slavery and the lived experiences of the enslaved.

Turning to the question of manners at the end of his *Notes on the State of Virginia,* for example, Thomas Jefferson worried loudly about what he called the "unhappy influence on the manners of our people produced by the existence of slavery among us"; he associated slavery with "a perpetual exercise of the most boisterous passions, the most unremitting despotism on the one part, and degrading submissions on the other."[5] Jefferson constantly worried that American children were being brought up in a culture in which the management of slavery demanded intemperance rather than restraint, a major precondition for a modern identity, and he often reflected on how slavery worked against the ordering of the passions that were essential to a culture of taste:

> If a parent could find no motive either in his philanthropy or his self-love for restraining the intemperance of passion towards his slave, it should always be a sufficient one that his child is present. But generally it is not sufficient. The parent storms, the child looks on, catches the lineaments of wrath, puts on the same airs in the circle of smaller slaves, gives a loose to his worst of passions, and thus nursed, educated, and daily exercised in tyranny, cannot but be stamped by it with odious peculiarities. The man must be a prodigy who can

retain his manners and morals undepraved by such circumstances. And with what execration should the statesman be loaded, who permitting one half the citizens thus to trample on the rights of the other, transforms those into despots, and these into enemies, destroys the morals of the one part, and the amor patriae of the other.[6]

Jefferson had a keen sense of how slavery challenged the tenets of the age of taste: it excited passions where constraint was required; it succored despotism where liberty was needed; it corrupted the manners and morals of white masters, transforming them into victims of despotic practices at odds with the tenets of a rational culture.

And yet in spite of these concerns, Jefferson couldn't imagine a way out of the cauldron of slavery; he seemed to have concluded that it was both the bedrock of the American polity and its curse. How, Jefferson wondered, could the liberties of a nation be considered sacrosanct when they were removed—or displaced—from the raison d'être of nation building, namely "a conviction in the minds of the people that these liberties are of the gift of God?"[7] In his reflections on such questions, Jefferson was acutely aware of the specific ways slavery haunted and undermined the sense of American self-being:

> Indeed I tremble for my country when I reflect that God is just; that his justice cannot sleep forever: that considering numbers, nature and natural means only, a revolution of the wheel of fortune, an exchange of situation, is among possible events: that it may become probable by supernatural interference! The Almighty has no attribute which can take side with us in such a contest.— But it is impossible to be temperate and to pursue this subject through the various considerations of policy, of morals, of history, natural and civil. We must be contented to hope they will force their way into every one's mind. I think a change already perceptible, since the origin of the present revolution. The spirit of the master is abating, that of the slave rising from the dust, his condition mollifying, the way I hope preparing, under the auspices of heaven, for a total emancipation, and that this is disposed, in the order of events, to he with the consent of the masters, rather than by their extirpation.[8]

Jefferson's agonizing on the status of liberty in a culture of slavery, as much as Morris's injunctive to Washington, provides a precise preface to the questions I want to discuss in this chapter: Could a culture of taste take root in the geography of slavery? And if so, how could it explain itself in the court of public opinion, since here in the Americas one could simply not repress or disavow the reality of enslavement? And why did violence become an important concordance to taste in different regions of the Americas?[9] To answer these questions, however, one must consider the peculiarity of American slavery in relation to the institutions of culture, conduct, and taste discussed in earlier chapters. In effect, one must start with a simple but foundational question: what makes American slavery in the modern period different from other institutions of bondage?

2

In the previous chapter, I suggested that the institutions of high culture in the English eighteenth century were enabled by money made in West Indian plantations. I argued that there was an important, though often unspoken, dialectic between the men of taste in London coffeehouses—and art galleries—and the West Indian planter at home. Men of taste, like Joseph Addison and Richard Steele, were directly or indirectly patronized by wealthy planters like Christopher Codrington, the heir to a Barbadian fortune. Cultural institutions benefited from the largesse of closeted colonial barons like William Beckford, who were able to commission artists, architects, and musicians to fulfill their ambition to become subjects of taste. It was the largesse of the planters that enabled the cultivation of polite conduct and the growth in consumption that was essential to the emergence of the culture of taste.

I further argued that West Indian planters derived cultural capital from their association with the men of taste. For example, it was through his sponsorship of cultural activities, ranging from plays on stage to conversational pieces, that Christopher Codrington entered English high society, endowed All Souls College, Oxford, and became an established figure in London cultural circles. Through their patronage of art and taste, the slave-owning plantocracy, like Indian nabobs, laundered its ill-gotten money and refashioned its identity. In even more extreme cases (my case study in the last chapter was William Beckford), living an aesthetic life, even an eccentric one, transformed one from being the son of a crass Jamaican planter to a person of taste. And as men of taste, West Indian planters could deploy a kind of repressive mechanism in which the power of art and good taste would transform them into a cultural aristocracy, far removed from the primal scene of slavery that was their inheritance and duty. In these circumstances, the purity and cleanliness of art would counter the danger and excreta of slavery.[10]

But the West Indian men of culture I discussed in the last chapter cannot be considered representative examples of how art and good taste could be used to laud unsavory social and commercial practices and turn them into acceptable modes of behavior. Indeed, one could argue that the reason why both Beckford and Codrington were able to contemplate purely aesthetic lives, existences ostensibly untouched by the dangers of the slaves that they owned in great numbers, was because they had managed to separate themselves physically from the regimen of the slave plantation. As absentee landlords, these West Indian planters could immerse themselves into the culture of taste, oblivious to the lived experience of slavery, which could be strictly quarantined from their consciousness and everyday existence. Could the person of taste who lived in close proximity to slaves separate his existence as a planter and slave master from his identity as a gentleman? Could the men of taste who presided over the slave plantations of Virginia and the Carolinas be able to sustain an aesthetic culture that was transcendental of slavery and its taint?[11]

A glance at the surviving images of the quintessential American gentleman, such as Washington, might suggest that there was no obvious contradiction between the pose of taste and the presence of the slave, that repression or disavowal of the kind discussed in the last chapter was unnecessary. As he undertook the voyage that was to usher in the American republic, a journey that began at the military academy at West Point, New York, and ultimately led to Mount Vernon, Virginia, Washington's constant companion was his slave William Lee, whom he had purchased in 1768. Since almost all antebellum gentlemen owned slaves, Washington's ownership of Lee is not a point of contention or dispute; what is intriguing is the presence of the enslaved in the portraits of his master. The figure of Lee is present in two of the most important surviving portraits of Washington, including John Trumbull's portrait of the young officer at West Point (fig. 4.2) and Edward Savage's portrait of the retired general at home in Mount Vernon (fig. 4.3).

Commenting on the marginal yet visible presence of Lee in these two paintings, Sidney Kaplan and Emma Nogrady Kaplan have argued that the representation of the slave in the imaginary world of the white master went well beyond conventional generic paintings of the period, suggesting that it "perhaps conceals the deep feeling that Washington had for his revolutionary comrade."[12] But this rather romantic view of race relations in the era of the American Revolution ignores the precarious location and status of the slave in the works of art from this period. Lee was, of course, one of Washington's slaves, not a comrade. He was bonded by law to serve the general from the moment of his birth until he was manumitted posthumously. At the same time, however, especially within the internal symbolism of the painting, there is no doubt that Lee was needed to add aura to the self-imagination of the American hero, aristocrat, and patriarch. His existence on the margins of the picture is an example of the presence/absence discussed in earlier chapters.

This presence/absence of the slave in the American world picture points to slavery's powerful haunting of the culture of taste, which has been the subject of this part of my book. And there is perhaps no better

4.2 John Trumbull,
George Washington.
1780.

4.3 Edward Savage, *George Washington.* 1804.

representation of this haunting than an anonymous painting from Virginia aptly called *Virginian Luxuries* (fig. 4.4).[13] Painted sometime in the first two decades of the eighteenth century, this was a picture in two sections, both representing the duplicity that characterized the relations between masters and slaves in the plantation complex. On one side was a black man being flogged; on the other side was a black woman being kissed. To the extent that the woman was a slave, we can safely assume that her relationship with the white man was already part of an enforced relationship, a form of sexual violence; the man was being subjected to whipping, the most common form of enforcing bondage. In this context, both parts of the picture represented two forms of disciplining.

While it is not clear what the intentions of the anonymous painter of this picture were, the coexistence of these two distinct modes of disciplining in the world of the Virginia elite would ultimately call attention to the duplicity of the institution of slavery itself, where masters presented blacks as the antithesis of cultured life while constantly engaging with them in intimate relations of one kind or another. Embedded in this picture and its doubleness, then, were some of the deepest anxieties driving the culture of the antebellum South—anxieties about gender, sexuality, and violence—and these anxieties were essential to the identity of the antebellum South as it tried to negotiate the line between white civilization and African barbarism.[14] We can detect them in *Notes on the State of Virginia*, where in addition to rehearsing the familiar biological arguments for black difference, Jefferson had underscored the role of passions in marking the slave as other. He had repeated Edward Long's slander about the "the preference of the Oranootan for the black women over those of his own species"; he had then gone on to argue that black males were "more ardent after their female," but "love seems with them to be more an eager desire, than a tender delicate mixture of sentiment and sensation."[15]

Ironically, *Virginian Luxuries* enacted "eager desire" as the province of the white male. In fact, one of the most curious aspects of the painting is how both "romance" and punishment acquired a sexualized character. It is in the interplay of race and gender that the painting exposed the duplicity of antebellum society in relation to the presence of the black body. Aware of the delicate nature of the subject, the painter sought to conceal his or her work, hiding *Virginian Luxuries* on the back of another painting, *Unidentified Man*. This duplicity was bound to transform the culture of taste in the slave colonies themselves, where the slave master or owner could not separate himself from the geography of slavery and was thus compelled to adopt various gestures of concealment.

Here, some contrasts between the adventure of taste in Britain and in the American colonies can clarify what physical proximity meant

4.4 Artist unknown, *Un-identified Man / Virginian Luxuries,* America, New England (probably). Circa 1815. Oil on canvas. Abby Aldrich Rockefeller Folk Art Museum, The Colonial Williamsburg Foundation, Williamsburg, Virginia.

for slaveholders who could not absent themselves from their holdings. Consider, for example, the role of social gatherings in the making of the subject of taste. As John Brewer has observed, high culture in the eighteenth century was "less a set of discrete works of art than a phenomenon shaped by circles of conversation and criticism formed by its creators, distributors and consumers."[16] And if one were looking for the specific institution that represented this gathering of the creators, distributors, and consumers of culture during this period, it would have to be the ubiquitous coffeehouse, which, in the eighteenth century, replaced the court as the center of high culture. It was in the coffeehouse that social and cultural life was shaped. Indeed, the coffeehouse was idealized by Richard Steele, Joseph Addison, and Dr. Samuel Johnson as the site of polite conversation, the place "in which the improving effects of decorous sociability formed men of taste and morality."[17]

The coffeehouse was not a place of casual cultural encounters. On the contrary, it was the space in which Addison and Steele "shaped an exemplary institution, fabricating an ideal of polite conduct and good taste developed in a convivial environment. They made the coffee house the representative institution of urban life."[18] These eminent men of letters and taste argued that the coffeehouse was the space where agents of commerce and art would meet and mutually inflect one another. This encounter would, in effect, become the philosophical gathering of commerce and virtue; an exposure to aesthetic culture would ameliorate the behavior of commercial subjects, pulling them away, as it were, from vulgar trade and alcohol to coffee and polite conversation, and the cultured subjects would presumably come to a bit of an understanding of trade. In the space of the coffeehouse, the uncouth habits generated by business activities would be processed through the mill of sensibility: "The coffee house was claimed as a new sort of urban territory, one which was accessible and orderly, a permeable, public institution where familiars and strangers could meet for polite conversation."[19] By the end of the long eighteenth century the coffeehouse was established enough to be the subject of burlesque in works by artists such as William Hogarth and Thomas Rowlandson, who effectively caricatured and inverted the idea of the institution as the gathering of the civilized.

In the colonial world of eighteenth-century America, however, the institution of the coffeehouse and the sensibilities associated with it were overshadowed by the powerful presence of the peculiar institution of slavery, which generated a different kind of space of sociability. The man of virtue was more likely than not to be a slaveholder; as such, he was more likely to be found transacting business in slave markets and taverns, not places of polite conversation.[20] The urban terrain of enslavement in many state capitals of the antebellum South was dominated by the slave auction, the equivalent of our modern stock or commodity exchange. In communities where the sale of African bodies was the central mode of exchange, neither commerce nor conversation were modulated through politeness; the violence of the slave trade and the rowdiness of the captains of this trade excluded polite conversation and conduct altogether. If slave traders were more likely to meet in the slave market than anywhere else in the slave-owning territory of the Americas, then it is fair to say that these encounters were mediated by the violence attendant to slavery rather than polite conversation.

Reflecting on the circumstances of her sale in a slave market in Bermuda, Mary Prince was to leave her readers a hallowing experience of the terror that mediated the social encounter between Europeans and Africans in the Americas:

> At length the vendue master, who was to offer us for sale like sheep or cattle, arrived, and asked my mother which was the eldest. She said nothing, but pointed to me. He took me by the hand, and led me out into the middle of the street, and, turning me slowly round, exposed me to the view of those who attended the vendue. I was soon surrounded by strange men, who examined and handled me in the same manner that a butcher would a calf or a lamb he was about to purchase, and who talked about my shape and size in like words—as if I could no more understand their meaning than the dumb beasts. I was then put up to sale. The bidding commenced at a few pounds, and gradually rose to fifty-seven, when I was knocked down to the highest bidder; and the people who stood by said that I had fetched a great sum for so young a slave.[21]

Prince acutely noted how the bidding for her family, which would ensure income for her sellers, was also the brutal unmaking of them as a social unit: "I then saw my sisters led forth, and sold to different owners; so that we had not the sad satisfaction of being partners in bondage. When the sale was over, my mother hugged and kissed us, and mourned over us, begging of us to keep up a good heart, and do our duty to our new masters. It was a sad parting; one went one way, one another, and our poor mammy went home with nothing."[22]

There was certainly no polite conversation to mitigate the fact that the sale of Mary Prince and her siblings was a brutal, instrumental form of exchange, a fact that was often borne by engravings of slave auctions that highlighted the plight of families on the auction block, on the verge of their separation. For the white gentlemen involved in these activities, however, the story was rather different. A day at the slave market was like one spent at the coffeehouse or the races. In fact, the paradox of one family unit being destroyed to enable the well-being of another was often what caught the imagination of European travelers to the antebellum South.

When Eyre Crowe accompanied William Thackeray on a trip to the United States in 1852–1853, for example, he had a chance to visit a slave market in Richmond, Virginia. He left behind a powerful description and series of illustrations on the impact of the business of buying and selling black slaves in the city market. In his account, published as *With Thackeray in America*, Crowe noticed how the business of selling slaves both dominated and suffused the cultural landscape of Virginia's capital. He remembered reading the local paper one day in March 1853: "It was not, however, the leaders or politics which attracted my eye, so much as the advertisement columns, containing the announcements of slave sales, some of which were to take place that morning in Wall Street, close at hand, at eleven o'clock."[23]

Crowe's description of the slave market on the day of an auction resembled a modern-day stock exchange, complete with clerks and agents. The auction rooms, he noted, were "low rooms, roughly white-washed, with worn and dirty flooring, open, as to doors and windows, to the street, which they lined in succession."[24] Crowe then went on to provide a vivid portrait of the sale of slaves and the radically different reactions of buyers and sellers:

> The sale was announced by hanging out a small red flag on a pole from the doorway. On each of these was pinned a manuscript notice of the lot to be sold. Thus I read:—"Fifteen likely negroes to be disposed of between half-past nine and twelve—five men, six women, two boys, and two girls." Then followed the dealer's signature, which corresponded to that inscribed over the doorway. . . . The ordeal gone through by the several negroes began by making a stalwart hand pace up and down the compartment, as would be done with a horse, to note his action. This proving satisfactory, some doubt was expressed as to his ocular soundness. This was met by one gentleman unceremoniously fixing one of his thumbs into the socket of the supposed valid eye, holding up a hair by his other hand, and asking the negro to state what was the object held up before him. He was evidently nonplussed, and in pain at the operation, and he went down in the bidding at once. More hands were put up; but by this time feeling a wish for fresh air, I walked out, passing intervening stores and the grouped expectant negroes there.[25]

Crowe even left behind a series of engravings that capture both the tragedy of the slave auction and its centrality in the political economy of the antebellum South (figs. 4.5 and 4.6). Here, the selling and buying of slaves was gentlemanly business; it was at least one of the ways in which the antebellum aristocracy took care of its bills.

One notably large slave auction held on the eve of the Civil War involved the disposal of 436 men, women, children, and infants belonging to Pierce M. Butler, which began on March 3, 1859. Butler, the owner

4.5 Eyre Crowe, *Slaves Waiting for Sale—Richmond, Virginia*. Painted upon an 1853 sketch. Oil painting exhibited at the Royal Academy, 1861.

4.6 Eyre Crowe, *After the Sale: Slaves Going South*. 1853.

of two plantations in Georgia, had run into debt (one of the vices of a gentleman), and he needed to dispose of some of his assets to pay off his creditors. The human assets were brought to a racetrack in Savannah, Georgia, where they were put in stalls for horses as they awaited buyers:

> The sale had been advertised for several weeks. Every hotel in Savannah was filled with potential buyers. In the days before the auction, potential buyers went to the racetrack to look over the people for sale. The slaves were humiliated when the buyers pulled open their mouths to see their teeth and they pinched their arms and legs to check for muscle strength. The slaves said nothing, unless they hoped to be bought by the person examining them. They knew they were to be sold in families, but "family" was defined as husband and wife, mother and young child, not brother or sister or parent. Some tried to convince prospective buyers to purchase their entire family.[26]

Within the next few weeks, families were broken up as diverse assets that were disposed of to different buyers. Slaveholders—all Southern gentlemen—had come to Savannah to make a good buy in what was considered to be the largest sale of slaves in the country; for the blacks in bondage, however, the event came to be referred to as "The Weeping Time."

The irony of American slavery, of course, was that the people Butler was selling off had hitherto been part of his extended "family" and lived within his community. As I noted earlier, while absentee West Indian planters such as Codrington and Beckford were insulated from slavery by its distance, American masters were forced by geography and circumstances to enter into an intimate relationship with those they considered nonsubjects. Thus, on the first day of his big slave sale in Savannah, Pierce Butler "walked among his people, speaking to them and shaking the hands of his favorite servants."[27] He owned them, and he was about to dispose of them to pay his debts, yet they were part of his "family."

And this kind of relationship was not unusual. William Lee was owned by George Washington, but the lives of the two men—and their world experiences—were intimately bound by the culture of slavery. It was as if the law that allowed one to own the other had also made them inseparable. Sometimes, as in the case of Thomas Jefferson and his personal slave, Jupiter Jefferson, this intimacy would almost be like a marriage, decreed and willed by law and social custom: "For over fifty years, the lives of Jupiter and Thomas Jefferson were bound together by law, for one man considered the other his property. In 1743, both were born at Shadwell, a newly opened plantation on Virginia's western frontier. As boys they may have fished in the Rivanna River, set trap lines along its banks, and shared hunting escapades in the surrounding woods. As young men they traveled the length and breadth of Virginia together and found wives on the

4.7 John Greenwood, *Sea Captains Carousing in Surinam*. Circa 1752–1758.

same plantation near Williamsburg."[28] The world of the master was intertwined with that of the slave; freedom and bondage went hand in hand.

As one moved from Europe to America, the social spaces in which the culture of taste operated also became different. For if the coffeehouse's primary function in Britain was to create a space in which polite conversation would replace the uncouth idiom of trade and thus enable those who had made money in commerce to differentiate means from ends, the slave auction denoted the conflation of brutal means and pleasurable ends. In the landscape of slavery, taste could not taper commerce; all it could do, perhaps, is confront it with its contradictions through irony. This is the kind of irony we see in John Greenwood's 1778 painting *Sea Captains Carousing in Surinam*, the portrait of a group of prominent sea captains whom the painter had encountered in Suriname (fig. 4.7).

Seen through critical eyes, the tortuous nature of the slave market and the unvirtuous carousing of slave traders would seem to function as the antithesis of taste. Indeed, according to the *Oxford English Dictionary*, to carouse is "to drink out; drink freely and repeatedly," the very activities that the London coffeehouse was intended to suppress and surpass. Rather than representing a measure of deportment, the behavior of the sea captains in Greenwood's painting reflected the carnivalesque and excessive, modes of behavior that were licensed by the cultural institutions of slave-owning cultures.[29] Here, carousing was not a social aberration, but a mode of behavior to be found even among respectable members of the slave-owning class. Hence, it was not a great surprise that the carousers caught in Greenwood's picture were not mere buccaneers, but prominent Newport slave traders, including Esek Hopkins, later commander of the United States Navy, and Joseph Wanton, soon to become governor of Rhode Island.[30] Could American slavery be compatible with the culture of taste? Could an aesthetic culture emerge in the shadow of slavery?

3

An aesthetic ideology did, of course, emerge in the antebellum South, but it was intimately bound to slavery. As Louis Wright has noted in *The First Gentlemen of Virginia*, by the end of the seventeenth century a "tight aristocracy" had developed in Virginia and "quickly gained a power and influence far in excess of the numerical importance of its numbers, who were vastly outnumbered by the yeoman class."[31] Like the West Indian planters discussed in the previous chapter, members of this colonial American class were constantly haunted by doubts about whether they could measure up to the English standard of gentility to which they aspired, and by lingering doubts about their aristocratic origins. It was not unusual for the Virginian aristocracy to wrap fantastical stories about royal genealogies around themselves, but this didn't stop taunts about other possible, nonaristocratic origins. As Marcus W. Jernegan caustically observed, the records of Newgate Prison and the Old Bailey, rather than Burke's peerage, might "prove a more fruitful source of genealogical information" on the antebellum aristocracy.[32]

When he wrote his book, Wright was eager to salvage the image of the American aristocracy as the worthy equal of its European counterpart, but the real achievement of his work was the recognition that a different set of social circumstances, including the code of honor that governed the lives of the slave-owning class, had led to the modification of the ideal of taste. Virginian gentlemen, Wright observed, thrived on a code that recognized "the inherent inequality in mankind"; they assumed that the upper class had "a natural and inherited right"; they embraced wealth as the precondition for rank; and they cultivated polite manners as the essence of selfhood.[33] Nevertheless, Wright noted that the introduction of what he called "the African slave system" was "the most important factor in the evolution of the Virginian aristocracy, for it enabled wealthy planters to crush, perhaps unconsciously, the economic power of small landowners who depended upon their own labor."[34] What he failed to underscore, however, were the specific and unprecedented ways in which the introduction of slaves into the colonial economy challenged, and then transformed, the culture of taste and the social imaginary of the American ruling class.

The transformations I have in mind here took place across many vectors. For example, the question of inequality and natural rights had to be changed or modified to enforce racial distinctions while maintaining class differences. From the early beginnings of the Virginia colony, notes Winthrop Jordan, even at a time when the working and living conditions of English yeomen and African slaves were relatively similar, "Negroes were set apart from white men by the word *Negroes*."[35] Set as a powerful figure of difference, the word *Negro* would also function as the most visible mark of social distinction, connoting debased status and "non-freedom" for those who bore it. And while this situation of debasement and non-freedom has been explained primarily in terms of changing conditions of labor, it had an important symbolic component: the debasement of Africans was necessary to establish the difference between black slaves and English yeoman; in turn, this difference secured the latter as a distinct category in opposition to the landowning class. Deprived of liberty, "Negroes" and "Indians" entered a social structure in which their condition was fixed and there was nothing they could do to affect the overall nature of social status within colonial society. Blacks could, of course, enter the realm of Englishness through conversion or assimilation, but by the 1680s, as racism became a bedrock of colonial American culture, Africans in America were encountering a new term—*white*—which they could not possess or claim.[36]

There is sometimes confusion over whether the slave codes were originally intended to police racial or class hierarchies, but laws against miscegenation were certainly designed to secure a newly invented white identity.[37] More significantly, the nature of hierarchies in colonial America, and the meaning of terms such as *equality*, *inequality*, and *natural rights*, was complicated by the culture of slavery; having excluded blacks from the symbolic economy of whiteness, as it were, distinctions of wealth and status could be applied only to Europeans. Indeed, the existence of a category of people whose identity was located in bondage complicated the terms of whiteness itself. One could not, for example, be a gentleman solely in relation to slaves, who were inherently excluded from "normal" social hierarchies by virtue of their color and status. As a class category, the status of being a gentleman was efficacious only in relation to poor whites; in relation to slaves, however, all whites had power and rank. As Orlando Patterson notes at the conclusion of *Slavery and Social Death*, the slave's "natal alienation and genealogical isolation" made him or her the ideal conduit for enhancing the slave-owner's status as a subject: "the slaveholder fed on the slave to gain the very direct satisfactions of power over another, honor enhancement, and authority. The slave, losing in the process all claim to autonomous power, was degraded and reduced to a state of liminality."[38]

Slavery also changed the meaning of wealth, a key ingredient in the theory and practice of modern identity. In terms of acquisition, only those

who owned slaves and land were able to aspire to the status of gentlemen.
Studies of the inventories of Jamaica by Richard S. Dunn clearly show
that "Negro slaves were the chief asset" in the colony.[39] An inheritance
of slaves was also central to social rank and the set of relationships that
bound the new world aristocracy through marriage. For example, in the
world in which Thomas Jefferson grew up and came of age, wealth was
reckoned in terms of slaves and land. As John Chester Miller notes, "one
of the pillars of the world of Thomas Jefferson was black slavery," and
"slaves were ubiquitous in the society in which Jefferson was reared and
in which he came to his majority."[40] In the privileged circles in which Jefferson moved, "it was difficult to find anyone who did not own slaves":
"His father was a slave owner from whom Thomas inherited both land
and slaves; all the Randolphs, to whom he was related through his
mother, held slaves. . . . Jefferson's wife's dowry consisted of 132 slaves
and many thousands of acres of land. Like other Virginia patricians, he
reckoned his wealth principally in slaves and land." By the time Jefferson
came into prominence as one of the great advocates of American freedom
and enlightenment, "he was by inheritance, purchase, and marriage, one
of the principal slave owners and one of the wealthiest men in Virginia."[41]
Here, slavery was the coin of the realm; it was located at the social juncture where inheritance, marriage, and social status converged, and the
use of slaves as dowry was indeed a salient indicator of its centrality to
domestic relationships.

One of the salient paradoxes of slave culture, then, was that while
slaves were considered to belong to a lower order of nature, and their
status deprived them of mobility in both the public and private spheres,
they were important markers of white identity in the new world. Another
paradox structured the relationship between white masters and black
slaves: private relations between masters and slaves were intimate, but
in public, strict moral and physical boundaries were maintained. One
of the most interesting aspects of antebellum architecture, for example,
was how its façade—the face of the colonial gentry that was available to
public scrutiny—concealed the private, domestic world, inside or behind
the great house, in which slavery thrived.[42]

Consider the case of William Byrd II of Virginia. When he returned
from his education in England in the late 1720s, Byrd considered his
father's plantation outpost in rural Virginia to be far removed from civilization and too remote from the culture of taste that he had acquired
abroad. He therefore set out to build a new house, Westover, that would
embody the culture of taste in the antebellum South. Westover was built
in an almost exact Georgian style, with "Ornate carved plaster railings,
hand-carved decorative woodwork, richly paneled rooms, and an unusual black mantelpiece add[ing] touches of elegance to the interior of

the mansion."[43] The building's Georgian façade, however, concealed the thriving political economy that enabled Byrd's taste, for not far behind the building, though not visible from the street or driveway, was to be found a line of slave houses. How did an antebellum gentleman like Byrd reconcile the physical presence of slaves and the institution of enslavement to imported ideals of taste?

Although American gentlemen sought to master the culture of taste that was circulating in England in the eighteenth century and strove to live up to a real or imagined English style, their aspirations often came up against the physical and cultural demands of a new-world cultural geography dominated by slavery. In the West Indies, for example, affluent planters put up buildings "after the English manner," hoping to impress their European peers. What this meant was the use of "brick or stone in preference to wood and plaster, building multi-storied houses in preference to wide, low bungalows, and using glazed windows rather than louvres or shutters."[44] A panoramic view of Bridgetown, Barbados, drawn by Samuel Copen around 1695, made "this Caribbean port look indistinguishable from a commercial town in England or Holland": "The houses press close to the wharves, leaving no room for gardens or shade trees. They are tall and narrow structures, three to five stories in height, without balconies or verandahs. This architectural style was better geared to Northern Europe than to the Caribbean." But this ostensibly elegant, ornate, or classical architecture was often at odds with the physical landscape of the Americas. Judging from the inventory of his household, Sir Henry Morgan, the buccaneer king, "slept in a silken nightgown on a costly bed equipped with mohair curtains, persian lining, and a 'musketo nett.' His servants, who slept in hammocks, and even his slaves, who slept on the ground, were very likely more comfortable."[45]

Yet it was precisely because they were surrounded by the enslaved, people considered to occupy the lowest echelons of nature and culture, that planters came to value, and to identify with, existing notions of high culture. Eager to model themselves on the English aristocracy, colonial gentlemen like Byrd often mobilized high culture to "evaluate or signal status or to create status and monopolize privileges."[46] This mobilization took both direct and indirect forms. Byrd, for example, was notorious for scrupulously following the cultural routine he had witnessed in England and reproducing the social spaces of British high culture. At Westover, for example, he built a library that held four thousand volumes, in English, French, Latin, Hebrew, and Greek. The library was the largest in Virginia and contained "almost any book that a cultivated and thoughtful aristocrat might want."[47]

This rehearsal of Englishness, however, reflected a deep anxiety, one that compelled Byrd, like many members of the colonial elite, to engage in what has come to be known as colonial mimicry: the imitation of English manners in situations of displacement.[48] Like William Beckford, Byrd seemed to have a good sense of his own troubled relationship to the culture of taste; he, too, was rehearsing culture to account for his own displaced position in the politics of taste. Indeed, there are striking similarities between the Beckfords of Jamaica and the Byrds of Virginia. Like the Beckfords, the Byrds came from poor London stock. They got involved in transatlantic trade in the seventeenth century, and with the proper marital and mercantile connections, they improved their assets and social standing, becoming one of the most prominent families in Virginia. In this sense, Byrd's life can be read as the progress from trade to elegance, from modest beginnings to wealth and status.

Still, it is important to note that the aristocratic conduct that has come to be associated with Byrd—his patriarchal attitude, his literary education, and even his rationalism—was driven by a certain oversensitivity toward rank and social standing. For example, he was upset when his name was omitted from the membership of the Royal Society in 1741, of which he had the honor "to be one of its ancientest members" and to which he had contributed a scientific paper on "the curious phenomenon of a negro with a dappled skin."[49] As indicated by the following letter from Byrd to the Earl of Orrery dated July 5, 1726, the colonial gentleman was eager to remind his European contemporaries that his location in the colonies did not exclude him from the domain of taste:

> I have a large family of my own, and my doors are open to every-body, yet I have no bills to pay, and half a crown will rest undisturbed in my pocket for many moons together. Like one of the patriarchs, I have my flocks and my herds, my bond-men and bond-women, and every sort of trade amongst my own servants, so that I live in a kind of independence of everyone but Providence. However, this sort of life is without expense, yet it is attended with a great deal of trouble. I must take care to keep all my people to their duty, to set all the springs in motion, and to make every-one draw his equal share to carry the machine forward. But then 'tis an amusement in this silent country and a continual exercise of our patience and economy. Another thing, my lord, that recommends this country very much: we sit securely under our vine and our fig trees without any danger to our property. We have neither public robbers nor private, which your lordship will think very strange when we have often needy governors and pilfering convicts sent amongst us. . . . Thus, my lord, we are very happy in our Canaans, if we could but forget the onions and fleshpots of Egypt.[50]

What we see here is the language of mimicry, which, as Jacques Lacan has noted, "reveals something in so far as it is distinct from what might be called an itself that is behind. The effect of mimicry is camouflage."[51]

Colonial mimicry performs its work through a double-entendre: it mimics and camouflages its desires and intentions in the same register. In the above example, then, Byrd was speaking the language of the Earl of Orrery—the language of providence, duty, and virtue—but in the process he was also concealing his other identity, his role as a hardened slave master. Sitting on what Homi Bhabha has aptly described as "the margins of metropolitan desire,"[52] Byrd would use language and self-presentation to conceal the fact that what he was calling "my people" were, in fact, African slaves.

Why did Byrd seek an identity in mimicry? To answer this question, we have to remember that culture, as Lamont and Fournier have taught us, is located in the world of organizations and institutions of power: "Culture is not only a code or mode of communication: it is also a form of domination, an ideology at the service of the dominant classes."[53] For Byrd, an overt acknowledgment of the value of African and Africanized cultures would be a form of social abnegation, a fatal threat to racial and class hierarchies. Like other members of the American plantocracy, Byrd needed European forms of art and culture that would enable him to maintain status in the midst of slavery. European high culture was associated with notions of order; it connoted "unity, harmony, balance, correctness, and rationality" and was assumed to emerge out of a "humane consensus," one that enabled "a harmonious community."[54] In these circumstances, Byrd's mimicry of Englishness was simultaneously a form of affiliation and expression of deep anxieties about belonging.

Yet Byrd lived in a world saturated by African slaves, and, like most planters, he had an intimate social relation with them.[55] But this intimacy bled fear and loathing. From the West Indies to the antebellum South, the black slave was considered to be the embodiment of what I will refer to in later chapters as a negative sensorium, their color, figure, and hair "physical distinctions proving a difference of race."[56] The black slave was the living embodiment of that which the planter class considered vulgar and distasteful. The slave-owning class often shared the fears, expressed most poignantly by Jefferson, that the existence of slavery depraved the "manners and morals" of the masters.[57] Byrd expressed the fear that Virginia might one day come to be known as "New Guinea."[58]

The specter of blackness would become manifest during the Haitian revolution, a spectacular and phantasmic event, one that was as apprehended as the threat to white civilization itself. Describing the destruction of the city of Cap Français in September 1791, the Jamaican planter and historian Bryan Edwards posited it as an event that was dreadful and horrific, "a sight more terrible than the mind of any man, unaccustomed to such a scene, can easily conceive."[59] For Edwards, the overpowering of white civilization by what Dayan has aptly described as "the horrors of

Africa" would be presented in aesthetic terms:[60] "Until those ravages and devastations which I have had the painful task of recording, deformed and destroyed, with undistinguishing barbarity, both the bounties of nature, and the labours of art, the possessions of France in this noble island were considered as the garden of the West Indies, and for beautiful scenery, richness of soil, might justly be deemed the Paradise of the New World."[61] The cultivation of culture had been one of the enabling conditions of white civilization in the tropics; its destruction by the revolting slaves signaled the precariousness of beauty in the theater of enslavement. More immediately for my discussion here, it was the apprehension that African barbarity might overcome the logic of civilization—the fear that Virginia might become a New Guinea—that prompted slave masters like Byrd to initiate "strenuous measures to maintain the civilized way of life of the social class to which they aspired."[62] But could this "civilized way of life," enacted through art, run parallel with slavery and enslavement?

4

The political economy of slavery made it difficult for a civilized way of life—or a culture of taste—to be simply transplanted to the American colonies. In the world of slavery, a new economy emerged that transformed notions of time and space and hence disturbed the subject's relation to its world. As Mechal Sobel has argued in her studies of black and white self-fashioning in colonial Virginia, in slavery almost all established European and African norms of selfhood, temporalities, and space were thrown askew.[63] The challenge for the slave-owning caste was to develop forms of art that conjured a pure and refined image of self and community and yet were rooted in the totality of plantation life.

As would-be civilized subjects, planters could not give up the idea of manners and morals, or even the cultivation of the arts, as the insignias of modern life; indeed, the emergence of painting as the most prestigious form of art coincided with the planter class's awareness of the significance of high culture in colonial self-fashioning. Painting would now be embraced in the American colonies as the art of prestige; but it would come to be structured by a paradox. On one hand, painting was the most prestigious form of art, because it was the least connected to the materiality and hardships of everyday life in the Americas and thus allowed for the enactment of an imaginary European identity in the colonies. On the other hand, because painting had no "use value," there was no incentive for artists to produce art for its own sake.[64] More specifically, there seemed no imperative for American paintings to account for their local identity or even to gesture to their geographical context. Compared to

their European counterparts, colonial American paintings seem amateur-
ish in character and of poor quality, a fact that has been explained in
terms of limited markets for works of art, the paucity of a leisured class
to consume it, and the plantocracy's sense of inferiority in relation to
European connoisseurs of art.

Some critics have also blamed the failure of American colonial art
on the cultured class's contentment with its identity as "a provincial reflection of the great styles of European paintings transmitted here via
England."[65] But even European models for art across the Atlantic were
themselves inadequate, for until the arrival of continental painters in the
late seventeenth century, American portraits were not based on actual
artistic styles but on what was imagined to be European art. Indeed, a
cursory look at some representative colonial American paintings underscores their limitation in relation to the ostensibly informing tradition;
these works now appear removed from the great European style of the
time and alienated from their immediate context.

Some comparisons are useful here. The most prominent portrait paintings of the English court by Sir Anthony van Dyck, for example, exhibit
a keen sense of place; they denote their distinctness from the paintings
of the Tudor court through the artist's ability to locate individuals within
their milieu. The genius of Van Dyck, the English art historian Ellis Waterhouse once noted, was his ability to understand the temperament of
the individual along "the lines of prevailing taste" and to direct his sensibility "towards nations and classes of society."[66] Waterhouse observed
that a Van Dyck portrait gestured to its context powerfully, carefully
pointing to the identity of the model: "Given the national temper and
the national costume, he devised a series of patterns appropriate to these
various classes. The individual appears only in the features of the face,
which Van Dyck studied and drew with meticulous fidelity."[67] In contrast,
even when they present expressive gestures and movements, American
portraits from the same period lack a sense of character and background.
Colonial American portraits, whether in New England or New Amsterdam, seem flat, belated, seeking proper models and contexts (often Elizabethan and Jacobite) that are far removed from the American experience.
Famous colonial American portraits are fashioned after a certain European style, but one either remembered vaguely or mastered poorly.

An excellent example of this kind of portrait is an anonymous portrait
of Elizabeth Freake and her child (fig. 4.8) now at the Worcester Art
Museum in Massachusetts. Commentators on this portrait have admired
the anonymous artist's mastery of the Elizabethan-Jacobite style, evident
in the frontal-posture presentation, the rigidity of the human form, and
the attention to details, especially in the dress and ornaments won by the
subjects. However, the portrait's focus on surface details is achieved at

4.8 Anonymous, *Mrs. Elizabeth Freake and Baby Mary.* Circa 1671 and 1674. American School. Oil on canvas.

the expense of the human form: the artist is almost oblivious to human anatomy so that although the subjects are sitting, they have no laps. The portrait was evidently produced without any concern for "modeling and realistic anatomy."[68] This colonial American portrait seeks to master a European style but ends up impoverishing its context and thus diminishing "the recognizable image of a particular person" that is supposed to be the enabling condition of portraiture.[69] The anonymous Freake painter represents the best of his time, but the limits in which he functions invite closer reflection.

There are two issues here, and both lead, directly and indirectly, to the aura of blackness embodied in the figure of the slave. The first issue concerns the belatedness of the Freake portrait. Although painted in New England at the end of the seventeenth century, the portrait reflects an Elizabethan and Jacobite style, which was already out of date even in England. The second issue is the portrait's lack of a dynamic relation to its context. In this picture, as in many others of its time and genre, there is no acknowledgment of colonial difference as the informing condition of the work of art or as a gesture to the objects that make up the fabric of colonial American life. When early colonial American portrait painters sought to commemorate the greatness of their subjects without inscribing or acknowledging the source and nature of this greatness in the painting, they deprived this picture of its auratic power, what Walter Benjamin famously called "the authority of the object."[70] And one of the things that was excluded from the world picture of colonial America, especially the antebellum South, was the figure of the slave, the subject/object that made the region distinctive from the Europe it worked hard to imitate.

Paradoxically, when the slave was allowed into the American world picture, either as an icon of American difference or as a symbol of the new-world context, an iconographic revolution would take place. A vivid illustration of this transformation can be found in the works of Justus Engelhardt Kühn, a German migrant painter who worked in Maryland. Sometime around 1710, Kühn, who specialized in paintings intended to enhance the status of "affluent colonialists in the developing landed aristocracy," painted a portrait of Henry Darnall III as a child (fig. 4.9). As in other Kühn portraits of the time, this representation was attuned to the client's need to be presented in a manner that mimicked a formal European style, one in which color, fashion, and ornamentation embodied wealth and status in society. The portrait gestured back to a seventeenth-century style of portraiture, especially in its use of ostentatious ornamentation to capture the regality of royalty and ennoblement. Kühn's painting of Henry Darnall, then, reflects the same sense of color and "romantic interpretation" that we have come to associate with the great European painters of the seventeenth and early eighteenth centuries, including Van Dyck and his contemporaries.[71]

Young Darnall was idealized in the Kühn painting; his status as a young gentleman was enhanced by his elegant and extravagant royal robes and exotic props, including the bird and the bow, all significant elements of what would later come to be known as the colonial Baroque.[72] The painting is a perfect fusion of color and aristocratic bearing and what Guy C. McElroy aptly calls the international Baroque: "Henry Darnall is dressed in a brocaded coat and lace scarf, jeweled platform shoes and a cape of lush fabric—finery that befits his wealth and status. Adopting the conventions of the international Baroque to satisfy the need of his clientele to see themselves as transplanted European gentry, Kühn used costume, physical accoutrements, and the palatial dwellings that serve as a backdrop to suggest wealth that was in fact rarely seen in eighteenth century America."[73]

This baroqueness emerges out of the artist's desire to inscribe his subject's rank and social standing within the colonial sphere, and it is this inscription that makes Kühn's painting similar to English court paintings

4.9 Justus Engelhardt Kühn, *Henry Darnall III*. Circa 1710. Oil on canvas. Maryland Historical Society.

from the end of the seventeenth century, such as Gerard Soest's painting of Cecil Calvert, Lord Baltimore. However, what ultimately gives Kühn's Darnall painting a sharper sense of person and setting than earlier colonial portraits is what is located on the margins of the frame rather than its center—namely, the figure of a black boy, considered to be "the earliest known depiction of an African-American subject in American painting."[74] It is this black boy who both enhances young Darnall's rank and character within colonial society and symbolizes the cultural and social context in which colonial-American notions of being and selfhood were established and elaborated. He is the mark of the American difference that was lacking in the Freake portrait discussed earlier.

How are we to read this difference, and what cultural work is it performing here? Most observers of Kühn's portrait of Henry Darnall III have focused on what McElroy calls the black boy's "position of obeisance": "His humble expression, inferior position within the composition, and the obvious disparity in rank vividly illustrate the chasm that existed between the landed aristocracy and the African-Americans whose enforced servitude allowed this system to flourish."[75] Other commentators have been struck by "the presence and the diminution" of the "slave boy."[76] The collar on the black boy's neck is often read as "a symbol of his servitude" while the palatial foreground of the picture represents the social ambitions of the Darnall family.[77]

These are accurate and powerful descriptive terms, but what I find fascinating in this picture is not the subservient status of the unnamed black boy in relation to Master Darnall, but the more vexing question of the sudden entry of slaves into the American world picture. Why did the Darnall family desire the representation of a slave in a composition whose goal was to enhance the status of their son? Why not settle for the dog that Kühn used in his painting of Henry's sister, Eleanor? Or a map of Maryland? Or simply foreground the palatial setting of the painting to point toward the Darnall's aspiration for grandeur?

There are two possible answers to this question. The first explanation is simply that by the end of the seventh century and the beginning of the eighteenth, the conventions of portrait painting had come to incorporate the black slave as a mark of wealth and prestige. From this perspective, the black was just another figure of ornamentation, a substitute for the dog or parrot that had always been an essential component of the aristocratic portrait. A second explanation is that blackness added a certain aura to the picture and transformed the function that art was asked to perform in the social imaginary. In the colonial sphere, the black slave would operate in a changed context and represent a bifurcated narrative. Located inside the frame of the painting but off center, he or she was necessary in endowing the American aristocrat with value and meaning; outside the picture, however, the enslaved was associated with abjection and danger and was often considered to represent whatever was distasteful in antebellum or colonial culture.[78] One of Kühn's signal achievements in the Darnall painting was to recognize the value and aura of black marginality and to deploy it effectively in realizing the baroqueness of the colonial gentleman as deeply connected to the colors and riches that enslavement enabled. This is the lesson that Kühn passed on to his

American successors, such as John Hesselius, who, in a 1760 painting of young Charles Calvert, another future Lord Baltimore, deployed the slave as part of the aura of mastering and mastery.

The claim that the slave on the margins of the portrait enhanced the standing of the master is not in itself unusual, nor was it a uniquely American phenomenon. Within the conventions of the seventeenth and early eighteenth centuries, the obligatory black in the portrait was the sign of a certain kind of eroticism, but one represented in the same splendor and color as that of the master or mistress. Occasionally a black would appear on the margins of the aristocratic portrait, not as a figure of status or standing, or even contrast, but of visual continuity. Black pages sit on the margins of paintings of Louise de Kéroualle, Duchess of Portsmouth and mistress of Charles II, by Sir Godfrey Kneller, Pierre Mignard, and other prominent artists, but here, as in most European portraits of the time, these figures are there for purely decorative purposes, disconnected from any meaningful context.

Like Kneller and Mignard, Kühn and Hesselius located their black subjects in a supplicant relationship to their masters; they used broadly similar colors; and the master's lace scarf and the slave's color of bondage were as elegant as the silk robes that draped the Duchess of Portsmouth or any aristocratic figure in a European painting. There is, however, a subtle difference between the Americans' aristocratic portraits and those of their European peers. The insignias of subordination may be similar in color or hue, but in terms of social or cultural value, the black children in these works were being asked to perform dissimilar tasks. In Pierre Mignard's portrait of Louise de Kéroualle (fig. 4.10), for example, the black boy wears a string of pearls around his neck; in the Kühn portrait, the black boy wears a collar around his neck. The change here is not simply one of ornamentation, but of a transformed context; the slave's collar was a powerful symbol of bondage, one that affirmed enslavement as the condition that made the young master's world of play and leisure possible.

But bondage was not what painters such as Kühn and Hesselius had in mind when they set out to incorporate the figure of the slave in their paintings. Indeed, if the American painters seemed keen to make the slave visible in their pictures, it was because they understood how blackness endowed aura and status to the self-made American aristocrat. Here, it was the presence of the slave that separated the slave owner from ordinary white subjects, making him an aristocrat worthy of a portrait as demanded by eighteenth-century theories of painting. And it is not an exaggeration to say that it was the presence of the slave in the frame that enabled the coming of age of the American portrait. Unlike the Freake painting discussed earlier, the Kühn paintings had a sense of character and context; the artist understood that the status of the young masters

4.10 Pierre Mignard, *Louise de Kéroualle, Duchess of Portsmouth.* 1682. Oil on canvas.

who occupied the center of the picture did not depend on inheritance and peerage alone; on the contrary, social rank depended on one's location at the heart of antebellum culture and its properties. Here, rather than being mere exotic subjects, slaves were the true sources of the wealth of the nation and hence the bedrock of status and character.

In focusing on this process of turning the black into an object of art, I have sought to shift interpretative interest from a now dominant concern with positive and negative images of the black in Western culture.[79] My contention is that irrespective of whether the images are positive or negative, the deployment of black subjects in the iconographic tradition is a symbolic activity that is often at odds with the real condition of the slave in the modern world but also transcendental of it. With specific reference to colonial slavery, it is interesting to note that the black body, broken down in holding pens, exhibited in slave markets, and considered to be chattel under the law, entered the European and American imaginary in elevated terms.

By calling attention to the aesthetic function of the slave in the economy of slavery, I am not suggesting that black bodies existed solely as figures of antebellum or planter desires. On the contrary, I have been trying to figure out the nature of the relationship between slaves as objects of art and the materiality of their lives—namely, their presence as an integral part of the fabric of American life. The figure of the slave exists in the aristocratic portrait as paraergon: "neither work (ergon) nor outside the work, neither inside nor outside, neither above nor below."[80] In this condition, however, the presence of the subjected body would inscribe "something which comes as an extra, exterior to the proper field," and its location on the margins of the frame would call attention to the exteriority that was absent from the picture, that which was "lacking in something and . . . lacking from itself."[81]

What is lacking in the artwork is, of course, the political economy of slavery, which is elided when the slave is turned into an object of art. The paradox of Kühn's portrait, then, is that it would give the slave the aura and standing he didn't have in real life but would also distract the viewer from the violence that was attendant to enslavement. In this context, the portrait would seem to have been playing what Walter Benjamin, in his famous discussion of aura, called a ritualistic role. Against the pressures of slavery, the masters could ennoble themselves by commissioning works in which the cult of power and authority would be enhanced by the ritualistic function of the slave; in turn, this secularized ritual would avert the crisis associated with slavery as a perverse mode of mechanical reproduction, one in which the human had been turned into chattel.[82] In short, the painters of slave masters would deploy the aura of blackness to defeat the logic driving dehumanized labor. And it is at this juncture—at the point where the auratic black body marks the absence of plantation labor within the frame of the picture but also calls attention to its transcendental presence as what enables the dreams of the masters—that violence becomes an essential counterpart to the work of art.

5

Violence was, of course, the dominant theme in the literature on slavery. Indeed, the perverse and systematic nature of the violence intended to enforce enslavement and subjection would appear to have acquired an aesthetic character of its own.[83] From the crude yokes that constituted the coffle in Africa as witnessed by Mungo Park and René Claude Geoffroy de Villeneuve in Africa in the 1780s and 1790s, to the iron shackles that now grace our exhibit museums, the act of enslavement conditioned the emergence and perfection of modes of subjugation.[84] Instruments of torture became works of art. As Marcus Wood has elaborately shown in *Blind Memory*, slavery, torture, and art went hand in hand.[85] The questions I want to raise in this section will focus on the direct relation between violence and what one may call the guilty pleasures of slavery and the modes of identity it generated: How did the violence that enabled and enforced enslavement become transformed into art itself? Was aesthetic pleasure possible in the scene of the horror that was slavery? Did the violence that was attendant to enslavement present any dangers to the slave owner's identity as a modern subject?

These are vexed questions for a number of reasons. For one, people involved in the slave trade, from agents to owners, tended to approach the task of enslavement as just another form of exchange in a world that considered trade to be part of good social relationships. John Newton, for example, saw the purchase and packaging of African slaves as a most ordinary and banal commercial transaction, where bags of rice and hog skins of rum intermixed with bodies of black men, women, and children. The entries from his journal denote this banality with frightening meticulousness:

> Saturday 23rd February. At 3 a.m. the yaul came on board, brought 4 slaves, 1 girl, 2 boys and an old woman. At daylight took the remaining goods out of her, pulled down her quarter deck and wash boards and fitted her with 6 oars to tend the ship. At 10 Mr Tucker came on board. Sent the yaul in shoar, brought of Joseph Tucker with a girl (4 foot) and a boy (3 foot 9 inches), bought them and sent the goods on shoar in the yaul in the afternoon. Received of Mr Harry a tooth, weight 37 lbs, on account. Buryed a man slave (No. 33), having been a fortnight ill of a flux, which has baffled all our medicines. Put more goods and provisions in the longboat and sent her away in the evening for St Pauls, there being some encouragement there, and the Kittam trade seems quite exhausted.[86]

Here we have an early example of what Hannah Arendt, in a different context, has called the banality of evil.[87]

Represented in its banality, the act of enslavement would become a quotidian event. Indeed, the only reason that we know violence was attendant to acts of enslavement is because of the powerful testimony left to us by former slaves. It was in the slaves' testimony that the ordinariness of the slave trade was challenged by powerful semantic gestures. For example, one of the most powerful counterpoints to Newton's journal was Olaudah Equiano's famous description of his first encounter with the slave ship:

> The stench of the hold while we were on the coast was so intolerably loath-some, that it was dangerous to remain there for any time, and some of us had been permitted to stay on the deck for the fresh air; but now that the whole ship's cargo were confined together, it became absolutely pestilential. The closeness of the place, and the heat of the climate, added to the number in the ship, which was so crowded that each had scarcely room to turn himself, almost suffocated us. This produced copious perspirations, so that the air soon became unfit for respiration, from a variety of loathsome smells, and brought on a sickness among the slaves, of which many died, thus falling victims to the improvident avarice, as I may call it, of their purchasers. This wretched situation was again aggravated by the galling of the chains, now become insupportable; and the filth of the necessary tubs, into which the children often fell, and were almost suffocated. The shrieks of the women, and the groans of the dying, rendered the whole a scene of horror almost inconceiveable.[88]

In Equiano's narrative, the act of enslavement, which was also his own forced entry into modernity, represented a violent form of disciplining in which the power of the masters was matched only by the powerlessness of the slave. The violent transformation of the self from a being into a commodity, which is the gist of the first sections of Equiano's narrative, was the essence of what Orlando Patterson has called social death.[89]

There is a second problem that emerges in the management of slaves within the culture of taste: slave masters cultivated the identity of gentlemen and thus did not want to be associated visibly with the violence that was essential to the effective running of a plantation. In *The History of Jamaica*, Edward Long described the native white men of the island, the white Creoles, as "in general sensible, of quick apprehension, brave, good natured, affable, generous, temperate, and sober; unsuspicious, lovers of freedom, fond of social enjoyments, tender fathers, humane and indulgent masters."[90] Long acknowledged that white Creoles had some foibles—such as indolence, temperament, and addiction to expensive living—but he was revolted by the suggestion that these slave masters treated their slaves with barbarity and angrily rejected their stigmatization as "West-Indian tyrants, inhuman oppressors, and bloody inquisitors." Leaping to the defense of his Creole compatriots, Long compared Jamaican slave masters to English country squires, going as far as to argue that there was no order of men in Britain "[p]ossessed of more-disinterested charity, philanthropy, and clemency than the Creole gentlemen of this island." Long noted that he had never known—"and rarely heard"—of "any cruelty either practiced or tolerated by them [the masters] over their Negroes."[91]

4.11 "An Interior View of a Jamaica House of Correction." 1837. Engraving.

How, then, could Long explain the many instances of torture in Jamaica, where new technologies of punishment such as the treadmill (fig. 4.11) had emerged in the eighteenth century?[92]

Long's apologia for the plantocracy was, of course, intended to oppose abolitionism and should be read in that context. But more than an apologia, the representation of the slave owner as a gentleman was an important mode of identity, a social mask that, as I suggested earlier in this chapter, enabled the men of taste to deal with the contradictions and anxieties of slavery, especially in relation to the indices of modernity and civilized behavior that were central to their European identity. For even if violence was considered to be a necessary instrument in the process of enslavement, an integral part of the technology of slavery, dirty work best left to others, didn't it at an existential level trouble those who were ultimately morally responsible for its existence and enforcement?

Still, neither art nor manners could entirely quarantine the planter class from the ugliness of slavery. Consider the reaction of the Dorset planter and merchant John Pinney on his first visit to a slave market in St. Kitts in a letter dated 1765, about a year after his arrival on the island: "Since my arrival I've purchased 9 Negro slaves in St Kitts and can assure you I was shocked at the first appearance of human flesh for sale. But surely God ordained 'em for the use and benefit of us' otherwise his Divine Will would have been made manifest to us by some particular sign or token."[93] Pinney's unsettledness at the site of flesh on sale is important not because it points to a lurking conscience in the slave master, but because it underscores one of the points I have been making throughout this book: that whatever we think about the actions of the slave-owning class, we must locate them solidly in the culture of the eighteenth century, a culture driven by a fundamental belief in the integrity and autonomy of the self but also eager to rationalize acts that seemed to be necessary but at odds with the doctrine of selfhood. What this means is that slavery haunted modern culture precisely because it called its ideals of selfhood and freedom into question. For if we accept Charles Taylor's claim that the coming into being of the category of the economic in the eighteenth century reflected the higher value put on the "dimension of human existence," then the slave trade did put into question the meaning of a transaction that was enabled by the devaluation and dehumanization of what was initially conceived as another human being.[94]

As modern subjects, slave traders, merchants, and planters operated within the parameters of an eighteenth-century doxa that privileged the self and its claims to freedom and liberty over other things. Thus, even as he bought and buried slaves, John Newton continued to insist that the greatest blessings "of which human nature was capable are undoubtedly religion, liberty, and love."[95] The slave trader was not an aberration from his milieu; he was not a callous person existing outside the culture and morality of the modern age, nor did he take the objectification of the slave for granted or consider its human identity ipso facto. If this were the case, neither the technologies deployed to dehumanize the African nor resorting to theories to justify the enslavement of others because of their race would have been necessary. It is not incidental, then, that no sooner had slave traders encountered the shock of the human body on sale that they fell back, almost instinctively, on theories of providence, which seem intended to rationalize their own uneasiness with the act of enslavement.

Indeed, it is a mark of the slavers' modern identity as free, self-reflective subjects that when confronted by human bodies on sale and compelled to justify their role in this dehumanizing transaction, they turned elsewhere, to religion and God, to explain enslavement. Alternatively, they shifted the burden of enslavement to the Africans themselves. For example, in order to reconcile the trade in human beings with the theories of liberty and freedom that enabled his own subjectivity, John Newton was quick to evacuate the African from the circle of the human. He foregrounded his identity as a religious man, one who valued his freedom and liberty, and upheld these qualities as the defining characteristics of human nature, against what he saw as the Africans' cultural and moral deficits:

> The three greatest blessings of which human nature is capable are undoubtedly religion, liberty, and love. In each of these how highly has God distinguished me! But here in Africa are whole nations around me, whose languages are entirely different from each other, yet I believe they all agree in this, that

they have no words among them expressive of these engaging ideas. . . . These poor creatures are not only strangers to the advantages which I enjoy, but are plunged in all the contrary evils . . . they are deceived and harassed by necromancing, magic, and all the train of superstitions that fear, combined with ignorance, can produce in the human mind. The only liberty of which they have any notion, is an exemption from being sold; and even from this very few are perfectly secure . . . for it often happens, that the man who sells another on board a ship, is himself bought and sold in the same manner, and perhaps in the same vessel, before the week is ended.[96]

And once he had recovered from the initial shock of "human flesh exposed on sale," John Pinney, who was committed to a humanistic project in his management of slaves, sought comfort in the designs of providence and the solace of divine will.

But even after enslavement had been presented as the cause and explanation of the African's debasement, and once violence had been accepted as necessary to enforcing God's will, it was still important to show that one could uphold what were ostensibly conflicting identities—those of a slave master and those of a person of virtue and taste. From ship captains to plantation masters, agents of slavery were often eager to argue and show, in the most forceful and dramatic manner possible, that a life in the political economy of slavery did not in itself preclude one from civilized culture or the aesthetic order. As a marker of modernity, the aesthetic idea attracted slave owners because it was built on powerful transcendental claims, just as notions of taste were justified through a compelling notion of disinterest. Transcendentalism and disinterest made it possible to separate the culture of taste and enslavement even in those spaces—the plantation, for example—where they were forced to coexist. Disinterest did not, of course, occlude the persistent violence that informed colonial culture. And since violence was a necessary condition of enslavement, it either needed to be explained away or turned into a perverse sense of pleasure. In fact, as Marcus Wood and other scholars of the iconography of slavery have shown, slavery was itself an aesthetic project, one located in the problematic of pain, torture, and suffering as it emerged in the modern period.[97]

Still, the theoretical literature on the aesthetics of pain has presented us with three complicated, if not intangible, problems. The first problem was raised, in a different context, by Elaine Scarry in *The Body in Pain*. In this groundbreaking book, Scarry argued that the fact that we continue to invoke "analogies to remote cosmologies" to explain painful experiences is itself a sign of the capacity of pain to achieve "its aversiveness in part by bringing about, even within the radius of several feet, this absolute split between one's sense of one's reality and the reality of other

persons."[98] How, for example, could slave masters and drivers sanction extreme suffering yet seek to live by humanitarian maxims? How could one live a life of pleasure when surrounded by an endless drama of terror and human suffering?

The second problem concerns the value of pain for those who inflicted it. Did those in power find it easy to inflict pain on others because they had been able to exclude their victims from the domain of the human through what Scarry would consider to be an act of anaesthetization, or was there a sense in which the infliction of suffering was turned into an aesthetic and pleasurable form? And how could pain be represented so that it was pleasurable? A characteristic aspect of pain, argues Scarry, is "its capacity to resist language"; indeed, physical pain "does not simply resist language but actively destroys it, bringing about an immediate reversion to a state anterior to language, to the sounds and cries a human being makes before a language is learned."[99] However, the ability of pain to shatter language is valid only on an abstract or conceptual level, because quite often, especially for victims of torture and other extreme forms of suffering, a testimonial to pain demands a summoning of the most radical forms of expressiveness. In the culture of slavery, for example, pain was not a state of consciousness with "referential content" nor was it a phenomenon that resisted "objectification in language."[100] On the contrary, the state of enslavement objectified pain by making a radical distinction, in the disciplinary apparatus, between those who meted it out and those who suffered it.

For slaves, the regimen of punishment, torture, and pain was a reminder that they existed outside the domain of the human; punishment was not the response to a radical departure from an established code of human behavior but a regulatory mechanism designed to enhance dehumanization through its domestication. For the masters, on the other hand, the regime of punishment, pain, and torture demanded the routinization of an efficient system of subjection. What this meant was that pain was not shared between masters and slaves nor did it demand or imply empathy. For masters, the affliction of pain on slaves was rarely a source of visible anguish; the fact that the objects of torture were not considered to be part of the human community that administered the punishment excluded empathy. In other words, unlike forms of punishment directed at criminals and the poor in Europe, or even poor whites in the Americas, the torture of the slave was considered to be of a different order, since the victim and the victimizer were not competing for the same rights of selfhood or liberty. It is in this context that the public spectacle of punishment came to acquire aesthetic value.[101]

The aesthetization of punishment constitutes an important part of the archival of enslavement. A vivid example of this can be found in the second volume of Bryan Edwards's *History Civil and Commercial of the British Colonies in the West Indies*, in a section where the planter historian describes Tacky's revolt of 1760 in Jamaica, an uprising started by slaves in Ballard Beckford's frontier plantation in St. Mary's County. After providing an elaborate description of the antics of the revolting Coromantee (or Koromantyn) slaves and their leader, Tacky, Edward would turn his attention to the punishment meted on the revolters:

> Tacky, the chief, was killed in the woods by one of the parties that went into pursuit of them; but some others of the ringleaders being taken, and a general inclination to revolt appearing among all the Koroman Negroes in the island, it was thought necessary to make a few terrible examples of some of the most guilty. Of three who were clearly proved to have been concerned in the murders committed at Ballard's Valley, one was condemned to be burnt, and the other two to be hung alive in irons and left to perish in this dreadful situation. The wretch that was burnt was made to sit on the ground, and his body being chained to an iron stake, the fire was applied to his feet. He uttered not a groan, and saw his legs reduced to ashes with the utmost firmness and composure; after which, one of his arms by some means getting loose, he snatched a brand from the fire that was consuming him, and flung it in the face of the executioner. The two that were hung up alive were indulged, at their own request, with a hearty meal immediately before they were suspended on the gibbet, which was erected in the parade of the town of Kingston. From that time, until they expired, they never uttered the least complaint, except only of cold in the night, but diverted themselves all day long in discourse with their countrymen, who were permitted, very improperly, to surround the gibbet. On the seventh day a notion prevailed among the spectators, that one of them wished to communicate an important secret to his master, my near relation; who being in St. Mary's, the commanding officer sent for me. I endeavoured, by means of an interpreter, to let him know that I was present; but I could not understand what he said in return. I remember that both he and his fellow sufferer laughed immoderately at something that occurred,—I know not what. The next morning one of them silently expired, as did the other on the morning of the ninth day.[102]

A year before the publication of his history, Edwards would turn the scene of the burning of a slave rebel into the centerpiece of a set of stanzas about freedom, the will of nature, and the power of love.[103] And like other poems that Edwards had written or commissioned, including Isaac Teale's "The Sable Venus," these stanzas were intended to summon poetry to act as a counterpart to a landscape of violence and bondage that the author thought was unjustly maligned in the British imagination.

But the act of punishing the slave went beyond aesthetic value—it was also sexualized and commingled with sensory needs. Frederick Douglass's clear understanding of the direct connection between sexualized violence prompted him to recall and narrate the beating of Aunt Hester by her predatory master at the beginning of his classic slave narrative:

> Before he commenced whipping Aunt Hester, he took her into the kitchen, and stripped her from neck to waist, leaving her neck, shoulders, and back, entirely naked. He then told her to cross her hands, calling her at the same time a d——d b——h. After crossing her hands, he tied them with a strong rope, and led her to a stool under a large hook in the joist, put in for the purpose. He made her get upon the stool, and tied her hands to the hook. She now stood fair for his infernal purpose. Her arms were stretched up at their full length, so that she stood upon the ends of her toes. He then said to her, "Now, you d——d b——h, I'll learn you how to disobey my orders!" and after rolling up his sleeves, he commenced to lay on the heavy cowskin, and soon the warm, red blood (amid heart-rending shrieks from her, and horrid oaths from him) came dripping to the floor. I was so terrified and horror-stricken at the sight, that I hid myself in a closet, and dared not venture out till long after the bloody transaction was over.[104]

Clearly, the act of punishing the slave was not purely instrumental—it was bound up with perverse pleasures. But how could the ravaged body of the slave invite pleasure?

A third problem in the discourse of pain—and and thus the persistence of punishment as part of an exhibitionary, aesthetic order—concerns the transformation of the economy of violence at the end of the eighteenth century, discussed at length by Michel Foucault in *Discipline and Punish: The Birth of the Prison*. In the introduction to his book, Foucault discusses the process by which, through a succession of penal reforms at the end of the century, the "tortured, dismembered, amputated body, symbolically branded on face or shoulder" disappeared from view as "the major target of penal repression."[105] In the new penal regimen, Foucault argued, punishment was sent underground and publicity was shifted to the process of trial and sentence. As a consequence, the body was deprived of the symbolic authority previously embodied by the spectacle of torture and punishment and was retained merely as an intermediary. Foucault concluded, "If the body now serves as an instrument or intermediary: if one intervenes upon it to imprison it, or to make it work, it is in order to deprive the individual of a liberty that is regarded both as a right and as a property."[106]

But the instruments of torture and the modes of punishment that Foucault assumed had been exorcised from the European penal system continued to thrive in many plantation societies in the Americas, a fact that prompted Marcus Wood to raise a provocative question: why would the spectacle of physical punishment be displaced from the European scene and yet thrive in the American and Caribbean colonies?[107] Wood's response to this question is to make a distinction between the question of power, a key term in Foucault's lexicon, and the economy of terror, which, as we have already seen, defined the relation between masters and slaves: "The slave codes, and the operation of large plantations, combined logic and efficiency with barbaric violence, and a display of power which was focused upon the public torture of the body of the slave."[108]

This legalistic and instrumental explanation of the persistence of physical torture in slave societies is convincing, but it doesn't explain the necessity of the spectacle and the exhibitionary order, the scopic regime of enslavement that I discussed in the introductory chapter. The issue here is not simply that the spectacle of the tortured body continued to have an authority in the Americas that it had lost in Europe; rather, the fact remains that a priori claims made for the body in a slave context were radically different from those in "free" society. At precisely the moment in European society that the destruction of the body came to be seen as a source of moral embarrassment, torture and mutilation were considered essential for the maintenance of symbolic domination in slave society.

6

To understand the role of punishment as perversely desirable, it is important to rehearse the spectacle of punishment and its inscription in the European text and to turn, like others have done before, to the works of John Gabriel Stedman, whose *Narrative of a Five Years' Expedition against the Revolted Negroes of Surinam* and the illustrations accompanying it provide an unrivaled witness to the use of violence as a part of an exhibitionary order.[109]

Early during his expedition in Suriname, Stedman was struck by the role played by torture in the management of rebellious slaves: "In 1730, a most shocking and barbarous execution of eleven of the unhappy negro captives was resolved upon, in the expectation that it might terrify their companions and induce them to submit. One man was hanged alive upon a gibbet by an iron hook stuck through his ribs; two others were chained to stakes and burnt to death by a slow fire. Six women were broken alive upon the rack, and two girls were decapitated. Such was their resolution under these tortures, that they endured them without even uttering a sigh."[110] Writing from a generally pro-abolitionist position after his tour of duty in Suriname, Stedman was fascinated by scenes of barbarity because of the powerful impression they had left on him—"the gloom which the infernal furnace had left upon my mind," as he put it.[111] William Blake's illustrations for Stedman's book were to become powerful

4.12 William Blake, *The Execution of Breaking on the Rack*. 1793. Engraving. From John Gabriel Stedman, *Narrative of a Five Years' Expedition against the Revolted Negroes of Surinam*.

4.13 William Blake, *A Negro hung alive by the Ribs to a Gallows*. Engraving. From John Gabriel Stedman, *Narrative of a Five Years' Expedition against the Revolted Negroes of Surinam*.

visual testimonies to the economy of terror at the end of the long eighteenth century (figs. 4.12 and 4.13).

Couldn't slaves be punished and their bodies destroyed without making a public spectacle of their punishment and death? While punishment in modern Europe was intended to deprive the body of liberty, the property of subjectivity, and the entitlement to life, the black slave had no rights to such rights or any claim to a unique identity. Quite often, torture was justified by the absence of any reference to the slave's right to liberty or human property; it was intended to reinforce the existence of the slave as chattel or to provide a public example of the power of the masters to control their property. Indeed, it is precisely because the slave was chattel—property without rights or entitlement to life—that it could be subjected to the most extremes forms of torture. Violence is what ensured that the slave's body could function as a useful force as what Foucault calls "a productive body and a subjected body."[112]

Moreover, what was crucial about the scenes witnessed by Stedman and graphically represented by his illustrators was that the power of these images depended on spectatorship and effect. In fact, spectatorship and effect would operate on two levels or planes. In the first instance, there was the record of the act of torture as it had been observed, represented here by Stedman's prose. In the second instance, the observed effect was re-represented, for tactical reasons, to affect readers who were far removed from the event in order to achieve a particular political goal, in this case abolitionism. Still, the question that needs to be addressed is why white observers such as Edwards and Stedman were attracted to these scenes of torture, why they presented them in such great detail, and why they made them central to their narratives irrespective of political positions.

Although Stedman's graphic representations of scenes of torture and execution were intended to force his readers to react against slavery, he also had an uncanny ability to connect scenes of barbarity with those of pleasure. He knew, for example, that his expedition was in Suriname to protect the sources of the coffee that had become a major source of pleasure in European high culture. Stedman easily recognized the connection between coffee, a valued stimulant, and the violence of slavery. During a visit to a coffee estate in Suriname, he witnessed what he described as "the unpardonable contempt with which the negro slaves are treated in this colony":

> I was an eye witness of His son, a boy not more than ten years old, when sitting at table, gave a slap in the face to a grey-headed black woman, who by accident touched his powdered hair as she was serving in a dish of kerry. I could not help blaming his father for overlooking the action, but he told me, with a smile, that the child should no longer offend me, as he was next day to sail for Holland for education. To this I answered that I thought it almost too late. At the same moment a sailor passing by, broke the head of a negro with a bludgeon, for not having saluted him with his hat. Such is the state of slavery, at least in this Dutch settlement![113]

Representations of scenes of barbarity by romantic writers, most notably William Blake in his illustrations for Stedman's book, tended to invoke a poetics of suffering in which, to use Hugh Honor's words, the tortured black was endowed with "the fortitude of Christian martyrs and thereby elevating them to a level of heroic suffering from which they were otherwise barred."[114]

A closer look at the engravings of the torture of slave women, which were often suffused with Christian overtones, may lead one to the conclusion that the female subject had been selected as the conduit through which violence could be sensualized or even eroticized. Indeed, in one of the most famous engravings of a mulatto woman being flogged (fig. 4.14), the subject under torture bears a resemblance to Joanna, Stedman's

4.14 William Blake, *Flagellation of a
Female Samboe Slave.* 1793. Engraving.
From John Gabriel Stedman, *Narrative
of a Five Years' Expedition against the
Revolted Negroes of Surinam.*

eroticized mistress and common-law wife. In this case, as in others, the
line that would come to divide abjection from sexual desire was not
clearly demarcated, and it is not clear whether, in watching these pictures,
the spectator was supposed to share the pain of the tortured body or to
admire its fortitude and suffering.[115]

Thus, while Stedman might have designed his prose to ascertain the
quotidianness of torture in the culture of slavery, he often ended up
turning the scene of suffering itself into a unique, heroic, and sexualized
event. For example, Stedman reports witnessing an African who "lost his
life under the most excruciating torments, which he supported without
heaving a sigh or making a complaint."[116] And in one of the most grue-
some scenes in his narrative, he repeated a story told to him by "a decent
looking man," who talked with relish about the quartering of a slave and
the entertainment provided by the stoic victim in his last moments:

> After four strong horses had been fastened to his legs and arms, and iron
> sprigs had been driven home underneath every one of his nails on hands and
> feet, he first asked a dram, and then bid them pull away, without a groan.

But what afforded us the greatest entertainment, were the fellow's jokes, by desiring the executioner to drink before him, in case there should chance to be poison in the glass, and bidding him take care of his horses, lest any of them should happen to strike backwards. As for old men being broken upon the rack, and young women roasted alive chained to stakes, there can be nothing more common in this colony.[117]

For Stedman, then, the renarrativization and apparent eroticization of such scenes of suffering was not merely intended to draw a distinction between the heroic slave and the callous master but to endow them with the power of abjection and sentimentality. This explains the subtle contrast he made between the "moral" of the stories told by the "decent young man" and his own reaction to this story: "I was petrified at the inhuman detail, and breaking away with execrations from this diabolical scene of laceration, made the best of my way home to my own lodgings."[118]

Undoubtedly, the representation of the slave as a stoic figure in suffering and death presented an image of Christian charity that enervated the case for the humanity of the African as a subject worthy of pity. The problem with these representations, however, was that they could easily mirror another discourse of violence that was emerging at about the same time and was to acquire currency after the abolition of the slave trade: the discourse in which the proponents of slavery would often rewrite the history of the African slave—in Africa and before enslavement—to make the claim that the blacks had never had any rights to liberty, that pain and suffering, and an unmitigated inhumanity, were their natural state.[119] While abolitionists displayed the violence of slavery to move public passions against enslavement, proponents of slavery called attention to the wantonness of African life to make the case that violence was inherent in the condition of the black, who was better off under the modern regimen of plantation life than the fetishistic economies of their homeland.

In both cases, iconography played a central role in the making of the American world picture and the place of the black in it. But what I have sought to bring together in this chapter is the play of two traditions of representation often separated in time and space, one claiming distance from the harsh materiality of slavery through invocation of taste, the other enmeshed in the unholy business of managing bodies that had been decreed socially dead. In the next two chapters I will consider how the slaves themselves responded to this strange conjuncture of violence and taste.

"Popping Sorrow":
Loss and the Transformation of Servitude

*I*f one were looking for an intimate connection between slavery and the culture of taste, there would be no better place to go than the series of paintings and engravings done by the Italian artist Agostino Brunias under the commission of Sir William Young, the governor of Dominica and commissioner of St. Vincent in the Windward Islands (figs. 5.1 and 5.2). On the surface, Brunias's images were colorful evocations of tropical landscapes, now familiar touristic pictures of a West Indian paradise where happy blacks and enchanting mulattoes encountered one another in markets, streets, and dance arenas against the picturesque background of the blue Caribbean sea. Here was the West Indies of the colonial imagination: ladies in colorful fabrics and parasols, market women in higgler headgear, and mulattoes mimicking the dance steps of European courts with blacks observing on the periphery. In this imaginary colonial paradise of markets, festivals, and promenades, the mulatto woman stood out as the quintessential figure of an attractive difference.[1]

These pictures do not, or course, depart from the planter image of the West Indies as a garden or a picturesque landscape "not much unlike to, nor less romantic than, the most wild and beautiful situations of the Frescati, Tivoli, and Albano."[2] But as Kay Dian Kriz has shown in her careful survey and study of Brunias's artwork, these paintings and engravings were summoned to do colonial work in two unexpected ways. First, they were intended to reproduce the West Indian islands, all slave colonies at the time, as intimate and desirable places of settlement. Second, they were expected to present the islands as spaces of cultivation and refinement.[3] In fact, it could be argued that one of the major goals of these images, and the whole process of reproducing the slave islands as pictures for European consumption, was driven by one overriding desire: to obviate the violent presence of slavery through the calculated production

5.1 Agostino Brunias, *The Linen Market at St. Domingo.* Engraved print of painting by Agostino Brunias, published by John P. Thompson (London), October 6, 1804.

5.2 Agostino Brunias, *A Negro Festival Drawn from Nature on the Island of St. Vincent.* Lithograph. From Bryan Edwards, *The History, Civil and Commercial of the British Colonies in the West Indies.*

of happiness. If the West Indies was to attract enough English settlers to counter French designs, it had to disavow its real identity as a place where social relationships were conducted through the brutal regimen of enforced labor or the modes of excess associated with the white Creoles. Through images of happy slaves, colonization would be reimagined as what Sir William Young called a "jovial party."[4] In these circumstances, the reproduction of the West Indies as a desirable aesthetic object was self-consciously mediated through the culture of taste and represented through its dominant idiom. Thus the mulatto women in these paintings would be imagined, very much like the ladies of taste discussed in chapter 2, as people located in a public space "actively disengaged from commercial transactions"; like "figures in English conversation pieces," the so-called mulatress would be "involved in conversation or polite recreations, such as dancing," almost oblivious to the marketplace as a site of exchange.[5]

And yet, given Brunias's careful deployment of the vocabulary of taste, the mulatress could not convincingly be represented as a surrogate for the absent slave, as Kriz claims; on the contrary, the mixed-race woman functioned as the stand-in, a supplement, as it were, for the absent white woman.[6] Far from pointing out the defining contradictions of slave society, a place where black bondage and white taste met in a contrapuntal relationship, the figure of the mulatress could be summoned to nudge readers and viewers of these scenes to see beyond their competing political and aesthetic ideologies. One could gaze on, or even consume, this figure of beauty without even noticing the unspeakable subject of slavery. In this sense, the mulatress could provide a new dimension to a discourse of black happiness that was being presented by supporters of the slave trade as an antidote to the abolitionist insistence on black pathos.

This discourse—the reproduction of the slave as a happy subject in bondage—can be found in the works of Robert Norris, one of the last great advocates of the slave trade in Britain, a man who continued to be puzzled and irritated by the abolitionists' association of enslavement with suffering and unhappiness. Norris, who assumed that the passage of blacks from the West African coast to the plantations of the Americas had liberated them from barbarism and bondage at home, could not understand how the enslaved could be unhappy in the Americas. At the end of *Memoirs of the Reign of Bossa Ahadeee, King of Dahomy*—ostensibly an account of the kingdom of Dahomey at the height of the slave trade, but in reality a rearguard attempt to defend slavery against the onslaught of abolitionism—Norris carefully observed how in the plantations of the West Indies, African slaves had found a home and sanctuary against the excesses of black despotism in their own country. After years of work in the plantation, noted Norris, the African slave would find, in old age, not wretchedness or "chilling penury" but help and consolation in the hands of "his children, and his children's children, his friends, and former fellow-laborers; his countrymen, and fellow passengers."[7] To support his claim, Norris noted that there had scarcely been a case where an enslaved black in the West Indies had expressed the desire to return to his or her country; there had not been instances of freed slaves returning home.

5.3 Princess Madia, Enslaved African from the Congo. June 2, 1860. *Harper's Weekly.*

On the contrary, "even newly imported Negroes, when threatened by the overseer, upon some fault or neglect of theirs, to be sent back again, are seriously alarmed at it."[8]

Slaves did not, of course, consider their condition to be one of freedom and happiness; instead, many enslaved Africans conceived and performed sorrow as the true representation of their state and drew on the reserves of their unhappiness and depression to find a language for expressing the integrity of the self against overwhelming conditions of oppression. This seems to have been the case with Madia, a Congolese woman aboard the slave ship *Wildfire* captured by the U.S. Navy off Key West, Florida, in 1860 (fig. 5.3). It is reported that because of the solemnity of her bearing, most notably the palm she always placed on her cheek, Madia was accorded the status of a princess.[9] In the culture of slavery, the performance of sorrow often went hand in hand with the arduous task of recovering the self from psychic bondage and re-representing it in public space.

And thus it is to Princess Madia, rather than the phantom figures of happiness imagined by Brunias, Norris, and the major planter historians, that we must turn in order to understand how slaves set out to cultivate a sensuous subjectivity outside the regimen of bondage and enforced labor. It is to the melancholy generated by slavery that we must seek not only discourses and performances of resistance but also what Joseph Roach has called "the vitality and sensuous presence of material forms."[10] Here,

5.4 *Propping Sorrow,* a moment in a dance by the National Dance Theater Company of Jamaica. Photo by Maria LaYacona, no date. From Rex Nettleford, *Dance Jamaica: Cultural Definition and Artistic Discovery the National Dance Theatre Company of Jamaica, 1962–1982.*

even the smallest physical gesture, such as the placement of the palm on the cheek, was to become the visible measure of a depressive affect, the pose of sorrow, loss, and mourning (see fig. 5.4).[11] Melancholy constituted an important aesthetic reaction to the violence of enslavement, an alternative to the sensibility of high European culture discussed at the beginning of this book.

As they sought an idiom for their captivity, the only comfort Equiano and his sister could find "was in being in one another's arms all that night, and bathing each other with our tears"; but the pathos of enslavement was deepened by the fact that soon they were "deprived of even the smallest comfort of weeping together."[12] In one of the most moving scenes in his narrative, the one describing his separation from his sister, Equiano would turn to the power of apostrophe to demarcate sorrow as the only logical emotional response to natal alienation:

> When these people knew we were brother and sister they indulged us to be together; and the man, to whom I supposed we belonged, lay with us, he in the middle, while she and I held one another by the hands across his breast all night; and thus for a while we forgot our misfortunes in the joy of being together: but even this small comfort was soon to have an end; for scarcely had the fatal morning appeared, when she was again torn from me for ever! I was now more miserable, if possible, than before. The small relief which her

presence gave me from pain was gone, and the wretchedness of my situation was redoubled by my anxiety after her fate, and my apprehensions lest her sufferings should be greater than mine, when I could not be with her to alleviate them. Yes, thou dear partner of all my childish sports! thou sharer of my joys and sorrows! happy should I have ever esteemed myself to encounter every misery for you, and to procure your freedom by the sacrifice of my own.[13]

The play of sorrow, then, was a persistent and pressing arsenal in the cause of abolitionism in both Europe and the Americas, constituting a significant counterpoint to the rationalized regimens of representing the African as either an object of trade or a figure whose goals and desires were anterior to the logic of modern identity.

2

The turn to melancholy as an aesthetic response invites several questions: How did African slaves respond to enforced labor, to the tortured life that was the signature of their displacement in the plantations of the Americas? What was their reaction to notions of taste and economies of pleasure in situations that seemed to negate the very idea of a black sensorium? And how could slaves, defined in modernity as property, cling to a subjective identity?[14] Perhaps the best way of responding to these questions is to turn to a work that has nothing whatsoever to do with slavery, but one that provides us with the most powerful and touching commentary on the condition of loss in the modern world—namely, Walter Benjamin's *The Origin of German Tragic Drama*.[15] Benjamin's book is a masterful reading of the aesthetics of the tragic in the modern world and of melancholy and allegory as the essential response to the loss and displacement of the human subject, one isolated from nature, history, and selfhood and thus forced to feed on its inner passions. It is a book that is particularly acute in its understanding of the play and display of human wretchedness as the only logical response to modernity's failure to live up to its redemptive claims.

Central to Benjamin's book is the argument that in a world in which the idealized and transfigured face of nature had failed to live up to its promise and had instead given in to the "*facies hippocratica* of history as a petrified, primordial landscape," sorrowfulness was the essential register of the negative historicity of the subject, the mark of its process of decline and decay in time:

Everything about history that, from the very beginning, has been untimely, sorrowful, unsuccessful, is expressed in a face—or rather in a death's head. And although such a thing lacks all "symbolic" freedom of expression, all classical proportion, all humanity—nevertheless, this is the form in which man's subjection to nature is most obvious and it significantly gives rise not only to the enigmatic question of the nature of human existence as such, but also of the biographical historicity of the individual. This is the heart of the allegorical way of seeing, of the baroque, secular explanation of history as the Passion of the world; its importance resides solely in the stations of its decline. The greater the significance, the greater the subjection to death, because death digs most deeply the jagged line of demarcation between physical nature and significance. But if nature has always been subject to the power of death, it is also true that it has always been allegorical. Significance and death both come to fruition in historical development, just as they are closely linked as seeds in the creature's graceless state of sin.[16]

For Benjamin, melancholy registered the stations of decline in what was supposed to be the redemptive history of the world. The play of sorrow, the *Trauerspiel*, would embody the semiosis of death and its power to dig, even deeper, the trench separating alienated nature and human capacity, thus marking the descent of the subject into nonbeing.

The world of slavery was, of course, nowhere near Benjamin's thinking when he was reflecting on the meaning of subjecthood in death; his immediate concern was the atrophy of the narrative of Western civilization as it slipped toward barbarism in the last years of the Weimar Republic. Still, the terms of Benjamin's discourse should resonate powerfully with the experience of enslavement, whose tortured worldliness stands out as the stain of modernity and its enabling condition. For the world of the African slave in the new world would come to be defined by loss and the power of death. Here, again, Equiano's reaction to the geography of enslavement is illustrative. Separated from the new colleagues he had formed on the slave ship, and finding himself without a common language to share his experiences with other slaves in the Americas, Equiano plunged into melancholy: "I was now exceedingly miserable, and thought myself worse off than any of the rest of my companions; for they could talk to each other, but I had no person to speak to that I could understand. In this state I was constantly grieving and pining, and wishing for death, rather than any thing else."[17]

And Equiano was not the only slave who found it hard to find a redemptive language for a deracinated experience, or to respond to the lack of a social point of reference with a combination of melancholy and fear. On her first night as a slave, Mary Prince was possessed by what she described as "a sad fright":

I was just going to sleep, when I heard a noise in my mistress's room; and she presently called out to inquire if some work was finished that she had ordered Hetty to do. "No, Ma'am, not yet," was Hetty's answer from below. On hearing this, my master started up from his bed, and just as he was, in his shirt, ran down stairs with a long cow-skin in his hand. I heard immediately after, the cracking of the thong, and the house rang to the shrieks of poor Hetty, who kept crying out, "Oh, Massa! Massa! me dead. Massa! have mercy upon me—don't kill me outright."—This was a sad beginning for me. I sat up upon my blanket, trembling with terror, like a frightened hound, and thinking that my turn would come next. At length the house became still, and I forgot for a little while all my sorrows by falling fast asleep.[18]

Sorrow would become the marker of separation of the self from the world. Paradoxically, for slaves like Equiano and Prince, the alienated nature of the new world, the primordial landscape of loss and unbelonging and the passion of sorrow that it generated, would be the first sign that they had become modern subjects. In this context, the play of sorrow, the passion drama of alienated nature, would appear to be the only condition the slave had inherited as the basis of a modern identity, and in order for the slave to become human, suffering itself needed to be transformed into a redemptive narrative, a story of being oneself against the violently imposed identity of being a slave.[19]

My operating premise here and for the rest of this chapter is that the condition of possibility of being black in the new world could not be realized until slavery, a sorrowful state of shame and negation, was transformed into a narrative of identity. It is probably this transformation that W.E.B. Du Bois had in mind when, in the concluding chapter of the *Souls of Black Folk*, he described Negro spirituals—the sorrow songs—as the medium of what was tantamount to a black logos. Through these songs, Du Bois asserted, "the soul of the black slave spoke to men"; they were "the most beautiful expression of human experience born of this side of the seas."[20] For Du Bois, the sorrow songs functioned as allegorical expressions of the repressed self and its yearning for a language of freedom out of the ruins of enslavement. While they denoted suffering as the essential historicity of the African slave in the new world, the songs of sorrow also had the capacity to secure the coupling of what Benjamin had cryptically called death and significance. Death represented the descent of the self into the sphere of nonbeing; significance was the desire for transcendence.

Du Bois identified the double play of allegory in his careful reading of the sorrow songs. He noted that they were signifiers of loss, of disconnection from Africa, and thus registered "the voice of exile."[21] But he also recognized the redemptive hermeneutics embedded in the sound of these sorrow songs:

What are these songs, and what do they mean? I know little of music and can say nothing in technical phrase, but I know something of men, and knowing them, I know that these songs are the articulate message of the slave to the world. They tell us in these eager days that life was joyous to the black slave, careless and happy. I can easily believe this of some, of many. But not all the past South, though it rose from the dead, can gainsay the heart-touching witness of these songs. They are the music of an unhappy people, of the children of disappointment; they tell of death and suffering and unvoiced longing toward a truer world, of misty wanderings and hidden ways.[22]

What did Du Bois mean when he said that the sorrow songs served as a "heart-touching witness"? Witness to what? To history? To suffering? Or to black being?

Du Bois did not elaborate what he meant when he said that sorrow songs were "the articulate message of the slave to the world," but it is not implausible that he was thinking of these songs functioning, very much like Benjamin's *Trauerspiel*, as an allegorical way of seeing and being in a world defined by pain and suffering. Here, witnessing sadness and sorrow, like the general play of melancholy, could operate as a weapon against the death drive, a total onslaught against alienation. In fact, if we agree with Julia Kristeva's assessment that a "depressive affect" operates as "a defense against parceling"—namely, the atomization of the self—then sadness can reconstitute "an affective cohesion of the self, which restores its unity within the framework of the affect."[23] Kristeva recognizes that the protection that melancholy affords the self is a flimsy one, but she nonetheless calls attention to the compensatory nature of depressive affect; those who have been invalidated in a symbolic sense can register the dignity of the self in adversity: "The depressive mood constitutes itself as a narcissistic support, negative to be sure, but nevertheless presenting the self with an integrity, nonverbal though it might be. Because of that, the depressive affect makes up for symbolic invalidation and interruption (the depressive's 'that's meaningless') and at the same time protects it against proceeding to the suicidal act."[24]

Slave narratives often staged melancholy as a negative anchor to the enslaved person's quest for identification. The staging of a sensibility of loss was often foregrounded as the counter to the picture of the happy slave in the European imaginary. Thus, at the end of her slave narrative, first published in 1831, Prince noted that she was vexed and saddened by people in England who believed that slaves were happy or even hinted that there was any cause or source for joy in enslavement:

I am often much vexed, and I feel great sorrow when I hear some people in this country say, that the slaves do not need better usage, and do not want to be free. They believe the foreign people, who deceive them, and say slaves are happy. I say, Not so. How can slaves be happy when they have the halter round their neck and the whip upon their back? and are disgraced and thought no more of than beasts?—and are separated from their mothers, and husbands, and children, and sisters, just as cattle are sold and separated? Is it happiness for a driver in the field to take down his wife or sister or child, and strip them, and whip them in such a disgraceful manner?—women that have had children exposed in the open field to shame! There is no modesty or decency shown by the owner to his slaves; men, women, and children are exposed alike.[25]

Although Prince directed her rhetoric at any suggestion that happiness and slavery were compatible, the closing paragraphs of the *History of Mary Prince* seem to suggest that much more than the question of happiness, or its absence, was at issue in debates about the emotional condition of the enslaved. For what Prince set out to present at the end of her book was a forceful denunciation of the ideology of the aesthetic that I have discussed in previous chapters, an ideology that assumed that "sensual recognition" was the key to subjectivity and that being happy was both the means and ends to a modern life.[26]

Prince's picture of the slave was that of a body deprived of its sensuous capacity, turned, often through brutal and sustained acts of violence, into a beast of burden, one regulated outside the norms of affective relationships such as family, kinship, and passion. When English people go to the West Indies, lamented Prince, "they forget God and all feeling of shame," and this forgetfulness of divinity was evident in the treatment of the slave as an animal: "They tie up slaves like hogs—moor them up like cattle, and they lick them, so as hogs, or cattle, or horses never were flogged;—and yet they come home and say, and make some good people believe, that slaves don't want to get out of slavery."[27] The mere suggestion that slavery was a place to seek fulfillment was, for Prince, incomprehensible and apprehensible: "I have been a slave myself—I know what slaves feel—I can tell by myself what other slaves feel, and by what they have told me. The man that says slaves be quite happy in slavery—that they don't want to be free—that man is either ignorant or a lying person. I never heard a slave say so. I never heard a Buckra man say so, till I heard tell of it in England. Such people ought to be ashamed of themselves."[28] Having thus displayed her own suffering in the course of her narrative, Prince was now in a position to shame her English readers and shift debates about the condition of slavery from the happiness adduced to them by the pro-slavery lobby to scenes of suffering, where, in her mind, questions of identity truly belonged.

And Prince was not alone in the privileging of sorrow and suffering as the lived experience of the black slave in the new world. Frederick Douglass detested any suggestion that the experience of slavery would generate any kind of pleasure for the enslaved, or that people in bondage could become sensuous beings, akin to the white subjects of taste that I discussed in previous chapters. Slave holidays and the entertainments associated with them, Douglass noted bitterly in *Life and Times* "served the

5.5 Portrait of Frederick Douglass as a Younger Man. 1855. Engraved by J. C. Buttre from a daguerreotype. Frontispiece. Frederick Douglass, *My Bondage and My Freedom.*

purpose of keeping the minds of the slaves occupied with thoughts and aspirations short of the liberty of which they are deprived."[29]

Douglass went on to provide a systematic indictment of modes of pleasure that were, in his view, created and enforced by masters to "secure the ends of injustice and oppression."[30] He argued that this kind of enforced pleasure in situations of bondage defied all notions of "rational enjoyment" and militated against "virtuous liberty": "The license allowed appeared to have no other objective than to disgust the slaves with their temporary freedom, and to make them as glad to return to their work as they had been to leave it."[31] Douglass believed that the only morally acceptable representation of slavery was one that took cognizance of its tragic dimension and identified and affirmed seriousness and unhappiness as the essential condition of the black in the modern world. Douglass's own self-presentation, both in his works and pictures, was intended to enforce the rule of pathos as the counterpoint to play (fig. 5.5).

In his fierce critique of slave performances, which he argued were inauthentic and un-redemptive, Douglass was indirectly assaulting the ideology of the aesthetic on two fronts. First, he was interrogating the claim, common in theories of taste and leisure since the eighteenth century, that people who had access to happiness, whether through consumption or leisure, were free subjects, irrespective of what was consumed and the circumstances in which leisure was enacted. Douglass's counterexample to the idea of happiness was his portrait of slaves in the antebellum South, often and insidiously compelled not only to be happy, but also to display this happiness as a mask for their real condition of existence. The performance of enforced happiness seemed to defeat the core foundation of freedom as an expression of sensuousness and affect. And Douglass was, of course, aware that from the moment they arrived on the slave ship, in their passage through the Atlantic and in their eventual placement in the plantation, enslaved Africans were subjected to degrading performances, including being made to dance on the deck of the slave ship (fig. 5.6).

Second, Douglass's harsh rejection of an imposed economy of pleasure among the enslaved served as an implicit questioning of the notion that sensuousness itself could have value outside the domain of rationality and reflection. As far as he was concerned, slave holidays and performances were part of the master's cunning, attempts to manipulate affect rather than provide a vehicle through which the real feelings and sensibilities of slaves could be expressed. Such enforced acts of play, or expressions of happiness, precluded a thinking or reflective subject. If taste and happiness could thus be manipulated, it was difficult, if not impossible, to posit the realm of the senses as the foundation of true feelings or real identity, as ideologues of the aesthetic such as Alexander Baumgarten had been arguing since the early eighteenth century.[32]

There were, of course, pragmatic and tactical reasons why melancholy was the preferred rhetorical mode in slave narratives and other accounts against enslavement. Within the context or aftermath of abolitionism, in which the books by Prince and Douglass were written and circulated, any contemplation of black pleasure in enslavement would fall right into the trap of the slave-owning class and its propaganda machine, which liked to display images of happy slaves as evidence of the good life they were having in the plantation. So if Douglass insisted that his image in public be surrounded by pathos, and if he would get upset when a

5.6 "Danse de Negres." From Amédée Grehan, ed., *La France Maritime* [Paris, 1855], vol. 3, facing p. 179. Copy in Princeton University Library.

daguerreotype or *carte de visite* presented him smiling, it was because he understood that images or stories of happy slaves could undermine the project of abolitionism, and the pathos on which it was constructed, faster than any philosophical argument.[33] Operating within the orbit of white desire and pleasure, black entertainments such as butting heads in Venezuela or dancing a jig in a Southern plantation came to be perceived as a further diminishment of the blacks' control over their economies of desire and pleasure.

However, the strategic deployment of pathos in the discourse of abolitionism did not necessarily mean that melancholy or the play of sorrow was, per se, the essential condition of the slave. In spite of Douglass's admonitions, slave holidays and the scenes of happiness that seemed to surround them were a dominant feature of the cultural and social geography of the plantation. And despite the hardships associated with enslavement, the lasting images of slaves, whether at home in their own quarters or in front of their masters', was one of subjects at play. Indeed, for a people who were the most brutalized in the culture of modernity, excluded from the category of personhood, separated from community and kin, and forced into a regime of labor enforced by continuous violence, African slaves in the new world appeared unusually happy.

It was this condition of happiness that struck Matthew Gregory Lewis when he arrived in Jamaica around the turn of 1815 to 1816 to visit his newly inherited West Indian plantations. On witnessing a New Year festival soon after his arrival in Jamaica, Lewis concluded that he had never seen "so many people who appeared to be so unaffectedly happy." Compared to the poor in the English marketplace, where attendance seemed to be based on social compulsion or the simple need to exchange goods and make money, Lewis described the West Indian fair as a site of "real pleasure," one that "seemed to consist in singing, dancing, and laughing, in seeing and being seen, in showing their own fine clothes, or in admiring those of others." Unlike the scenes of enforced bacchanal described by Douglass in his retrospective view of slave festivals, Lewis's version of Jamaican festivals was one of a self-willed orderliness: "There were no people selling or buying; no servants and landladies bustling and passing about; and at eight o'clock, as we passed through the market-place, where was the greatest illumination, and which, of course, was most thronged, I did not see a single person drunk, nor had I observed a single quarrel through the course of the day."[34]

Similar scenes had been reported by earlier European travelers in the landscape of slavery. Traveling in Antigua and St. Christopher in December 1724, Janet Schaw described the appearance of black slaves on their way to market as "one of the most beautiful sights I ever saw," and went on to describe a scene so picturesque that it seemed at odds with the wretchedness of slavery she had witnessed elsewhere on the island:

> They were universally clad in white Muslin: the men in loose drawers and waistcoats, the women in jackets and petticoats; the men wore black caps, the women had handkerchiefs of gauze or silk, which they wore in the fashion of turbans. Both men and women carried neat white wicker-baskets on their heads, which they balanced as our Milk maids do their pails. These contained the various articles for Market, in one a little kid raised its head from amongst flowers of every hue, which were thrown over to guard it from the heat; here a lamb, there a Turkey or a pig, all covered up in the same elegant manner, While others had their baskets filled with fruit, pine-apples reared over each other; Grapes dangling over the loaded basket; oranges, Shaddacks, water lemons, pomegranates, granadillas, with twenty others, whose names I forget.[35]

These scenes were to enter the paintings and prints by Brunias that opened my discussion.

The interplay between melancholy and such scenes of gaiety seems to lead to a theoretical or analytical caesura and to raise troubling questions: How are we to explain these consistent images of black slaves as happy and sensuous subjects in the theater of brutality and abjection? Were they mere expressions of white fantasies intended to counteract the violence of slavery? Were they part of a grand design to eroticize the body in bondage to make the colonial scene worthy of settlement? Or did these scenes reflect the feelings and passions of the slaves, who, in spite of their condition, found means of expressing sensuousness and created aesthetic spaces where none were supposed to exist? Given the slaves' investment in the work of pleasure and the carnivalesque atmosphere that surrounded their gatherings, markets, and squares on weekends and holidays, one cannot dismiss these images and accounts of happy slaves at play as the simple projection of white fantasies. The persistence of accounts of slaves as subjects of pleasure cannot be assumed to represent the partial view of a group of interested observers merely focused on the beauty of the human and natural landscape at the expense of its torrid ruins. On the contrary, they function as important signals to the complex and often contradictory ways that slaves presented themselves in the public sphere, the subject of my next chapter.

One could argue that Lewis, Brunias, and others—including the slaves they observed at play—were caught in the frenzy of a festival, a social space outside lived experience and "now" time, and that the scenes of happiness observed and presented to the outside world were mere performatives, separated from the empirical world of enslavement. One could then conclude—following the arguments of Mikhail Bakhtin—that the slaves were engaging in speech forms that had been liberated from the "norms, hierarchies, and prohibitions of established idiom."[36] Such speech forms would hence not be called upon to bear witness to the condition of enslavement.

My overall concern in this chapter and the next, however, is on the meaning of the scenes of merrymaking that dominate descriptive accounts of West Indian and American slavery and how they should be read or interpreted. Should these scenes be interpreted as occasions for leisure and sources of pleasure and, by extension, as expressions of local identity? Could one, then, see slave performances and related forms of expression, many of them sensuous, as essential and indispensable cultural weapons in the African slave's long journey from the bowels of the slave ship (the zero ground of modernity) to the public sphere, the square, the market, the fair, where their phenomenological presence could be acknowledged?[37] Or should we look at them as forms of enforced pleasure, modes of false consciousness, what Douglass called "safety-valves," whose sole intention was to "carry off the explosive elements inseparable from the human mind when reduced to the conditions of slavery"?[38]

Simply put, our challenge here is how to provide a descriptive and analytic response to these scenes of happiness, not so much to figure out whether they were genuine or affected, but to understand the role they played as a means of recoding social life for a people excluded from multiple domains of freedom and the aesthetic life that came with it. Even within these parameters, however, the task of the analyst is made even more difficult by the absence, within slavery itself, of independent black voices that might provide us with an inside view of what slaves themselves thought when they performed happiness. The black voices that we hear from the archive of slavery come to us mediated by white interlocutors or the powerful idiom of abolitionism; they thus tell only partial stories. These limits, however, also offer at least two theoretical or conceptual opportunities. First, if slave performances were inventions of the masters—gestures and tasks that had been chaperoned either to create the semblance of pleasure in enslavement, or to provide escapism from the drudgery of enforced labor—couldn't they also be transformed into spaces of leisure, populated by the slaves' own needs and desires? We should be cautious in treating cultural activities that are enforced as essentially antithetical to the interests of the oppressed, for even within domination, slaves could transform enforced play into a set of what Michel de Certeau has called tactics.[39] Second, there is the problem of what I will call a mangled semantics, the confusion of the performative and the truth-value of slave cultural activities and utterances: did the continuous presentations of happiness witnessed by observers in the slave plantation reflect the moral geography of servitude, or were they mere performatives, speech acts that were not intended to describe or represent an existing situation?[40]

3

The anonymous author of *Marly*, a description of Jamaican plantation culture, was astounded to discover, on arrival at the island, that all the slaves he encountered were fawning on him as if he were King George himself, although he was apparently just a bookkeeper. Indeed, Jamaican slaves saw the bookkeeper as the link between them and the English king, whom they referred to as Brother George.[41] Even the urbane and often cynical Matthew Gregory Lewis was startled by the affections (or affectations) of the slaves who celebrated his arrival, happy to meet the man who owned them and even happier to belong to "Massa George," the king: "On my arrival, every woman who had a child held it up to show to me, exclaiming,—'See massa, see! here nice new neger me bring for work for massa'; and those who had more than one did not fail to boast of the number, and make it a claim to the greater merit with me."[42]

Why would slave mothers show off the children they had produced to work for the master and be happy about the inevitable bondage of their progeny? Lewis was puzzled by these gestures, but the more this fawning was piled on him, the more he began to recognize that it was part of a subtle and insidious reversal of the structure of control. He slowly came to understand that the slaves who flattered him most were those who had transgressed in his absence or needed favors from him. Here, the performance of happiness in the face of servitude was a calculated tactic, a means to a specific end.

Now, given the confusion between genuine affect and a manipulative play of feelings, the question of semantics or speech acts is an important one. It is important because when we listen to slaves flattering their masters or expressing the pleasure of belonging to a particular owner—and by extension Massa George, the king himself—it is difficult for us to tell whether they were rehearsing conventions expected of them, whether they were involved in a kind of play, sucking up, as it were, to the often absentee master, or whether their happiness was linked somehow, in a deeper sense and meaning, to their referential and experiential world. Indeed, white visitors to the slave colonies were highly disturbed by their incapacity to draw the line between the semantics of authenticity and sincerity and self-interested performance. For many white observers and other outsiders, understanding the affective nature of the slave, either in private meetings or in public gatherings, did not seem to cohere with the general condition of enforced labor, which was one of unmitigated suffering. Many observers of slavery in the West Indies wondered what the meaning of these scenes of pleasure was in relation to dominant notions about freedom, especially the assumption that only free people could be happy. More particularly, liberal observers struggled to reconcile the slaves' momentary sense of freedom, expressed mostly on Sundays and the Christmas holidays, with the overall condition of enslavement. J. B. Moreton, writing on Jamaica, was struck by the fact that slaves engaged in the hardest labor were commonly singing; he was moved by the "deep melancholy of their songs."[43] And Lewis, who seemed to thrive on scenes of slaves at play as a validation of his own role as a liberal slave owner, found the presentation of happiness and affection to be the source of some doubt and confusion: "Whether the pleasure of the negroes was sincere may be doubted; but certainly it was the loudest that I ever witnessed: they all talked together, sang, danced, shouted, and, in the violence of their gesticulations, tumbled over each other, and rolled about upon the ground. Twenty voices at once enquired after uncles, and aunts, and grandfathers, and great-grandmothers of mine, who had been buried long before I was in existence, and whom, I believe, most of them only knew by tradition."[44]

Lewis was probably involved in a subtle defense of slavery; the rhetoric of his journal reflected a modish attempt to represent enslavement as a benign, almost harmless, institution and thus to ameliorate the discourse of abolitionism.[45] Still, his observations raise important questions about how slaves themselves came to redefine the condition of servitude and how we should read the performances that must now be seen as the key to their own aesthetic ideology. For going by even secondhand accounts of both the enslaved men and women and observers of their daily lives, it is apparent that even within the instrumental culture of the plantation, African slaves were able to create a site of pleasure and leisure at odds with their lived experience; in these sites of play, they could be temporarily liberated "from the prevailing truth of the established order."[46] In fact, while Douglass's reservations about festivals cannot be dismissed offhand, slaves did seem to recognize the power and value of the fair, the marketplace, or the carnival as what Stallybrass and White have called "the epitome of local identity."[47]

At issue here, then, is a process defined by apparent contradictions, one in which two equally compelling cultural logics seem to be at work, against each other or in tandem. There was, on one hand, the recognition that the process of enslavement represented the radical evacuation of the African from the central categories of cultural identity, morality, selfhood, and even the capacity for pleasure. Within this logic, Douglass's distaste for slave performances as just another form of servitude makes perfect sense. Making those deprived of the capacity for pleasure perform happiness would indeed strike us as a cruel form of punishment and a foreclosure of what Douglass called "virtuous liberty."[48] On the other hand, however, performances represented the clearest and most palpable evidence of the emergence of an alternative aesthetic or culture among the slaves. It is not accidental that all the leading studies on slave cultures have focused on performance as the essence of black self-making in the very sites of control that sought to deny them agency.[49] The overriding question, however, is this: How could the slaves turn the nothingness in which they found themselves into the consciousness of their own being? And how do we now read the inscription of being in the structure of negativity?

A useful first step here is to understand the origin of nothingness itself. Jean Paul Sartre, who is my guide on identity as a form of dissociation, notes that there are "an infinite number of realities which are not only objects of judgment, but which are experienced, opposed, feared . . . by the human being and which in their inner structure are inhabited by negation, as their necessary condition."[50] Realities that are defined by negation, what Sartre calls *négatités* (his neologism) are caught between their existence as expressions of "wholly positive realities," which are still defined by negation, and a realm of experience in which "the positivity is only an appearance concealing a hole of nothingness."[51] To the extent that slave performances and other material forms were ways of being in the world, they could be described as positive realities; but since the world that produced these experiences and to which they were a reaction were defined by radical negativity, they could well have been mere appearances, concealing the deep hole of that enslavement.

And there is no doubt that slaves conceived their existential condition as structured by negativity, as depressive of the body and mind as it was exhaustive of being. Equiano presented this structure of nothingness in the form of a question: "Does not slavery itself depress the mind, and extinguish all its fire, and every noble sentiment?"[52] Quobna Ottobah Cugoano conceived his enslavement as a descent from "a state of innocence and freedom" into a world of terror and barbarism, of "oppression and calamities" that seemed excessive of descriptive language.[53] For Mary Prince, slavery was an affliction and terror.[54] And when her infant son fell sick, Harriet Jacobs was torn between her love for her baby and the thought that death was better than slavery. What seemed to hurt her most, Jacobs noted, was the cruel fact that the child would not bear his real father's name, because her master had decreed against it: "It was a sad thought that I had no name to give my child. His father caressed him and treated him kindly, whenever he had a chance to see him. He was not unwilling that he should bear his name; but he had no legal claim to it; and if I had bestowed it upon him, my master would have regarded it as a new crime, of insolence, and would, perhaps, revenge it on the boy. O, the serpent of Slavery has many and poisonous fangs!"[55] For the slave, the breakdown of the body and mind signaled the beginning of the descent to nothingness, a point underscored by Douglass in his retrospective narration of the first six months of his stay with Mr. Covey, where he had been sent to be broken like a horse:

> If at any one time of my life more than another, I was made to drink the bitterest dregs of slavery, that time was during the first six months of my stay with Mr. Covey. We were worked in all weathers. It was never too hot or too cold; it could never rain, blow, hail, or snow, too hard for us to work in the field. Work, work, work, was scarcely more the order of the day than of the night. The longest days were too short for him, and the shortest nights too long for him. I was somewhat unmanageable when I first went there, but a few months of this discipline tamed me. Mr. Covey succeeded in breaking me. I was broken in body, soul, and spirit. My natural elasticity was crushed, my intellect languished, the disposition to read departed, the cheerful spark that lingered about my eye died; the dark night of slavery closed in upon me; and behold a man transformed into a brute![56]

All of these are accounts of the negativity that slaves needed to comprehend and overcome in order to come into being as subjects.

But a question still remains to be addressed: Was the play of sorrow—and performance—in general, a way of apprehending the nothingness of slavery and negating it at the same time? And if so, how does one map out a structure for the enslaved African body in these zones of nonbeing? How does one write of the space of enslavement as both a radical form of debasement, the site of undoing identity, and as a place where new modes of being, new identities were constructed, elaborated, and represented in an altered public sphere?

It is true, of course, that the culture of modernity posited enslavement as the symbolic extremity of refinement. And as I have argued in considerable detail in previous chapters, in order for European high culture to be exalted and elevated to the place it has come to occupy since the early modern period, it needed to debase the black other and to rehearse and display this debasement as the counterpoint to refinement. But focusing on the instrumental nature of debasement alone is not enough, because if we were to reduce slaves to their functions, we would end up espousing the thesis that they were culturally rootless, total victims of a system of domination that did not or could not allow for the Africans' agency.[57] Since this was not the case, the subjective identity of the enslaved must be seen to emerge as a calculated negation of economies of control, especially the symbolic ones.

The power of symbolism in the management of African slaves in the Americas has been well documented. We know, for example, that what might have appeared to be simple instruments for enforcing servitude—the whip, the chain, and the muzzle, for example—were simultaneously valued for their capacity to inflict pain and their symbolic measure. As Orlando Patterson notes in *Slavery and Social Death*, "symbolic instruments" were critical factors in the control of the slave's body: "In much the same way that the literal whips were fashioned from different materials, the symbolic whips of slavery were woven from many areas of culture. Masters all over the world used special rituals of enslavement upon first acquiring slaves: the symbolism of naming, of clothing, of hairstyle, of language, and of body."[58] From William Blake's illustrations for Stedman's *Narrative of a Five Years' Expedition* to the portrait of a whipped slave named Gordon featured prominently in *Harper's Magazine* (July 11, 1863), punishment was most effective when it was made visible.[59]

These images of the mutilated or tortured black body would become popular in the public imagination, as they concealed a more surreptitious and complicated form of control, one that actually sought to destroy the spirit and preserve the body. After all, the slave's valuable asset—his or her labor—depended on the destruction of the spirit and the preservation of the body. And thus, in looking back at the forms of punishment popular in slave culture, and indeed the instruments of torture perfected by the slave-owning class, it is striking to note that control was directed not at the body as a whole but at those parts of it that might provide symbolic resistance. Muzzles, for example, were favored instruments of controlling speech while the chain restricted physical and social mobility. There are, therefore, useful lessons to be learned from a reflection of the invisible, psychological forms of control, including those that deprived the body of its capacity for pleasure and its sensuousness, which would thus lead it to disorientation in both moral and physical space.

Consider, for example, the question of physical space. In *Discipline and Punish*, Michel Foucault has noted that in its ambition to produce docile bodies, "discipline proceeds from the distribution of individuals in space."[60] He has isolated several techniques perfected in the eighteenth century by institutions of power as they sought better ways of producing docile subjects. These techniques, according to Foucault, included the confinement of bodies in enclosures of monotony, the partitioning of spaces to break up "collective dispositions," and the assignment of individuals to spaces limited to particular functions.[61] While all of those means of controlling space are discernible in the transformation of the African from a free person into a slave, Foucault's analysis of space cannot account for the extreme nature of the slave's confinement, because it presupposes a free subject. Indeed, for Foucault, the disciplining project, as he called it, did not set out to destroy the subjectivity of its victims but to produce a different kind of being—a docile subject. In this sense, disciplining would become a project of producing subjects whose docility would make them function better within the institutions of modern culture. If, for example, one were a soldier, the disciplining project did not take away that role; it just made the subject function according to "constraints, prohibitions or obligations" imposed by those in power.[62] In contrast, enslavement was premised on the forced displacement of human subjects from prior functions and identities. Slavery was a form of moral and spatial disorientation.

And in order to understand the significance of this dissociation, we need to recall Charles Taylor's claim that there is an essential link between social identity and orientation: "To know who you are is to be oriented in moral space, a space in which questions arise about what is good or bad, what is worth doing and what not, what has meaning and importance for you and what is trivial and secondary."[63] If one's sense of being depends on spatial orientation, the disordering of space leads to "a radical uncertainty about oneself and about what is of value to one" and to "disorientation and uncertainty about where one stands as a person seems to spill over into a loss of grip on one's stance in physical space."[64]

There are certainly many examples of how the enslavement of the African commenced with a spatial disorientation that, in turn, led to an acute crisis of identity and a sense of moral devaluation. Accounts of people involved in the slave trade as both slavers or enslaved have provided detailed accounts of the slaves' painful transition from the open to the confined space. A vivid and detailed eyewitness account of the slaves' spatial confinement and its attendant crises was provided by Alexander Falconbridge, who served as a surgeon on a slave ship. Falconbridge acutely noted the close relationship between spatial confinement and the act of bondage:

> They are brought from the places where they are purchased to Bonny, &c. in canoes; at the bottom of which they lie, having their hands tied with a kind of willow twigs, and a strict watch is kept over them. Their usage in other respects, during the time of the passage, which generally lasts several days, is equally cruel. Their allowance of food is so scanty, that it is barely sufficient to support nature. They are, besides, much exposed to the violent rains which frequently fall here, being covered only with mats that afford but a slight defense; and as there is usually water at the bottom of the canoes, from their leaking, they are scarcely ever dry.[65]

He then went on to show how, on being brought abroad the slave ship, the bound slaves would be put in positions that distorted the form of the human body:

> [T]hey are frequently stowed so close, as to admit of no other posture than lying on their sides. Neither will the height between the decks, unless directly under the grating, permit them the indulgence of an erect posture; especially where there are platforms, which is generally the case. These platforms are a kind of shelf, about eight or nine feet in breadth, extending from the side of the ship towards the centre. They are placed nearly midway between the decks, at the distance of two or three feet from each deck. Upon these the negroes are stowed in the same manner as they are on the deck underneath.[66]

Former slaves, too, would recall the point of confinement in the hull of the slave ship as emblematic of a frightening disorientation in moral space and a violation of the codes that had hitherto defined their identity. Here is Quobna Ottobah Cugoano's recollection of his confinement in *Thoughts and Sentiments on the Evil of the Slave Trade*:

> [W]hen a vessel arrived to conduct us away to the ship, it was a most horrible scene; there was nothing to be heard but rattling of chains, smacking of whips, and the groans and cries of our fellow-men. Some would not stir from the ground, when they were lashed and beat in the most horrible manner. I have forgotten the name of this infernal fort; but we were taken in the ship that came for us, to another that was ready to sail from Cape Coast. When we were put into the ship, we saw several black merchants coming on board, but we were all drove into our holes, and not suffered to speak to any of them. In this situation we continued several days in sight of our native land;

5.7 "Slaves Packed Below and On Deck." *Illustrated London News* (June 20, 1857), vol. 30, p. 595. Copy in Princeton University Library.

but I could find no good person to give any information of my situation to Accasa at Agimaque. And when we found ourselves at last taken away, death was more preferable than life, and a plan was concerted amongst us, that we might burn and blow up the ship, and to perish all together in the flames; but we were betrayed by one of our own countrywomen, who slept with some of the head men of the ship, for it was common for the dirty filthy sailors to take the African women and lie upon their bodies; but the men were chained and pent up in holes.[67]

Though located at different ends of the slavery continuum, both Falconbridge and Cugoano were testifying to a new relationship between bodies and spaces. As a rule, African slaves, considered nothing more than commodities after they had been sold at coastal markets, would commence their journey into the new world as packed bodies rather than subjects; and crammed to maximize space, these bodies would be supervised by cadres who were oblivious to kinship ties, genealogy, social status, or even the integrity of the human being. As objects of trade, rather than as social beings, the slaves would not be permitted what Falconbridge calls "the indulgence of an erect posture."[68] In this "anomalous intimacy," slaves were not entirely commodities, but their relation to constricted spaces did not denote a phenomenological relation between selves and landscapes (fig. 5.7).[69] The confinement of African slaves in these spaces quickly came to be understood as a form of disembodiment and dismemberment. This point was understood and underscored by abolitionists who used the model of the slave ship—most famously the *Brookes*—as evidence of the degraded physical condition of the slave. Displaying slaves in their physical confinement disturbed the modern imagination, its norms of social space, and its conscience.[70] Thus in Francis Meynell's color drawings of both the above and below deck of the slave ship *Albaroz*, slaves were intermixed with other objects of trade and supplies such as barrels of water and sacks of food (figs. 5.8 and 5.9).

4

The constriction and redefinition of the slaves' physical and social spaces was often followed by other modes of symbolic negation, including stripping a slave's body and denying his or her natal name. Agents in the slave trade understood the significance of the symbolic undressing of the body. To take the clothes off a slave's back, the governor of the Dutch West Indian Company noted in 1705, was to reduce him to cultural tabula rasa: "we send them on Board our ships with the very first opportunity; before which their masters strip them of all they have on their Backs; so that they come Aboard stark-naked as well Women and Men."[71] For the slaves, entering the hold of a ship meant more than the removal of the clothes on their backs; it was tantamount to being stripped away of the vestiges of what they used to be, the style, or mode of self-presentation that had once marked them as members of a community. This state of being culturally undressed struck Mahommah Gardo Baquaqua as a radical gesture of alienation: "We were thrust into the hold of the vessel in a state of nudity, the males being crammed to one side, and the females on the other."[72]

A complex semiotics was evident in this art of undressing, and there is no doubt that stripping a black's body was in itself a paradox of the cultural encounter between Africans and Europeans on the colonial frontier. Consider this: throughout the period of their adventures in Africa in the early modern period and especially in the era of enslavement, European travelers and agents had consistently remarked on the nakedness of the African as a sign of cultural lack, of the state of barbarism that was endemic on the continent. Jean Barbot's description of the natives of what he called "Senegal," first published in 1688, is typical of this view of the African as a naked and uncultured self: "Men and women of the common sort for the most part go about naked, or if they cover themselves, it is only with a pagne (length of cloth) or a scrap of cloth, over the parts modesty requires them to hide. Men have merely a loincloth around the

5.8 Francis Meynell, "Slave deck of the *Albaroz,* 1845." Album of Lt. Meynell's watercolors, National Maritime Museum, London.

waist and some have only a little strip of leather around the loins to which they attach behind and before a strip of cloth which hides what it is not decent to name. This cloth hangs at the rear like the tail of a horse."[73] Significantly, Barbot's account of African nakedness—and the illustrations he provided to go with his narrative—were not original or even accurate. As the editors of the Hakluyt edition of his account note, the descriptions and illustrations had been copied from the accounts of prior travelers, including Pieter de Marees Olfert Dapper and perhaps Alain Manesson Mallet, and "relate not to Senegal, but to the dress of the Gold Coast."[74]

5.9 Francis Meynell, "The Slave Deck of the *Albaroz*, Prize to the *Albatross*, 1845." Album of Lt. Meynell's watercolors (circa 1860), National Maritime Museum.

What was plagiarized often, however, was what was considered central in the differentiation of Africans from other human beings; African nakedness was recycled as evidence of moral and cultural lack. Yet almost all the illustrations of the Africans in seventeenth- and eighteenth-century travel narratives show people dressed—or half dressed—for their environment or occasion. Even the so-called Hottentots of southern Africa, who would later be demonized in nineteenth-century colonial narratives for their nakedness, would appear in most accounts in ceremonial dress or the appropriate apparel for their environment and social world.

Why, then, did the sight of half-dressed Africans seem to have generated deep cultural anxieties among European observers and slave agents? And why did the slave agents, given their revulsion to nakedness, undertake the systematic act of undressing the African as a prelude to enslavement? A compelling response to these questions is provided by Steve Buckridge in his study of the language of dress in colonial Jamaica, where he probes the duality of undressing among the slavers and the enslaved in the negotiation of the landscape of slavery:

> The Africans' clothing reflected identity and relational ties with others within the community. Being stripped, having the naked body exposed, represented for African slaves their painful reality: discontinuity and the enforced severance of cultural and kinship ties. For Europeans, this became a symbolic act of

ridding their captives of their "wildness," of humiliating and enfeebling Africans to gain control. Europeans, who had equated African nudity with backwardness, were now enforcing on Africans the very act they once condemned. This reflected Europeans' ambivalence about the black body—simultaneous fascination and abhorrence.[75]

For the slaves, nakedness was not in itself the source of shame or trauma; what seemed devastating was the act of enforced undressing, which became a part of an elaborate, symbolic undoing of selfhood. What about the enslavers? What did they feel when they undressed their captives? Although this point may not be apparent, dress and undressing had a deep and complex meaning in the world of the slave traders and their moral economies. The majority of the European agents on the West African coast and leading captains on slave ships were often products of the Protestant Reformation. Barbot, who had become involved in the African slave trade as an employee of the French Royal African Company, was a Huguenot, a French Calvinist. On October 1685, the Edict of Nantes, which had been passed in 1598 by Henry IV, guaranteeing French Calvinists rights of citizenship, was revoked, Protestant beliefs were condemned, and Barbot and his family fled to England. It was in his capacity as a Protestant fugitive that Barbot undertook the two voyages (1678–1679 and 1681–1682) that were the basis of his narrative.

More generally, when slave traders and captains like Barbot, Hugh Crow, and John Newton invoked providence in their justifications of the slave trade, they were drawing from an established Protestant tradition. And as children of the Reformation, Protestants in the slave business must have had a keen sense of the meaning and significance of nakedness in the economy of faith and salvation. If they had read John Milton— and there is evidence many of them had—captains of slave ships would have been acquainted with the centrality of what Ann Rosalind Jones and Peter Stallybrass have called the "material mnemonics of livery," an essential aspect of the Renaissance account of Genesis; they would have known that to be naked was to be reduced to the skins of beasts, that to be clothed in livery was to wear what Milton called the "robe of righteousness."[76]

Having associated clothing with the state of culture or civilization, European slavers understood, perhaps more than their African captors, what was at stake in the stripping of the body. They especially understood the cultural capital and symbolic value, which Jones and Stallybrass have identified in their exploration of the politics of dress in early modern culture:

> The "value" of livery, though, cannot be fully calculated in monetary terms. Livery was a form of incorporation, a material mnemonic that inscribed

obligations and indebtedness upon the body. As cloth exchanged hands, it bound people in networks of obligation. In most modern societies, dominated by neutral exchanges of money, the creation of bonds, of debts, and of liberties through the physical medium of clothes appears increasingly strange. We are rarely connected in any personal way to our employers by our wages, any more than we are personally connected to the supermarket through the plastic cards or the pieces of paper and metal with which we trade. In a livery society, though, things take on a life of their own. Payment is made not only in the "neutral" currency of money but also in material which is richly absorbent of symbolic meaning and in which memories and social relations are literally embodied.[77]

It is, of course, possible that when European slavers undressed African slaves and paraded them naked on deck or on arrival at the slave markets of the Americas, they were not pondering the theological meaning of this gesture, its connection to Genesis, or the puritanical reading of it, but it is unlikely that they did not consider the act of undressing the slave in terms of symbolic debasement, just as today's torturers begin their task by reducing their victims to a state of nakedness. What is apparent, however, is that when slaves stepped out of the slave ship, they were often naked, or almost naked, and this nakedness did not represent uncleanliness, or even the absence of righteousness, but cultural lack. Slave traders perceived such acts of undressing as a key precondition for enslavement. Here, the slavers were not simply reducing slaves to a state of beastliness but also depriving them of the capacity for memory and social connection. In short, from their own experiences as early modern subjects, the slave traders understood that clothing was "a form of material memory," one that "incorporated the wearer into a system of obligations."[78] Thus the representations of the slaves' arrival and sale in America captured in images such as William Blake's illustration *Group of Negroes, as imported to be sold for slaves* (fig. 5.10) could call attention to the two profound ironies in the exhibition of the naked body—or half-naked body—in the public square. First, there was the elaborate and colorful dress of the slave agents, which would stand in stark contrast to the nakedness or semi-nakedness of their merchandise. Second, there was the irony of symbolic reversal: the Europeans were parading the Africans in the very states they had condemned as un-Christian and barbaric.

The project of disciplining the African into docility went hand in hand with his or her reduction to a state of pure functionality as a body. A dual process seems to have been at work here: the impoverishment of the meaning of work through the establishment of routines, and the violent marking of the body as an object of ownership. Many slave accounts call attention to what it meant to work according to rules and regulations

5.10 William Blake, *Group of Negroes, as imported to be sold for slaves*. 1796.
From John Gabriel Stedman, *Narrative of a Five Years' Expedition against the
Revolted Negroes of Surinam*. Copy in Princeton University Library.

5.11 *Branding Slaves.* From William O. Blake, *The History of Slavery and the Slave Trade* (Columbus, Ohio, 1857), p. 97.

outside one's set of desires or norms. For example, reflecting on her new regimen the morning after the auction block, Mary Prince noted the connection between work and violence in the following words:

> The next morning my mistress set about instructing me in my tasks. She taught me to do all sorts of household work; to wash and bake, pick cotton and wool, and wash floors, and cook. And she taught me (how can I ever forget it!) more things than these; she caused me to know the exact difference between the smart of the rope, the cart-whip, and the cow-skin, when applied to my naked body by her own cruel hand. And there was scarcely any punishment more dreadful than the blows I received on my face and head from her hard heavy fist. She was a fearful woman, and a savage mistress to her slaves.[79]

As for the marking of the slave as an object of ownership, there is perhaps no better representation of the complex semiotics involved here than the branding of the enslaved (fig. 5.11). Here, in the inaugural site of enslavement, the brand would distinguish slaves from free subjects. Marked with the insignia of their owners, either a company or an individual, the slaves' relation to their labor would be alienated; to a slave, work and task would not be forms of fulfilling desire but modes of objectification. For the enslaved, like the laborers discussed by Marx in the *Economic and Philosophic Manuscripts of 1844*, this objectification would appear as a process of displacement from reality, and alienated labor would manifest itself as estrangement because the more objects the laborer produces, "the less he can possess and the more he falls under the sway of his product, capital."[80]

The final stage in the process of the Africans' objectification—of becoming a stranger to oneself, as it were—was renaming the slaves. For most African slaves this was a significant loss, because in the cultures from which they came, names, perhaps more than livery, represented cultural capital, with the immense capacity to embody memory and link subjects to a set of social and moral obligations that, in turn, signaled the subject's connection to what French anthropologist Pierre Bourdieu once called a habitus—a set of socially acquired dispositions and predispositions.[81] In fact, it should be noted that in most of the African communities that the slaves were coming from—Akan, Mandingo, Yoruba, Congo, and Igbo, just to mention a few—names were the carriers of heavy symbolic meaning, joining individuals to families, communities, and, as in the case of the patronym, to the foundations of a polity. Africans valued names and what they connoted more than their European captors did; for Africans, the name was the core of a subject's basic relationship to a community and history.[82]

We can deduce, for example, that for slaves such as Equiano, the process of imposed naming, renaming, and unnaming signaled the radical disorientation of the slave in moral space: "While I was on board this ship, my captain and master named me Gustavus Vassa. I at that time began to understand him a little, and refused to be called so, and told him as well as I could that I would be called Jacob; but he said I should not, and still called me Gustavus; and when I refused to answer to my new name, which at first I did, it gained me many a cuff; so at length I submitted, and by which I have been known ever since."[83] To be turned into slaves, Africans like Equiano had to give up their spaces of emplacement and try to seek orientation in regulated confinement; they had to be subjected to a process of symbolic stripping that reduced them to raw nature, outside culture, outside moral spaces; and through the process of unnaming, they had to be unhinged from communities of kinship.

What did this string of negations add up to? It is easy to imagine the "middle passage," like the sea in which it was enacted, as a big empty space, a place without monuments, where tribal memories were interred and locked up, a place where those looking for history would only encounter "the men with eyes heavy as anchors / who sank without tombs."[84] Alternatively, the middle passage could be seen as "the passage through death / to life upon these shores."[85] In either case, it is hard to find any value that one can adduce to the slaves' passage of transition from Africa to the Americas except to describe it as a state of non-culture, one only available to us through the negative language of loss and wordlessness. Still, reflections on extremely negative experiences, sites of traumatic transition, do invite important questions: What does the negativity of cultural being, the sense of living without cultural capital, value, or the sense of obligations that come with it, do to the self? When the slaves were reduced to bodies in the purely functional sense described above, what happened to their prior senses, forms of habit, or patterns of behavior? What was the relation between their old signs and the phenomena in front of them? In short, could a sensorium survive the middle passage? Stephanie Smallwood has posed these questions in a slightly different way: "To what extent, if at all, were Africans able to work free of the slave ship, the saltwater, and the agenda of the Atlantic market?"[86]

The semiosis of this transformation, rather than its history or political economy, is my focus here. Slave testimony constantly referred to the sense of bewilderment and shock slaves felt on encountering a world they were not prepared to comprehend or even place in perspective, a world in which signs and signifiers seemed out of joint. In Virginia, Equiano would recall his first encounter with objects and activities that, though banal and quotidian aspects of his master's modern life, struck fear and terror in him because they caused sensual disorientation. Equiano felt adrift in the new world, bereft of the deep experiences for which he had a descriptive vocabulary or cultural grammar, struggling to produce meanings for the new and to endow it with significance. Here, in the American slave plantation, Equiano found that the integers of time, emotion, and everydayness that had made him an African were of no value; indeed, a prior language for describing cultural experience often impeded Equiano's capacity to develop a grammar of modern identity:

> While I was in this plantation, the gentleman, to whom I supposed the estate belonged, being unwell, I was one day sent for to his dwelling house to fan him: when I came into the room where he was, I was very much affrighted at some things I saw, and the more so as I had seen a black woman slave as I came through the house, who was cooking the dinner, and the poor creature was cruelly loaded with various kinds of iron machines; she had one particularly on her head, which locked her mouth so fast that she could scarcely speak; and could not eat nor drink. I was much astonished and shocked at this contrivance, which I afterwards learned was called the iron muzzle. Soon after I had a fan put into my hand, to fan the gentleman while he slept; and so I did indeed with great fear. While he was fast asleep I indulged myself a great deal in looking about the room, which to me appeared very fine and curious. The first object that engaged my attention was a watch which hung on the chimney, and was going. I was quite surprised at the noise it made, and was afraid it would tell the gentleman any thing I might do amiss: and when I immediately after observed a picture hanging in the room, which appeared constantly to look at me, I was still more affrighted, having never seen such things as these before. At one time I thought it was something relative to magic; and not seeing it move, I thought it might be some way the whites had to keep their great

men when they died, and offer them libations as we used to do our friendly spirits. In this state of anxiety I remained till my master awoke, when I was dismissed out of the room, to my no small satisfaction and relief, for I thought that these people were all made of wonders.[87]

In the eyes of the slave masters, the objects that had frightened Equiano, including the dreadful muzzle, were easily explicable and functional. But the slave found it difficult to find descriptive terms for these previously unknown things, and unable to adduce some deep meaning to instruments of dehumanization, or even to provide a linguistic accounting for the strange and mechanical, the slave was marooned in cultural space.

In this particular instance, Equiano's description of the watch and its assumed function could only serve to call attention to the dissonance between the thing and its meaning, the sign and the signifier. Nothing in the slave's earlier life could help him make this new world intelligible; he could neither invoke his Igbo past nor the Englishness that he would later aspire to in order to make sense of the geography of enslavement. In effect, when it came to the production of meaning, an essential condition of being a subject, Equiano was living in a state of cultural limbo. He was in a world where the relation between words and things was one of incommensurability, the result of which was a negative hermeneutics. To put it another way, the slave could only articulate the meaning of things by expressing what he could not know or understand, what appeared to be at odds with his own apparatus of understanding. This negative hermeneutics was, however, not simply a case of linguistic inadequacy; rather, it was informed by several factors that go directly to the role of melancholy in the structuring of identity and cultural experience. In the scene represented above, for example, Equiano was lost for words, not emotions.

And yet the slave was keen to make sense of his new world, because the expression of feelings without thoughts seemed to him inadequate. For example, Equiano knew, almost intuitively, that the things that didn't make sense to him played an important role in the culture of enslavement. He sensed, for example, that the iron muzzle was a powerful insignia of the disciplinary project of enslavement; that the watch symbolized the temporality of modernity itself; that the iron pots were instruments of daily living. So in order to have bearing in this world, Equiano desperately needed to be able to make sense of the objects that defined it yet eluded his African vocabulary. But when he was unable to produce meanings, to make sense of things with mere words, Equiano turned to the weapon of affect, keenly telling his readers how he felt—"exceedingly miserable and lonely."

It is this link between the loss of words and the buildup of emotion that I find intriguing. Why is it that Equiano, finding himself with no way of apprehending the world of slavery through what linguistics calls pragmatics (a context for creating and shaping meaning), could only make sense of the objects and experiences he was encountering by expressing his emotional response to them? The answer to this question has already been denoted at the beginning of this chapter: it was melancholia, the emotion of loss and desire, that most effectively provided a language for expressing moral disorientation. And so long as the slave could express powerful emotions in response to his or her condition of bondage, it would appear that the middle passage had not numbed the senses and sensations of the slave.

5

But this last claim—that the middle passage did not rob the slave of the power of the senses—leads to another puzzle: If slaves reacted to their condition of enslavement in such powerful and often melancholic gestures, including suicide, why were they often considered by observers to be subjects without sense and sensibility in the terms defined by the culture of taste discussed in earlier chapters? Why were they only associated with a negative sensorium, a ratio of senses that could not be construed to be a source of identity?[88] This question cannot be answered by a simple archeology of the slaves' emotions or their affective response to enslavement. On the contrary, in order to understand the exile of slaves from the order of the senses, we must shift focus from the experiences of the Africans themselves to the moral and symbolic economies of their masters. After all, one of the operative premises in this book is that narratives that separate the worlds—and words—of slaves and masters miss their informative and sometimes fatal intersection.

The senses occupied an important place in the domain of the masters. In fact, the order of the senses (and the discourses that surrounded them) was not a neutral term in the eighteenth century; rather, sensuousness was a category with a particular value in the self-understanding of modern European culture. For many European writers and intellectuals in the culture of taste, the period in which African slaves found themselves transformed into bodies in bondage, *sentiment* and *sensibility* were key cultural terms.[89] Initially developed as technical terms in medicine, philosophy, and psychology, by the middle of the eighteenth century *sentiment* and *sensibility* had come to be used "to describe the expression of heightened intense human feeling, of a new sort of refinement" and a sign of a sense of inwardness, of a selfhood whose standing was, unlike in the case of politeness, dependent on one's relation to others.[90] Thus if one is looking for a term that bridges the well-known divide between continental European philosophy and British ideas of the aesthetic, it is *sensuousness*—the singular investment in the senses as a mode of understanding human experience—as what one critic has called "the analogon to reason."[91]

When Alexander Baumgarten coined the term *aesthetic* in 1735, his goal was to show that sensuality was not inferior to reason. In this context, Baumgarten's ambition was to develop a new "science of sensual recognition" to complement "the rationalist focus of analysis on the 'higher' or 'rational' forms of recognition." The ambition of Baumgarten's aesthetic project was to show "that sensuality, in some contexts and for some objects, provides an adequate 'representation' of reality the same way reason does for rationalist philosophy." He then goes on to show how the aesthetic, as sensuous cognition, underwent a radical transformation, one that turned it into an alternative to rationality: "Sensual cognition—this is the basic insight of Baumgarten's new discipline of aesthetics—could not be shown to possess right or significance equal to rational cognition by analyzing it according to the model rationalist philosophy had developed. The goal of aesthetics—the enlargement of the realm of legitimate cognition, including sensual forms—required an epistemological break with the very understanding of legitimate cognition as such."[92]

Within the Scottish Enlightenment, the senses were associated with innate moral values or virtues that were essential to the maintenance of a modern self. In his *Inquiry into the Original of Our Ideas of Beauty and Virtue*, Francis Hutcheson argued that there was an implicit connection between pleasant ideas and sound; subjects with a good ear were able, through their superior perception of sound, to derive pleasure from ideas. Now the order of the senses was the key to understanding modern identity:

> It is of no consequence whether we call these ideas of beauty and harmony perceptions of the external senses of seeing and hearing, or not. I should rather choose to call our power of perceiving these ideas, internal sense, were it only for the convenience of distinguishing the from other sensations of seeing and hearing, which men may have with out perception of beauty and harmony. It is plain from experience, many men have in the common meaning, the senses of seeing, and hearing perfect enough; they perceive all the simple ideas separately, and have their pleasures; they distinguish them from each other, such as one color from another, either quite different, or the stronger or fainter of the same color, when they are placed beside each other, although they may often confound their names, when they occur apart from each other; as some do the names of green and blue: they can tell in separate notes, the higher, lower, sharper or flatter, when separately sounded; in figures they discern the length, breadth, wideness of each line, surface angle; and may be as capable of

hearing and seeing at great distances as any men whatsoever; and yet perhaps they shall find no pleasure in musical compositions, in painting, architecture, natural landscape; or but a very weak one in comparison of what others enjoy from the same objects. This greater capacity of receiving such pleasant ideas we commonly call a fine genius or taste: in music we seem universally to acknowledge something like a distinct sense from the external one of hearing, and call it a good ear; and the like distinction we should probably acknowledge in other objects, had we also got distinct names to denote these powers of perception by.[93]

Here, Hutcheson assembled a whole economy of the senses—taste, feelings, color, and pleasure—and turned this sensorium into the key for a modern identity and universal truth claims.

There is one more thing to be added to this repertoire of senses and sensations before the negative sensorium of blackness can be measured against it, and that is the representational value of labor and its connection to the moral order. In their attempt to establish a link between political economy and moral value, some of the most influential theorists of the eighteenth century, most notably Adam Smith, appropriated the aesthetic as the category that mediated economics and morality. For Smith, an aesthetic sensibility was "often the secret motive of the most serious and important pursuits of both private and public life."[94] But Smith's most important contribution to modern philosophy was perhaps his introduction, into debates on political economy, of the concept of labor as what Foucault has called "a domain of reflection not previously aware of it."[95] Smith's achievement, argues Foucault, was to relate the notion of wealth to that of labor, making it the "means of analysing exchangeable wealth" and a "functioning representation element," even a pleasurable pursuit. By locating work in the "interior time of an organic structure which grows in accordance with its own necessity and develops in accordance with autochthonous laws—the time of capital and production," the Scottish moral philosopher had made a breakthrough in the valuation of what might previously have been considered simple taste.[96]

Smith's breakthrough theory of labor arose from two critical shifts that he made in *The Wealth of Nations*. First, he understood that the annual labor of a nation was the aggregate total of "all the necessaries and conveniences of life which it annually consumes, and which consist always, either in the immediate produce of that labour, or in what is purchased with that produce from other nations."[97] Second, Smith was able to connect the value of labor to that of need and exchange: "The value of any commodity, therefore, to the person who possesses it and who means not to use or consume it himself, but to exchange it for other commodities, is equal to the quantity of labour which it enables him to purchase or command."[98] For Smith, then, a labor theory of value represented an advancement of sociability. Labor could not be valued solely on the basis of its utilitarianism; its value also needed to take into account the larger social and communal goals that enabled sociability. Connected to sentiments and actions that could be conceived or imagined to reflect the wisdom of God, work would become virtuous, a manifestation, to borrow Charles Taylor's words, of a providential design; here, the "self-regulating system of production and exchange is a prime manifestation of the interlocking providential order of nature; it binds the productive, that is, those who follow the designated human vocation, into a mutually sustaining harmony."[99]

Now, if one keeps in mind the tripartite connection between a productive subject, a designated human vocation, and the desire for mutual social harmony, one can clearly understand the necessity and paradox of the slave's exclusion from the modern sensorium in the same way he had been excluded from the order of reason and the culture of taste. The necessity for exclusion was that one could not assign a set of affirmative attributes such as reason or taste to a group of people—African slaves, for example—and continue claiming that slavery was their natural condition. The paradox arises out of the slaves' primary identity as subjects of labor, for here modern culture had to confront the fact that slaves worked, yet most derived no pleasure from their work; that they contributed immensely to the wealth of the nation, yet their labor worked against their self-interest since it led to the breakup of their families, alienation of their communities, and the truncation of their history.

In order to understand this exclusion in more specific terms, one needs to recall the fact that in all of its manifestations, as it emerged and was recycled in the eighteenth century and after, the aesthetic ideology presupposed a subject, a human being with the capacity to reflect, to say I.[100] The subject who emerged in the eighteenth century—or rather the ways of talking about the subject that emerged in this period—was one who was capable of reflecting on his or her condition of existence, one who was able to ground phenomena to "an underlying activity" and, in turn, to explain its relation to that world. In this context, the act of reflection would function as "the free act of an I and its acts."[101] The subject of modernity was a subject who could act freely. All debates on aesthetic theory seem to be agreed on this point.[102] However, if subjectivity was premised on the capacity for individual autonomy and self-reflection—the ability to say I—then the slave, defined as socially dead or as chattel, would have no such status in theory or discourse. And by extension or implication, the African, whether free or enslaved, could not have the capacity for sense and sensibility that was a precondition for understanding. "The Negroes of Africa have by nature no feeling that rises above the trifling,"

Kant asserted in a passage from *The Feeling of the Beautiful and Sublime*, because they were beholden to the religion of fetishism, which, by its very nature, precluded self-consciousness or reflection.[103] And it was precisely this ostensible incapacity for autonomous judgment that locked African slaves in the negative dialectic of modernity. Defined as nonsubjects in European discourses on art, culture, and taste, African slaves were not capable of reflection, and because they were incapable of reflection they fell short of subjecthood. This insidious dialectic would continue to drive pro-slavery ideologies and, more devastatingly, the logic of the laws that regulated slavery.

Two famous cases support this contention. In a landmark, though not well known, decision issued in the North Carolina Circuit Court in 1829, Judge Thomas Ruffin ruled that the intentional injuring of a slave was not a crime, because the enslaved, as property, existed outside the domain of subjecthood and by implication the realm of feelings:

> With slavery . . . the end is the profit of the master, his security and the public safety; the subject, one doomed in his own person, and his posterity, to live without knowledge, and without the capacity to make anything his own, and to toil that another may reap his fruits. What moral considerations such as a father might give to a son shall be addressed to such a being, to convince him what it is impossible but that the most stupid must feel and know can never be true—that he is thus to labour upon a principle of natural duty, or for the sake of his own personal happiness. Such services can only be expected from one who has no will of his own; who surrenders his will in implicit obedience in the consequence only of uncontrolled authority over the body. There is nothing else which can operate to produce the effect. The power of the master must be absolute, to render the submission of the slave perfect.[104]

"The power of the master must be absolute, to render the submission of the slave perfect"—that phrase alone sums up the doctrine of power in the culture of slavery.

And Ruffin's was not the last word on the legality and necessity of subordination and thus the foreclosure of the slaves from the domain of freedom. The presupposition that slaves had no rights, that as far as the law was concerned they were already nonsubjects, would find its most famous resonance in the Dred Scott decision of 1857. In a landmark ruling that was to dominate American law concerning freedom and the Bill of Rights for almost a century, the chief justice of the United States, Robert B. Taney, declared that the black "had no rights which the white man was bound to respect":

> They had for more than a century before been regarded as beings of an inferior order, and altogether unfit to associate with the white race, either in social

or political relations; and so far inferior, that they had no rights which the white man was bound to respect; and that the negro might justly and lawfully be reduced to slavery for his benefit. He was bought and sold, and treated as an ordinary article of merchandise and traffic, whenever a profit could be made by it. This opinion was at that time fixed and universal in the civilized portion of the white race. It was regarded as an axiom in morals as well as in politics, which no one thought of disputing, or supposed to be open to dispute; and men in every grade and position in society daily and habitually acted upon it in their private pursuits, as well as in matters of public concern, without doubting for a moment the correctness of this opinion.[105]

Beneath this inflammatory rhetoric, however, was a mode of reasoning that reflected a masterful understanding of the terms of the exclusion of the black subject—what Taney called "the unfortunate race"—from the domain of the human. He understood that race, rather than the mere act of enslavement, was the basis of the blacks' exclusion from the realm of law, freedom, and rights.

6

What counterclaims could black slaves make against the power of the law that already presupposed their exclusion from its purview? What philosophical and juridical categories could they deploy to counter what Orlando Patterson has aptly described as their "secular excommunication"?[106] Throughout the nineteenth century, there was a sustained aesthetic and conceptual attempt by blacks in colonial Africa and the Americas to emerge out of the confinement of the law and the ideology of the aesthetic that associated Africans and people of African descent with ugliness. Unfortunately, the invocation of black rights under the law and the domain of taste would dissolve when confronted by the power of a negative sensorium that the institutions of racial categorization had developed to explain African difference. For when it came to matters of sentiment, or sense and sensibility, the general tendency among the custodians of European Africanism was not to focus on black lack, as had been the case in debates about reason and rationality, but to consign the African to a sensory order mired in dirt, mud, odor, and simple bad taste. Not surprisingly, the association of blackness with uncleanliness—and, by implication, moral disorder—would come from not only those who had a specific interest in maligning the enslaved African in order to sustain the profits made in sugar cane, cotton, or rice fields, but also those engaged in the intellectual project of taste as supposedly an autonomous domain of modern identity.

Belonging solidly in the first category was Edward Long, the historian and apologist of the West Indian planter class, who insisted that the "rancid exhalation" of the blacks was innate, a sign of their bestial nature. For Long, the "bestial or fetid smell" of the African was a sign of stupidity; he was not in doubt that "the most stupid of the Negroe race, are the most offensive."[107] As if this were not enough, Long went on to support his theory of innate black uncleanliness and stupidity by retelling the story of a Jamaican slave who had tried to observe the rules of hygiene to no avail, her desire for absolution constantly defeated by the olfactory order of blackness. In an attempt to get rid of her odor, the slave in question, a household maid, had washed her body twice a day and observed strict diet rules to no avail. Long dismissed such efforts at cleanliness as futile challenges against the order of blackness, comparing them to the proverbial attempt to "wash the Black-a-moor white." All the black maid's efforts at cleanliness, Long noted gleefully, had come to no purpose, and "her mistress found there was no remedy but to change her for another attendant, somewhat less odoriferous."[108]

Debates about black smell, however, went beyond the planters' desire to malign the slave in order to rationalize the order of enslavement. The general association of blacks with an offensive sensory order, what Mark Smith has called an "olfactory ontology," was, together with theories about color, an important instrument in the arsenal of philosophers of taste. Lord Kames, the distinguished Scottish philosopher, argued, "The black color of the Negroes, thick lips, flat nose, crisped woolly hair, and rank smell, distinguish them from every other race of men."[109] And when Oliver Goldsmith argued that black skin had "strength of which gives a roughness to the feel," his mind was most probably focused on the color of whiteness, the fair complexion, which, he asserted, was "the most beautiful to the eye" and "a transparent covering to the soul."[110] Similarly, ideals of honor, considered by Bertram Wyatt-Brown, among others, to be the key to white identity in the antebellum South, "existed in intimate relation to its opposite: shame";"the fears and projections of ignominy" could not be understood apart from "the usages of honor."[111] And crucially, the fear of shame and ignominy was projected onto the black slave, who became, as it were, the *Pharmakon*, the scapegoat who would function as both the remedy and poison of white slave culture.[112] Now the desire for honor as a subscription to communal standards of judgment and the necessity of a ritual scapegoat onto which notions of shame would be ascribed was the fulcrum around which the moral economy of slaveholding cultures revolved. To quote Wyatt-Brown, "In slaveholding cultures, the contrast between the free and the unfree—the autonomy of one, the abjectness of the other—prompts an awareness of moral, as well as political and social stratification. Not all honor societies were slaveholding. Yet no slaveholding culture could casually set aside the strictures of honor. The very de-basement of the slave added much to the master's honor, since the latter's claim to self-sufficiency rested upon the prestige, power, and wealth that accrued from the benefits of controlling others."[113] The slave was thus locked in a distorted sensorium, and black difference, whether embodied in color or smell, and the deep and continuous desire to provide scientific or philosophical explanations of it were attempts to secure white identity in the drama of what anthropologist Mary Douglas has termed ritual cleanliness.[114]

But how did slaves themselves confront this negative sensorium and its associated technologies of exclusion? How did they overcome their confinement to the order of dirt and scum to affirm their being in the public arena? Indeed, what do scholars mean when they say that African slaves crossing the Atlantic brought with them what Rex Nettleford, the Jamaican cultural scholar, has called "cultural equipage"?[115] Two of the most important visual representations to come out of the world of African slavery—*Slave Play in Suriname*, a 1707 painting by the Dutch artist Dirk van Valkenburg (fig. 5.12), and *The Old Plantation*, a late eighteenth-century work by an anonymous artist from South Carolina (fig. 5.13)—provide fascinating clues to the meaning of the terms *culture* and *equipage*. They are also indices of the changing form of slave work and play as counterpoints to the negative sensorium that enhanced white moral order in the culture of slavery.

Van Valkenburg's painting is considered to be one of the earliest representations of the role of performance in the reconstruction of African subjects and communities in the Americas. The painting contains several elements that suggest an aesthetic culture among the enslaved was closely connected to the task of community building: For one, there is the simple conception of the scene of play as the gathering of a community, one that was self-conscious of both its horizontal and vertical relationships.[116] Here, all the important ingredients of a vibrant community—from everyday objects of play, such as drums, pets, and gourds, to couples and children in active relationships—are inscribed in what would appear to be their ordinariness.

It is perhaps the case that Van Valkenburg, like most European painters of his generation, was probably more interested in the black body for its visual effect rather than its social presence. This explains his use of color to contrast the well-oiled bodies of the Africans with their simple white, blue, and red garments. However, what is most compelling about his picture is its presentation of the site of play as one of autonomy and self-assertion. In *Slave Play*, then, there are no signs of slave masters or the infrastructure of enslavement; on the contrary, what is being displayed and thus re-created are song and dance as activities that were

5.12 Dirk van Valken-burg, *Slave Play in Suriname.*" 1707. Oil on canvas.

5.13 Anonymous, *The Old Plantation, South Carolina.* Circa 1790.

transcendental of the slave economy of colonial Suriname. This sense of autonomy is evident in the relation of parts to the whole: everything seems to be part of a larger pattern of communal life, one that moves to its own rhyme and rhythm, oblivious to the larger structure of control, which has been excluded from the picture. The picture represents the presence of the circle of Africanist cultures that has been observed across the geography of slavery.[117]

A second facet in the representation of the Africans in Van Valkenburg's work is that it contains no docile bodies; rather, what is highlighted is the movement of peoples who have breadth and depth and a sense of inwardness that seems to go against the record of cultural deracination discussed in the earlier sections of this chapter. These are not the naked bodies of the middle passage or Long's odiferous slaves. This is not a portrait of cultural lack. In fact, several aspects of the painting seem deliberately intended to emphasize the deeply symbolic cultural presence of Africa in the plantation. There is, for example, the portrait of two sparring men (in the front of the hut door) engaged in what Robert Farris Thompson has identified as "a game of footwork that derives from the Kongo *nsunsa* dance."[118] Then there is the portrait of a kissing couple to the right of the picture, a rare erotic moment in the iconography of slavery, and surely the sign of another kind of sensuousness at odds with the toxicology described by Long.

Finally, there is a subtle signal of cultural connection in the painting. This is the white flag flying over the hut, which Thompson has read as a shrine, understood as a ritual mark of belonging, an altar, a place of primal identification. If we consider the altar to be the centerpiece of the picture, then what we see in Van Valkenburg's painting are the key ingredients of a community that, in spite of its harrowing passage across the Atlantic, has retained or recaptured its moral orientation enough to recall and rehearse African cultural forms in their most intimate details, sustain an autonomous community, engage in sensuous relationships, and establish ritual markers of kinship and ancestry. In short, the slaves observed by Van Valkenburg in Suriname at the beginning of the eighteenth century display an African cultural equipage that would become important in the making of an alternative imagined community of the African in America in a diachronic process of remembering and forgetting.[119]

The second painting, *The Old Plantation*, represents a slave dance in South Carolina at the end of the eighteenth century and is considered one of the earliest representations of Yoruba culture in North America. It, too, represents a scene in which the performance of an African dance has become an alibi for the gathering of community. But while many discussions of this picture have revolved around the sources and meaning of its African-derived objects, something important had changed in this rehearsal of Africanness.[120] Here, the landscape and setting is not wholly autonomous; on the contrary, the dance takes place against the background of the plantation, represented by the fields and the slave cabins. We are no longer in the landscape of an imagined Africa with thatched huts, altar flags, *nsunsa* dances, and, by implication, cultural distinctiveness; rather, the slave cottages in the painting are similar to many others in the antebellum South. So if Van Valkenburg's picture represents a culture trying to replicate its old world in a new setting, *The Old Plantation* is a visual record of an emerging Creole culture.[121] One painting captures a community, the Djuka of Suriname, rehearsing the African cultures they will later make the basis of their maroonage from Dutch control; the other represents another community in the American South performing a hybrid dance as a signal of their own peculiar relationship to the plantation.

How do we explain these transformations? Perhaps we can account for the distinctive styles of these two paintings in terms of time. The community observed and represented by Van Valkenburg in 1707 could remember Africa in a phenomenological sense and replay its rituals from memory. In contrast, for slaves in the low country of South Carolina (the subjects of *The Old Plantation*) at the end of the same century, Africa could not be retrieved from memory; it could only be imagined as a set of fragments that, significantly, needed to be patched together to have meaning. Is the dance represented in the picture a Mende Shegura, a West Indian Hipsaw, or a Yoruba Juba? Are the musical instruments Yoruba or Hausa? Are the headdresses African or American? Attempts to read *The Old Plantation* as the performance of an African dance, whether Yoruba or Mende, are bound to be incomplete, because the subject of the painting, and the culture it claims to represent, is cultural hybridity itself.

I want to conclude this chapter, however, by arguing that the two paintings represent diverse responses to the trauma of enslavement and the work of reconstructing community in its aftermath; thus they mark the first step in developing a response to the acts of de-arting and de-aesthetization associated with enslavement. In Van Valkenburg's painting, Africa and its Africanisms are recalled through memory and elevated to high symbolism. In symbolism, as Walter Benjamin noted, destruction "is idealized and the transfigured face of nature is fleetingly revealed in the light of redemption."[122]

Although we cannot tell whether Van Valkenburg was accurately representing what he saw in front of him as he traveled in the Dombi plantation, or whether he was projecting his own vision on his subjects, evidence seems to suggest that the community he was observing in Suriname was engaged in an elaborate reconstruction of Africa through symbol and ritual.[123] Here and elsewhere, remembering Africa was an important part of the slaves' moral orientation. But the work of memory is often fickle, and it was hard for Africans in enslavement to sustain the task of remembrance over time; it is in this context that works such as *The Old Plantation*, which seem to proffer impoverished and messy versions of Africa, become important. As I argue in the next chapter, this messier, sometimes truncated, often phantasmal, and always performed African imaginary, one at odds with the culture of taste itself, would provide the allegories through which the slave confronted the ugly face of history.

The Ontology of Play:
Mimicry and the Counterculture of Taste

Sometime between 1730 and 1745, an African drum was collected
in Virginia by a certain Reverend Clarke on behalf of Sir Hans Sloane,
distinguished English naturalist and founder of the British Museum (fig.
6.1). The drum, now at the British Museum, is a remarkable piece of
work, one whose meaning is suspended somewhere between the aura of
art and ritual. Constructed in the Akan style, and made of wood (Cordia
and Baphia) native to Africa, deerskin, and vegetable fiber, it is considered
to be one of the earliest known surviving examples of African objects in
North America.[1] If the drum was made in Africa, as the physical evidence
suggests, then it would appear to counter the argument that no art, no
history, no memories survived the middle passage of enslavement. But
the drum also raises an issue that is more complicated than the idiom of
cultural survival might suggest: who brought it to Virginia, and what was
its use or value?

It is highly unlikely that slaves themselves loaded the object on board
the slave ship as a mnemonic of the world they had left behind, for, as
mentioned earlier, the first and most decisive step in the process of enslavement was stripping the body of all its accoutrements and returning it
to a state of cultural nakedness. More likely, the drum was brought to the
Americas by the captain of a slave ship or one of the sailors on board. If
this is the case, it is hard to tell what worth the object had in the owner's
mind: Did it attract in itself, as a work of art, one valuable enough to be
dissociated from the people who had constructed it, who were now considered nonsubjects? Or was the drum a mere curiosity piece, something
to be added to the ever-expanding cabinet of curios? And what would
slaves in Virginia, confronting this object and perhaps trying to replicate
it, consider its use value to be—a figure of memory, its loss, or both?

6.1 Akan-style drum, African, eighteenth century AD, from Virginia.

The best way of responding to these questions is to see this African drum, very much like the paintings of two African dances discussed at the end of the previous chapter, as what Walter Benjamin would refer to as the allegory of ruins. For like other remnants of African culture in the Americas, the drum was a mere fragment of a lost culture, a figure that had survived the human equivalent of what Benjamin calls "the most elemental forces of destruction, lightning and earthquakes."[2] Within the context of slavery, what had survived destruction could not be recuperated as a figure of beauty nor as an impeccable showpiece of a lost antiquity; rather, it was just one of the many entangled pieces out of which a new Creole culture could be constructed. As an assemblage of fragments, a creolized culture could only emerge as part of what the Caribbean scholar Édouard Glissant has called a "Forced Poetics"—a mode of expression that occurs "whenever a drive for expression confronts something impossible to express."[3] The notion of a forced poetics does not, of course, imply that Creole cultures were enforced by the masters as part of the business of managing slaves; on the contrary, argues Glissant, a creolized culture was "the original creation by the uprooted African, who, faced with the limited linguistic implements imposed on him, chose to limit it further, to warp it, to untune it, in order to make it an idiom of his own."[4]

Under this postulation, two elements are central to the emergence of a slave-driven aesthetic in the new world. First, for the subjects stripped of native cultures and ruptured from former systems of pleasure and sensuousness, the work of art was predicated on the undoing, warping, and unraveling, even inverting, of the imposed idiom. Second, within the plantation system, the project of pleasure and sensuousness was underwritten by an awareness of the continuous opposition between the idiom that was forced on the slaves and the language that they needed in order to express their selfhood outside the grammar of bondage discussed in the previous chapters. Conscious of the incommensurability of the enforced means of expression and their desires, slaves were forced to develop a counter-poetics. This counter-poetics was, in turn, informed both by its self-awareness of the alienation that had engendered it in the first place and by the slaves' desire to fashion a language that might express their personhood outside the authorized idiom, be it the law or the rule of taste. Aware that their new cultures could not be authorized by a native language, culture, or genealogy, slaves were compelled to turn their "familiar foreignness" into a work of art.[5] But the task of turning slavery into a speakable event, a *representam,* as it were, faced a double challenge: how to recognize the impossibility of belonging to a place yet claim one's presence in it; of how to strive and yearn for emplacement yet live in a world in which rights and ideals were constantly thwarted. This would create what W.E.B. Du Bois would later call "the peculiar ethical paradox" of African American life.[6]

Within the reigning ideologies of culture, slaves were systematically excluded from the realm of beauty and taste; their relationship to objects that would be considered beautiful was hence tenuous; and given the regimen of labor and control, their notions of pleasure were radically different from those of their masters. This does not mean that works of art could not be sources of pleasure in the context of enslavement; the problem was that where subjects were not free, or even allowed the capacity for self-reflection because they were considered to be property, the idea and practice of pleasure would require a different form and meaning. In fact, my contention in this chapter is that slaves would come to value works of art as ruins and fragments—broken bowls, jars and quilts, and half-remembered African dances—because only the fragmentary and incomplete had the capacity to denote the doubleness that was the mark of African identities in the new world, the sign of a presence and absence both in time and space.

Slaves were located in spaces they did not desire, and they often yearned for a lost world, yet it was the presentness of the plantation system that commanded daily attention. In the circumstances, the works of culture that emerged in slave cultures tended to be caught between the need to denote an Africa that existed only in the imagination or dim memories, and the regimen of the plantation and its powerful and often brutal demands—the persistence of American everydayness. This division or duality was to become the signature of new-world blackness, what W.E.B. Du Bois famously called "double-consciousness."[7] The peculiar sensation of doubleness, Du Bois noted, arose from the condition of living in "two-ness," of being "an American, a Negro; two souls, two thoughts, two unreconciled strivings; two ideals in one dark body."[8]

Ironically, it was through its incommensurability with the world it inhabited that the slaves' aesthetic could be connected to a channel of life that existed outside enslavement. For slaves, culture itself had to start as a ruin, a fragment that represented both connection and disconnection from Africa. Out of the ruins of Africanism, slaves could have a vision of their location and dislocation in both the new and old worlds. Bodies could be broken, memories could be deracinated, but thoughts, or fragments of thoughts, could be used to summon new identities or to ward off the pains of living under the whip. Against the bitter dregs of slavery, the enslaved would turn to sound (the shout) as the building block of what was denied them: selfhood, community, and family.

One of the earlier memories of Frederick Douglass, who was often averse to slave revelry, was that of slaves marching to the great house for their monthly allowance, their "wild songs" reverberating in the dense woods "revealing at once the highest joy and the deepest sadness."[9] Douglass went on to observe how these songs used sound—not words—to sustain what we now call a hermeneutics of suspicion by contrasting the surface reality of the plantation with the deep wounds in the souls of the slaves.[10] For the slaves, a questioning of the order of the plantation was achieved through what amounted to a chiasmus of passion: "They would sometimes sing the most pathetic sentiment in the most rapturous tone, and the most rapturous sentiment in the most pathetic tone."[11] Douglass noted how these sorrow songs led him to understand what enslavement meant by affect; through the "affliction" of feelings that they triggered, these songs to spoke to him and others. But these feelings also secured a measure of reflection, providing the "first glimmering conception of the dehumanizing character of slavery."[12] And at the end of *The Souls of Black Folks*, trying to ward off the despair that had overcome Alexander Crummell, his hero, Du Bois would turn to the spirituals, the sorrow songs, as "the articulate message of the slave to the world," expressions of what had eluded rationality and a disorganized sociology; they were the conduit to the unspoken, telling "of death and suffering and unvoiced longing toward a truer world, of misty wanderings and hidden ways."[13] However, Du Bois wanted more than mere emotions from these songs: he needed them to stand in for a past, an Africanism outside the instrumentality of racial bondage. So he turned to the fragment of an African song sung by his great-grandmother, Violet, and posited it as the string of lineage. The song would be passed from generation to generation, its words unknown, but the meaning of its music intuitively comprehended.[14]

This turn to sound as a mode of meaning raises intriguing questions: Could negative or affective understanding provide the scaffold for community building? And if so, how could a tenuous Africanism be turned into the basis of a new set of structures and identities? Among the Akan, the drum that opened my discussion was deeply connected to profound rituals and meanings, tied up with the work of imagining and building communities, and to the individual's deep sense of belonging. Drums, like other regal works of art, were part of a whole complexity of ideas and ideals, the elaboration of cosmologies and genealogies, of associative relationships rather than structures of alienation. In the Americas, however, this same drum, like Violet's song, was a reminder of what had been or what could have been; it was condemned to exist at once as an insignia of identity and alienation, part of a redemptive hermeneutics and also a mark of the crisis of meaning for the black as a modern subject.[15] How, then, could one be a self in a place of enforced nonbeing, a state where all the integers of selfhood, including time and space, were owned by another? How could the self be a self in a place of radical alienation? And could a site of pleasure be hallowed in the midst of pain and suffering? These questions lie at the heart of the aesthetic that sought to imagine the unspeakable experience of slavery. And in order to understand what it meant to construct a sensorium in the space of death, we need to reflect on how slaves sought to undo the idiom of taste described in the beginning of this book and how, in this undoing, they developed alternative modes of expressiveness.

At the end of the last chapter I argued that by the end of the eighteenth century, African slaves in the Americas had started to construct a new kind of aesthetic in response to their condition of enslavement. They had established modes of ritual and forms of performance that would reorient them in the new world and locate them in a both moral and public space, and modes of pleasure that would counter their representation as mere chattel. I argued that when slaves in the Dombi plantation in Suriname or in the South Carolina rice country rehearsed elaborate Kongo dances or danced the Juba, they were staking a moral claim to the public sphere. But I left two questions unaddressed: Why was the staking of these claims important to modern identity? And why did enslavement demand, among other things, an aesthetic response?

These are difficult questions to answer, because as noted earlier, the act of enslavement was predicated on the exclusion of the slave from the moral and aesthetic realm. Indeed, all the categories used by Europeans to exclude slaves from modern civic culture—from the devaluation of their labor, the imprisonment of their bodies in a language of violence and ugliness, and the condemnation of their culture to ritual uncleanliness—had powerful moral connotations. Even when technologies of exclusion were not explicitly moral, they had to be moralized for affect. In fact, the practice of associating blackness with dirt was to continue with uncanny persistence through Jim Crow and the right-wing reaction against the civil rights movement in the 1950s. Lynching, for example, was articulated as a form of white defense against black licentiousness directed against the cleanliness of white women.[16] Within the culture of modernity, of course, the privileging of moral categories is not unusual. As Charles Taylor has shown, there was an essential link "between identity and a kind of moral orientation": "To know who you are is to be oriented in moral space, a space in which questions arise about what is good or bad, what is worth doing and what not, what has meaning and importance for you and what is trivial and secondary."[17] But this assertion assumes a set of meanings and values predicated on a free, self-reflective subject. How do questions of moral orientation play out in the world of the dominated and unfree? How did slaves come to emplace themselves in the places of exile?

One might argue that the enslaved had no say in moral matters because bondage precluded any form of control over would-be spaces of identity. Yet what was striking about spatial configurations in slave communities, especially in the Caribbean and the antebellum South, was the slaves' determination and capacity to create real and imaginary spaces of placement, to presuppose "a space-analogue within which one finds one's way."[18] One remarkable aspect of slave life was the capacity of the enslaved to create dynamic neighborhoods that "encompassed the bonds of kinship, the practice of Christianity, the geography of sociability, the field of labor and discipline, the grounds of solidarity, the terrain of struggle."[19] As Sylvia Wynter has argued in a classic essay on folk art in Jamaica, slaves, alienated from Africa in "space, time or degree," and faced equally with "the more total alienation of the New World," developed a cultural response that transformed them into "the indigenous" inhabitants of their new land: they indigenized the new world by humanizing the landscape through what amounts to an aesthetic response—"peopling it with gods and spirits, with demons and duppies, with all the panoply of man's imagination."[20]

Slaves seem to have recognized early that although they were part of an alienating infrastructure, they could still create, within this complex, an ontological space in which an alternative identity and aesthetics could be inscribed. As early as the seventeenth century, in the infancy of the slave complex, observers of the West Indian landscape noted that slaves were transforming the terms of their enslavement by claiming—sometimes demanding—spaces of cultivation that they could control outside the plantation system. An act passed in Jamaica in 1678 required masters to provide "one acre of ground well planted in provision for every five Negroes."[21] And this gesture, initially intended to placate slaves so that they could submit to the regimen of forced labor, would rapidly transform the character of West Indian slavery and the identities that emerged out of it; in regard to questions of land and emplacement, the provision ground helped restore a measure of autonomy to the African slave. By the end of the seventeenth century, West Indian slaves were investing cultural and moral value in the provision ground, making it the site in which what I term a counter-aesthetic would later emerge.

Initially, white masters and observers were not clued in to the revolutionary nature of the simple plots of land allotted to slaves. Oblivious to the aesthetic and moral value of the provision ground, white observers tended to evaluate the system in terms of its economic efficiency and its capacity to supply the basic needs of slaves. Writing from Port Royal, Jamaica, in 1685, John Taylor called attention to the utilitarian demand that had led to the emergence of the provision ground as an essential part of the landscape but missed the moral dimension: "When a planter hath purchased some 20, 30-or more Negro slaves, he first gives to each man a wife without which they will not be content or work. Then he gives to each man and his wife an half acre of land for them to plant for themselves maize, potatoes, yam etc.; which land they cleared in their Leisure hours and build them a wigwam on it, and then plant it as fast as they can."[22]

The unintended consequence of these plots of land was astounding. By the time slavery was consolidated in Jamaica in the eighteenth century, the provision ground had become the site of an alternative way of life, a place where bonds of family were maintained and notions of both labor and cultural value were cultivated and recalibrated in spite of the harsh logic of enslavement. Even advocates of slavery such as Bryan Edwards recognized the centrality of the provision ground in the cultivation of a "humane" culture among Jamaican slaves. As a writer and later Member of Parliament, Edwards was a strong critic of what he considered the "odious severity of the Roman law," which allowed the sale of slaves as payment of debts, a practice that was singularly responsible for the breakup of families and displacement of communities. What irked

Edwards most about the sale of slaves to cover their master's debts was that it uprooted them from their spaces of identity and belonging:

> In a few years a good Negro gets comfortably established, has built himself a house, obtained a wife, and begins to see a young family rising about him. His provision-ground, the creation of his own industry, and the staff of his existence, affords him not only support, but the means also of adding something to the mere necessaries of life. In this situation, he is seized on by the sheriff's officer, forcibly separated from his wife and children, dragged to publick auction, purchased by a stranger, and perhaps sent to terminate his miserable existence in the mines of Mexico, excluded for ever from the light of heaven; and all this without any crime or demerit on his part, real or pretended. He is punished because his master is unfortunate.[23]

Edwards considered the statute allowing the sale of slaves to cover their masters' debt "injurious to the national character" and "a disgrace to humanity"; as a member of the British parliament, he worked hard to have the statute repealed in the belief that a happy slave was one who was given the opportunity to become attached to the land and to "fold with it."[24] But even long before Edwards pushed for the repeal of the "Roman law" allowing slaves to be sold to cover their masters' debts, Africans in bondage had come to consider the provision ground to be a form of entitlement bound up with their own changing notions of labor and family. Indeed, one of the reasons the provision ground has come to mark the distinctiveness of West Indian slavery—and the communities that emerged from its ruins—was because it enabled the reversal of the social, moral, and epistemological categories that had been constructed to enforce slavery.

Consider, for example, the question of labor. As I have argued in previous chapters, the act of enslavement was at odds with accepted theories of value. In terms of labor value, slavery was the performance of work that did not provide any benefits to the enslaved. The profits that came out of this work—the cultivation of sugar, for example—went to a master who, in the West Indian case, was often absent from the plantation. Within the provision ground, however, this configuration of value was ameliorated if not changed. Here, slaves were allowed to plant crops for their use, to generate a surplus, and to retain the profits. Indeed, the terms of value were radically transformed. Masters came to value the system because it relieved them of the burden of feeding their slaves, while the slaves valued it because it permitted them "a degree of independence at odds with the notion of being chattels."[25] For the slaves, however, the provision ground was also the means to a larger end—a measure of control over time and space and hence part of the process of moral reorientation I noted earlier. The existence of the provision grounds under law mandated a rethinking of temporality. Whereas in other places in the slave world planters sought to maximize time, sometimes going out of their way to try to increase the number of working hours in a week, Jamaican slaves used the provisional ground as a form of temporal leverage, one that enabled them to put Saturday afternoons, Sundays, and the Christmas and Easter holidays under their own control.

There was an aesthetic dimension to the provision ground, too, one that was comparable, if only by default, to the transformation of spaces of leisure in the European metropolis. Let us recall that debates on slaves and their relationship to social and physical space were taking place at a time when architects and designers in Britain were striving to transform landscapes into scenes of pleasure informed by "particular moral and political precepts."[26] During this period, leading British architects like William Chambers were trying to embellish landscapes in order "to evoke a particular emotion in the spectator."[27] While slaves did not make an explicit connection between their small plots and the British gardens, and there is no evidence that any of them had heard of English gardens of pleasure such as Vauxhall or Kew, they seemed to recognize the aesthetic value of their own tiny spaces and to maintain the provisional ground as a source of food, money, and pleasure.

Some scholars of slave gardens, most notably Jill Casid, have argued that provision grounds were self-consciously "artificed" as a "justification for the plantation system."[28] Although Casid recognizes how the slaves used these gardens to transform the Caribbean market, she cites many instances in which the planter class pointed to the existence of the provision ground to enhance the myth of happy slaves in a picturesque setting. Moreover, as prints and engravings of famous Jamaican plantations such as Montpelier Estate illustrate (fig. 6.2), the visual representation of the scene of slavery was intended to produce a pastoral discourse that concealed the brutal realities of slavery.[29] But slaves were not always virtual prisoners of the other's gaze, and their relationship to the provision ground or the neighborhood was informed by a calculus—it could be "a way for slaves to recalibrate the balance of power in society."[30] Thus, even under the gaze of their masters and infrastructure of the plantations, slaves could engage in cultural practices whose ends and means were at odds with the representational regimen of the masters.

To understand the full scope of practices that denoted a measure of freedom in an unfree society, however, we need to shift interpretative interest from resistance as the organizing principle of slave life to what Michel de Certeau has called a tactic.[31] Key to this shift in analytical terms is Certeau's recognition that a tactic is "a calculated action determined by the absence of a proper locus"; that it does not control its own spaces, but must "play on a terrain imposed on it and organized by the law of a

6.2 James Hakewill, *Montpelier Estate, St. James.* From James Hakewill, *A Picturesque Tour of the Island of Jamaica* (London, 1825).

foreign power"; and that it does not have the means to maintain its distance and must thus deploy maneuvers "within enemy territory."[32] One of the tactics and maneuvers the slaves could deploy was to transform the provision ground from a utilitarian space to an aesthetic object.

Evidence that the provision ground was more than a utilitarian space can be gleaned from the writings of Jamaican planter historians, most prominently Long, Edwards, and William Beckford, who often complained that slaves tended to invest too much time and effort in crops that had no exchange value. The misfortune of African slaves as cultivators, noted Edwards, was that "they trust more to plantain-groves, corn and other vegetables, that are liable to be destroyed by storms, than to what are called *ground-provisions*; such as yams, eddoes, potatoes, cassava, and other esculent roots; all which are out of the reach of hurricanes."[33] In matters of which crops to plant, Edwards lamented, "prudence" was a term "that has no place in the Negro-vocabulary." The colonial government seemed to share Edwards's view; under the Consolidated Slave Act of 1787, every planter in Jamaica was required, under penalty of law, "to keep, properly cultivated in ground-provisions, one acre for every ten Negroes, exclusive of the Negro grounds."[34]

In complaining that the slaves preferred "useless"—above-ground— crops to utilizable plants, both Edwards and the colonial government missed the ontological and aesthetic function of the provision ground and its emergence as an essential feature of the enslaved Africans' project of redefining their own spaces of bondage. At the center of this redefinition was the transformation of the landscape of death and suffering into a space of pleasure, of aesthetic value, one that could be made visible only through above-ground crops. Indeed, these were the crops that enchanted observers who, on encountering the provision ground for the first time, were struck by its beauty and its forceful sublimity. The sublime power of these gardens was captured vividly by Michael Scott in the *Journal of Tom Cringle*, in a scene where the title character encounters a Jamaican village for the first time:

> At a distance it had the appearance of one entire orchard of fruit-trees, where were mingled together the pyramidal orange, in fruit and in flower, the former in all its stages from green to dropping ripe,—the citron, lemon, and lime trees, the stately, glossy-leaved star-apple, the golden shaddock and grape-fruit, with their slender branches bending under their ponderous yellow fruit,—the cashew, with its apple like those of the cities of the plain, fair to look at, but acrid to the taste, to which the far-famed nut is appended like a bud,—the avocada, with its Brobdingnag pear, as large as a purser's lantern,—the bread-fruit, with a leaf, one of which would have covered Adam like a bishop's apron, and a fruit for all the world in size and shape like a blackamoor's head; while for underwood you had the green, fresh, dew-spangled plantain, round which in the hottest day there is always a halo of coolness,—the coco root, the yam and granadillo, with their long vines twining up the neighbouring trees and shrubs like hop tendrils,—and peas and beans, in all their endless variety of blossom and of odour, from the Lima bean, with a stalk as thick as my arm, to the mouse pea, three inches high,—the pine-apple, literally growing in, and constituting, with its prickly leaves, part of the hedgerows,—the custard-apple, like russet bags of cold pudding,—the cocoa and coffee bushes, and the devil knows what all, that is delightful in nature besides; while aloft, the tall graceful cocoa-nut, the majestic palm, and the gigantic wild cotton-tree, shot up here and there like minarets far above the rest, high into the blue heavens.[35]

For Tom Cringle, the provision ground was an aesthetic space that transcended the landscape of slavery.

But to have a proper understanding of the centrality of the provision system in slaves' attempts to construct their own aesthetic, or even a counterculture of taste, we need to turn to where its presence was most tenuous: in the American colonies, more specifically in the low country of South Carolina. Here, in the early decades of the eighteenth century, a work practice described as the task system developed in the rice plantations of the region. At the center of this system, as Philip Morgan has shown, was the slaves' control over time and labor.[36] Slaves, many of them possibly familiar with rice growing even before arriving in the Americas, had developed a system in which their time was differentiated from that of their masters.[37] There are no obvious reasons why this system developed in the rice country and not the tobacco or cotton "kingdoms" of Virginia and Mississippi, but there is clear evidence that the slaves' determination to take possession of their time, land, and labor posed a threat to the established order. Numerous legal attempts were initiated to control the spread of the task system. As early as 1686, a law had been passed in South Carolina prohibiting the exchange of goods between slaves and other slaves or freemen without the consent of the masters. In 1714 the South Carolina legislature passed a law prohibiting slaves from planting for themselves corn, rice, or peas.[38] Morgan argues that these laws were ineffective and that the task system dominated agricultural life in the low country well into the middle of the nineteenth century. Still, legal attempts to curtail this kind of "free work" and to control "free time" points to its significance in the slaves' attempt to develop an ontology of space.

The task system in South Carolina, like the provision ground in Jamaica, was tied up with a significant politics of time. Through these systems, slaves could transcend the rigorous regimen of forced labor to evolve what one may call surplus time, one controlled by the enslaved and deployed toward ends that were at odds with the political economy of servitude. A "fugitive" system of labor enabled a measure of autonomy for the enslaved. In South Carolina the slaves' control over time and space "increased their autonomy, allowed them to accumulate (and bequeath) wealth, fed individual initiative, sponsored collective discipline and esteem, and otherwise benefited them economically and socially."[39] Perhaps masters allowed this system to continue because they recognized that the slaves' attachment to the land and the property it generated for them facilitated the regimen of enslavement, but what needs to be underscored is that the slaves embraced the provision ground because it enabled cultural autonomy in what might have been places of absolute deracination.

It is easy to underestimate the huge phenomenological gap between free and forced labor even within the culture of slavery. As numerous illustrations from the eighteenth century show, free labor, and its attendant notions of time and space, was centered on the wishes and desires of slaves as individuals; even when it was hard work, it was unbounded. A vivid sense of leisure and joy would characterize descriptions and scenes of the West Indian market, the culmination of the process of unfettered labor and the free and profitable exchange of its produce, or Sunday dress, when slaves owned their time (fig. 6.3). Working in the plantation was, in contrast, labor under strict control and surveillance, with the ubiquitous planter and driver in the foreground or background (fig. 6.4).

I do not think it is pure coincidence that Africanisms survived, or were most prominently invoked, in those slave cultures where the provision ground or task system was a salient part of the landscape, for autonomous spaces of time and task could be secured only outside the gaze of

6.3 *Female Negro Peasant in Her Sun-day and Working Dress.* From James M. Phillippo, *Jamaica: Its Past and Present State* (London, 1843).

6.4 *Planter, Attended by Negro Driver.* From James M. Phillippo, *Jamaica: Its Past and Present State* (London, 1843).

the master. The outstanding question, however, concerns the meaning and scope of these spaces and their relation to the slaves' aspiration to freedom: how could they be sustained within the infrastructure of the plantation? But perhaps there is a prior question that needs to be addressed: what does the existence of these autonomous spaces mean for the widely held view that to be enslaved was to be socially dead?[40]

2

In earlier parts of this book, I cited and rehearsed Orlando Patterson's famous definition of the slave as socially dead and his reflections on the slaves' natal alienation, their exclusion from the claims and obligation of a community, and their genealogical isolation.[41] Significantly, Patterson's thesis was founded on the concept of time, or temporality, as an instrument of exclusion. One of his most radical claims was that slaves "differed from other human beings in that they were not allowed freely to integrate the experience of their ancestors into their lives, to inform their understanding of social reality with the inherited meanings of their natural forebears, or to anchor the living present in any conscious community of memory." Patterson conceded that slaves strove to reach back in time and to connect with a past, but such efforts came up against "the iron curtain of the master, his community, his laws, his policemen or patrollers, and his heritage."[42] He concluded that the "genealogical and historical memory of the slaves" was shallow, citing examples from Michael Craton's study of the descendants of slaves at the Worthy Park sugar plantation in Jamaica to prove his point.[43] At the end of his study of the lives of slaves on a Jamaican plantation, Craton had noted that attempts to get descendants of slaves to talk about "antecedents dating back to slavery days" or to trace "precise lineage" led to "disappointment in nearly every case": "At best the information was inaccurate; at worst there was ignorance of even indifference."[44] What are we to make of this genealogical ignorance or shallowness of memory? Or, as Saidiya Hartman has asked poignantly, "What is it we choose to remember about the past and what is it we will to forget?"[45]

If we are looking for memory as history, as a process of genealogical continuity and reconstruction, which is the way Patterson and Craton posit it, then it is inevitable that the descendants of Worthy Park, like their slave ancestors, had little of it left. However, if we are to locate the process of remembering in what Pierre Nora has called *lieux de mémoire* (sites of memory), then what made the past important and meaningful, even in its fragmentation, was much more than the subject's connection to a real environment of historical continuity or reconstruction; rather, separated from history, this kind of memory would remain in "permanent evolution, open to the dialectic of remembering and forgetting, unconscious of its successive deformations, vulnerable to manipulation and appropriation, susceptible to being long dormant and periodically revived."[46] What would appear to have been the shallow memory of slaves and their descendants, then, was also what enabled the dialectic of remembering and forgetting. The shallowness of memory and the thinness of genealogy would give slaves a space for maneuver; to have a shallow memory was to be liberated from the burden of genealogy; without concrete claims to historical antecedence, slaves could be free to imagine an alternative world of space and play. In turn, loose ties to the past would enable the symbolic inversion of the meaning of work and time on the plantation.[47] My assumption here is that the search for genealogical connections and cultural antecedents or the quest for "real memory" could hinder rather than enhance the slaves' phenomenological presence in the new world; in this context, shallow memory, rather than complete forgetfulness, was one way the enslaved could reorient themselves in social space.[48]

What this reorientation demanded, among other things, was the slaves' recognition that memory was best doing its work when it was affective, magical, and ritualistic. As Nora aptly notes, memory, "insofar as it is affective and magical, only accommodates those facts that suit it; it nourishes recollections that may be out of focus or telescopic, global or detached, particular or symbolic—responsive to each avenue of conveyance or phenomenal screen, to every censorship or projection."[49] As magic, memory would be summoned to respond to the lived condition of the slave rather than a real past. So when they were asked by researchers to remember their "real" history, slaves were probably aware that what was at stake was not just the meaning of the past but also the meaning of the present—the site of enunciation and interrogation. As a speech act or performative, the act of remembering had the capacity to either censor memory or enhance it. In neither case were truth claims paramount.

There is another dimension to this debate on the shallowness of recollection: the slaves' capacity to differentiate their own sites of memory from the larger plantation complex and thus to exist as "self-interpreting beings."[50] Writing on the category of the person, Taylor has argued that what is involved in "being a person" is not simply consciousness or self-awareness but also what he calls "holding values"—the capacity to form representations that are invested with "peculiarly human significances."[51] Those are the kinds of self-interpretation and holding of other value implicit in the slaves' capacity to define their own time and to separate it from the regimen of forced labor. The most important insignias of the slaves' self-interpretation and their capacity to hold values at odds with their enslavement were precisely those objects of representation whose connection to Africa was most tenuous, the Juba dance mentioned in the last chapter and the Sloane drum above being some of the most prominent examples. These were objects of remembering/forgetting—they enabled both the censorship and projection of memory.[52] For example, accounts exist of slaves who chose to build their individually designed houses in what they considered to be the "African" style of their ancestors, often against environmental odds and the wishes of planters, rejecting the European log cabin for "clay floors, wattle-and-daub walls, and thatched roofs"[53]

Why did slaves go out of their way to build and maintain these allegories of ruins? Apparently, for those born in Africa, building in the "African style" was often a concerted attempt to deploy fragments of African architecture to claim the affective and magical possession of space. A former slave, Ben Sullivan, would later remember this struggle over the meaning of the place of dwelling among his peers: "Old man Okra said he wanted a place like he had in Africa, so he built himself a hut. I remember it well. It was about 12 by 14 feet, it had a dirt floor, and he built the sides like a woven basket with clay plaster on it. It had a flat roof that he made from brush and palmetto, and it had one door and no windows. But Master made him pull it down. He said he didn't want an African hut on his place."[54] Here, building a hut in the "African style," such as the one belonging to Tahro, "a native Bakongo, one of the last slaves imported

6.5 House built by Romeo, an African. From Charles J. Montgomery, "Survivors from the Cargo of the Negro Slave Yacht *Wanderer*," plate 10.

6.6 Thomas Coram, *View of Mulberry House and Street*. Circa 1800. Oil on paper. Gibbes Museum of Art, Charleston, South Carolina.

into the United States" (fig. 6.5), or the cabins at Mulberry Plantation in North Carolina, painted by Thomas Coram around 1770 (fig. 6.6), was a calculated way of laying claim to the American landscape.[55] Within the landscape of slavery, these places of dwelling were crucial to the reconstruction of black selfhood. With their African symmetry, these cabins were intended to turn the place of enslavement into a habitat, that place which, in Gaston Bachelard's formulation, "transcends geometric space."[56]

In *Back of the Big House*, his study of the architecture of plantation slavery, John Vlach makes several points that are crucial to what I am calling the ontology of space. First, he argues that slaves were engaged in their own definition of space, investing the landscape of slavery with their own thoughts and deeds. Second, he shows that the creation of slave landscapes was a strategy of survival: "Taking advantage of numerous opportunities to assert counterclaims over the spaces and buildings to which they were confined, slaves found that they could blunt some of the harsh edges of slavery's brutality."[57] Third, Vlach notes that the creation of these slave landscapes amounted to a counterclaim, "a reactive expression, a response to the plans enacted by white landowners" who had set out to mark the landscape both as a geometric and aesthetic space, one expressing their "tastes, values, and attitudes."[58]

The masters' idea of organizing space was, of course, explicitly connected to their power over the slaves; it was a play of order. Vlach quotes a Mississippi planter who, in an 1851 article, expressed the first rule of running a plantation as follows: "There shall be a place for every thing and everything shall be kept in its place." The rule was spelled in bold and capital letters. In fact, slave masters considered order to be essential to their mastery of the landscape, and order was about power and control: "The ideal order among planters was a rigorous order intended to confirm their final authority in all matters. It was important that their domains be planned with care, defined with clear and certain boundaries, and run on efficient, unwavering schedules. Striving constantly toward this goal, planters used every means—but especially the manipulation of the built environment—to convince themselves that they were both physically and symbolically above their slaves and other less wealthy whites as well." Vlach concludes that slaves "overturned the logic that their owners used to place themselves well up in the social landscape" and, in the process, affirmed their self-worth.[59]

Still, something more than a structural reversal was involved in the process of redefining space: overturning the logic of the masters also implied an appeal to African disorder as the counterpoint of the culture of taste. Consider the "African House" that Marie Thèrése Metoyer, the matriarch of a free Creole slave-owning family, built in Melrose (Yucca),

6.7 African House, ca. 1798–1800. Natchitoches Parish, Louisiana. Picture by Billy Hathorn. Courtesy Billy Hathorn / Wikimedia Commons.

Louisiana, sometime in the early 1830s (fig. 6.7) The house was built using local materials; the basic construction of its walls and lower level was in the existing *bousillage entre poteaux* (mud in the wall) French style, but its overhanging roof reflected a distinctively African style, more specifically the hanging roof of West African adobe granaries.[60] It is the only building of its kind recorded in Louisiana. Other buildings built by the Metoyer family were strictly in the French Creole planter style.[61] How do we explain this brazen Africanism in the middle of a thriving planter culture? Why would Marie Thèrése, a free woman of color, desire such a provocative symbol of Africa on her property at a time when Louisiana Creoles were keener to identify with France?

The brazen expression of difference in this house becomes even more perplexing when the house is located in its in its social geography, for in all other aspects of their lives the Metoyers cultivated the habits and tastes of the Louisiana plantocracy, and apart from their touch of color they were not very different from other slave owners. Traveling in the Deep South in the years 1853–1854, Frederick Law Olmstead noted that although the owners of the Yucca plantation were "a nearly full-blooded Negro," their plantations appeared "no way different from the generality of white Creoles; and on some of them were large, handsome, and comfortable houses."[62] The main house at the Melrose Plantation (fig. 6.8) affirmed similitude, not difference.

6.8 Melrose Plantation, State Highway 119, Melrose, Natchitoches Parish, Lousiana. General View of Plantation House. Library of Congress, Prints and Photographs Division, Historic American Buildings Survey or Historic American Engineering Record, Reproduction Number (HABS LA,35-MELRO,1-4).

Why, then, would a wealthy woman, the owner of more than eighteen thousand acres of land and hundreds of slaves—the largest number owned by a black planter—want to construct a house that would recall the ontology of African architecture? There are no obvious social or political reasons why Marie Thèrése Metoyer would have wanted to invoke African difference in colonial Louisiana, nor did she have a compulsion to subvert the spatial logic of the plantation system or its systems of values, to which she apparently subscribed. It has been suggested that Marie Thèrése had fond memories of her African great-grandmother and that she might have built the house as a memorial, but legend also has it that the African House was conceived as a ghost house, a place for spooking rebellious slaves. Did she, then, want a building that stood out in its environment in memoriam to an imagined Africa? Or was the African House intended to be the depository of an unknown and thus frightening ghost?

Either way the house would serve as a place of psychological habitation and deep cultural mapping, of the assemblage and disassemblage of memory, a site of comfort and terror. In this house, built in the style of African granaries, Marie Thèrése Metoyer could psychologically dwell in the house of imaginary ancestors without occupying it; this habitation in absentia, as it were, was a way of marking another space of identity outside the plantation house, what the philosopher Martin Heidegger would term "that domain to which everything that *is* belongs."[63] Far from using the house to reorder her world symbolically, Metoyer was inserting herself in an ontological order that was independent of even the institution of plantation slavery to which she belonged. And if we recall that her goal was not to abolish slavery but to thrive in it, then it is highly possible that she valued the African House for its pure symbolism, the measure of an essence of being that was above the political economy of slavery. Disconnected from utilitarian goals, the African House would become a work of art.

What do I mean by this? Most of the theoretical attention to space that has dominated cultural studies under the influence of Michel Foucault, Michel de Certeau, and postmodern geographers such as David Harvey and Edward Soja has explored the functional symbolism of the spatial, focusing on its openness to human creativity, its function as a marker of identity and as a vector defined by its users, what Certeau aptly called "space as a practiced place."[64] In all of these accounts, symbols function as a medium of ordering social space. What is often missing in these post-modern stories, however, is the notion of a symbolic space as something that exists, to borrow Hans-Georg Gadamer's words, outside the logos, one that has meaning in itself. According to Gadamer, the symbol, unlike other hermeneutical figures, "is not related by its meaning to another meaning, but its own sensuous nature has meaning"; it is "something which is shown and enables one to recognise something else." Through the sensuousness of the symbol, argues Gadamer, "members of a community recognise one another," and irrespective of the context in which it appears, "the meaning of the symbolon depends on its physical presence and acquires its representative function only through the fact of its being shown or spoken."[65]

As a symbol, then, the Metoyer African House did not denote a connection to a real or imagined Africa, nor did it represent collective yearnings; on the contrary, it was valued for strictly personal reasons. It was almost like a family chapel, a place of solitary worship. Perhaps the only meaning the building held for Marie Thérése Metoyer was her sensuous desires as a master who was also the other; like an ancient shrine, the African House enabled her to map out whatever private grievances she may have had about the system that she presided over. We do not know what these grievances were, of course; so in the end we have to see pure symbolism as an alternative to other, allegorical projections of the African self in the public spaces of enslavement, such as the *nsunsu* and Juba dances discussed in the previous chapter.

The obvious contrast to be drawn here, then, is between forms of desire that were collective and public, such as dances, and others that were strictly private, such as houses built in the "African style." My contention, however, is that desires cultivated in private could not perform the work of memory or identity, because they were locked in the interiority of the

self. While it is true that it was in these private shrines that a radical subjectivity could be asserted, desires that were expressed privately would be
cut off from the larger project of community building, an essential aspect
of the slaves' self-fashioning in the Americas. African-style houses, unlike
their Creole counterparts, could appear estranged from their localities
and could thus be cut off from the project of creating new identities and
meanings for the enslaved. For this reason, slaves needed to find ways
in which private desires and anxieties could be projected in the public
sphere, because publicness was one of the essential conditions of being a
modern subject, and slaves had indeed been conscripted into modernity.[66]
Rituals and performances would become important weapons of resistance and of coping with imposed identities.

3

From the very beginning of slavery in the Americas, observers of slave
cultures were struck by what appeared to be the centrality of ritual and
festivity among the Africans who were struggling to reconstruct their lives
in the new world. Reporting from Barbados around 1647, Richard Ligon
was one of the first eyewitnesses to note the connection between modes
of performance and the Africans' attempt to clear a cultural space in the
harsh regimen of the plantation. Ligon noted that on Sundays, their day
of rest and pleasure, the slaves would gather under the mangroves and
make ropes out of the bark. In the afternoon they would sing songs and
perform dances. Ligon complained that the Africans' drum had only one
tone, but their singing was impressive, although he wished he was able to
give the slaves "some hints of tunes" to add to their harmony, because "if
they had the variety of tune, which gives the greater scope in Musicke, as
they have of time, they would do wonders in that art."[67] Similarly, writing
on his experiences in the West Indies in 1707, Hans Sloane noted that the
slaves were "much given to Venery, and although hard wrought, will at
nights, or on Feast days Dance and Sing."[68]

Slaves were so passionate about their songs and dances, George Pinckard noted in 1806, and devoted so much time to amusement on Sunday
that "instead of remaining in tranquil rest, they undergo more fatigue,
or at least more personal exertion."[69] Even Thomas Jefferson, who had
excluded blacks from the realm of taste, declared that they were "more
generally gifted than the whites" in music.[70] Clearly the preponderance of
singing and the role of music in the slaves' lives occupy almost every major
description of slave society from the early accounts by Ligon and Sloane
to later works by leading African American cultural historians such as
John Blassingame and Sterling Stuckey.[71] Almost all major descriptions of

slave culture have underscored the use of music and dance as mechanisms for ameliorating the difficult conditions in which African slaves worked.

White praise for black performances should be enough to raise suspicion. This is especially the case when the praise came from members of the powerful planter class, who rarely had anything positive to say about black slaves when it came to matters of culture and taste. And because of the context in which these observations were made and the interests of the eyewitnesses scholars, there are at least three specific reasons why we should be suspicious of the privileging of rituals in the aesthetic of slavery. First, because music and the rituals surrounding it attracted the attention of plantation owners and defenders of slavery more than any cultural event, there has been a tendency to see them as an imposition, from above, of the masters' cultural ideology. This is particularly the case in the West Indies and the antebellum South, where, for most of the eighteenth century, masters pointed to ritual performances by slaves as either evidence of African bestiality or a sign of their contentment. Second, because most of the observations on ritual that are available to us from the archive of slavery are by white observers who were not clued in to the inner lives of slaves, we are not sure how to use them as evidence. Rarely do we find testimony on ritual from the enslaved themselves. In fact, the slaves who ended up producing narratives about their experiences were largely silent on cultural activities that they considered inimical to their identities as modern subjects. Writing in the context of abolitionism or the vantage point of Christian conversion, former slaves were defensive about Africanism in their communities and fearful that a recentering of African rituals in the plantations might detract from the project of abolitionism by reviving the slander of African barbarism. Frederick Douglass simply consigned such rituals to the domain of superstition.[72] Third, there have been doubts that rituals and performances, often produced within the infrastructure of slavery and white consent, could actually have been able to subvert the cultural system that enabled them in the first place. Claims that rituals and performances represent a form of revolt against the established culture are troubled by the possibility that the revolt embedded in them was limited and could actually end up enforcing that order.

My premise, however, is that although there is a need to question the centrality of rituals to locate them within the overall context of bondage, it is hard to ignore the value slaves invested in cultural performances as a mode of resistance against the order of enslavement and the ideologies that informed it, including aesthetic ones. Simply put, performances represented the most visible presence of the slave on the public stage; it was in the field of play that slaves asserted their own sense of being in the world; it was here that they presented themselves in a public sphere and oriented themselves in time and space, often against the desire of the masters, to control the moral geography of the plantation. So while slave masters had their own reasons for focusing on rituals, their agenda should not detract us from the value of performed Africanisms as a tactic of survival, a mode of remembering, and, ultimately, a kind of antidote to enslavement.[73]

Moreover, the planters' acknowledgment of, and sometimes enthusiasm for, African musical forms did not amount to an endorsement of a black aesthetic. Indeed, what often gives white witnesses credence is that their minute observation of Africanist cultural practices was motivated by the malignant desire to exclude slaves from the domain of modern culture and reason. Thus, even those witnesses who conceded that slaves had musical talent often went out of their way to point out what they considered to be the disjunctive, abnormal, and sometimes pathological nature of the end product. Ligon was struck by the fact that the music that seemed to give the greatest pleasure to the slaves was "one of the strangest noises that ever I heard made of one tone."[74] Sloane equated black singing to noise. Charles Leslie was startled by what he considered the promiscuity of the black dances that he observed in Jamaica in 1745 and was especially repelled by what he called the "very barbarous Melody."[75] Even the musical instruments used by slaves seemed to white observers to be perverted versions of well-known instruments, and this pervasion, it was argued, distorted musical form. Leslie noted that the slaves he had seen in Jamaica used an instrument he called a "Bangil" (banjo), which was "not unlike our Lute in anything but the Musik."[76] And writing from Antigua in 1789, John Lufman lamented, "Negroes are very fond of the discordant notes of the banjar, and the hollow sound of the toombah."[77] Neither observer bothered to reflect on the aesthetic possibilities of this deformation of accepted form.

White testimony on black performances was underwritten by a paradox. On one hand, white observers were clearly fascinated by black music, dance, rituals, and other performances; otherwise they would not have devoted so much time and space to their representation. On the other hand, however, they considered black music and dance to be at odds with all accepted aesthetic norms. Music was one of the most prominent forms of art in eighteenth-century Britain, and it was expressed and performed in a variety of media, from chamber orchestra to theatrical musicals. But it was underwritten by what amounted to an aesthetic consensus, an implicit assumption that musical form, and the energies that informed it, should be harnessed through melody, rhythm, and harmony.[78] Indeed, the discordance of African music—and its performance—seemed an affront to the ideology of music promoted by the culture of taste. The boisterousness of a black ensemble on a Cuban plantation (fig. 6.9) would appear

6.9 *Negro Dance on a Cuban Plantation*. *Harper's Weekly* (January 29, 1859), vol. 3, p. 73.

6.10 Philippe Mercier, *"The Music Party": Frederick, Prince of Wales, with his Three Eldest Sisters, 1733*. Oil on canvas. The Royal Collection © 2009, Her Majesty Queen Elizabeth II.

to be far removed and at odds with the ordered structure of a concert or music party on the lawn of English royalty and the serene deportment of both performers and listeners (fig. 6.10).

When European observers, then, complained that African musical forms in the new world were devoid of rhythm, they assumed that harmony and order were the essence of true musical expression. In more extreme cases, pro-slavery observers were not even willing to concede the notion, popular in Europe since the early modern period, that Africans had musical gifts; the lack of harmony was used to deprive them of even this old claim. From his observations in Jamaica, Bryan Edwards complained that the prevailing opinion in Europe that blacks "possess organs peculiarly adapted to the science of musicke" was "an ill-founded idea."[79] Edwards argued that blacks did not have vocal harmony or a proper ability to play instruments. He asserted that he could "not recollect ever to have seen or heard of a Negro who could truly be called a fine performer on any capital instrument," concluding that in general they preferred "a loud and long-continued noise to the finest harmony, and frequently consume the whole night in beating on a board with a stick."[80] As far as white observers were concerned, slave performances seemed to be discordant with established norms about art, morality, and associative behavior, and this provided the alibi for the evacuation of black expressive culture from the domain of taste. And yet these same observers continued, almost obsessively, to write about black performances, often creating the impression that they were the essence of slave life. Did planters and other white observers of slave culture focus on these performances because they were the most visible signifiers of black cultural expression, or were they insidiously attracted to them because they reflected white anxieties about play and the outward display of feelings?

I think the case can be made for both perspectives. Performances were an essential part of African identity in the new world, but perhaps because of this very fact, they triggered deep anxieties among the planter class and its supporters, many of whom subscribed to the dominant aesthetic ideology of order and restraint. For example, travelers to Africa in the early modern period had noticed the significance of dance and festival as signifiers of community, cultural connections, and the cycle of life. Writing on his observations of the cultures of the Gambia in 1623, the English trader Richard Jobson insisted that there were "without doubt, no people on the earth more naturally affected to the sound of musicke than these people." He noted that music permeated all aspects of social life and was central to the practice of statecraft. Wherever one went in the region, Jobson observed, court musicians, whom he compared to the "Irish Rimer," would be found singing the praises of the king, his lineage, and his deeds. If the king or any important person came to visit the

European traders on the banks of the Gambia, Jobson noted, "they will have their musicke playing before them, and will follow in order after their manner, presenting a shew of State."[81] Out of such reports, and perhaps from his own recollections of childhood, Olaudah Equiano concluded that his people were "almost a nation of dancers, musicians, and poets. Thus every great event, such as a triumphant return from battle, or other cause of public rejoicing, is celebrated in public dances, which are accompanied with songs and music suited to the occasion."[82]

When white observers described black festival arts in the plantations, however, they were also expressing a deeply rooted fear of the sensual as expressed through the black body. In other words, what frightened white observers about slave dances, for example, was its affirmation of sensuousness and the celebration of the body, elements that the culture of taste had tried to control, if not exclude from its domain. We see this fear of sensuousness in George Pinckard's description of a black dance in Jamaica at the end of the eighteenth century,

> The dance consists of stamping of the feet, twisting of the body, and a number of strange indecent attitudes. It is a severe bodily exertion—more bodily indeed than you can well imagine, for the limbs have little to do in it. The head is held erect, or, occasionally, inclined a little forward—the hands nearly meet before—the elbows are fixed, pointing from the sides—and the lower extremities being held rigid, the whole person is moved without lifting the feet from the ground. Making the head and limbs fixed points, they writhe and turn the body upon its own axis, slowly advancing towards each other, or re-treating to the outer parts of the ring. Their approaches, with the figure of the dance, and the attitudes and inflexions in which they are made, are highly indecent; but of this they seem to be wholly unconscious, for the gravity—I might say the solemnity of countenance, under which all this passes, is peculiarly striking, indeed almost ridiculous. Not a smile—not a significant glance, nor an immodest look escapes from either sex; but they meet, in very indecent attitudes, under the most settled, and unmeaning gravity of countenance.[83]

And yet, even as they expressed horror at the sounds they were hearing, white observers were quick to note the important cultural work being performed by disharmonious sound. Pinckard, for example, noted that although the songs were "harsh and wholly deficient in softness and melody," they provided the slaves an alibi for associative behavior: "They assemble, in crowds, upon the open green, or in any square or corner of the town, and, forming a ring in the centre of the throng, dance to the sound of their beloved music, and the singing of their favorite African yell."[84] Songs and dances were clearly associated with the work of community building. As an anonymous writer observed in 1797, in Jamaica, song and dance provided occasions for different African groups to affirm their identity—"on these occasions the Negroes of each tribe or nation assemble in distinct groups with their several instruments."[85]

White observers were also fascinated by black performances because they provided a conduit for deeper cultural anxieties, those located in the zones of expression and affectivity, repressed by the culture of taste. This is evident in their obsession with Obeah or other occult practices among African slaves. In fact, descriptions of Obeah and other forms of magic functioned in a fascinating dialectic of attraction and revulsion. Observers sought to represent the practice as a mark of black difference and to locate it in the realm of the irrational, which, in their mind, defined the African. Obeah, which Bryan Edwards described as an "extraordinary superstition," was considered so central to understanding the underside of the slave in Jamaica that detailed research on it was transmitted to the Lords of the Committee of the Privy Council in its discussions of the slave trade.[86] Obeah was such a great source of fear among the colonial ruling class that its practitioners were often sentenced to death by burning or transported to penal colonies.[87]

However, despite the attention it was getting from the highest levels of the British government and members of the planter class alike, Obeah was an occult practice that was barely accessible to white observers; indeed, it drew most of its power from its invisibility. Paradoxically, this invisibility also made it even more appealing to the white imagination; inaccessible in a descriptive sense, it could be rewritten as a ghost story. This was at least the case with Matthew Gregory Lewis, who was already a renown Gothic novelist by the time he arrived in Jamaica to inspect his properties twice between 1815 and 1818. In his representations of Jamaican slave society, Lewis put his imagination to good use. Writing in the *Journal of a West Indian Proprietor*, Lewis represented Obeah as what Errol Hill, writing in a different context, has aptly described as "a drawn-out theatrical performance."[88] Not only did Obeah practices dominate Lewis's journal, but they were also often retold as ghost stories.

One such story revolved around the exploits of a slave named Plato, the organizer of a revolt in Jamaica, who had been sentenced to death for his actions but somehow still managed to deploy the power of magic posthumously. Lewis retold Plato's story with the imaginary prowess of a Gothic novelist:

> He died most heroically; kept up the terrors of his imposture to his last moment; told the magistrates, who condemned him, that his death should be revenged by a storm, which would lay waste the whole island, that year; and, when his negro goaler was binding him to the stake at which he was destined to suffer, he assured him that he should not live long to triumph in his death, for that he had taken good care to Obeah him before his quitting the prison.

It certainly did happen, strangely enough, that, before the year was over, the most violent storm took place ever known in Jamaica; and as to the goaler, his imagination was so forcibly struck by the threats of the dying man, that, although every care was taken of him, the power of medicine exhausted, and even a voyage to America undertaken, in hopes that a change of scene might change the course of his ideas, still, from the moment of Plato's death, he gradually pined and withered away, and finally expired before the completion of the twelvemonth.[89]

Reading Lewis's journal one might conclude that Obeah was the key to understanding the moral economy of Jamaican slaves—but was it? As a Gothic novelist, Lewis was, of course, attracted to the ghostly as a source of stories, and his descriptions of Obeah are comical and ironical, often at odds with the terror associated with magic in the official narrative of Jamaican slavery. Nevertheless, his version of Obeah tells us more about his fertile imagination than about the lives of Jamaican slaves. Indeed, the role assigned to Obeah, as a source of either enchantment or danger, was based on a crucial misunderstanding. Planters and government officials alike seemed to believe that the African resistance to slavery and their determination to hold on to a set of values outside the regimen of labor were embedded in magic.

Posited as a threat to the moral order and a display of a dreaded Africanism, Obeah was under constant surveillance on the plantation; but it was perhaps not as powerful as it was projected to be. According to students of Jamaican slavery, the real center of occult power among the slaves was Myal, a cult that resembled West African secret societies and which white planters often confused with Obeah. It was in Myalism that the African resistance to slavery was enshrined and an alternative set of beliefs cultivated. In fact, Myalism emerged as a counter to Obeah, developed its own complex, and, more importantly, was "shaped by a Christian presence."[90]

The often subtle but important differences between Obeah and Myal have been summarized by Orlando Patterson in *The Sociology of Slavery*. Patterson draws three distinctions between the two cultural practices. First, he notes that Obeah was primarily centered on individuals who acted on their own while Myalism had a corporate or group character. Second, he notes that Obeah was essentially "a type of sorcery which largely involved harming others" while Myalism was "a form of anti-witchcraft and anti-sorcery."[91] Third, while Obeah was discernible through the activities of its practitioners, Myalism was a secret cult centered on a special dance.

These distinctions are important because they help us understand why planters, as products of the culture of taste, needed the manifestation of an irrational Africanism as a counterpoint to the cognitive faculties embedded in the aesthetic ideology. Simply put, planters were attracted to Obeah because they could associate it with what they considered an un-Christian, residual Africanism and because they could readily connect it with death and destruction and radical irrationalism. In contrast, Myalism was not easily classified, having always been part of a secret cult, deep underground, and, as Patterson notes, often associated with anti-witchcraft. While Obeah could easily be rewritten as a ghost story revolving around the activities of one individual (Lewis's Plato, for example), Myalism was spread across communities and was not easily contained; the secrets of the Myal fraternity, noted Edward Long, were guarded by oath.[92]

From the slaves' perspective, Myalism was powerfully associated with life and community in two senses. In one sense, from the genesis of the cult, Myal priests had always claimed invulnerability. The 1760 Kromanti Rebellion in Jamaica was instigated by priests who provided the warriors with medicines that they claimed would protect them from bullets.[93] In another sense, Myal priests were supposed to have the power to raise the dead. Lewis, who tended to confuse his Obeah and Myal, provided an insightful description of the task of raising the dead. He described a scene where, in the midst of "the Myal dance," a priest would oblige a "devoted victim" to drink a liquor that would turn him or her into what he called "A perfect corpse":

> The chief Myal-man then utters loud shrieks, rushes out of the house with wild and frantic gestures, and conceals himself in some neighbouring wood. At the end of two or three hours he returns with a large bundle of herbs, from some of which he squeezes the juice into the mouth of the dead person; with others he anoints his eyes and stains the tips of his fingers, accompanying the ceremony with a great variety of grotesque actions, and chanting all the while something between a song and a howl, while the assistants hand in hand dance slowly round them in a circle, stamping the ground loudly with their feet to keep time with his chant. A considerable time elapses before the desired effect is produced, but at length the corpse gradually recovers animation, rises from the ground perfectly recovered, and the Myal dance concludes.[94]

What Lewis did not understand was that the Myal dance, the centerpiece of the ritualizing of slave life that he was describing, was a form of both revelation and concealment. Indeed, by the first half of the nineteenth century, Myalism, its secret codes still undeciphered by the disciplinary powers, had appropriated a Christian idiom, which further concealed its mission. In 1842 what Patterson has described as "a remarkable outbreak of Myalism" took place in Jamaica. According to one eyewitness, Myal people, also calling themselves "angel men," went around the island proclaiming the end of the world and vowing to root out the evils of Obeah.[95] Yet few white observers, obsessed with the danger of Obeah, noticed the purifying claims of Myal.

4

One can see why forms of ritual such as Obeah and Myal (and Vodun in Haiti and Santeria in Cuba), which seemed excessive in the eyes of typical eighteenth-century Europeans, products of the culture of taste that opened this book, would become the centerpiece of the slaves' alternative aesthetic.[96] On encountering the world of the slave, the men of taste found cultural practices that were at odds with the integers of civilized society. A good part of this oddity was the invisibility and inscrutability of ritual. Finding themselves in the midst of slave cultures and eager to produce a discourse that would explain the new-world African, gentlemen of taste such as Bryan Edwards were constantly exasperated by the genesis of secrecy that surrounded the governing codes of the enslaved: "A veil of mystery is studiously thrown over their incantations, to which the midnight hours are allotted, and every precaution is taken to conceal them from the knowledge and discovery of the White people."[97] Edwards then went on to underscore how the fetishes that had been used to demonize the Africans in West Africa had now become a source of their power in the Americas: "The deluded Negroes, who thoroughly believe in their supernatural power, become the willing accomplices in this concealment, and the stoutest among them tremble at the very sight of the ragged bundle, the bottle or the egg-shells, which are stuck in the thatch or hung over the door of a hut, or upon the branch of a plantain tree, to deter marauders."[98]

Edward's complaint that slaves in Jamaica were involved in deluded practices that were, nonetheless, outside the realm of white knowledge is central to the argument I have been developing so far regarding the emergence of a space of cultural expression outside the hermeneutics of modernity. For what seemed to frustrate Edwards was not simply African delusions among the enslaved, but the inability of white proprietors to penetrate the ritual codes of slaves and bring them under the regimen of modern knowledge. Edwards was particularly irked by the inability of the governing class to isolate Obeah men and women from "any other Negro"; he was equally exasperated by the power Obeah people had over both "ignorant" and "wiser" Negroes.

What Edwards did not countenance is the possibility that part of the power of Obeah and other forms of magic among the enslaved was derived not from ignorance or fear of vengeance, but from the slaves' investment in these practices as part of a larger cognitive apparatus in the project of self-making and community building. This explains his infatu-ation with what, for the modern mind, appeared injurious and irrational, the opposite of the rationality and order of modern civility and the cul-ture of sensibility. Furthermore, Edwards failed to recognize the power of the spectacle itself and indeed the compulsion of what seemed to exist outside the order of rationality. For it is quite apparent that slave perfor-mances were spectacles that eluded the power of vision or, as Foucault would put it, the power of surveillance.

In *Discipline and Punish*, Foucault makes a crucial distinction between spectacle and surveillance. Modern society, he argues, uses surveillance as a technology of forces and bodies whose goal is to conscript individuals into the service of the institutions of power. In the field of power and its systems of representation, argues Foucault, subjects are not simply am-putated, repressed, and altered by the social order; rather, the individual is "fabricated" according to "a whole technique of forces and bodies."[99] In the regime of surveillance, subjects are on display to be observed, but observation is also a form of control. In the world of spectacle, on the other hand, the subject is no longer observable since, as Guy Debord puts it, "the spectacle's job is to cause a world that is no longer directly per-ceptible to be *seen* via different specialized mediations."[100]

What I am arguing is that those forms of play that frightened white planters because they took place in a dark, secretive world—one that was imperceptible to their eyes and seemed outside the realm of European reason—were the essence of the slaves' revolt against the political and cultural order that rationalized bondage. Furthermore, forms of cultural expression that were the most likely to be dismissed as meaningless spec-tacle were also those that were valued by slaves themselves as they sought to produce a counterculture, including one that went against the grain of sense and sensibility. What is at issue here, then, is the slaves' perfor-mance as an assemblage of values that were inaccessible to their masters and dissociated from the accepted social order, the realm of surveillance. Dance, song, and sound represented what had clarity for the slaves but was inaudible to the masters. Herein lies the significance of those ac-counts coming from the archive of slavery where witnesses, confronted by black sound, song, or dance, could discern the significance of what they saw but were not sure what it meant and were then left pondering the meaning of a spectacle that was disharmonious and at odds with Eu-ropean aesthetic practices.

Let us look at some examples: On February 21, 1819, Benjamin Latrobe, the distinguished architect and engineer, "accidentally stumbled upon" a group of blacks playing a jumble of instruments that "made an incredible noise."[101] The most curious contraption, noted Latrobe, "was a string instrument which no doubt was imported from Africa"; on the top of the finger board "was the rude figure of a Man in a sitting position, and two pegs behind him to which the strings were fastened."[102] The Africans beat these instruments to a song that only seemed to add to the cacophony: "A Man sung an uncouth song to the dancing which I supposed was in some African language, for it was not French, and the Women screamed a detestable burthen on one single note."[103] What Latrobe didn't recognize was that behind the dissociation of notes, and beneath the noise that caught the observer's attention, slaves had found ways of perpetuating an African idiom where it was not supposed to exist, that the jumbled instruments and notes that annoyed him, and the scene of performance or dance that irked him because they were at odds with the culture of taste, were what enabled Africans to transcend the ontology of enslavement.

Students of slave culture have been unanimous in their claim that dance and the noise that accompanied it marked the phenomenological presence of Africanness among the slaves and masked this other cultural self from the gaze of the planters. Sterling Stuckey aptly notes that as a form of expression, dance "was the most difficult for slaveholders to suppress."[104] And Sylvia Wynter has observed that the drum, "central to African religion and belief, became a focal point of the physical and cultural resistance" among the slaves.[105] Because of its sense of deviance, this black sound and the movement it provoked—the drum and the dance—became a source of anxiety and fear across the slave world. The drum and dance became the targets of repression by the apparatus of enslavement, and the institutions of white power lived in fear of the African sound, which they went about repressing systematically and uniformly. Drumming, for example, was banned in South Carolina in the aftermath of the Stono Rebellion of 1739. Farther south, in Argentina, public dances by slaves, known as *candombes*, were banned three times in the last half of the eighteenth century.[106] In Brazil, *candomble*, the dance of the slaves, was banned at the beginning of the eighteenth century.[107] In many states in the antebellum South, black dancing was controlled by acts of the legislature.

What threat did the drum and dance pose? The explanation that quickly comes to mind is pragmatic: drums were used to signal insurrection, and dances provided cover for organized resistance. And there is no doubt that in the major slave rebellions from Haiti to South Carolina, drums were used to spread the language of insurgency, and dance would provide an alibi for prohibited assembly. But pragmatic explanations should not detract us from the aesthetic or counter-aesthetic work performed by the drum and dance in articulating the ontological authority of a much-maligned blackness. Simply put, the drum and dance were performing aesthetic work that was invisible to the naked eye of white observers, who were already prisoners of their own standards of judgment and taste.

Where white masters saw African barbarism or instruments of revolt, slaves perceived the work of art as their last connection to lost and soon to be forgotten homelands. Observers of slave culture were struck by the fact that in both its style and function, the African dance deployed movement as part of an aggressive claim to physical space and as a community-building project. One of the stylistic features of the dance in West Africa, which American slaves came to value immensely, was the organization of the dancers in a circle. Writing of West African dance at the beginning of the eighteenth century, Barbot noted that black dances were performed in a circular movement, and this is what enabled their sensuousness: "Some of them stand in the middle of the ring, holding one hand on their head, and the other behind their waist, advancing and strutting out their belly forwards, and beating very hard with their feet on the ground. Others clap their hands to the noise of a kettle, or a calabash fitted for a musical instrument. When young men, or boys, dance with maidens, or women, both sides always made abundance of lascivious gestures; and every now and then each takes a draught of palmwine to encourage the sport."[108]

This so-called circle of culture was to become even more important in the slave plantation, where enslaved Africans, deprived of their sovereignty and "the deep, horizontal comradeship" that enabled the imagined community of the nation, considered an aesthetic community to be an imperative for survival.[109] Slaves used dance to clear or create a social space where new connections could be made and rehearsed in public. With enslavement experienced and conceived as a traumatic moment of rupture, dance was embraced as the visible form of the black aesthetic and a technology of reconnection. Reporting on the West Indies, the French priest Jean Pierre Labat, did not find the Calenda, a Congolese ring dance, entertaining, but he did notice both the organization of the dancers in a circle and the intimacy it engendered: "The dancers, men and women, form a circle and without moving about they do nothing else but to raise their feet in the air and strike the ground with a sort of cadence, holding their bodies bent toward the ground, each in front of the other. They intone some story that one of their number tells, to which the dancers respond with a refrain while the spectators clap their hands."[110] And in his description of Congo Square in New Orleans, Latrobe, who found black dance generally repulsive was nevertheless struck by its symmetry: "They were formed into circular groupes in the midst of four of which, which I examined (but there were more of them) was a ring, the largest not 10 feet in diameter. In the first were two women dancing. They held each a coarse handkerchief extended by the corners in their hands, and set to each other in a miserably dull and slow figure, hardly moving their feet or bodies."[111] Latrobe was probably describing the Bamboula dance, which was later drawn by E. W. Kemble for the February 1886 issue of *Century Illustrated Monthly Magazine* (fig. 6.11).

What did these circular, intimate, sensuousness motions mean? Were they expressions of an African aesthetic—or even metaphysics—or simply the slaves' performance of the remnants of imaginary homelands? Performance and being seem to have been conjoined in dance, for wherever one went in the landscape of slavery in the Americas, Africans in bondage had a keen sense of how dancing—and the performance of identity in general—helped them articulate an imaginary homeland that was transcendental of the lived experience of enslavement. Thus dominant slave dances—the Calenda, the Bamboula, or the Juba, for example—were often given national designations; in their choreography and conception, dances were usually identified as belonging to a specific cultural group, not an amorphous mass. In a 1795 petition to the viceroy of Argentina, Congolese slaves in Buenos Aires invoked their right to "hold their functions in the manner of their respective Nations," reminding the potentate that "each Nation performs its Dances according to its style and with all due propriety."[112]

A complaint from the Buenos Aires town council from the same period indicates that colonial authorities recognized the association between dance and the performance of nationhood and the dangers it posed to the established moral order: "It has been observed that in these dances the Blacks perform Gentile Rites of the places in which they were born, with certain ceremonies and speeches that they perform in their Languages. They put on the various Dances by which each Nation distinguishes itself."[113] And observing a slave dance in New Orleans in 1807, a bewildered Christian Schultz recorded the antics of what he described as "wretched Africans" performing "their *worship* after the manner of their country": "They have their own national music, consisting for the most part of a long kind of narrow drum of various sizes, from two to eight feet in length, three or four of which make a band. The principal dancers or leaders are dressed in a variety of wild and savage fashions, always ornamented with a number of tails of the smaller wild beasts, and those who appeared most horrible always attracted the largest circle of company."[114]

But perhaps even more than their role in sustaining an *ethne*, black ceremonies functioned as a means of bringing together fragments of a scattered people, united as a social body, suspended above the pain of the everyday. The use of dance and ceremony as a counterpoint to the cruel and diabolical festivals of punishment and enforced labor discussed in previous chapters caught the attention of the French naturalist Alcides d'Orbigny as he observed a *candombe* in Montevideo in 1827:

> All the blacks born on the coasts of Africa gathered in tribes, each one of which elected a king and a queen. Dressed in the most striking manner, with the most brilliant outfits that one can imagine, and preceded by all the subjects of their respective tribes, these monarchs-for-a-day made their way to mass, then paraded through the city, and, gathered at last in the small square near the market, every one performed, each in his own way, a dance characteristic

6.11 E. W. Kemble, *The Bamboula. Century Illustrated Monthly Magazine,* February 1886.

> of his nation. I saw in rapid succession war dances, representations of agricul-
> tural work, and steps of the most lascivious type. There more than six hundred
> blacks seemed to have regained for a moment their nationality, in the heart of
> that imaginary country, whose memory alone, . . . in the midst of that noisy
> saturnalia of another world, made them forget, for one single day of pleasure,
> the pains and sufferings of long years of slavery.[115]

More than an aesthetic palliative, however, the performance of national dances could be read as an orchestration of horizontal social relationships at odds with the hierarchical structure of enslavement. In terms of movement, slave dances could be interpreted as audacious attempts to rewrite the terms of the master/slave relationship, a repositioning of what was supposed to be instrumental control into a tactic of liberation. These performances could thus be construed to be what Certeau has defined as "transverse tactic"—strategies for survival that "do not obey the law of the place, for they are not defined or identified by it."[116]

Although it was considered indecent or transverse, this performance of black sensuousness demanded attention, and sometimes admiration, even from the planter class. Edward Long, who considered blacks to have no aesthetic sense at all, and whose overall project was to evacuate Africans from the order of culture and the human by associating them with pure negativity, grudgingly came to recognize poetry, style, and order in the dances of Jamaican slaves. Long's conclusion, which comes in a rare and odd passage in a work committed to the demonology of blackness, is worth quoting in detail:

> Their tunes for dancing are usually brisk, and have an agreeable compound
> of the *vivace* and *larghetto*, gay and grave, pursued alternately. They seem
> also well-adapted to keep their dancers in just time and regular movements.

The female dancer is all languishing, and easy in her motions; the man, all action, fire, and gesture; his whole person is variously turned and writhed every
moment, and his limbs agitated with such lively exertions, as serve to display
before his partner the vigour and elasticity of his muscles. The lady keeps her
face towards him, and puts on a modest demure look, which she counterfeits
with great difficulty. In her paces she exhibits a wonderful address, particularly in the motion of her hips, and Heady position of the upper part of her
person: the right execution of this wriggle, keeping exact time with the music,
is esteemed among them a particular excellence; and on this account they
begin to practise it so early in life, that few are without it in their ordinary
walking. As the dance proceeds, the musician introduces now and then a pause
or rest, or dwells on two or three *pianissimo* notes; then strikes out again on a
sudden into a more spirited air; the dancers, in the mean while, corresponding
in their movements with a great correctness of ear, and propriety of attitude;
all which has a very pleasing effect.[117]

After spending considerable time in his book denouncing all aspects
of black life, it is ironic that Long was willing to endow black dance
with the values reserved for the culture of taste, applying a technical language to its movement, acknowledging slaves as masters of their bodies,
and even admitting that effects could be pleasing. But my interest here
is not what might have motivated Long and other white observers to
recognize in dance what they had negated in other spheres of slave life;
rather, I want to probe some of the ways African-derived performances
in the landscape of slavery exemplified what Eugen Fink, Ute Saine, and
Thomas Saine have called "the ontology of play."[118]

Writing on the relation between play and the nature of being, Fink and
the Saines have argued that play is not simply an occasional interruption
of the serious business of living, nor is it "frivolous and pleasurable non-
sense" or an escape into the realm of fantasy; rather, play is "an essential
element of man's ontological makeup, a basic existential phenomenon . . .
a clearly identifiable and autonomous one that cannot be explained as de-
riving from other existential phenomena."[119] The ontological value of play
is implicit in its capacity to function as a spontaneous act and vital im-
pulse, one denoting a mode of "existence centered in itself."[120] And there
is no doubt that spontaneous acts and vital impulses were salient features
of the slaves' aesthetic and that rather than representing dissonance, the
resulting free play enabled communal bonds. In one of the earliest descriptions of the Calenda, Labat noted that in the dance, the "ablest person
sings a song which he composes on the spot on any subject he considers
appropriate. The refrain of this song is sung by everyone and is accompanied by great handclapping."[121] Labat went on to describe the movements
of the dance, which, he concluded, were "contrary to all modesty."[122]

What Labat failed to see, however, is how in its immodesty, the dance was aggressively challenging the social codes associated with the culture of the masters and in the process affirming a space of existence that the slaves controlled. When the city of New Orleans banned dancing the Calenda in 1843, it seemed to have recognized the subversive potential of play. If dances like the Calenda constituted a threat to the established order, it was not just because they challenged conventional morality or provided the cover for revolt and rebellion, but also because they transformed what Fanon would call "the lived experience of blackness" or, more precisely, its terms of representation.[123]

If I may adopt Fanon's formulation further, the challenge facing the slave in the plantation complex was not how to assume the attitude of the master, but to initiate a "cycle of freedom" that went beyond the historical and instrumental condition of enslavement.[124] The slaves' aesthetic did not just depend on a reimagination of Africa, as many scholars have suggested, but on a self-conscious act of *dédoublement*, a dissociation from the regime of work (hence the value of play) and a reversal of the lived condition of a blackness bonded to unpaid labor and an enforced morality. In their dances, complained town officials in Buenos Aires, slaves forgot the sentiments of the Catholic religion and renewed "the rites of the gentiles"; they then perverted "the good customs that their Owners have taught them, learn nothing but vices," and, in the process, "the Republic is very badly served."[125]

But this was precisely the point: African performances in the new world could function as forms of resistance only if they were deployed as "gentile rites" at odds with the dictates of taste and its privileging of order and cleanliness. As a matter of fact, African festivals in the new world, ranging from the John Canoe (Jonkonnu) festival in Jamaica to the Pinkster festival in Albany, New York, seemed to consistently confirm the claim, associated with Bakhtin, that festivals enable a domain of cultural expression outside "official order and official ideology."[126] One of the central assertions in Bakhtin's *Rabelais and His World* was that the festival constituted an extraterritorial space of identity: "Abuses, curses, profanities, and improprieties are the unofficial elements of speech.... Such speech forms, liberated from norms, hierarchies, and prohibitions of established idiom, become themselves a peculiar argot and create a special collectivity, a group of people initiated in familiar intercourse, who are frank and free in expressing themselves verbally. The marketplace crowd was such a collectivity, especially the festive, carnivalesque crowd at the fair."[127]

Given what appears to be the totality of domination engendered by the plantation system, which regulated everything from romance to labor, childbirth to leisure, the prevalence of the carnivalesque among the slaves is an attractive place for what Max Gluckman once called "rituals of rebellion."[128] A striking feature of the organization of rituals of rebellion, Gluckman argued, was "the way in which they openly express social tensions: women have to assert license and dominance against their formal subordination to men, princes have to behave to the king as they covet the throne, and subjects openly state their resentment of authority."[129] But there was a powerful caveat in Gluckman's study of ritualized forms of rebellion: they expressed social tensions and incited debates about the distribution of power but did not question "the structure of the system itself"; ritual enabled institutionalized protest, which ended up renewing "the unity of the system."[130]

5

And thus two questions arise: What could forms of play and rituals of rebellion do to the powerful system of enslavement, one in which the masters had total power and the slaves none? Could symbolic work leave a dent on this totalitarian edifice of modernity? Since my goal and challenge in the last two chapters of this book has been to recuperate existential freedom within enslavement, it is imperative that I raise the question of the subjunctive nature of play in relation to the institutions of power. And the first step in the process is to rehearse and question the general claim that the slaves' festivals represented an oasis of happiness and freedom in the midst of suffering and bondage. There is a need here to interrogate the accepted view that the carnivalesque in itself represents an alternative to the hegemonic system.

This view is, of course, dominant in the study of European carnivals. In addition to Bakhtin, scholars such as Emmanuel Le Roy Ladurie and Peter Burke have called attention to the role of carnival in reversing the established social order in terms that bear comparison to the situation of African slaves in the modern world. Le Roy Ladurie has described carnival in early modern France as "a prodigious cultural grafting," as a perjurer of "various ills and sins," and as a form of ritual cleansing.[131] And in his study of popular culture in early modern Europe, Peter Burke describes carnival as the subalterns' symbolic inversion of the dominant regimen of representation and their opposition "to the everyday."[132] But did the transgressive nature of festivals in situations of bonded labor lead to a realm of freedom?

For some scholars of slavery, play and performance enabled slaves to transcend their deracinating everydayness to enter into what Roger Abrahams called the elevated "experience of celebration."[133] Posited against the pressures of bondage, festivals could be used to recapture what Robert Farris Thompson labeled "heaven's glamour."[134] The distinguished Congolese scholar K. Kia Bunseki Fu-Kiau has gone as far as to endow the festival with the capacity to transform the nature of meaning and truth itself. Festivals, argues Fu-Kiau, bring about change because they allow people "to say not only what they voice in ordinary life but what is going on within their minds, their inner grief, and their inner resentments"; parades "alter truth" and "see true meaning."[135] Still, one has to ask whether the extraordinary circumstances of enslavement in which the Africans found themselves in the plantations of the Americas could allow for an alternative regimen of truth.

Slaves did not, of course, acquire real freedom through play, but there is compelling evidence that the performance of a counterculture of taste was essential to the transformation of enslaved Africans from chattel to subjects. A compelling example of performance as a form of symbolic resistance can be found in the history and transformation of John Canoe, a unique festival that sought to create an alternative social space through the appropriation and mimicry of inherited aesthetic forms. What makes John Canoe exemplary is that it presents us with a paradox. On one hand, as Sylvia Wynter has noted, John Canoe constitutes, in its persistence, longevity, and power, one of the most important cultural forms to have come out of slavery in the West Indies. Wynter has rightly labeled it a counterculture or counter-aesthetic.[136] On the other hand, John Canoe had only a tangential relation to Africa. In fact, what struck most observers about its form was it indebtedness to European performances, especially Christmas festivals and, in its mimicry of the European saturnalia, John Canoe would appear to be just a displaced European aesthetic, just another version of the Christmas masque common in Europe since the Middle Ages, now transplanted to the slave cultures of the West Indies.[137]

However, John Canoe was more than the slaves' version of the European saturnalia. According to Jamaican lexicographer Frederick Cassidy, the festival had a complex development and uncertain meaning, one that provides important pointers to the cultural entanglement that created the African diaspora.[138] Consider, for example, the enigmatic geography of the festival. In one form or another, John Canoe was spread across several West Indian islands from the beginning of slavery in the late seventeenth century to the dawn of independence in the 1960s. The essential features of John Canoe were first identified by Sir Hans Sloane in 1707 and definitively named by Edward Long in 1774 and Peter Marsden in 1788, suggesting that the festival had been part of West Indian slave culture throughout the eighteenth century. John Canoe was present in almost all prominent accounts of Jamaica through the long eighteenth century, the nineteenth century, and the early twentieth century, attracting the attention of a diverse group of observers from Matthew Gregory Lewis; Lady

Nugent, the wife of the governor; and the American anthropologist Mary Beckwith.

In contrast, reports of John Canoe in United States are scanty; the only traces of the festival are found in a tiny part of North Carolina, where its life was short.[139] Why did John Canoe not take root in the antebellum South? Or to put it another way, why did John Canoe become such an important feature of West Indian slave society and not of the American South? Questions of geography are further complicated by the lack of consensus about the meaning and origins of John Canoe. Edward Long considered the dance to be "an honourable memorial of John Conny," a West African slave trader and representative of the Prussian government at Axim on the Gold Coast.[140] Cassidy traces the etymology of the word to the Ewe people of Ghana and speculates that it is a corruption of "Sorcerer Man."[141]

My concerns here are not, however, philological; rather, I am interested in the cultural work the festival was asked to perform as an aesthetic response to enslavement, which depended as much on the appropriation of the European Christmas festival as its mockery or deformation. In this context, three aspects of John Canoe demand particular attention. First, like other dances and festivals, John Canoe was perceived as a temporary respite from the regimen of slavery. It took place during the Christmas break, a season when, Janet Schaw noted, "the crack of the inhuman whip must not to be heard . . . nothing but joy and pleasantry to be seen or heard."[142] Lady Nugent, in the patronizing tone expected of the governor's wife, described the John Canoe festivities that she witnessed in Jamaica on December 25, 1801, as evidence of the slaves' "short-lived and baby-like pleasure."[143] All observers noted that this was the season of bacchanal and unbound pleasure; with its masked figures and exuberant music, John Canoe was a form of off-season carnival.

Second, the character and meaning of the festival was predicated on its brazen imitation of what the slaves considered European—more specifically, English—forms of entertainment. Observing a John Canoe festival in Jamaica in the mid-1780s, Marsden noted that the men dressed in "the English mode, with cocked hats, cloth coats, silk stockings, white waistcoats, Holland shirts, and pumps" in a perfect imitation or mimicry of the eighteenth-century person of taste, and black male slaves danced minuets with "the mulattoes and other brown women."[144] Crucially, this imitation of the English mode was also a form of deformation. When slaves danced the minuet, Marsden noted, they did so with "a degree of affectation that renders the whole truly laughable and ridiculous."[145] Writing about ten years later, William Beckford noted that during John Canoe, mulattoes in Jamaica would hold public balls and "view with each other in the splendour of their appearance; and it will hardly be credited how very expensive their dress and ornaments are, and what pains they take to disfigure themselves with powder and with other unbecoming imitations of European dress."[146]

Third, John Canoe stood out as a cultural form because of its apparent disfiguration of the very aesthetic forms that the slaves were imitating. From its very beginning, Long noted in 1774, John Canoe, perhaps drawing on African masquerade arts, thrived on the grotesque. He further observed that during the Christmas holidays, in all the towns of Jamaica "appeared several tall robust fellows dressed up in grotesque habits, and a pair of ox-horns on their head, sprouting from the top of a horrid sort of vizor or mask, which about the mouth is rendered very terrific with big boar-tusks."[147] Among these fellows was a masquerader, "carrying a wooden sword in his hand … followed with a numerous crowd of drunken women, who refresh him frequently with a cup of aniseed-water, whilst he dances at every door, bellowing out John Connu! with great vehemence; so that, what with the liquor and the exercise, most of them are thrown into dangerous fevers; and some examples have happened of their dying."[148]

John Canoe had two faces and functions: one imitated the culture of taste; the other mocked it. The title character in the masque, the figure of John Canoe, tended to have what one anonymous observer called "two faces, different from each other."[149] One face imitated the measured manners of the European court; the other face, which was notable for its hideousness, was a distortion of the symmetrical form of the accepted aesthetic. Even when the John Canoe figure did not have two faces, its doubleness was implicit in the split between the masked head, "which is often rendered hideous by beards and boar's tasks," and the "fantastic cut of their cloaths, often of silk and sometimes enriched with lace" (fig. 6.12).[150] How does one explain this doubleness? One could argue that the economy of mimicry in John Canoe was also a form of mockery, one that enabled the slave to parody the culture of taste by confronting it with its ridiculous, unacknowledged side. In its menacing presence, John Canoe would mark black difference from the very culture that it was ostensibly imitating.[151] On another level, however, John Canoe had a significant, though sublimated, relation to the Africa of the slaves' imagination.

The latter aspect of the festival can be discerned more clearly if we reflect on the key transformations that were taking place in the structure and meaning of John Canoe in the course of the eighteenth century. For if John Canoe had indeed started an Africanist festival, one indebted to West African masking traditions, its name, whether drawn from the Ewe or, as Long had speculated, after a slave trader at Axim, registered the slaves' sense of belonging and unbelonging; it designated both the tenacity of African memory and its displacement, both continuity and rupture.

Cynric Williams presented the acute bifurcation of John Canoe when he noted, in an 1827 account, that the custom was "African and religious, although the purpose is forgotten."[152]

Certainly some of the most apparent transformations in the festival were closely connected to fading African memories, but as slaves born in Africa died and were succeeded by Creoles, so did the semiotics of the festival change. Indeed, by the beginning of the nineteenth century, the aesthetic of John Canoe was primarily determined by a competition between African- and West Indian–born slaves, a fact that was accentuated by the arrival of Creoles fleeing from Haiti in the aftermath of the revolution in the early 1790s. Thus at precisely the point when John Canoe had become a central feature of colonial culture, one acknowledged by the rich and powerful who were now keen to show off the masquerade to European visitors, it had become a mark of the absence of Africa and its memories. And it was the festival's tenuous relation to Africa and its memories as much as the arrival of Haitian Creoles in Jamaica that enabled the semiotic transformations that were evident for most of the nineteenth century. In the early days of slavery, for example, John Canoe derived its moral value from an implicit association with African ceremonies, including the Yam festivals, which had attracted the attention of slavers on the West African coast as perverted forms of pleasure and religious ritual. Significantly, like earlier slave dances, the early John Canoe festival was an occasion to inscribe the distinctiveness of the different nationalities that had been brought together under the yoke of slavery. In 1769, Long records, "several new masks appeared; the Ebos, the Pawpaws, etc. having their respective Connus, male and female, who were dressed in a very laughable style."[153] As late as the 1790s, slaves were deploying the festival as a symbol of their real or imagined African nationalities, a point noted by an anonymous observer in the *Colombian Magazine* of April–October 1797: "The negroes from different districts in Guinea associate in parties and wander about the town, diverting themselves with their own peculiar singing, instruments."[154]

Increasingly, however, the festivals observed at the end of the eighteenth century and for most of the early nineteenth century were no longer part of the slave's attempt to commemorate Africa or to hold on to national identities. Significant changes were apparent even in the material objects of the festival and its costumes. Errol Hill notes that as the festival evolved in response to the changing institutions of the plantation, what had been previously seen as insignias of Africa—animal skins and horns, for example—were replaced by symbols of what could be described as the modern: "Military apparel replaced animal skins, models of ships and great houses were carried on the head instead of horns."[155] Or as Richardson Wright put it, "John Canoe assumed a much more picturesque air."[156]

6.12 I. M. Belisario, "Jaw-Bone, or House John-Canoe, 1837–38." From Isaac Mendes Belisario, *Sketches of character, in illustration of the habits, occupation, and costume of the Negro population, in the island of Jamaica.*

By 1823, when Cynric Williams observed John Canoe in Jamaica, the festival seemed to have lost all of its oppositional force, reduced, as noted earlier, to pure mimicry. Indeed, Williams's description suggests that John Canoe had become a minstrel show performed to entertain the planter class and their guests rather than to affirm the slaves' sense of identity or being:

> They were all dressed in their best; some of the men in long-tailed coats, one of the gombayers in old regimentals; the women in muslins and cambrics, with coloured handkerchiefs tastefully disposed round their heads, and ear-rings, necklaces, and bracelets of all sorts, in profusion. The entertainment was kept up till nine or ten o'clock in the evening, and during the time they were regaled with punch and santa in abundance; they came occasionally and asked for porter and wine. Indeed a perfect equality seemed to reign among all parties; many came and shook hands with their master and mistress, nor did the young ladies refuse this salutation any more than the gentlemen. The merriment became rather boisterous as the punch operated, and the slaves sang satirical philippics against their master, communicating a little free advice now and then; but they never lost sight of decorum and at last retired, apparently quite satisfied with their saturnalia, to dance the rest of the night at their own habitations.[157]

Moreover, the process of creolization—and the imminent end of slavery—presented the festival with a new set of pressures that forced it to develop new forms to account for its relevance. These pressures were most manifest in the evolution of another Christmas festival in the West Indies, the so-called Set-Girls, groups of glamorous performances associated with Haitian Creoles. At a time when the authority of Africanism had diminished, the Set-Girls, who appeared more European, presented an alternative aesthetic, a counter-counter-aesthetic, as it were. If the masked figures of John Canoe embodied an imaginary Africa, the descriptions and sketches of the Set-Girls looked toward an imaginary Europe. When the English painter Isaac Mendes Belisario presented the world with his glamorous lithographs of the Set-Girls on the eve of emancipation, the Christmas festival had become part of a pure exhibition order that no longer claimed to be connected to ancestral worlds (fig. 6.13). By the time John Canoe retreated into the Jamaican countryside in the second half of the nineteenth century, it had come to be perceived, together with the Set-Girls, at best as pure play and at worst as a pale imitation of Englishness.

Had John Canoe been transformed from a performance whose goal was to disturb the established rule of taste and good manners to a harmless minstrel show? Once again, white reaction to the festival offers some useful clues to its changing contexts. In its beginnings, John Canoe set out to terrorize white sensibility. Writing from Jamaica in 1687, for example, Sloane noted that slaves tied cow tails and other "odd things" to their bodies in order to give them what he called "an extraordinary appearance."[158] By the beginning of the nineteenth century, however, John Canoe was being described as a colorful costume party. If in the early years of enslavement, John Canoe costumes were deliberately intended to call attention to black distinctiveness, by the end of the slave period in the West Indies festival participants sought ornaments that repressed Africanness; it had become a medium of displaying the black's mastery and possession of white fashion. Describing a John Canoe festival in 1806, John Stewart was struck by how the slaves were able to alter their "race of being" through ornamentation: "They show themselves off to the greatest advantage, by fine clothes and a profusion of trinkets; they affect a more polished behaviour and mode of speech; they address the whites with greater familiarity."[159]

When the slaves appeared in front of Lewis's house to perform in a festival ostensibly in his honor, they turned up in ornaments that seemed to defy their "natural" order, striving to cover their blackness with the veneer of Englishness:

About two o'clock they began to assemble round the house, all drest in their holiday clothes, which, both for men and women, were chiefly white; only that the women were decked out with a profusion of beads and corals, and gold ornaments of all descriptions; and that while the blacks wore jackets, the mulattoes generally wore cloth coats; and inasmuch as they were all plainly clean

6.13 I. M. Belisario, "Red Set-Girls, and Jack-in-the-Green, 1837–38." From Isaac Mendes Belisario, *Sketches of character, in illustration of the habits, occupation, and costume of the Negro population, in the island of Jamaica.*

instead of being shabbily fashionable, and affected to be nothing except that which they really were, they looked twenty times more like gentlemen than nine tenths of the bankers' clerks who swagger up and down Bond Street.[160]

If the African masks of the early John Canoe were alien and alienating, like the fetishes that haunted early modern travelers to the West African coast, the ornaments of the late festival seemed easy to explain in familiar terms, such as bankers swaggering up and down Bond Street, or Creoles dancing familiar European steps such as the aire and bolero. The bullroarers of the old John Canoe might have scared well-bred ladies, but when they appeared before Lady Nugent in December 25, 1801, they were easily fitted into an existing grid of explanation: the "blackies" dancing with "the greatest glee amused," she noted in her journal.[161] It is erroneous, however, to argue that the later, creolized version of John Canoe was just a misplaced form of entertainment. Beneath the mimicry of European form, the festival seemed to have been calibrated to account for changed circumstances, for transformed moral economies.

Let me clarify this point: In his famous essay on the moral economy of the English crowd in the eighteenth century, E. P. Thompson has noted that grievances of ordinary people in the English countryside were structured or overdetermined by a popular consensus as to what was legitimate and illegitimate in the political economy of food production and distribution. What enabled this consensus, Thompson argued, was not so much the presence of tangible grievances but a general understanding of a set of communal expectations. Social consensus, then, was "grounded upon a consistent traditional view of social norms and obligations, of the proper economic functions of several parties within the community, which, taken together, can be said to constitute the moral economy of the poor."[162] Thompson further noted that "an outrage to these moral assumptions, quite as much as actual deprivation was the usual occasion for direct action."[163]

Slaves, too, had a consensual sense of their grievances, and they had a deep understanding of the "social norms and obligations" that ensured their selfhood in conditions that tended to abnegate their identity. What we see in the transformation of John Canoe, as a field of play intended to clear a space of identity in the midst of its denial, is how an even keener sense of norms and obligations would change as the idea of Africa came to be supplemented by the reality of the new-world plantation. The early John Canoe favored the grotesque exhibition of the body, adopting and rehearsing the elements of the African that the culture of taste feared most. It was seditious. The later John Canoe favored mimicry; it preferred the familiar over the distant, making European ornaments central to its cultural project. However, what might have appeared to be an emptiness of meaning in this later version was also a form of resistance, because, as Jones and Stallybrass have shown, clothes, like masks, are informed by an economy of "animatedness," an "ability to 'pick up' subjects, to shape them both physically and socially, to constitute subjects through their power as material memories."[164]

The irony, of course, is that in both its two guises—as a form of extreme ugliness or affected beauty—John Canoe, like other slave festivals, enabled the displaced Africans to assert their sensorium and thus to constitute themselves as feeling subjects. This claim is ironic in a double sense: First, in recognizing the space of play as a site of identity, the slaves were deploying the field of the aesthetic, of manners, of sense and sensibility, from which they had been excluded by the ideologists of taste, to imagine an alternative way of being, detouring slavery and displacing the claim that they were mere objects. The second irony is that in mastering and presenting what white observers saw as mere noise, rudeness, and boisterousness, the slaves had unwittingly recognized and invested in one of the original premises of the aesthetic ideology—namely Alexander Baumgarten's claim that the aesthetic constituted "the science of sensual cognition."[165]

Does this mean that the slaves' aesthetic could will into being an alternative, transcendental space, above the conditions that generated it in the first place? Clearly, nothing the slaves did during the Christmas festival could alter the condition of enslavement itself or the phenomenology of bondage. But in the realm of the aesthetic, or simply of sensuousness, slaves could deceive reality itself by performing happiness in place of suffering and sorrow or by generating and sustaining pathos where they were supposed to be content. But there are some outstanding questions: did the performance of happiness (or melancholy) ameliorate enslavement, thus enabling slaves to acquire a measure of humanity, or was the so-called consolation of art itself an illusion, a form of false consciousness, the opium of beauty in conditions of abjection?

Paradoxically, it is the culture of taste itself that had made the palliative of art central to the autonomy of the self in conditions of subjection, and the simulation of happiness a key condition of modern identity. In the *Theory of Moral Sentiments*, Adam Smith had argued that the simulation of happiness, one animated by desire and imagination, was crucial to the development of civilization. For Smith, the simulation of happiness was the deception that aroused and kept "in continual motion the industry of mankind": "It is this which first prompted them to cultivate the ground, to build houses, to found cities and commonwealths, and to invent and improve all the sciences and arts, which ennoble and embellish human life; which have entirely changed the whole face of the globe, have turned the rude forests of nature into agreeable and fertile plains, and made the trackless and barren ocean a new fund of subsistence, and the great high road of communication to the different nations of the earth."[166]

A similar act of dissimulation seemed to be at work in the ontology of African slaves in the West Indies and elsewhere. In the days of festivities, slaves imagined themselves living somewhere else, back home in Guinea, or performing in European courts, free and happy. In reality, however, they knew that the work of art articulated the absence of these imaginary homelands and the lack of freedom, the essential condition of a modern identity. A Jamaican slave song aptly called "If Me Want for Go in a Ebo" captured this absence well:

> If me want for go in a Ebo,
> Me can't go there!
> Since dem tief me from a Guinea,
> Me can't go there!
>
> If me want for go in a Congo,
> Me can't go there!
> Since dem tief me from my tatta,
> Me can't go there!
>
> If me want for go in a Kingston,
> Me can't go there!
> Since massa go in a England,
> Me can't go there![167]

This slave song in Jamaican Creole was calling attention to the state of unhomeliness that defined the condition of the black as a modern subject: when they wanted to go back home to the Ebo of their imagination, the slaves found themselves stranded, because they had already been stolen from Guinea; they couldn't go back to Congo or Kingston either, and they would not go to England, where the master had retreated. How, then, could the slaves, given this perpetual homelessness, inscribe their identity?

My argument in this chapter is that whether they were produced in defiance or imitation of the culture of taste, the works of art imagined and implemented by slaves, from buildings to dances and festivals, enabled the enslaved to redefine their relation to time and space, to reconstitute their own bodies and social relationships outside the shadow of their masters, and thus to display bodies that were not mere chattel. The animatedness of the slave in festival, the explosiveness of the body, the celebration of excess, was at odds with all the assumptions that governed white taste and polite behavior, the essence of Englishness and modern identity.

In positioning itself against the norms of polite behavior and its regimes of controlled or regulated feelings, the slaves' negative sensorium became one of the most important arsenals in the making of the black self. As Sigmund Freud noted in his study of negativity, symbolic negation has the capacity to free the self from "the limitations of repression."[168] It was through this kind of negation that African slaves positioned themselves against the systems that excluded them and found a way out of social death. But as one colonialist discovered to his dismay, aesthetic autonomy was not a substitute for true freedom, nor was dissimulation an alternative to the real condition of enslavement and its pathologies.

In June 1834, in the "apprenticeship period" leading to the emancipation of slaves in the British West Indies, Richard Robert Madden, an Irish doctor and special magistrate in Jamaica, set out on a sentimental journey to the town of Claremont to seek an old slave previously owned by his grand-uncle. Given the long years the old African had faithfully served his uncle (forty as a "waiting boy"), Madden approached the encounter like a family reunion, and his first goal was to establish a genealogy between dead masters and surviving slaves and to share what he assumed were common memories. On meeting the old slave, Madden wanted to know, among other things, whether the old slave was sorry to hear that his old master had died in England; he also wanted to explore their common past as a way of reconnecting with the other side of his "family." After all, as noted earlier, West Indian and antebellum masters considered their slaves to be kith and kin, and Madden had no reason to doubt that masters and slaves shared a common bond.

But this family drama did not turn out the way Madden had expected. Much to Madden's chagrin and puzzlement, the old slave would not have anything to do with this family romance or be a willing participant in what he perhaps considered to be contrived sentimental encounters or re-creations of painful pasts under the guise of shared memory. Simply put, the old African slave went out of his way to deflate any filial connections to his old master and to renounce any empathy for the gentleman he had served and ostensibly revered for forty years. In fact, the old slave had nothing but scorn for the man who had "brought him out of a Guinea ship when a piccanini boy."[169] This is how the encounter ended:

> The man was now becoming impatient. I thought it time to awaken his sensibility by telling him at once that I was the nearest relative of old master he had seen for forty years. I was ready to extend my hand for a hearty shake. I was prepared, as I have said before, for an affecting scene; judge of my disappointment—
>
> "For true! you belong old massa: well, what you want here? you come to carry away old stones from Marley—plenty of old stones on grounds at Marley—you come carry away more old massa's money—whara you find it?—no more poor niggers to sell at Marley."
>
> The old man, as he made the concluding observation, gave me a look which I would not willingly meet at the day of judgment. He turned away with the greatest indifference, humming to himself as he toddled toward the garden that sentimental negro air:
>
> "Hi, massa buckra, sorry for your loss,
> Better go to Lunnon town, and buy another oss."[170]

This encounter between Madden, a reluctant heir to a ruined plantation, and an African slave in the apprenticeship of freedom contains useful insights into what an air of real freedom could do to the human soul. Madden, a man of liberal sympathies presiding over the end of slavery in a Jamaican county, had misjudged the nature of slavery and its mnemonics. He had mistaken the old man's affectation of happiness in bondage as affection. He had mistaken the master/slave relationship for kinship. Above all, he had misjudged the moral economy of freedom, the transformation of obligations and responsibilities engendered by the passage of the Emancipation Act of 1833 and the coming of freedom, which, painfully in the West Indian case, was to be put in abeyance for five years. The old African's indifference—and his mocking air—was his recognition that freedom, even when it was postponed to save the plantation system, had changed his status and his sense of expectations. Freedom had created a different context for the "sentimental negro air." Negro airs, as aesthetic objects (songs) or expressions of attitudes, had already anticipated this moment, conjuring another way of being in the world, a counter-aesthetic. The ghost of slavery, however, would have a long life—a life as long as that of the category of taste, one of its twins in the making of modern identity.

Coda:
Three Fragments

Fragment I

On February 13, 1819, James Tallmadge Jr., the Republican representative from New York, rose in the U.S. Congress to introduce an amendment to the bill seeking to grant statehood to Missouri. He proposed that "the further introduction of slavery or involuntary servitude be prohibited" in Missouri as a condition for its entry into the union and that "all children of slaves, born within the said state, after admission thereof into the union, shall be free at the age of twenty-five years."[1] Since Alabama, a slave-owning state, had recently been admitted into the union, the overt goal of the amendment was to ensure that the balance of power between slave-owning and non-slave-owning states was maintained.

Tallmadge's amendment had more dramatic consequences than the congressman had intended, for rather than leading to a simple resolution of the question of power and its balance between the states, it provoked what has been described as the most "remarkable week of debate in the history of Congress."[2] The amendment put slavery at the center of debates on the nature of the union and its republican virtues, and by the end of 1819 and continuing into 1820, the Missouri issue provided a forum for the most candid discussion of slavery, caught between the guilt and shame it provoked and its value as a special form of property. For if Tallmadge's motives for introducing the amendment were driven by the moral sense that slavery was wrong, or that it went against Christian values and republican virtues, his opponents from the slaveholding states considered the institution central to the well-being of their economies and a key pillar of the Southern way of life and its civilization.

7.1 A Slave-Coffle Passing the Capitol. From William Cullen
Bryant and Sidney Howard Gay, *A Popular History of the
United States* (New York, 1881), vol. 4, p. 266.

But whether it was considered an absence in the North or a presence in
the South, slavery informed the ideologies of the new republic; it constituted that powerful American Africanism that, in Toni Morrison's words,
has "provided the staging ground and arena for the elaboration of the
quintessential American identity."[3] In fact, even as the Missouri debate
was in progress, the ghost of slavery—the figure that enabled and disas-
sembled modern identity—would appear on the streets of Washington,
D.C., in the form of a slave coffle (fig. 7.1).

The very appearance of a procession of slaves in the nation's capital,
noted Tallmadge, was a vivid illustration of the way of life the South
wanted to preserve:

> Since we have been engaged in this debate, we have witnessed an elucidation
> of this argument, of bettering the condition of slaves, by spreading them over
> the country. A slave driver, a trafficker in human flesh, as if sent by Provi-
> dence, has passed the door of your Capitol, on his way to the West, driving
> before him about fifteen of these wretched victims of his power, collected in
> the course of his traffic, and, by their removal, torn from every relation, and
> from every tie which the human heart can hold dear. The males, who might
> raise the arm of vengeance and retaliate for their wrongs, were hand-cuffed,
> and chained to each other, while the females and children were marched in
> their rear, under the guidance of the driver's whip! Yes, sir, such has been the

scene witnessed from the windows of Congress Hall, and viewed by members who compose the legislative councils of Republican America.[4]

Could any state of freedom be imagined outside the shadow of slavery?

FRAGMENT II

Sometimes the repressed histories of the enslaved would emerge out of their places of entombment to question the drive of modernity and modernization. At least that seems to have been the case in June 1991when excavations for a new federal government office building in New York City revealed the remains of four hundred Africans, mostly slaves, who had been buried there, some as early as the 1690s. Here, below the ground in Lower Manhattan, a place intimately associated with a triumphant culture of consumption and taste, on the site where the logic of modernization and capitalism rose as high as the glass and steel buildings that protruded over the Atlantic Ocean and the Hudson River, lay the allegory of the ruin of modernity, its petrified life hidden so that its glories would shine.[5]

In these remains of African slaves in New York, the peculiar institution had been preserved as, to borrow words from Susan Burck-Morss, "a skeletal residue with its empty stare that was once, an animated face."[6] These stories—of skeletons in the closet of modernity—can be found everywhere modernity has taken root from Vera Cruz, Mexico, to Cape Town, South Africa. Here, too, the insignias of modern civilization—the ports and the cruise ships, the modern university, and the vineyards—rise over the bones of the enslaved. How can these ghosts be laid to rest? Can civilization be freed from the specter of difference?

FRAGMENT III

On January 20, 2009, around noon Eastern Standard Time, Barack Hussein Obama was inaugurated as the forty-fourth president of the United States, an event attended by a million people and watched by around 600 million worldwide. Among the many meanings adduced to this historic event, the most poignant was perhaps the claim that it had raised the ghost of slavery and then put it to rest. For if slavery was the mark of the exclusion of the African from the institutions of modern culture, then it could be said that the election of a black person to the highest office in the land, an act that guaranteed that the son of an African was now the custodian of late modernity and its problems, seemed to be proof that the catastrophe of history was also the condition of possibility of the idea of human freedom.

Obama was sworn in before a monument built by African slaves; his historical procession walked on ground trodden by coffles of black men, women, and children in shackles; a slave market once stood on the same mall where the masses had gathered to serenade the new president; many of his illustrious predecessors had assumed that their standing as members of the American aristocracy was connected to the ownership of slaves. Did the election of a black president imply that the continuum of history had exploded and that the dream of freedom as the universal right of all human beings had been realized? Had the story of slavery, as some commentators suggested, turned full circle?[7]

Derek Walcott, who had started his illustrious poetic career agonizing over the meaning of the vault of new world experience, would see lyrical possibilities in the breakup of history:

> Out of the turmoil emerges one emblem, an engraving —
> a young Negro at dawn in straw hat and overalls,
> an emblem of impossible prophecy, a crowd
> dividing like the furrow which a mule has ploughed,
> parting for their president.[8]

Was it possible that slavery, which had functioned as the threshold of modernity, would no longer haunt the present? Only time would tell. What seemed obvious was that the ghosts in the archives and tombs of the modern world would perhaps need a new language to account for the "impossible prophecy" signified by the Obama moment. Hence the aura of blackness would need to be cast in new terms, new idioms, and new vocabularies; it would have to be displaced from its traditional inscription as the stigmata of modernity. Then the turmoil of slavery would give way to what was always assumed, by masters and slaves alike, to be the impossible prophecy of a common modern identity.

Notes

PREFACE

1. Walcott, "The Sea Is History," *Collected Poems*, 364.
2. Abraham and Torok, "Mourning *or* Melancholia," 125–38.
3. Ibid., 130.
4. Douglas, *Purity and Danger*, 3.
5. Ibid., 7.
6. Said, *Culture and Imperialism*, 41–42.
7. Fanon, *Wretched of the Earth*, 227.

CHAPTER ONE. OVERTURE: SENSIBILITY IN THE AGE OF SLAVERY

1. Bosman, *New and Accurate Description*, 117.
2. The image of the black in the early modern period is outside the scope of this book, but see the following general surveys by Erickson, "Representations of Blacks and Blackness," 499–527, and "Moment of Race," 27–36; and the essays collected in *Black Africans in Renaissance Europe*, ed. Earler and Lowe. See also the pioneering work of E. Jones, *Elizabethan Image* and *Othello's Countrymen*. See also K. Hall, *Things of Darkness*; Loomba, *Shakespeare, Race, and Colonialism*; and the essays collected in Hendricks and Parker, *Women, "Race," and Writing*.
3. Kunst, *African in European Art*, 23. Kunst's view is challenged or qualified by Kim Hall in "Object into Object?" 346–79. For a biography of Rembrandt, see Schama, *Rembrandt's Eyes*.
4. Donnan in *Documents Illustrative of the History* 1:149–50. The book was first published by the Carnegie Institution of Washington, D.C., 1930–1935.
5. The civilizing process is discussed by Elias in *Civilizing Process*, 363–448.
6. This point has been underscored by Allison Blakely in *Blacks in the Dutch World*, 119. Kim Hall provides a compelling reading of the role of the black figure on the margins of the early modern portrait in "Object into Object?" 321–24.

7. Benjamin, "Work of Art," 17–52. Here I'm thinking of Karl Marx's famous use of a religious analogy to describe the emergence, in capitalism, of a relationship "between men, that assumes, in their eyes, the fantastic form of a relation between things" and his precise conclusion: "This I call the Fetishism which attaches itself to the products of labour, so soon as they are produced as commodities, and which is therefore inseparable from the production of commodities." See *Capital* 1:165. What Marx forgot to say was that the concept of the fetish (Portuguese *fetissio*) was invented to describe trade relations on the West African slave coast. This is the subject of a series of remarkable essays by William Pietz: "Problem of the Fetish, I," "Problem of the Fetish, II," "Problem of the Fetish, IIIa." See also his "Fetishism and Materialism."

8. Mauss, "Category of the Human Mind." See also Charles Taylor's essay, "The Person." The literature on modernity is too extensive to cite here, but I have relied on the classical philosophical texts, including C. Taylor, *Sources of the Self* and *Secular Age*; Blumenberg, *Legitimacy of the Modern Age*; Cassirer, *Philosophy of the Enlightenment*; and Habermas, *Philosophical Discourse*. For a historical exploration of the making of the self in a specifically eighteenth-century English context, see Wahrman, *Making of the Modern Self.*

9. The key documents here, which I will be referring to throughout this chapter and the next, are Mendelssohn, "On the Question: What is Enlightenment?" Kant, "An Answer to the Question: What is Enlightenment?" Hume, *Treatise on Human Nature*; Hutcheson, *Inquiry into the Original of Our Ideas*; Kames, *Essays on the Principles*; and A. Smith, *Theory of Moral Sentiments.*

10. Kant, "Answer to the Question," 55.

11. Outram, *Enlightenment*, 3. See also her *Panorama of the Enlightenment.* As will become apparent, the debates surrounding the project of Enlightenment do not occupy the center of my project, which will focus on the British tradition of taste, but the larger philosophical debates are pertinent. For these, see the essays collected in Schmidt, *What is Enlightenment?* See also Habermas, "Modernity," 3–15. For the Enlightenment outside the North European circuit, see Venturi, *Italy and the Enlightenment*; Hulme and Jordanova, *Enlightenment and Its Shadows*; and Eze, *Race and the Enlightenment.* For slavery and the Enlightenment, see Duchet, *Anthropologie et historie*; and Cohen, *French Encounter with Africans.*

12. Kant, "Answer to the Question," 55.

13. Kant, *Observations on the Feeling*, 110–11. The question of racism in Kant is outside the scope of my discussion, but it has generated significant debate in revisionary histories of the Enlightenment. Thomas Hill and Bernard Boxill focus on Kant's concern for universal freedom and consider racism tangential to his project; see their "Kant and Race." For a contrary view, see Eze, "Color of Reason"; and Bernasconi, "Who Invented the Concept of Race?" See also Neugerbauer, "Racism of Hegel and Kant"; and Judy, "Kant and the Negro."

14. Stallybrass and White, *Politics and Poetics*, 3.

15. Cited in Eze, *Race and the Enlightenment*, 91.

16. Quoted in Kramnick, *Portable Enlightenment Reader*, 669.

17. Wahrman, *Making of the Modern Self*, xv.

18. Reiss, introduction to *Kant: Political Writings*, 18.

19. A. Smith, *Theory of Moral Sentiments*, 216–17. My discussion here is indebted to Howard Caygill, *Art of Judgement*, 38–97.

20. Cassirer, *Philosophy of the Enlightenment*, 9.

21. Here, I provide a synopsis of a debate that has generated a lot of literature. In addition to Cassirer, see Eagleton, *Ideology of the Aesthetic*; Bernstein, *Fate of Art*; Osborne, *From an Aesthetic Point of View*; Hammermeister, *German Aesthetic Tradition*; Guyer, *Kant and the Claims of Taste*; and Woodmansee, *Author, Art, and the Market*.

22. Hulme and Jordanova, introduction to *Enlightenment and Its Shadows*, 7.

23. Outram, *Panorama of the Enlightenment*, 142–46.

24. Decorse, *Archeology of Elmina*, 25. See also Boxer, *Portuguese Seaborne Empire, 1415–1825*.

25. Blakely, *Blacks*, 104–5.

26. Ibid., 105.

27. Said, *Culture and Imperialism*, 66. For a discussion of the black Atlantic as a counterculture of modernity, see Gilroy, *Black Atlantic*, 1–40.

28. Kristeller, *Renaissance Thought and the Arts*, 164. For a philosophical/historical exploration of the system of art, see Preben Mortensen in *Art in the Social Order*, 1–12, and the essays collected in Mattick, *Eighteenth-Century Aesthetics*.

29. Kristeller, *Renaissance Thought*, 164.

30. Ibid., 225. For Kristeller, a key element in the transformation of the arts was the emergence of the amateur as a critic: "The origin of modern aesthetics in amateur criticism would go a long way to explain why works of art have until recently been analyzed by aestheticians from the point of view of the spectator, reader and listener rather than of the producing artist" (225).

31. Addison and Steele, *Spectator* 1:31.

32. Danto, *Philosophical Disenfranchisement*, 166.

33. Cassirer, *Philosophy of the Enlightenment*, 278.

34. Ibid., 339.

35. In addition to Cassirer, the question of criticism in the Enlightenment has been discussed by Anthony Cascardi in *Consequences of Enlightenment*, 49–91.

36. When I commenced work on this book, the major division in the field of aesthetic criticisms was between those who insisted on the redemptive work of art—its capacity to make truth claims—and those who dismissed its function as an alternative mode of knowledge. For the cognitive claims of art and aesthetic alienation, see Bernstein, *Fate of Art*, 1–16; and Osborne, introduction to *From an Aesthetic Point of View*, 1–12. Terry Eagleton dismisses the political project of the aesthetics as part of the middle-class search for political hegemony; see *Ideology of the Aesthetic*, 3. See also T. Bennett, *Outside Literature*; and Beech and Roberts, "Spectres of the Aesthetic."

37. Jay, "'Aesthetic Ideology' as Ideology," 46.

38. Horkheimer and Adorno, *Dialectic of Enlightenment*, 19.

39. Menke, "Modernity, Subjectivity," 46.

40. For a discussion of Sterne's rhetoric and ethics of sensibility in relation to slavery, see Wood, *Slavery, Empathy and Pornography*, 12–18.

41. Sancho, *Letters of the Late Ignatius Sancho,* 31. See also Sancho, *New Light on the Life of Ignatius Sancho*.

42. In addition to his letters, Sancho's investment in the culture of taste can be detected in his musical compositions. See J. Wright, *Ignatius Sancho* and the essays collected in King, et al., *Ignatius Sancho*. For a study of the role of black writing during the period, see Sandiford, *Measuring the Moment* and *Genius in Bondage*; Ellis, "Ignatius Sancho's Letters"; and Ogude, *Genius in Bondage*.

43. Adorno, *Prisms*, 34.

44. Ashton, *Negative Dialectics*.

45. Caygill, *Art of Judgement*, 98.

46. Kant, *Critique of the Power of Judgment*, 38.

47. E. Burke, *Philosophical Enquiry*, 160–61.

48. A. Smith, *Theory of Moral Sentiments*, 211.

49. Brewer, "'Most Polite Age'," 349.

50. For the histories and discourses of taste and modern subjectivity in Britain, I have relied on the following: Barker-Benfield, *Culture of Sensibility*; De Bolla, *Discourse of the Sublime*; De Bolla et al., *Land, Nation and Culture*; Ashfield and de Bolla, *Sublime Reader*; Bermingham and Brewer, ed., *Consumption of Culture*; Langford, *Polite and Commercial People*; McKendrick, Brewer, and Plumb, *Birth of a Consumer Society*; Paulson, *Breaking and Remaking*; Sekora, *Luxury*; and Todd, *Sensibility*.

51. Bermingham, introduction to *Consumption of Culture*, 4.

52. McKendrick, "Consumer Revolution" in *Birth of a Consumer Society*, 2.

53. Ibid., 9.

54. A detailed exploration of this process can be found in Brewer, *Pleasures of the Imagination*; Mortensen, *Art in the Social*, especially part 2; McKendrick, Brewer, and Plumb, *Birth of a Consumer Society*; Sekora, *Luxury*; and Solkin, *Painting for Money*.

55. Hogarth, *Analysis of Beauty*.

56. R. Jones, *Gender and the Formation of Taste*, 11.

57. In addition to Jones's *Gender and the Formation of Taste*, De Bolla, *Discourse of the Sublime*, and Mortensen, *Art in the Social Order*, excellent discussions of the politics and the discourse of politeness can be found in Barrell, *Political Theory of Painting*; Klein, "Third Earl of Shaftesbury," *Shaftesbury and the Culture of Politeness* and "Politeness for Plebes"; and Pocock, *Virtue, Commerce, and History*.

58. For the way these debates played out in Scotland, see the essays collected in Hont and Ignatieff, *Wealth and Virtue*; and Dwyer and Sher, *Sociability and Society*. For the English provinces, see Wilson, *Sense of the People*.

59. For debates on civility and taste before this period, see Bryson, *From Courtesy to Civility*.

60. A famous example of the mercantile code as the mediator of social relationships can be found at the beginning of Sterne's *Sentimental Journey* where Yorick slips a crown to the French chambermaid, a reward that, observes Robert Markley, "puts a price on her virtue." See Markley, "Sentimentality as Performance."

61. Mortensen, *Art in the Social Order*, 95; and McKendrick, "Consumer Revolution," 14.

62. See Berry, *Idea of Luxury*, 241; and Castronovo, *English Gentleman*.

63. McKendrick, "Consumer Revolution," 10.

64. Steele, *Spectator* 6 (March 7, 1711), in Addison and Steele, *Spectator* 1:26.

65. Quoted in Mortensen, *Art in the Social Order*, 80.

66. Pocock, *Virtue, Commerce and History*, 66.

67. Mortensen, *Art in the Social Order*, 83. For the August desire for order, see Humphreys, "Arts in Eighteenth-Century Britain," 5–7. See also Lipking, *Ordering of the Arts*.

68. Shaftesbury, *Characteristics of Men*, 218. See also Mortensen, *Art in the Social Order*, 107–17; and Klein, *Shaftesbury and the Culture of Politeness*.

69. Hume, "Of the Standard of Taste," 231.

70. Ibid., 231–332.

71. S. Johnson, *Rambler*, no. 92 (February 2, 1751), in *The Rambler* 2:128.

72. E. Burke, *Philosophical Enquiry*, 12.

73. Ibid., 1.

74. E. Burke, *Letters on a Regicide Peace*, 126.

75. Porter, "Enlightenment in England," 11.

76. Lamont and Fournier, *Cultivating Differences*, 9.

77. This point is made powerfully by Bermingham in her introduction to *Consumption of Culture*, 5. I will return to the notion of disavowal later in this chapter, but I am using it strictly in the Freudian sense, not as a reference to negation, but to the subjects' refusal to embrace the consequences, social or psychic, of experiences that they clearly perceived. See Laplanche and Pontalis, *Language of Psycho-Analysis*, 118–21.

78. Ibid., 353.

79. McKendrick, in *Birth of a Consumer Society*, 108.

80. Daniels, *Fields of Vision*, 48. See also McKendrick, "Josiah Wedgwood," in McKendrick et al., *Birth of a Consumer Society*, 100–45.

81. For a discussion of Wright and the spectacle of power and the industrial revolution, see Daniels, *Field of Vision*, 43–79.

82. See McKendrick, "Josiah Wedgwood."

83. Quoted in Honour, *Image of the Black*, 62.

84. Ibid., 62–63.

85. Quoted in Brewer, *Pleasures of the Imagination*, xv.

86. Langford, *Polite and Commercial People*, 5.

87. A. Smith, *Theory of Moral Sentiments*, 214.

88. Ibid., 216.

89. Hume, "Of Refinement in the Arts," 278.

90. The essays collected in Bermingham and Brewer, *Consumption of Culture*, provide solid evidence of the interplay of affirmation and denial in the construction of the culture of taste.

91. Caygill, *Art of Judgement*, 43.

92. Brewer, "'Most Polite Age'," 353. For the ways in which gender could disturb the epistemological boundaries of the culture of taste, see L. Brown, *Fables of Modernity* and *Ends of Empire*; Castle, *Female Thermometer* and *Masquerade and Civilization*; and Nussbaum, *Autobiographical Subject, Torrid Zones*, and *Limits of the Human*.

93. Wilson, introduction to *New Imperial History*. See also Wilson, *Island Race*; Armitage, *Ideological Origins*; and Colley, *Britons*.

94. Nussbaum and Brown, *New Eighteenth Century*, 14. See also Nussbaum, *Global Eighteenth Century*; and Aravamudan, *Tropicopolitans*.

95. See Derrida, *Speech and Phenomena*, 70–71.

96. Mortensen, *Art in the Social Order*, 116.

97. Barrell, *Dark Side of the Landscape*, 5.

98. Wood, *Blind Memory*, 7. For the relation between aesthetics and the culture of pain, see Hartman, *Scenes of Subjection*; and Scarry, *Body in Pain*.

99. For William Blake, see Bindman et al., *Mind-forg'd Manacles*; for visual culture in the slave zones, see Quilley and Kriz, *Economy of Colour*; Kriz, *Slavery, Sugar*; and Tobin, *Picturing Imperial Power*.

100. Walvin, *England, Slaves, and Freedom*. See also Walvin's earlier works: *Black and White*; *Black Ivory*; and *Black Presence*. The literature on blacks in Britain is extensive, but I have found the following useful for this chapter: Gerzina, *Black England* and *Black London*; Fryer, *Staying Power*; Shyllon, *Black Britannia* and *Black Slaves in Britain*; P. Edwards and Walvin, *Black Personalities*; Walvin, *Black Presence*; and Little, *Negroes in Britain*.

101. Walvin, *England, Slaves, and Freedom*, 27.

102. I borrow the concept of "political unconscious" from Jameson, *Political Unconscious*, 17–102.

103. Walvin, *England, Slaves, and Freedom*, 27. Walvin is discussing the specific examples of England here, but his example could be said to apply to the whole of Britain after the Act of Union. If there is slippage between Britishness and Englishness here and elsewhere, it is because after the Act of Union of 1707, Scottish interests tended to be sublimated to English debates, especially in matters of empire. I discuss this problem in Gikandi, *Maps of Englishness*. See also Colley, *Britons*, 11–12.

104. Walvin, *England, Slaves, and Freedom*, 33. A similar set of paradoxes and complexities were at work in France, too, where the emergence and consolidation of a culture of liberty went hand in hand with the development of the slave trade. For this, see McCloy, *Negro in France*; Peabody, *There Are No Slaves in France*; and C. Miller, *French Atlantic Triangle*.

105. Foucault, *History of Sexuality*, 35.

106. For Marx's classical terms, see the preface to his *Contribution to the Critique of Political Economy*, 9–15.

107. Brewer, "Culture as Commodity," 353.

108. C. Miller, *French Atlantic Triangle*, 9.

109. The terms here are borrowed from Mary Douglas's *Purity and Danger*, 1–6, and *In the Wilderness*, especially chapter 3.

110. I return to this topic in subsequent chapters, but see Wyatt-Brown, *Honor and Violence*, and M. Smith, *How Race Is Made*.

111. Douglas, *In the Wilderness*, 25.

112. Finley, *Ancient Slavery*, 60.

113. Garnsey, *Ideas of Slavery*, 5.

114. Wish, "Aristotle, Plato," 83.

115. Garnsey, *Ideas of Slavery*, 5.

116. Fitzhugh, *Sociology for the South*, 244.

117. Quoted in J. White and R. White, *Slavery in the American South*, 113. My argument here is indebted to Page DuBois's, *Slaves and Other Objects*, 3–31.

118. Indigenous African slavery is the subject of Perbi's excellent book, *A History of Indigenous Slavery*. Other important studies of slavery in Africa can be found in Miers and Kopytoff, *Slavery in Africa*.

119. Debates on the political economy of slavery are outside the scope of this project, but for a long historical view, see Anstey, *Atlantic Slave Trade*; Blackburn, *Making of New World Slavery*; Barker, *African Link*; Eltis, *Rise of African Slavery*; Searing, *West African Slavery*; E. Williams, *Capitalism and Slavery*.

120. Derrida, *Specters of Marx*, 4–5. See also Baucom, *Specters of the Atlantic*.

121. Quoted in Jordan, *White over Black*, 74. My discussion of the haunting of freedom by the ghosts of slavery relies heavily on Jordan's discussion of colonial encounters in America. See also Davis's *Problem of Slavery in Western Culture*; and Vaughan, *Roots of American Racism*. For colonial encounters in the Atlantic world, see the essays collected in Canny and Pagden, *Colonial Identity*; Canny, *Oxford History*; and Marshall, *Oxford History*. For the cultural traffic between Africa and the Americas, see Thornton, *Africa and Africans*.

122. Quoted in Eltis, *Rise of African Slavery*, 15.

123. Ibid.

124. Davis, *Problem of Slavery in Western Culture*, 13.

125. Schama, *Embarrassment of Riches*. There were important counterpoints to Schama's history, including Blakely, *Blacks in the Dutch World*; and Burck-Morss, "Hegel and Haiti." Schama's later work on slavery and abolitionism, *Rough Crossings*, can be read as a rectification of his prior omissions, but it begs one of the questions informing my study: why and how can European domestic culture and slavery be treated as part of the same register?

126. Slavery is barely mentioned in C. Taylor, *Sources of the Self* and *Secular Age*, or in Blumenberg, *Legitimacy of the Modern Age*; Cassirer, *Philosophy of the Enlightenment*; or Habermas, *Philosophical Discourse*; it is barely present in Porter, *Enlightenment* or *English Society*; Wahrman's revisionist work, *Making of the Modern Self*, devotes only a few pages to the question of slavery itself.

127. Scarry, *On Beauty and Being Just*, 31.

128. De Bolla, *Art Matters*, 143.

129. Colley, *Britons*, 6. I had taken up and developed this point in *Maps of Englishness*.

130. Aravamudan, *Tropicopolitans*, 12.

131. Nussbaum and Brown, *New Eighteenth Century*, 5.

132. Wilson, introduction to *New Imperial History*, 1, 3. Wilson provides an outstanding revisionist account of nations, empires, and identities in the eighteenth century in *Island Race*.

133. Ibid., 1.

134. Wahrman, *Making of the Modern Self*, xv.

135. Ibid.; emphasis is mine.

136. For Wahrman, see ibid; for Foucault, see afterword to *Michel Foucault*.

137. The work on slave culture is too extensive to cover here, but for antebellum slavery, I have found the following general studies useful: Berlin, *Many Thousands Gone*; Blassingame, *Slave Community* and *Slave Testimony*; Genovese, *Roll, Jordan, Roll*; Levine, *Black Culture and Black Consciousness*; Stuckey, *Slave Culture*; and D. White, *Ar'n't I a Woman?* For slave culture in Jamaica, my

West Indian case study, see Brathwaite, *Folk Culture of the Slaves in Jamaica*; and Patterson, *Sociology of Slavery.*

138. Morrison, *Playing in the Dark*, 13.

139. Dayan, *Haiti, History, and the Gods*, 242.

140. Brathwaite, *Contradictory Omens.*

141. Spillers, "Mama's Baby, Papa's Maybe," 6.

142. Sharpe, *Ghosts of Slavery*, 1–2.

143. Hartman, *Lose Your Mother*, 13.

144. Daston, "Historical Epistemology," 282.

145. Quoted in C. Miller, *French Atlantic Triangle*, 39.

146. Ricoeur, *Symbolism of Evil*, 37.

147. Wilson, introduction to *New Imperial History*, 16.

148. Trouillot, "Anthropology and the Savage Slot."

149. Lyotard, *Postmodern Condition*, 82. Modern rationality is vigorously defended by Habermas in "Modernity: An Incomplete Project."

150. Lyotard, *Postmodern Condition,* xxiv.

151. Foucault, introduction to *On the Normal and the Pathological*, 12.

152. Ibid.

153. For the role of small stories in the larger history of empire, see Colley, *Captives Britain,* 12; for the vulnerability of the imperial center, see Wilson, introduction, 17; for minorities and ethnics within Britain and the Atlantic world, see Kidd, "Ethnicity in the British Atlantic World" and his earlier *British Identities before Nationalism.*

154. Nussbaum and Brown, *New Eighteenth Century*, 3.

155. C. Hall, *Civilising Subjects*, 16–17.

156. Said, *Culture and Imperialism*, 62–80.

157. Ibid., 74.

158. Bhabha, *Location of Culture*, 114–15. These questions have been raised by others, including D. Scott in *Refashioning Futures* and *Conscripts of Modernity.* See also Casid, *Sowing Empire*, especially chapter 1.

159. Aravamudan, *Tropicopolitans*, 10.

160. For the structure of difference before the eighteenth century, see Bartra, *Wild Men in the Looking Glass*; E. Hall, *Inventing the Barbarian*; Hartog, *Mirror of Herodotus*; and Hodgen, *Early Anthropology.*

161. Dupré, *Passage to Modernity*, 3.

162. This is the subject of important work by Curtin, *Image of Africa*; Cohen, *French Encounter with Africans*; and Hammond and Jablow, *Africa That Never Was.*

163. Gilman, "Figure of the Black," 373. My discussion here is heavily indebted to Gilman. See also Popkin, "Philosophical Basis," 245–62.

164. Gilman, "Figure of the Black," 374.

165. Quoted in Ibid., 374–75.

166. E. Burke, *Philosophical Enquiry*, 131–32. For Burke and the Chelsden experiment, see Gilman, "Figure of the Black"; M. Armstrong, "Effects of Blackness," 213–36; and Aravamudan, *Tropicopolitans*, 192–200.

167. For these two versions of the sublime, see De Bolla, *Discourse of the Sublime*; and Paulson, "Burke's Sublime," 241–69.

168. Wheeler, *Complexion of Race*, 7; emphasis in the original.

169. Ibid.

170. Metz, *Imaginary Signifier*, 61.

171. Jay, "Scopic Regimes of Modernity," 3. See also Crary, *Techniques of the Observer*.

172. For these terms, see Lloyd, *Polarity and Analogy*.

173. See Cavazzi de Montecúccolo, *Descrição histórica dos três reinos do Congo*; Pifagetta, *Report of the Kingdom of Congo*; and Dapper, *Description de l'Afrique*. For a study of these colonial encounters, see Mudimbe-Boyi, *Essais sur les Cultures en Contact*.

174. This point has been made by Bassani and Fagg in *Africa and the Renaissance Art*, 45.

175. Rafael, *Contracting Colonialism*, 210. See also Segal, *Solo in the New Order*.

176. Rafael, *Contracting Colonialism*, 210.

177. Jordan, *White over Black*, 11.

178. See Reilly, "Race and Racism," 126. For Hawkins and his crest, see E. Jones, *Elizabethan Image of Africa*, 17, illustration 6. Hawkins's role in the beginning of the slave trade is discussed by Hazlewood, *Queen's Slave Trader*; and Pollitt, "John Hawkins's Troublesome Voyages," 26–40.

179. Davis, *Problem of Slavery*, 447. Eric Williams, in *Capitalism and Slavery*, argues that debates on the origins of slavery had given a "racial twist" to what was "basically an economic phenomenon" and that slavery "was not born of racism; rather racism was the consequence of slavery" (7), but the centrality of anti-black racism in the development of the peculiar institution is now established in the canonical literature, especially on the antebellum South and the West Indies. In addition to Jordan and Davis, see the conclusions by E. Morgan, *American Slavery, American Freedom*, especially chapter 16; Vaughan, *Roots of American Racism*, chapter 7; and Eltis, *Rise of African Slavery*, chapter 1.

180. E. Morgan, *American Slavery*, 44–70.

181. Vaughan, *Roots of American Racism*, 11, 13. See also Parry, *Image of the Indian and the Black Man*.

182. John C. Miller, *Wolf by the Ears*, 65. See also Jordan, *White over Black*, 429–81.

183. Jefferson, *Notes on the State of Virginia*, 138.

184. Ibid., 140.

185. Quoted in John C. Miller, *Wolf by the Ears*, 62.

186. See Long, *History of Jamaica* 2:351–53.

187. Wahrman, *Making of the Modern Self*, 13.

CHAPTER TWO. INTERSECTIONS: TASTE, SLAVERY, AND THE MODERN SELF

1. Larpent, *Woman's View of Drama,* entry for April 24, 1797. For a discussion of the diaries and Larpent's interest in performance, see Colombo in "This Pen of Mine Will Say Too Much." Useful background for women in the period can be found in Vickery's *Gentleman's Daughter*.

2. Brewer, *Pleasures of the Imagination*, 56–75.

3. Derrida, *Archive Fever*, 3.

4. Park, *Travels in the Interior Districts of Africa*, 375–76.

5. Ibid., 482.

6. Ibid., 491.

7. Ibid., 493.

8. Ibid., 494–95.

9. Kristeva, *Powers of Horror*, 1–2.

10. Brewer, *Pleasures of the Imagination*, 56.

11. Ibid., 57.

12. Ibid.

13. For the centrality of the eighteenth century in the making of modern identity, see C. Taylor, *Sources of the Self*; Habermas, *Structural Transformation*; and Wahrman, *Making of the Modern Self*.

14. R. Williams, *Keywords*, 99.

15. Larpent, *Woman's View of Drama*, entry for April 26, 1797.

16. The major work on the concept of the public sphere is Habermas, *Structural Transformation*. For debates on Habermas's definition of the public sphere, see Calhoun, *Habermas and the Public Sphere*.

17. Bermingham, "Elegant Females," 509. For the paradox of feminine sensibility, see Nussbaum, *Limits of the Human*, especially chapter 2.

18. At the beginning of the novel, Jane Eyre compares her oppressors to slave masters and her revolting mood to that "of the revolted slave . . . bracing me with its bitter vigour." See Brontë, *Jane Eyre*, 18.

19. If we are to argue that the aestheticization of women imprisoned them in the prison house of irrational male desires, as Bermingham seems to suggest, then we will miss the opening that the culture of taste provided for them. I think this is the point Nancy Armstrong was making in her revisionist account of the English novel: "I know of no history of the English novel that can explain why women began to write respectable fiction near the end of the eighteenth century, became prominent novelists during the nineteenth century, and on this basis achieved the status of artists during the modern period. Yet that they suddenly began writing and were recognized as women writers strikes me as a central event in the history of the novel." See *Desire and Domestic Fiction*, 7.

20. Brewer, *Pleasures of the Imagination*, 59.

21. The link between identity and moral orientation has been made by Charles Taylor: "To know who you are is to be oriented in moral space, a space in which questions arise about what is good or bad what is worth doing and what not, what has meaning and importance for you and what is trivial and secondary." See *Sources of the Self*, 28.

22. Reynolds's painting is discussed by Pawlowicz in "Reading Women," 47. For a majestic exploration of the relation between the book, the painting, and the text, see G. Stewart, *The Look of Reading*; and Warner, "Staging Readers Reading."

23. For an overview of Hogarth's career, see Hallett and Riding, *Hogarth*.

24. Brewer, *Pleasures of the Imagination*, 59.

25. I use the term "world picture" in the Heideggerian sense; it does not mean "a picture of the world but the world conceived and grasped as picture." See Heidegger, "Age of the World Picture," 129.

26. Humphreys, "Arts in Eighteenth-Century Britain," 5.

27. See Brewer, *Sinews of Power*, xv. See also Langford, *Polite and Commercial People*; and Marshall, *Eighteenth Century*.

28. Heidegger, "Age of the World Picture," 128.

29. See De Bolla, *Discourse of the Sublime*, 4–23.

30. Quoted by Caygill, *Art of Judgement*, 38. My discussion here is indebted to Caygill.

31. Kames, *Elements of Criticism*, front matter, 6.

32. Eagleton, *Ideology of the Aesthetic*, 37.

33. See Althusser and Balibar, *Reading Capital*, 13–69.

34. Blackstone, *Commentaries on the Laws of England*, 3:362.

35. Langford, *Polite and Commercial People*, 1. For the long architectural history of Castle Howard, see Summerson, *Architecture in Britain*, 259–68.

36. Langford, *Polite and Commercial People*, 1.

37. McKendrick, Brewer, and Plumb, *Birth of a Consumer Society*, 9.

38. Elias, *Civilizing Process*.

39. Habermas, *Philosophical Discourse*, 42–44.

40. Brewer, "'Most Polite Age'," 348.

41. Shaftesbury, "Sensus Communis," in *Characteristics of Men*, 1:46. See also Klein, *Shaftesbury and the Culture of Politeness* and "Politeness for Plebes."

42. Shaftesbury, "Sensus Communis," in *Characteristics of Men*, 1:46.

43. Ibid.

44. Summerson, *Architecture in Britain*, 260, 264.

45. See Addison and Steele, *Spectator*, 1:31.

46. For writing under erasure (*sous rature*) as it has evolved from Martin Heidegger to Jacques Derrida, see Spivak, translator's preface to *Of Grammatology*, xiv-xvii. On the repertoire and the archive, see D. Taylor, *Archive and the Repertoire*, 1–52.

47. See Miers and Kopytoff, *Slavery in Africa*.

48. Park, *Travels*, 473.

49. Ibid.

50. Ibid., 474.

51. I use the term *moral luck* loosely here to refer to Park's inability to assign blame to any of the agents in the transactions he was observing. For the origin and meaning of the term in philosophy, see B. Williams, *Moral Luck*, 20–39.

52. In *Sources of the Self*, Charles Taylor uses the term *ordinary life* "to designate those aspects of human life concerned with production and reproduction, that is, the labour, the making of the things needed for life" (211). In the society described by Park, slaves were some of the important things needed for life as they would be in the European and colonial societies that purchased them.

53. Park, *Travels*, 475–76.

54. Ibid., 475.

55. Ibid.

56. This distinction has been highlighted by C. Miller in *French Atlantic Triangle*, 11–13.

57. Park, *Travels*, 495.

58. Ibid., 497.

59. Ibid.

60. For this argument, see Eagleton, *Ideology of the Aesthetic*, 7–8, and De Man, *Aesthetic Ideology*, 70–90.

61. On slavery and modern time, see Gilroy, *Black Atlantic*; W. Johnson, "Time and Revolution in African America," 197–215; and Hartman, "Time of Slavery."

62. Foucault, *Discipline and Punish*, 23. The ideas driving subjection in the cultures of enslavement are discussed by Patterson, *Slavery and Social Death*, 1–14. Subjection and slavery are the topics of Hartman's *Scenes of Subjection*.

63. Foucault, *Discipline and Punish*, 25–26.

64. Hartman provides one of the most compelling accounts of the mechanisms of subjection and economies of power and desire in *Scenes of Subjection*, 105–12.

65. Park, *Travels*, 499.

66. This point is underscored by Marsters in her introduction to a new edition of *Travels in the Interior Districts of Africa*, 1–38. The story of Park's life can be found in Lupton, *Mungo Park*. For Park and women, see Nussbaum, *Torrid Zones*, 64–65. Park's contribution to imperial travel writing is considered by Pratt in *Imperial Eyes*, 69–85.

67. Park, *Travels*, 499.

68. Georgiana, Duchess of Cavendish, "Anonymous," 21.

69. My notion of a rhetoric of reading is derived from De Man's *Allegories of Reading*, 3–19.

70. Patterson, *Slavery and Social Death*, 35–76. For identity or nonidentity in the space of death, see Taussig, *Shamanism, Colonialism, and the Wild Man*, 3–36.

71. Althusser and Balibar, *Reading Capital*, 106.

72. For the relationship between conviviality and melancholy, see Gilroy, *Postcolonial Melancholia*, 121–52.

73. For the political unconscious, see Jameson, *Political Unconscious*; emphasis in the original.

74. Langford, *Polite and Commercial People*, 59–60; emphasis in the original.

75. Kristeva, *Black Sun*, 21.

76. Ibid.; emphasis in the original.

77. Hayden, "Middle Passage," 48.

78. A detailed discussion of happiness as a category of virtue can be found in Potkay, *Passion for Happiness*.

79. Plumb, *Commercialization of Leisure*, 3; see also McKendrick, Brewer, and Plumb, *Birth of a Consumer Society*.

80. Porter, "Enlightenment in England," 10.

81. Plumb, *Commercialization of Leisure*, 18.

82. Porter, "Enlightenment in England," 14.

83. For Scotland, see the essays collected in Dwyer and Sher, *Sociability and Society*. Johnson and Hume are discussed in Potkay, *Passion for Happiness*, chapter 3.

84. Addison, *Spectator*, vol. 2, no. 383 (1712). A brief history of Vauxhall Gardens can be found in Edelstein, "Vauxhall Gardens," 203–15.

85. See Cameron and Crooke, *Liverpool*; and Dresser and Giles, *Bristol and Transatlantic Slavery*. See also D. Richardson, "Liverpool and the English Slave Trade."

86. Thornton, "Africa: The Source," 42.

87. R. Williams, *Country and the City*, 165.

88. Decorse, *Archeology of Elmina*, 28.

89. Van Dantzig, *Forts and Castles of Ghana*, 15. See also Feinberg, *Africans and Europeans in West Africa*; Lawrence, *Fortified Trade-Posts*; and Hansen, *Coast of Slaves*.

90. Van Dantzig, *Forts and Castles of Ghana*, 13.

91. Bosman, *New and Accurate Description*, 42.

92. Ibid., 47.

93. It is important to underscore the fact that the slave trade began as a business interest, a fact reflected in the charter setting up the Royal African Company and in the minutes of many boards of trade engaged in this enterprise. For the complete text of the charter, see Donnan, *Documents Illustrative of the History*, 1:180; examples of the minutes of the company can be found at 2:250. A comprehensive history of the company can be found in K. Davies, *Royal African Company*.

94. The account is reproduced in Dow, *Slave Ships and Slaving*, 63.

95. Newton, *Journal of a Slave Trader*, 58.

96. Ibid.

97. Ibid., 95.

98. For Newton's paradoxical life in the slave trade, see Hochschild, *Bury the Chains*, 11–29; and Rediker, *Slave Ship*, 157–86.

99. Quoted in Cameron and Crooke, *Liverpool*, 41.

100. In addition to Newton's journal, see Snelgrave, *New Account of Guinea*; and Gamble, *Slaving Voyage to Africa and Jamaica*.

101. Newton, *Journal of a Slave Trader*, 84.

102. Locke, *Second Treatise of Government*, 8.

103. For a summary of the arguments and debates, see Lawson, "Locke and the Legal Obligations," 131–50.

104. Long, *Candid Reflections*, 4.

105. Equiano, *Interesting Narrative*, 53. My concern here is not the real-lived life of these slaves but the way they imagined their experiences. An excellent investigation of Equiano's complicated life can be found in Carretta, *Equiano the African*. For background and detailed studies of early African American writing, see Carretta and Gould, *Genius in Bondage*; Sidbury, *Becoming African in America*; and Sandiford, *Measuring the Moment*.

106. Cugoano, *Thoughts and Sentiments*, 15.

107. Wheatley, *Complete Writings*, 13; emphasis added to title, original emphasis on "*Pagan* land."

108. Equiano, *Interesting Narrative*, 68. The idea of the "talking book" has been explored by Gates in *Signifying Monkey*, 127–69; and Callahan, *Talking Book*, 1–19.

109. Douglass, *Narrative of the Life*, 96.

110. Habermas, *Philosophical Discourse*, 5.

111. Hegel, preface to *Phenomenology*, 20.

112. Habermas, *Philosophical Discourse*, 6.

113. The observer is James Barbot from a journal kept in 1698–1699, parts of which are abstracted in Dow, *Slave Ships and Slaving*, 83.

114. Cugoano, *Thoughts and Sentiment*, 15.

115. Snelgrave, *New Account of Guinea*, 171.

116. Wilson, introduction to *New Imperial Histories*, 5.

117. Douglass, *Narrative of the Life*, 19. This argument has been made powerfully by Hartman in *Scenes of Subjection*; and Patterson, *Rituals of Blood*.

118. Foucault, *Discipline and Punish*, 129–30. Foucault's argument is that in the eighteenth century this spectacle disappeared from the public view, considered to be at odds with modern sensibilities (perhaps); I will argue in later chapters that it was just exported to slave cultures. For the symbolism of violence, see Patterson, *Slavery and Social Death*, 3.

119. Snelgrave, *New Account of Guinea*, 183–84.

120. Foucault, *Discipline and Punish,* 25.

121. Ricoeur, *Symbolism of Evil*, 37.

122. Goveia, *West Indian Slave Laws*, 19.

123. Ibid., 21.

124. For a detailed discussion of the case, see Shyllon, *Black People*, chapters 6 and 7.

125. National Archives, "Somersett Case, Howell's State Trials."

126. Goveia, *West Indian Slave Law*, 20.

127. Quoted in ibid. On English reactions to the Stowell decision vis. Grace Jones, see Shyllon, *Black People,* 210–29.

128. Blackstone, *Commentaries on the Laws*, Avalon Project, ch. 1, p. 123. My discussion here is indebted to Shyllon.

129. Ibid., ch. 14, p. 412.

130. Quoted in Shyllon, *Black People*, 60.

131. Ibid., 61.

132. The irony in this wrangle is that Lord Mansfield himself was a Scot, educated at Oxford.

133. Quoted in Shyllon, *Black People*, 179.

134. Boswell, *Life of Johnson*, 877–78.

135. Ibid., 878.

136. Ibid.

137. Shyllon, *Black People*, 177.

CHAPTER THREE. UNSPEAKABLE EVENTS: SLAVERY AND WHITE SELF-FASHIONING

1. Equiano, *Interesting Narrative*, 96–97. For Equiano's aspirations toward culture, see Carretta, *Equiano, the African* and "Property of Author"; Nussbaum, "Being a Man"; Sandiford, *Measuring the Moment*; and Sidbury, *Becoming African in America*.

2. Equiano, *Interesting Narrative*, 99.

3. Ibid., 129.

4. Quoted in Schlereth, *Cosmopolitan Ideal*, 1.

5. See ibid., xiii.

6. Ricoeur, *Symbolism of Evil*, 37.

7. Ibid., 36.

8. For the terms of debate here, see Douglas, *Purity and Danger*, 2–4.

9. Hartman, *Scenes of Subjection*.

10. Caygill, *Art of Judgement*, 75.
11. Hume, "Of the Standard of Taste."
12. Mortensen, *Art in the Social Order*, 101.
13. Hume, "Of the Standard of Taste," 326.
14. Ibid., 328.
15. Ibid.
16. Ibid., 325; emphasis in the original.
17. Ibid. 326.
18. Hume, "Of National Characters," 213.
19. Ibid.
20. Ibid.
21. The literature on the imbrication of the colonies in the making of English high culture is too extensive to cite here, but see Aravamudan, *Tropicopolitans*; Armitage, *Ideological Origins*; Colley, *Britons*; C. Hall, *Civilising Subjects*; and the essays collected in Wilson, *New Imperial History*.
22. Kant, "Observations," 638.
23. For the shift from physical nature to culture as a signifier of difference, see Wheeler, *Complexion of Race*, 177–233; and Wahrman, *Making of the Modern Self*, 113–17. As I argued in chapter 1, the distinction between blackness as a physical category and as a sign of cultural distinctiveness seems more blurred in the aesthetic ideology than Wheeler and Warhman have suggested.
24. This argument has made by Morrison in *Playing in the Dark*, 6.
25. See Ronnick, "Francis Williams," 4.
26. See, for example, Grégoire, *Enquiry Concerning the Intellectual and Moral Faculties*.
27. Long, *History of Jamaica*, 2:484.
28. Ibid. For contrasting views on Long's place in the changing economies of race, see Wheeler, *Complexion of Race*, 177–233; and Dayan, *Haiti, History and the Gods*.
29. For Williams's function in Long's attempt to fix the moral character of the black subject, see Long, *History of Jamaica*, 476–85. For latter-day attempts to recognize Williams as one of the founding fathers of a black Atlantic literary tradition, see D'Costa and Lalla, *Voices in Exile*, 9–12; see also Gates and McKay, *Norton Anthology of African American Literature*, xxx.
30. See Warhman, *Making of the Modern Self*, 13. My position here is closer to that articulated by Dayan in *Haiti, History, and the Gods*, 194.
31. Goveia, *Study on the Historiography*, 61. My discussion here is indebted to Dayan.
32. Hume's footnote represented then, as it does now, a form of prejudice that went against his whole philosophical project, against his insistence on the rule of evidence as an antidote to prejudice. The distinguished American philosopher Richard Popkin captured the paradox at issue here in an intriguing parenthesis to an essay on Hume's racism:

(How could an alleged empiricist like Hume make such sweeping generalizations and ignore evidence to the contrary? Hume himself explained the matter in his discussion of general rules in the chapter of the Treatise on "unphilosophical probability." He showed the psychological factors involved in people believing prejudicial general rules, such as "All Irishmen are quarrelsome," in spite of counter-evidence. And, Hume seems to have been a perfect case of his own explanation of how prejudices can over-ride any evidence. In a letter he referred to his friend Isaac de Pinto, the Dutch economist and philosopher, as a good man "tho a Jew." With Hume's prejudices, it is easy to see that he was a fine choice to run the Colonial office in 1766.)

Popkin, "Hume's Racism." For Popkin's other work on Hume and the question of race, see "Philosophical Basis," 245–62, and "Hume's Racism Reconsidered," 64–75.

33. John C. Miller, *Wolf by the Ears*, 77.

34. Quoted in ibid.

35. Gates, *Trials of Phillis Wheatley*, 51; and Jefferson, *Notes on the State of Virginia*, 139. Jefferson's tortured views on black lack are discussed by Jordan in *White over Black*, 429–81.

36. Jefferson, *Notes on the State of Virginia*, 139.

37. Ibid., 140.

38. Ibid.

39. Laplanche and Pontalis, *Language of Psychoanalysis*, 362.

40. Ibid., 103.

41. Ibid., 292. For the structuralist or Marxist version of this sense of contradiction, see Althusser, "Contradiction and Over-Determination."

42. Walvin, *Fruits of Empire*, ix.

43. Mintz, *Sweetness and Power*, xxv.

44. Ibid.

45. Walvin, *Fruits of Empire*, 122–23.

46. Dunn, *Sugar and Slaves*, 190.

47. E. Williams, *Capitalism and Slavery*, 23. See also Blackburn, *Overthrow of Colonial Slavery*, 1–32, and *Making of New World Slavery*, especially chapter 10.

48. Calder, *Revolutionary Empire*, 254.

49. Dunn, *Sugar and Slaves*, 189.

50. Quoted in E. Williams, *Capitalism and Slavery*, 85.

51. Ragatz, *Fall of the Planter Class*, vii.

52. Calder, *Revolutionary Empire*, 473.

53. Quoted in E. Williams, *Capitalism and Slavery*, 44.

54. See International Slavery Museum, "Liverpool and the Slave Trade," International Slavery Museum. My sources on Liverpool and the slave trade include Tibbles, *Transatlantic Slavery*; and Cameron and Crooke, *Liverpool*.

55. Bohls, "Disinterestedness and Denial," 16.

56. Dunn, *Sugar and Slaves*, 211.

57. Quoted in ibid.

58. I owe this argument to Charles Taylor; see *Sources of the Self*, especially chapter 17.

59. Dunn, *Sugar and Slaves*, 201.

60. Schaw, *Journal of a Lady of Quality*, 99–100.

61. Dunn, *Sugar and Slaves*, 290.

62. See Alleyne and Fraser, *Barbados Carolina Connection*, 53–55.

63. Ibid., 291.
64. Ragatz, *Fall of the Planter Class*, 6.
65. Long, *History of Jamaica*, 2:76.
66. Summerson, *Architecture in Britain*, 383.
67. Ibid., 297.
68. Ibid., 301.
69. Harlow, *Christopher Codrington*, 91.
70. Calder, *Revolutionary Empire*, 412.
71. For this account see Bennett, *Bondsmen and Bishops*; and Puckrein, *Little England*. The Codrington estate is discussed briefly in Hochschild, *Bury the Chains*, 64–68; and Calder, *Revolutionary Empire*, 413.
72. Harlow, *Christopher Codrington*, passim.
73. Long, *History of Jamaica*, 2:269.
74. Calder, *Revolutionary Empire*, 413.
75. Schiller, *On the Aesthetic Education of Man*, 9. For Schiller's aesthetic project, see Woodmansee, *Author, Art, and the Market*, chapter 3; and Docherty, *Criticism and Modernity*, chapter 6.
76. Harlow, *Christopher Codrington*, 11.
77. Ibid., 47.
78. Ibid., 42.
79. White Creoles were people of European descent born in the Americas or the colonial Caribbean. Their cultural history can be found in Long, *History of Jamaica*, 2:260–319. The most authoritative studies of Creole culture in the Caribbean are Brathwaite, *Development of Creole Society*; and Lambert, *White Creole Culture*. See also Dayan, *Haiti, History and the Gods*, especially chapter 3. For the anxieties of West Indian Creoles, see Lambert, *White Creole Culture*, chapter 6; Sandiford, *Cultural Politics of Sugar*, 150–76; and Aravamudan, *Tropicopolitans*, 214–29. Lewis is discussed by Sandiford in *Cultural Politics of Sugar*, 150–74.
80. Edwardes, *Nabobs at Home*, 13.
81. See Warren, "The Building of Dodington Park."
82. Hume, "Of the Standard of Taste," 328.
83. De Bolla, *Discourse of the Sublime*, 28.
84. Bhabha, *Location of Culture*, 89.
85. Byron, "Childe Harold's Pilgrimage," Canto I, XXIL, p. 6.
86. Quoted by Hewat-Jaboor in "Fonthill House," 51.
87. Mannings, "Visual Arts," 133.
88. Boswell, *Life of Johnson*, 742.
89. P. Anderson, *Over the Alps*, 118.
90. Hauptman, "Clinging Fast," 73.
91. Beckford, *Dreams, Waking Thoughts*, 191.
92. Ibid.
93. Shaffer, "'To Remind us of China'."
94. Ibid., 210.
95. Quoted in ibid., 216.
96. See ibid., 217.
97. Ibid.

98. Wordsworth, quote from "Preface to *Lyrical Ballads*," 21.

99. Shaffer, "'To Remind Us of China'," 220.

100. For detailed discussions of the Beckford collection, see the essays by David Watkin, Bet McLeod, and Oliver Impey and John Whitehead in Ostergard, *William Beckford*.

    101. Fothergill in *Beckford of Fonthill*, 126.

    102. Quoted in Lees-Milne, *William Beckford*, 7.

    103. For the political unconscious, see Jameson, *Political Unconscious*, 17–60.

    104. Hewat-Jaboor, "Fonthill House," 51.

    105. Ibid.

    106. Hauptman in *William Beckford*, 73.

    107. McLeod, "Celebrated Collector," 155.

    108. Fothergill, *Beckford of Fonthill*, 14.

    109. See Mowl, "William Beckford."

    110. Fothergill, *Beckford of Fonthill*, 16.

    111. Jeffery, "Architecture," 234.

    112. Quoted in Lees-Milne, *William Beckford*, 13.

    113. Edwardes, *Nabobs at Home*, 34.

    114. Lees-Milne, *William Beckford*, 13.

115. For Horace Walpole and the culture of gardening, see Symes, "English Taste in Gardening," 260. A brief discussion of the West Indian "great house" can be found in Buisseret, *Historic Architecture*, 10–16.

116. My terms here are borrowed from R. Williams, "Forms of Fiction," 1–7.

    117. Watkin, "Beckford, Soane, and Hope," 33.

    118. Ibid.

    119. D. Armstrong, *Old Village and the Great House*, 27.

    120. R. Williams, "Forms of Fiction," 5.

    121. Melville, *Life and Letters*, 350.

    122. Laplanche and Pontalis, *Dictionary of Psychoanalysis*, 118.

    123. Alexander, *England's Wealthiest Son*, 156–57.

    124. Alexander, *Life at Fonthill*, 268.

    125. Melville, *Life and Letters*, 28.

    126. Elsner and Cardinal, introduction to *Cultures of Collecting*, 5.

127. This is the view expressed by Fothergill in *Beckford of Fonthill*, 70, 170. Beckford's relationship with Courtney is discussed in detail by Alexander in *England's Wealthiest Son*; see especially chapters 5 and 12. For William Beckford's aesthetic life, see Lees-Milne, *William Beckford*.

    128. Ostergard, *William Beckford*, 33.

    129. Baudrillard, "Culture of Collecting," 7.

    130. McLeod, "Celebrated Collector," 161.

    131. Ibid.

    132. Baudrillard, "Culture of Collecting," 8.

    133. Ibid., 10.

    134. Lees-Milne, *William Beckford*, 44.

    135. Ibid., 49.

136. Summerson, *Architecture in Britain*, 428.

137. Ibid., 426.

138. For a discussion of Beckford's Gothic works in a colonial context, see Srinivas Aravamudan, *Tropicopolitans*, 214–29. Lewis is discussed by Sandiford in *Cultural Politics of Sugar*, 150–76.

139. For a detailed study of the causes of the fall of the Caribbean plantocracy, see Ragatz, *Fall of the Planter Class*.

140. Alexander, *England's Wealthiest Son*, 40.

141. Hazlitt, "Fonthill Abbey," 287–91.

142. The terms are borrowed from Starobinski's examination of strikingly similar monuments to art in the French Revolution; see *1789: The Emblems of Reason*, 91.

143. Hazlitt, "Fonthill Abbey," 287; emphasis in the original.

144. Quoted by Aldrich, "William Beckford's Abbey," 132.

145. Ibid.

146. Ibid., 117.

CHAPTER FOUR. CLOSE ENCOUNTERS: TASTE AND THE TAINT OF SLAVERY

1. Quoted in L. Wright et al., *Arts in America*, 11–12. For the culture and attitudes of the antebellum elite, see L. Wright, *First Gentlemen of Virginia*; Sobel, *World They Made Together*, 54–63; Sugrue, "South Carolina College"; McInnis, *Politics of Taste*; and Kilbride, *American Aristocracy*.

2. L. Wright et al., *Arts in America*, 11.

3. For Morris's life see, Adams, *Gouverneur Morris*; and Brookhiser, *Gentleman Revolutionary*.

4. Quoted in Phillips, *The Constitution a Pro-Slavery Compact*, 48.

5. Jefferson, *Notes on the State of Virginia*, 162. For Jefferson's paradoxical relation to slavery see Onuf, "'To Declare Them," and *Mind of Thomas Jefferson*.

6. Jefferson, *Notes on the State of Virginia*, 162.

7. Ibid.

8. Ibid., 163.

9. This last question is taken up in Wyatt-Brown, *Honor and Violence*, especially chapter 7.

10. The terminology here is borrowed from Freud, *Civilization and Its Discontents*, especially chapter 4; and Douglas, *Purity and Danger*.

11. Given the close commercial ties between the mid-Atlantic colonies of Maryland, Virginia, the Carolinas, and the Caribbean, I use the term *America* to refer to both territories.

12. Kaplan and Kaplan, *Black Presence*, 36.

13. See also Bontemps, "Seeing Slavery."

14. Juster, "Virginian Luxuries"; K. Brown, *Good Wives*, 107–36.

15. Jefferson, *Notes on the State of Virginia*, 138, 139.

16. Brewer, *Pleasures of the Imagination*, 3.

17. Ibid., 38.

18. Ibid.

19. Ibid.

20. A discussion of the relationship between virtue, commerce, and history can be found in Pocock, *Virtue, Commerce, and History*; see especially chapter 2, where he discusses the "patriot's virtue" in a culture of slavery. For American debates on the relation between citizenship, slavery, and virtue, see Tucker, *Treatise Concerning Civil Government*.

21. Prince, *History of Mary Prince*, 11–12. For explorations of Prince, slave narratives, and the economies of gender, see Ferguson, *Subject to Others*; Feischner, *Mastering Slavery*; Sandiford, *Measuring the Moment*; and Salih, introduction to *History of Mary Prince*, vii–xxxiv.

22. Prince, *History of Mary Prince*, 11–12.

23. Crowe, *With Thackeray in America*, 183.

24. Ibid.

25. Ibid.

26. Library of Congress, "Largest Slave Auction."

27. Ibid.

28. Stanton, *Free Some Day*, 19.

29. According to the *Oxford English Dictionary*, one of the earliest uses of the word "carouse" to denote excess is to be found in the work of François Rabelais, the master of the carnivalesque. For Rabelais and the carnival, see Bakhtin, *Rabelais and His World*.

30. This information comes from the caption to Greenwood's painting in Thomas, *Slave Trade*.

31. L. Wright, *First Gentlemen of Virginia*, 2. See also Scarborough, *Masters of the Big House*; and Oakes, *Ruling Race*.

32. Quoted in L. Wright, *First Gentlemen of Virginia*, 4.

33. Ibid., 45.

34. Ibid.

35. Jordan, *White over Black*, 73.

36. Ibid., 78.

37. Writing on the policing of status in Maryland and Virginia in the 1660s, Jordan notes that "when slavery was gaining statutory recognition, the assemblies acted with full-throated indignation against miscegenation"; see *White over Black*, 79. For slave laws in the Caribbean during the eighteenth century, see Goveia, *West Indian Slave Laws*.

38. Patterson, *Slavery and Social Death*, 337. There is perhaps no better illustration of how the degradation of the slave enhanced the status and honor of the master than the example of Sutpen in Faulkner, *Absalom Absalom*.

39. Dunn, "English Sugar Islands," 55.

40. John C. Miller, *Wolf by the Ears*, 2.

41. Ibid.

42. See Vlach, *Planter's Prospect*.

43. Roberts, *Plantation Homes*, 53.

44. Dunn, "English Sugar Islands," 55.

45. Ibid.

46. See Lamont and Fournier, introduction to *Cultivating Differences*, 9.

47. L. Wright, *First Gentlemen of Virginia*, 335.

48. I borrow the concept of colonial mimicry from Homi Bhabha. See "Of Mimicry and Man."

49. L. Wright, *First Gentlemen of Virginia,* 332.

50. Quoted in ibid., 330–31.

51. Lacan, *Four Fundamental Concepts,* 99.

52. Bhabha, *Location of Culture,* 92.

53. Lamont and Fournier, *Cultivating Differences,* 3.

54. A comprehensive discussion of the doctrine of art and order is provided by Humphreys in "Arts in Eighteenth-Century Britain," 3– 5. See also J. Burke, *English Art.*

55. This intimacy is documented in many studies of plantation life. Sobel, for example, notes that in eighteenth-century Virginia, blacks and whites lived together "in great intimacy, affecting each other in both small and large ways"; see *World They Made Together,* 3. The process of cultural exchange between Africans and Europeans is underscored in the essays collected in Ownby, *Black and White Cultural Interaction.* For a detailed discussion of Byrd and the culture of slavery, see Bontemps, *Punished Self.* For Byrd's life as a gentleman, see Bolton, "Architecture of Slavery," chapter 2; Berland, Gilliam, and Lockridge, *Commonplace Book of William Byrd II*; Lockridge, *Diary and Life of William Byrd II* and *On the Sources of Patriarchal Rage,* 1–28; and Marambaud, *William Byrd of Westover.* Questions of gender and sexual relations in the colonies are taken up by K. Brown in *Good Wives, Nasty Wenches,* especially chapter 10.

56. Jefferson, *Notes on the State of Virginia,* 138.

57. Ibid.

58. Quoted in Sobel, *World They Made Together,* 3.

59. B. Edwards, *Historical Survey,* preface, v.

60. Dayan, *Haiti, History, and the Gods,* 149. For Haiti, race, and the crisis of modernity, the following texts have been invaluable: James, *Black Jacobins*; Trouillot, *Silencing the Past*; L. Dubois, *Avengers of the New World*; D. Scott, *Conscripts of Modernity*; Fischer, *Modernity Disavowed*; Geggus, *Impact of the Haitian Revolution*; and Burck-Morss, "Hegel and Haiti."

61. B. Edwards, *Historical Survey,* 143.

62. The relationship between the planters' isolation and their craving for "civilized culture" is discussed by L. Wright in "From Wilderness to Republic," 12.

63. In addition to Sobel's *World They Made Together,* already cited, see L. Wright *Teach Me Dreams.*

64. For this argument, see McCoubrey, "Painting."

65. Ibid., 50.

66. Waterhouse, *Painting in Britain,* 74.

67. Ibid.

68. Roarke, *Artists of Colonial America,* 43–44. See also Craven, *American Art.*

69. Mannings, "Visual Arts," 133.

70. Benjamin, "Work of Art," 221.

71. Waterhouse, *Painting in Britain,* 60.

72. Blackburn has aptly noted that one term "for evoking the ethos and aspirations of early European colonialism is 'the baroque'"; see *Making of New*

World Slavery, 20. According to Rubert de Ventós, the baroque was an attempt "to retain the classical ideals in a world in which everything seems to overwhelm them: a portentous effort to contain elements from overflowing any figurative perimeter." See *Hispanic Labyrinth*, 116.

73. McElroy, *Facing History*, 3.

74. Ibid.

75. Ibid.

76. P. DuBois, *Slaves and Other Objects*, 79.

77. Craven, *American Art*, 74–75.

78. Derrida, *Truth in Painting*, 9.

79. This is the approach represented in Honour, *Image of the Black*.

80. Derrida, *Truth in Painting*, 9

81. Ibid.

82. I paraphrase and simplify Benjamin's claims on aura. Here is the relevant quote from "The Work of Art in the Age of Mechanical Reproduction," 223–24:

> Originally the contextual integration of art in tradition found its expression in the cult. We know that the earliest art works originated in the service of a ritual—first the magical, then the religious kind. It is significant that the existence of the work of art with reference to its aura is never entirely separated from its ritual function. In other words, the unique value of the "authentic" work of art has its basis in ritual, the location of its original use value. This ritualistic basis, however remote, is still recognizable as secularized ritual even in the most profane forms of the cult of beauty. The secular cult of beauty, developed during the Renaissance and prevailing for three centuries, clearly showed that ritualistic basis in its decline and the first deep crisis which befell it. With the advent of the first truly revolutionary means of reproduction, photography, simultaneously with the rise of socialism, art sensed the approaching crisis which has become evident a century later.

83. For the relation between enslavement, subjection and violence, see Hartman, *Scenes of Subjection*, especially chapter 2.

84. See Park, *Travels in the Interior Districts*, chapters 24 and 25; De Villeneuve, *L'Afrique, ou histoire,* vol. 4.

85. Wood, *Blind Memory,* especially chapter 5.

86. Newton, *Journal of a Slave Trader,* 37–38. For Newton and the slave ship, see Rediker, *Slave Ship*, 157–86.

87. Arendt, *Eichmann in Jerusalem,* 252.

88. Equiano, *Interesting Narrative*, 85. Equiano's encounter with the slave ship and his subsequent life as a sailor are discussed in detail in Rediker, *Slave Ship*, 108–31; and in Carretta, *Equiano,* chapters 2 and 3.

89. Patterson, *Slavery and Social Death*, 4–7.

90. Long, *History of Jamaica,* 2:262.

91. Ibid.

92. For the treadmill as a form of punishment, see Holt, *Problem of Freedom*, 106–10; and Paton, *No Bond but the Law*, 83–120.

93. Nash, "John Pinney." For Pinney and Bristol merchants in the West Indies, see Pares, *Merchants and Planters*; K. Morgan, "Bristol West India Merchants," 185–208; and Dresser and Giles, *Bristol & Transatlantic Slavery.*

94. C. Taylor, *Sources of the Self*, 286.

95. Newton, *Journal of a Slave Trader*, xii.

96. Ibid.

97. A curious aspect of the experience of slavery is that it is now represented most vividly in iconographic terms, meaning it is now available to us primarily through its images. Wood's *Blind Memory* provides a useful genealogy of this iconographical tradition. For the exhibiting of slavery, see Tibbles, *Transatlantic Slavery*; Burnside, *Spirits of the Passage*; and McMillan, *Captive Passage.*

98. Scarry, *Body in Pain*, 4.

99. Ibid.

100. Ibid., 5.

101. My discussion here is indebted to Hartman's *Scenes of Subjection*, especially chapters 2 and 3, and Salih, "Putting Down Rebellion."

102. B. Edwards, *History Civil and Commercial*, 78–79.

103. B. Edwards, *Poems, Written Chiefly in the West-Indies*, 40.

104. Douglass, *Narrative of the Life*, 19. In *Scenes of Subjection*, Hartman refuses to quote this scene "in order to call attention to the ease with which such scenes are usually reiterated, the casualness with which they are circulated, and the consequences of this routine display of the slave's ravaged body" (3). But Douglass uses this "terrible exhibition" (18) to call attention to the uses of the ravaged body beyond instrumental control. I cite this passage and the images discussed below to make the same point.

105. Foucault, *Discipline and Punish*, 8.

106. Ibid, 11.

107. Wood, *Blind Memory*, 228–30.

108. Ibid., 230.

109. Stedman, *Narrative of a Five Years' Expedition* (1963). For discussions of Stedman's work, see Wood, *Blind Memory*, 234–39; Sharpe, *Ghosts of Slavery*; Gwilliam, "'Scenes of Horror.'" For background to Stedman's life in Surinam, see Price and Price, *Stedman's Surinam*; and Stedman, *Narrative of a Five Years' Expedition* (1988).

110. Stedman, *Narrative of a Five Years' Expedition* (1963), 18.

111. Ibid., 38.

112. Foucault, *Discipline and Punish*, 26.

113. Ibid., 38.

114. Honour, *Image of the Black*, 19. See also Dykes, *Negro in English Romantic Thought*; and Baum, *Mind-Forg'd Manacles.*

115. The figure of Joanna is discussed by Sharpe in *Ghosts of Slavery*, 54–86.

116. Stedman, *Narrative of a Five Years' Expedition* (1963), 43.

117. Ibid., 44.

118. Ibid.

119. This discourse dominated, indeed motivated, the revisionist histories of African slavery among slave agents and their supporters. The most notorious

examples are the works of Long, *History of Jamaica;* Dalzell, *History of Dahomy;* and Norris, *Memoirs of the Reign.* For pro-slavery thought in the United States, see Tise, *Proslavery;* and Faust, *Ideology of Slavery.*

CHAPTER FIVE. "POPPING SORROW": LOSS AND THE TRANSFORMATION OF SERVITUDE

1. Detailed readings of these images can be found in Tobin, *Picturing Imperial Power*, 139–73; Kriz, "Marketing Mulatresses," 195–96, and *Slavery, Sugar.*
2. Beckford, *Descriptive Account*, 8–9. For landscape and conquest, see Seed, *Ceremonies of Possession*, 16–40; and Casid, *Sowing Empire*, 43–93.
3. Kriz, "Marketing Mulatresses," 195–96.
4. Young, *Observations*, 20.
5. Kriz, "Marketing Mulatresses," 208.
6. Kriz recognizes the absence of the white Creole woman from the West Indian public sphere and the difficulties of presenting them as signifiers of white civilization ("Marketing Mulatresses," 203). My point is that the space left open by the absent white woman rather than the black slave is the one the mulatress is asked to occupy, as a supplement. For the idea of a supplement as a stand-in for the original and a "mark of an emptiness," see Derrida, *Of Grammatology*, 144.
7. Norris, *Memoirs of the Reign*, 179.
8. Ibid., 179–80.
9. G. Hall, *Slavery and African Ethnicities*, 162.
10. Roach, *Cities of the Dead*, xiii.
11. See Nettleford, *Dance Jamaica;* and Warner-Lewis, *Central Africa in the Caribbean.*
12. Equiano, *Interesting Narrative*, 48.
13. Ibid., 51. A useful discussion of the structure of apostrophe can be found in Culler, *Pursuit of Signs*, 135–54.
14. Useful works on slavery and subjectivity, race and affect include Hartman, *Scenes of Subjection*, 17–48; Sharpe, *Ghosts of Slavery*, especially the introduction; and Cheng, *Melancholy of Race*, 3–30.
15. Benjamin, *Origin of German Tragic Drama.* Benjamin's book was written between 1924 and 1925 and published in Berlin in 1928. The circumstances in which it was written and published are discussed by George Steiner in the introduction to the Verso edition, 7–24.
16. Ibid., 166.
17. Equiano, *Interesting Narrative*, 62. See Gomez, "Quality of Anguish."
18. Prince, *History of Mary Prince*, 37.
19. For the idea of being in negation, see Sartre, *Being and Nothingness*, 33–85; and Fanon, *Black Skin, White Masks*, 210–22.
20. W.E.B. Du Bois, *Souls of Black Folk*, 180–81. The definitive historical and ethnomusicological accounts are by Southern, *Music of Black Americans*, 150–76; Floyd, *Power of Black Music*, 35–57; and Cone, *Spirituals and the Blues*, 9–19.
21. W.E.B. Du Bois, *Souls of Black Folk,* 183.
22. Ibid., 182.

23. Kristeva, *Black Sun*, 19.

24. Ibid.

25. Prince, *History of Mary Prince*, 37.

26. Menke, "Modernity, Subjectivity," 40. Potkay discusses happiness as a moral good in *Passion for Happiness*, 1–26, 61–75.

27. Prince, *History of Mary Prince*, 38.

28. Ibid., 34.

29. Douglass, *Life and Times*, 596. This point is discussed by Hartmann, *Scenes of Subjection*, 47.

30. Douglass, *Life and Times*, 596.

31. Ibid., 148.

32. See Menke, "Modernity, Subjectivity," 40.

33. I owe this point to Stauffer, "Creating an Image in Black." See also his *Black Hearts of Men*.

34. Lewis, *Journal of a West Indian Proprietor*, 40.

35. Schaw, *Journal of a Lady of Quality*, 107–8. Similar scenes are described by almost all European travelers to Jamaica in the eighteenth and early nineteenth century, including Nugent, *Lady Nugent's Journal*, 48–49; M. Scott, *Tom Cringle's Log*, 63–65; and Carmichael, *Domestic Manners and Social Conditions*, 161–201.

36. Bakhtin, *Rabelais and His World*, 187. For the history, form, and structure of carnival in the Caribbean, see Hill, *Trinidad Carnival*; and Crowley, "Traditional Masques of Carnival." For the United States, see Kinser, *Carnival, American Style*; and Roach, *Cities of the Dead*, especially chapter 5.

37. My terms here, as elsewhere in this study, are indebted to Stallybrass and White, *Politics and Poetics*, 27–31.

38. Douglass, *Life and Times*, 147.

39. Certeau, *Practice of Everyday Life*, xviii-xxii. According to Certeau, a tactic "insinuates itself into the other's place, fragmentarily, without taking it over in its entirety, without being able to keep it at a distance" (xix).

40. My understanding of performatives is informed by Austin, *How to Do Things with Words*, 4–11.

41. Anonymous, *Marly*, 88. See Burton, *Afro-Creole*, 57.

42. Lewis, *Journal of a West Indian Proprietor*, 133.

43. Moreton, *West India Customs and Manners*, 152–53.

44. Lewis, *Journal of a West Indian Proprietor*, 41–42.

45. Sandiford, "'Monk' Lewis and the Slavery Sublime."

46. Bakhtin, *Rabelais and His World*, 10.

47. Stallybrass and White, *Politics and Poetics*, 27. The most complete and compelling discussion of Douglass's reservations about the "fraught pleasures" of slave entertainment can be found in Hartman, *Scenes of Subjection*, 47–50.

48. Douglass, *Life and Times*, 596.

49. A distinctive mark of slave studies since the 1970s is the role assigned to culture in general—and performance in particular—as evidence of the African's capacity to evade social death. Culture is the subject of influential works, including Stuckey, *Slave Culture*; and Levine, *Black Culture*. Culture occupies a pivotal role in revisionist works on slavery such as Blassingame, *Slave*

Community; and Genovese, *Roll, Jordan, Roll*. A specific engagement with forms of performance as the essence of slave cultural life is evident in Abrahams and Zwed, *After Africa*; and Abrahams, *Singing the Master*. See also White and White, *Stylin'*.

50. Sartre, *Being and Nothingness*, 56.
51. Ibid.
52. Equiano, *Interesting Narrative*, 45.
53. Cugoano, *Thoughts and Sentiments*, 15–16.
54. Prince, *History of Mary Prince*, 13–14.
55. Jacobs, *Incidents in the Life*, 53.
56. Douglass, *Narrative of the Life*, 58.
57. This was the view espoused by Elkins in *Slavery*. Its most powerful counterpoint was perhaps Blassingame, *Slave Community*.
58. Patterson, *Slavery and Social Death*, 8–9.
59. This is the subject of two books by Wood: *Blind Memory* and *Slavery, Empathy, and Pornography*.
60. Foucault, *Discipline and Punish*, 141.
61. Ibid., 135.
62. Ibid., 136.
63. C. Taylor, *Sources of the Self*, 28.
64. Ibid.
65. Falconbridge, *Account of the Slave Trade*, 19–20.
66. Ibid., 20.
67. Cugoano, *Thoughts and Sentiments*, 15.
68. Falconbridge, *Account of the Slave Trade*, 20.
69. Smallwood, *Saltwater Slavery*, 101–9. For slavery and space, see Kaye, *Joining Places*, 1–29.
70. Clarkson, *History of the Rise*, 115–17. On the history of the slave ship *Brookes* and anti-abolitionist imagery, see Lapsansky, "Graphic Discord," 201–30; Finley, "Committed to Memory," 2–21; Wood, *Blind Memory*, 14–77; and Rediker, *Slave Ship*, 308–42.
71. Quoted in Foster, *"New Raiments of Self,"* 69.
72. Lovejoy and Law, *Biography of Mahommah Gardo Baquaqua*, 153. See also Buckridge, *Language of Dress*, 16–66.
73. Hair, Jones, and Law, *Barbot on Guinea*, 85.
74. Ibid, 93.
75. Buckridge, *Language of Dress*, 26.
76. A. Jones and Stallybrass, *Renaissance Clothing*, 20.
77. Ibid.
78. Ibid, 22.
79. Prince, *History of Mary Prince*, 14.
80. Marx, *Economic and Philosophic Manuscripts*, 108.
81. Bourdieu, *Logic of Practice*, 53.
82. In West African societies such as the Mande, where there were no visible divisions of race, class, or religion, cultural hierarchies were maintained and enforced through patronyms, which often were transformed into what Perinbam terms "enduring universal signifiers." See *Family Identity and the State*, 13. See

also Lovejoy, "Ethnic Designations," 9–42; Searing, "'No Kings, No Lords, No Slaves'"; McLaughlin, "Senegal," 91; and Conrad, *Status and Identity*, 150.

83. Equiano, *Interesting Narrative*, 63.

84. Walcott, "The Sea History," in *Collected Poems*, 365. For a powerful representation of this vast emptiness, see Huggins, *Black Odyssey*, 50–53; and Smallwood, *Saltwater Slavery*, 33–64.

85. Hayden, "Middle Passage," in *Collected Poems*, 48. For other poetic and artistic invocations of the "unspeakable event" see Brathwaite, *Arrivants*; C. Johnson, *Middle Passage*; Feelings, *Middle Passage*; and Dawes, *Requiem*. On slavery and the political economy of death, see Joseph C. Miller, *Way of Death*; and V. Brown, *Reaper's Garden*. 2008.

86. Smallwood, *Saltwater Slavery*, 182.

87. Equiano, *Interesting Narrative*, 62–63.

88. The issue here is not that black slaves were not associated with powerful negative senses; the point is that the economy of senses adduced to them was precisely what excluded them from the domain of the human subject. For race, slavery, and the senses, see M. Smith, *How Race Is Made*, 11–28.

89. Ellis notes that the terms *sensibility* and *sentiment* "denote a complex field of meanings and connotations in the late eighteenth century, overlapping and coinciding to such an extent as to offer no obvious distinction"; see *Politics of Sensibility*, 7.

90. Brewer, *Pleasures of the Imagination*, 114; 118.

91. Menke, "Modernity, Subjectivity," 40.

92. Ibid.

93. In Kramnick, *Portable Enlightenment Reader*, 318–19. C. Taylor discusses Hutcheson's moral philosophy in relation to the senses in *Sources of the Self*, 259–65.

94. Caygill, *Art of Judgement*, 85.

95. Foucault, *Order of Things*, 222.

96. Ibid., 223, 226.

97. A. Smith, *Inquiry into the Nature*, front matter, 8.

98. Ibid., 36.

99. C. Taylor, *Sources of the Self*, 286.

100. Menke, "Modernity, Subjectivity," 35.

101. Ibid., 36.

102. See, for example, De Bolla, *Discourse of the Sublime*.

103. In Kramnick, *Portable Enlightenment Reader*, 638.

104. Quoted in Patterson, *Slavery and Social Death*, 3–4.

105. Cited in Blaustein and Zangrando, *Civil Rights and African Americans*, 149.

106. Patterson, *Slavery and Social Death*, 5.

107. Long, *History of Jamaica*, 2:352.

108. Ibid., 2:425–26. My discussion here is indebted to M. Smith, *How Race Is Made*.

109. Kames, *Sketches of the History of Man*, 1:14. Kames is discussed by Jordan in *White over Black*, 245; and M. Smith, *How Race Is Made*, 14.

110. Goldsmith, *History of the Earth*, 106.

111. Wyatt-Brown, *Honor and Violence*, viii.

112. The most elaborate discussion of the *Pharmakon* as both remedy and cure is perhaps Derrida's "Plato's Pharmacy."

113. Wyatt-Brown, *Honor and Violence*, ix.

114. Douglas, *Purity and Danger*, especially chapter 1.

115. Nettleford, *Caribbean Cultural Identity*, 1.

116. Irrespective of the inequality and exploitation that exists in a nation, argues B. Anderson, it "is always conceived as a deep, horizontal comradeship." *Imagined Communities*, 7.

117. Stuckey, *Slave Culture*, 3–97.

118. R. Thompson, *Faces of the Gods*, 127–31.

119. B. Anderson, *Imagined Communities*, 187–206.

120. Lawal, "Reclaiming the African Past," 292–98; R. Thompson, "African Art in Motion," 17; and P. Morgan, *Slave Counterpoint*, 585–87.

121. Creolization in the Caribbean is the subject of seminal books by Brathwaite, *Development of Creole Society*; Glissant, *Caribbean Discourse*; and Warner-Lewis, *Central Africa in the Caribbean*.

122. Benjamin, *Origin of German Tragic Drama*, 166.

123. In addition to R. Thompson, *Faces of the Gods*, see Price, *First Time*; and Price and Price, *Two Evenings in Saramaka*.

CHAPTER SIX. THE ONTOLOGY OF PLAY: MIMICRY AND THE COUNTERCULTURE OF TASTE

1. British Museum, "Akan Drum"; J. King, *First Peoples, First Contacts*; Delbourgo, "Slavery in the Cabinet of Curiosities"; Sloan, *Discovering the Enlightenment*; and MacGregor, *Sir Hans Sloane*.

2. Benjamin, *Origin of German Tragic Drama*, 178.

3. Glissant, "Free and Forced Poetics," 95.

4. Ibid.

5. My argument here is adopted from Certeau, *Writing of History*, 320. On the process by which Africans became American, see Gomez, *Reversing Sail*; G. Hall, *Slavery and African Ethnicities*; Sidbury, *Becoming African in America*; Thornton, *Africa and Africans*; and Smallwood, *Saltwater Slavery*.

6. W.E.B. Du Bois, *Souls of Black Folk*, 146. For historical consciousness and the loss of place, see Certeau, *Writing of History*, 318–21.

7. W.E.B. Du Bois, *Souls of Black Folk*, 8–9.

8. Ibid.

9. Douglass, *Narrative of the Life*, 23.

10. Ibid. I'm working here with the concept of a hermeneutics of suspicion, borrowed from Ricoeur, who writes in relation to Freud that, "over against interpretation as restoration of meaning we shall oppose interpretation according to what I collectively call the school of suspicion." See *Freud and Philosophy*, 32.

11. Douglass, *Narrative of the Life*, 23.

12. Ibid., 30.

13. W.E.B. Du Bois, *Souls of Black Folk*, 182.

14. Ibid., 182–83; and W.E.B. Du Bois, *Dusk of Dawn*, 114–15.

15. W.E.B. Du Bois, *Dusk of Dawn*, 114–15.

16. For detailed discussion of these issues see Wyatt-Brown, *Honor and Violence*; and Patterson, *Rituals of Blood*, especially chapter 2.

17. C. Taylor, *Sources of the Self*, 28.

18. Ibid., 29.

19. Kaye, *Joining Places*, 4.

20. Wynter, "Jonkonnu in Jamaica," 35.

21. Patterson, *Sociology of Slavery*, 217.

22. Quoted in Wynter, "Jonkonnu in Jamaica," 35.

23. B. Edwards, *History Civil and Commercial*, 183.

24. Ibid., 184.

25. McDonald, *Goods and Chattels*, 19; see also Patterson, *Sociology of Slavery*, 217.

26. Edelstein, "Vauxhall Gardens," 203.

27. Jeffery, "Architecture," 253.

28. Casid, *Sowing Empire*, 198. Other important studies of the "English" garden in the West Indies include Higman, *Slave Populations*, 210–13; D. Hall, *In Miserable Slavery*, chapter 8; and Tobin, "'And there raise yams.'"

29. Casid, *Sowing Empire*, 196. For case studies of Jamaican plantations, see Higman, *Montpelier, Jamaica*, and *Plantation Jamaica*.

30. Kaye, *Joining Places*, 12.

31. Certeau, *Practice of Everyday Life*, 36–37. A summary of this debate can be found in Harvey, *Condition of Postmodernity*, chapter 13. I owe my argument here to Ross Chambers, who first introduced me to Certeau and the theory of tactics. See his *Room for Maneuver*, xi–xx. For the play of oppositionality in the Caribbean, see Burton, *Afro-Creole*.

32. Certeau, *Practice*, 37.

33. B. Edwards, *History Civil and Commercial*, 161–62; emphasis in the original.

34. Ibid.

35. M. Scott, *Tom Cringle's Log*, 252.

36. P. Morgan, "Work and Culture." See also P. Morgan, *Slave Counterpoint*, especially part 1.

37. Littlefield, *Rice and Slaves*; and Carney, *Black Rice*.

38. My discussion here is indebted to P. Morgan, "Work and Culture," 206–8.

39. Ibid., 223.

40. The problem of autonomy continues to plague the study of culture among the slaves, and the control or lack thereof of neighborhoods and provision gardens remains crucial to these debates. In the West Indies it seems logical to claim, after Patterson, that "there was a wide area in which the slaves' activities were economically and socially irrelevant to the masters." See Patterson, *Slavery and Social Death: A Comparative Study*, 93. But even here, the absolute control that the masters had in matters of punishment, sexual violence, and social regulation is indisputable. In the antebellum South, there does not seem to be agreement on the degree of freedom that slaves could retain even when they secured some measure of control over what Kaye describes as "their intimate relations, work, trade, and religious practice" (*Joining Places*, 10). Kaye provides an excellent summary

of American historiographic debates on the question of autonomy in his book and provides a plausible middle position between "autonomy and universal solidarity" (10). See also R. Scott, *Degrees of Freedom*, 253–69.

41. Patterson, *Slavery and Social Death*, 5.

42. Ibid.

43. Ibid., 6.

44. Craton, *Searching for the Invisible Man*, 374. For slaves and their memories in the United States, see Yetman, *Voices from Slavery*; Berlin, Favreau, and Miller, *Remembering Slavery*; and Fabre and O'Meally, *History and Memory*.

45. Hartman, *Lose Your Mother*, 15.

46. Nora, "Between Memory and History," 285.

47. I borrow the notion of symbolic inversion from Barbara A. Babcock, who, following on the rhetoric work of Kenneth Burke, has elaborated how figures of speech work as forms of cultural negation and aesthetic reversal. Symbolic inversion is defined here "as any act of expressive behavior which inverts, contradicts, abrogates, or in some fashion presents an alternative to commonly held cultural codes, values, and norms be they linguistic, literary or artistic, religious, or social and political." See Babcock, introduction to *Reversible World*, 14.

48. Nora, "Between Memory and History," 285.

49. Ibid.

50. C. Taylor, "Person," 263.

51. Ibid., 266–67.

52. For the relationship between remembering, forgetting, and nation building, see B. Anderson, *Invented Communities*, chapter 11.

53. Ferguson, *Uncommon Ground*, 57.

54. Work Projects Administration, *Drums and Shadows*, 179.

55. Ferguson, *Uncommon Ground*, 75. See also Montgomery, *Survivors from the Cargo*.

56. Bachelard, *Poetics of Space*, 47.

57. Vlach, *Afro-American Tradition*, 122–38, and *Back of the Big House*, 1.

58. Vlach, *Afro-American Tradition*, 122–38.

59. Ibid., 282.

60. In his discussion of the African house, Vlach rejects attempts to link its architecture to specific African cultures, arguing that the linguistic evidence does not support such a linkage in "either form or mode of construction" (*Back of the Big House*, 86). My interest is not in African and African American correspondences or influences but in the adducement of an Africanist origin as a way of countering the plantation complex and its hegemonic claims. I focus on the ontology of architecture, not its epistemology. For a discussion of the form, structure, and ontology of African architecture, see Denyer, *African Traditional Architecture*; Bourdier and Minh-Ha, *African Spaces*; Blair, *Anatomy of Architecture*; Prussin, "Introduction to Indigenous African Architecture"; and Elleh, *African Architecture*.

61. See Patton, *African-American Art*, 33. For a comprehensive history of Creoles and slaves in Louisiana, see G. Hall, *Africans in Colonial Louisiana*. The Metoyer dynasty is the subject of Mill's *Forgotten People*.

62. Olmstead, *Journeys in the Seaboard Negro Slave States*, 641.

63. Heidegger, "Building Dwelling Thinking," 323; emphasis in the original.

64. Certeau, *Practice of Everyday Life*, 117. A summary of this debate can be found in Harvey, *Condition of Postmodernity*, chapter 13.

65. Gadamer, *Truth and Method*, 65.

66. D. Scott, *Conscripts of Modernity.*

67. Ligon, *True and Exact History*, 48.

68. Sloane, *Voyage to the Islands*, xlviii-xlix.

69. Pinckard, *Notes on the West Indies*, 263.

70. Jefferson, *Notes on the State of Virginia*, 140.

71. See Blassingame, *Slave Community*; and Stuckey, *Slave Culture.*

72. Douglass, *Life and Times*, 498.

73. For the role of performance in African American culture, see Elam and Krasner, *African American Performance*; and Brooks, *Bodies in Dissent.*

74. Ligon, *True and Exact History*, 280.

75. Leslie, *New and Exact Account*, 326.

76. Ibid., 327.

77. Lufman, *Brief Account of the Island*, 135.

78. For the background, see N. Anderson, "Music."

79. B. Edwards, *History Civil and Commercial*, 102.

80. Ibid.

81. Jobson, *Golden Trade*, 133.

82. Equiano, *Interesting Narrative*, 34.

83. Pinckard, *Notes on the West Indies*, 265–66.

84. Ibid., 265.

85. Reprinted in Abrahams and Zwed, *After Africa*, 293.

86. B. Edwards, *History Civil and Commercial*, 106.

87. See Lewis, *Journal of a West Indian Proprietor*, 62. Obeah is the subject of Earle's novel *Obi; or, The History of Three-Fingered Jack*. For the literary context, see Aravamudan, introduction to *Obi*, 7–52; and A. Richardson, "Romantic Voodoo." For the religious context, see Paravisini-Gebert and Fernandez-Olmos, *Sacred Possessions*; and *Creole Religions of the Caribbean.*

88. Hill, *Jamaican Stage*, 228.

89. Lewis, *Journal of a West Indian Proprietor*, 61.

90. Austin-Broos, *Jamaica Genesis*, 43. Myalism is the subject of Brodber's novel, *Myal*. In addition to Patterson's *Sociology of Slavery*, detailed historical explorations of Obeah and Myalism can be found in D. Stewart, *Three Eyes for the Journey*, chapters 2 and 3; Schuler, *Alas, Alas, Kongo*; and Turner, *Slaves and Missionaries*, 36–65.

91. Patterson, *Sociology of Slavery*, 188.

92. Long, *History of Jamaica*, 4:416–17.

93. Beckwith, *Black Roadways*, 143.

94. Lewis, *Journal of a West Indian Proprietor*, 222–23.

95. Patterson, *Sociology of Slavery*, 187.

96. Some of my interlocutors have accepted my contention that the work of culture among the slaves constituted a form of resistance but have disagreed with my description of performances as a counter-aesthetic. I insist on these forms of expressiveness as a counter-aesthetic for two reasons: First, slaves were aware

of the aesthetic economies circulating in white culture. Evidence of this is that they sought to appropriate them (sensibility in the slave narrative, for example) or to mimic them (as in the case of the later John Canoe). Second, rituals and performances were not just responses against the established order; they also sought to discover a realm of experience outside that order seeking to affirm, in Joan Dayan's words, a way "back to the self, to an identity lost, submerged and denigrated." This search for an alternative, imaginary experience was "nothing other than the ability to keep expressing the self, and acceding, if only temporarily, to a form of power that defies compromise." See Dayan, *Haiti, History, and the Gods*, 74.

97. B. Edwards, *History Civil and Commercial*, 109. The critical terminology is from Kermode, *Genesis of Secrecy*.

98. B. Edwards, *History Civil and Commercial*, 109.

99. Foucault, *Discipline and Punish*, 217.

100. Debord, *Society of the Spectacle*, 17; emphasis in the original.

101. Latrobe, *Journals of Benjamin Henry Latrobe*, 204. For the cultural significance of Congo Square, see Roach, "Deep Skin," 101–13.

102. Latrobe, *Journals of Benjamin Henry Latrobe*, 204. Latrobe's reaction to an Afro-Catholic funeral is discussed by Roach, *Cities of the Dead*, 60–62.

103. Latrobe, *Journals of Benjamin Henry Latrobe*, 204.

104. Stuckey, *Going through the Storm*, 53. See also White and White, *Sounds of Slavery*, 8–9.

105. Wynter, "Jonkonnu in Jamaica," 36.

106. Andrews, *Afro-Argentines*, 157.

107. Karasch, *Slave Life in Rio de Janeiro*, 243.

108. Quoted by Emery, *Black Dance*, 3. Emery's book has been central in my understanding of the role of dance in slave culture.

109. For the "circle of culture" and its centrality in the remaking of black experiences in slavery, see Stuckey, *Slave Culture*, chapter 1. For "horizontal" relationships and the construction of communities, see B. Anderson, *Invented Communities*, 7.

110. Quoted in Emery, *Black Dance*, 29.

111. Latrobe, *Journals of Benjamin Henry Latrobe*, 203–4.

112. Quoted in Andrews, *Afro-Argentines*, 161.

113. Ibid.

114. Quoted in Emery, *Black Dance*, 157; emphasis in the original.

115. Quoted in Andrews, *Afro-Argentines*, 162–63.

116. Certeau, *Practice of Everyday Life*, 29.

117. Long, *History of Jamaica*, 2:424; emphasis in the original.

118. Fink, Saine, and Saine, "Oasis of Happiness."

119. Ibid., 19.

120. Ibid., 20.

121. Quoted in Emery, *Black Dance*, 21.

122. Ibid., 22.

123. Fanon, *Black Skin, White Masks*, 109–40.

124. Ibid., 231.

125. Quoted in Andrews, *Afro-Argentines*, 162.

126. Bakhtin, *Rabelais and His World*, 154.
127. Ibid., 187–88.
128. Gluckman, *Rituals of Rebellion*, 3.
129. Ibid.
130. Ibid. N. Davies writing about female disorder and ceremonies in early modern Europe has affirmed Gluckman's conclusion: "'female disorderliness' clarified the patriarchal structure in the process of reversing it but it did not change the system"; see "Women on Top."
131. Ladurie, *Carnival in Romans*, 308.
132. P. Burke, *Popular Culture*, 188.
133. Abrahams, *Singing the Master*, 87.
134. R. Thompson, "Recapturing Heaven's Glamour."
135. Quoted in ibid., 23.
136. See Wynter, "Jonkonnu in Jamaica," 35–36.
137. This is generally the view adopted by Dirks in *Black Saturnalia*.
138. Cassidy, *Jamaica Talk*, chapter 12.
139. For a general survey of the festival across the Atlantic, see Reid, "John Canoe Festival."
140. Long, *History of Jamaica*, 2:424.
141. Cassidy, *Jamaica Talk*, 259.
142. Schaw, *Journal of a Lady of Quality*, 108.
143. See Nugent, *Lady Nugent's Journal*, 49.
144. Quoted in Abrahams, *After Africa*, 230.
145. Ibid.
146. Quoted in ibid., 231.
147. Long, *History of Jamaica*, 2:424.
148. Ibid.
149. Quoted in Abrahams, *After Africa*, 233.
150. Ibid.
151. My argument here is indebted to Bhabha's theory of mimicry; see *Location of Culture*, chapter 4.
152. C. Williams, *Tour through the Island*, 26.
153. Long, *History of Jamaica*, 2:424–25. These transformations are discussed by Patterson in *Sociology of Slavery*, 242–45. For the aesthetic strategies of John Canoe and associated festivals, see Burton, *Afro-Creole*, 61–81.
154. C. Williams, *Tour through the Island*, 22.
155. Hill, *Jamaican Stage*, 236.
156. R. Wright, *Revels in Jamaica*, 240.
157. C. Williams, *Tour through the Island*, 23.
158. Sloane, *Voyage to the Islands*, xlvix.
159. J. Stewart, *View of the Past*, 270–71.
160. Lewis, *Journal of a West Indian Proprietor*, 49–50.
161. Nugent, *Lady Nugent's Journal*, 49.
162. E. Thompson, "Moral Economy," 80.
163. Ibid.
164. A. Jones and Stallybrass, *Renaissance Clothing*, 2. For dress and costume in eighteenth-century England, see Styles, *Dress of the People*.

165. Hammermeister, *German Aesthetic Tradition*, 7.
166. A. Smith, *Theory of Moral Sentiments*, 214–15.
167. Collected in Moreton, *West Indian Customs and Manners*, 153.
168. Freud, "Negation," 181.
169. Madden, *Twelvemonth's Residence*, 160–61.
170. Ibid., 161.

Coda

1. Tallmadge, "Speech of the Hon. James Tallmadge."
2. Forbes, *Missouri Compromise*, 36.
3. Morrison, *Playing in the Dark*, 45.
4. Tallmadge, "Speech of the Hon. James Tallmadge."
5. See Berlin and Harris, *Slavery in New York*.
6. Burck-Morss, *Dialectics of Seeing*, 161.
7. See, for example, Kranish, "At Capitol, Slavery's Story Turns."
8. Walcott, "Forty Acres."

Bibliography

Abraham, Nicolas, and Maria Torok. "Mourning *or* Melancholia: Introjection *versus* Incorporation." In *The Shell and the Kernel: Renewals of Psychoanalysis*, edited and translated by Nicholas T. Rand, 1:125–38. Chicago: University of Chicago Press, 1994.

Abrahams, Roger D. *Singing the Master: The Emergence of African American Culture in the Plantation South*. New York: Pantheon, 1992.

Abrahams, Roger D., and John F. Zwed, eds. *After Africa*. New Haven, CT: Yale University Press, 1983.

Adams, William Howard. *Gouverneur Morris: An Independent Life*. New Haven, CT: Yale University Press, 2003.

Addison, Joseph, and Richard Steele. *The Spectator*. Vol. 1. London: J. J. Woodward, 1830.

———. *The Spectator*. Vol. 2. London: J. J. Woodward, 1830.

Adorno, Theodor W. *Negative Dialectics*. Translated by E. B. Ashton. New York: Continuum, 1973.

———. *Prisms*. Translated by Samuel Weber and Shierry Weber. Cambridge: MIT Press, 1967.

Aldrich, Megan. "William Beckford's Abbey at Fonthill: From the Picturesque to the Sublime." In Ostergard, *William Beckford*, 117–36.

Alexander, Boyd. *England's Wealthiest Son: A Study of William Beckford*. London: Centaur Press, 1962.

———. *Life at Fonthill, 1807–1822: Letters of William Beckford*. London: Robert Hart-Davis, 1957.

Alleyne, W., and Henry Fraser. *Barbados Carolina Connection*. London: Macmillan Caribbean, 1989.

Althusser, Louis. "Contradiction and Overdetermination." In *For Marx*, translated by Ben Brewster, 87–128. London: Verso, 1969.

Althusser, Louis, and Etienne Balibar. *Reading Capital*. Translated by Ben Brewster. London: New Left Books, 1970.

Anderson, Benedict. *Imagined Communities: Reflections on the Origin and Spread of Nationalism*. Rev. ed. London: Verso, 1991.

Anderson, Nicholas. "Music." In Ford, *Cambridge Cultural History*, 275–303.

Anderson, Patrick. *Over the Alps: Reflections on Travel and Travel Writing, with Special Reference to the Grand Tours of Boswell, Beckford and Byron*. London: Hart Davies, 1969.

Andrews, George Reid. *The Afro-Argentines of Buenos Aires, 1800–1900*. Madison: University of Wisconsin Press, 1980.

Anonymous. *Marly; or, a Planter's Life in Jamaica*. Glasgow: Richard Griffin, 1928.

Anstey, Roger. *The Atlantic Slave Trade and British Abolition, 1760–1810*. Atlantic Highlands, NJ: Humanities Press, 1975.

Apter, Emily, and William Pietz, eds. *Fetishism as Cultural Discourse*. Ithaca, NY: Cornell University Press, 1993.

Aravamudan, Srinivas. Introduction to *Obi; or, The History of Three-Fingered Jack*, by William Earle, 7–52. Peterborough, Ontario: Broadview Press, 2005.

———. *Tropicopolitans: Colonialism and Agency, 1688–1804*. Durham, NC: Duke University Press, 1999.

Arendt, Hannah. *Eichmann in Jerusalem: A Report on the Banality of Evil*. New York: Viking Press, 1964.

Armitage, David. *The Ideological Origins of the British Empire*. Cambridge: Cambridge University Press, 2000.

Armstrong, Douglas V. *The Old Village and the Great House: An Archaeological and Historical Examination of Drax Hall Plantation, St. Ann's Bay, Jamaica*. Urbana: University of Illinois Press, 1990.

Armstrong, Meg. "The Effects of Blackness: Gender, Race, and the Sublime in Aesthetic Theories of Burke and Kant." *Journal of Aesthetics and Art Criticism* 54, no. 3 (1996): 213–36.

Armstrong, Nancy. *Desire and Domestic Fiction: A Political History of the Novel*. New York: Oxford University Press, 1987.

Ashfield, Andrew, and Peter de Bolla, eds. *The Sublime Reader: Eighteenth-Century British Sources and Contexts*. Cambridge: Cambridge University Press, 1996.

Austin-Broos, Diane. *Jamaica Genesis: Religion and the Politics of Moral Orders*. Chicago: University of Chicago Press, 1997.

Babcock, Barbara A. Introduction to *The Reversible World: Symbolic Inversion in Art and Society*. Ithaca, NY: Cornell University Press, 1978.

Bachelard, Gaston. *The Poetics of Space*. Translated by Maria Jolas. Boston: Beacon Press, 1994.

Bakhtin, Mikhail. *Rabelais and His World*. Translated by Helene Iswolsky. Bloomington: Indiana University Press, 1984.

Barker, Anthony J. *The African Link: British Attitudes to the Negro in the Era of the Atlantic Slave Trade, 1550–1807*. London: F. Cass, 1978.

Barker, Francis, Peter Hulme, Margaret Iverson, and Diana Loxley, eds. *Literature, Politics, and Theory: Papers from the Essex Conference, 1976–84*. London: Methuen, 1986.

Barker-Benfield, G. J. *The Culture of Sensibility: Sex and Society in Eighteenth-Century Britain*. Chicago: University of Chicago Press, 1992.

Barrell, John. *The Dark Side of the Landscape: The Rural Poor in English Painting, 1730–1840*. Cambridge: Cambridge University Press, 1983.

———. *The Political Theory of Painting from Reynolds to Hazlitt: "The Body of the Public."* New Haven, CT: Yale University Press, 1986.

Bartra, Roger. *Wild Men in the Looking Glass: The Mythic Origins of European Otherness.* Translated by Carl T. Berrisford. Ann Arbor: University of Michigan Press, 1994.

Bassani, Ezio, and William B. Fagg. *Africa and the Renaissance Art in Ivory.* New York: Center for African Art, 1988.

Baucom, Ian. *Specters of the Atlantic: Finance Capital, Slavery, and the Philosophy of History.* Durham, NC: Duke University Press, 2005.

Baudrillard, Jean. "The Culture of Collecting." In Elsner and Cardinal, *Cultures of Collecting,* 7–24.

Baum, Joan. *Mind-Forg'd Manacles: Slavery and the English Romantic Poets.* North Haven, CT: Shoe String Press, 1994.

Baumgarten, Alexander Gottlieb. *Reflections on poetry: Alexander Gottlieb Baumgarten's Meditationes philosophicae de nonnullis ad poema pertinentibus.* Berkeley: University of California Press, 1954.

Beckford, William. *A Descriptive Account of the Island of Jamaica.* London: T. and J. Egerton, 1790.

———. *Dreams, Waking Thoughts, and Incidents,* ed. Robert J. Gemmett. Rutherford, NJ: Fairleigh Dickinson University Press, 1971.

Beech, David, and John Roberts. "Spectres of the Aesthetic." *New Left Review* 218 (July-August 1996): 102–27.

Benjamin, Walter. *The Origin of German Tragic Drama.* Translated by John Osborne. London: Verso, 1998.

———. "The Work of Art in the Age of Mechanical Reproduction." In *Illumination: Essays and Reflections,* edited by Hannah Arendt, 83–110. New York: Harcourt Brace, 1968.

Bennett, J. Harry, Jr. *Bondsmen and Bishops: Slavery and Apprenticeship on the Codrington Plantations of Barbados, 1710–1838.* Berkeley: University of California Press, 1958.

Bennett, Tony. *Outside Literature.* London: Routledge, 1990.

Berland, Kevin, Jan Kirsten Gilliam, and Kenneth A. Lockridge, eds. *The Commonplace Book of William Byrd II of Westover.* Chapel Hill: University of North Carolina Press, 2001.

Berlin, Ira. *Many Thousands Gone: The First Two Centuries of Slavery in North America.* Cambridge, MA: Belknap Press, 2000.

Berlin, Ira, Marc Favreau, and Steven F. Miller, eds. *Remembering Slavery: African Americans Talk about Their Personal Experiences of Slavery and Freedom.* New York: New Press, 1998.

Berlin, Ira, and Leslie M. Harris, eds. *Slavery in New York.* New York: New Press, 2005.

Bermingham, Ann, and John Brewer. *The Consumption of Culture, 1600–1800: Image, Object, Text.* London: Routledge, 1997.

———. "Elegant Females and Gentlemen Connoisseurs." In Bermingham and Brewer, *Consumption of Culture,* 489–513.

———. Introduction to *Consumption of Culture,* 1–22.

Bernasconi, Robert. "Who Invented the Concept of Race? Kant's Role in the Enlightenment Construction of Race." In *Race and Racism,* edited by Robert Bernasconi, 11–36. Oxford: Blackwell, 2001.

Bernstein, J. M. *The Fate of Art: Aesthetic Alienation from Kant to Derrida and Adorno.* Cambridge, MA: Polity Press, 1992.

Berry, Christopher J. *The Idea of Luxury: A Conceptual and Historical Investigation.* Cambridge: Cambridge University Press, 1994.

Bhabha, Homi. *The Location of Culture.* London: Routledge, 1994.

———. "Of Mimicry and Man: The Ambivalence of Colonial Discourse." In Bhabha, *Location of Culture,* 85–92.

Bindman, David, et al. *Mind-forg'd Manacles: William Blake and Slavery.* London: Hayward Gallery, 2007.

Blackburn, Robin. *The Making of New World Slavery: From the Baroque to the Modern.* London: Verso, 1997.

———. *The Overthrow of Colonial Slavery.* London: Verso, 1988.

Blackstone, William. *Commentaries on the Laws of England.* Vol. 3. 1778. San Francisco: Bancroft and Witney, 1890.

———. *Commentaries on the Laws of England.* Avalon Project, Yale Law School. http://avalon.law.yale.edu/18th_century/blackstone_bk1ch1.asp, ch. 1, and http://avalon.law.yale.edu/18th_century/blackstone_bk1ch14.asp, ch. 14.

Blakely, Allison. *Blacks in the Dutch World: The Evolution of Racial Imagery in a Modern Society.* Bloomington: Indiana University Press, 1993.

Blassingame, John. *The Slave Community: Plantation Life in the Antebellum South.* New York: Oxford University Press, 1979.

———. *Slave Testimony: Two Centuries of Letters, Speeches, Interviews, and Autobiographies.* Baton Rouge: Louisiana State University Press, 1977.

Blumenberg, Hans. *The Legitimacy of the Modern Age.* Translated by Robert M. Wallace. Cambridge: MIT Press, 1983.

Bohls, Elizabeth A. "Disinterestedness and Denial of the Particular: Locke, Adam Smith, and the Subject of Aesthetics." In *Eighteenth-Century Aesthetics and the Reconstitution of Art,* edited by Paul Mattick Jr., 16–51. New York: Cambridge University Press, 1993.

Bolla, Peter de. *Art Matters.* Cambridge, MA: Harvard University Press, 2001.

———. *The Discourse of the Sublime: Readings in History, Aesthetics, and the Subject.* Oxford: B. Blackwell, 1989.

Bolla, Peter de, Nigel Leask, and David Simpson, eds. *Land, Nation and Culture, 1740–1840: Thinking the Republic of Taste.* Houndmills, Eng.: Palgrave Macmillan, 2005.

Bolton, Ormond. "The Architecture of Slavery: Art, Language, and Society in Early Virginia." PhD diss., College of William and Mary, 1991.

Bontemps, Alex. *The Punished Self: Surviving Slavery in the Colonial South.* Ithaca, NY: Cornell University Press, 2001.

———. "Seeing Slavery: How Paintings Make Words Look Different." In "Representing Slavery: A Roundtable Discussion," *Common-Place* (July 2001). http://www.historycooperative.org/journals/cp/vol-01/no-04/slavery/bontemps.shtml (accessed June 26, 2010).

Bosman, William. *A New and Accurate Description of the Coast of Guinea*. Edited by John Ralph Willis. 1704. New York: Barnes and Noble, 1967.

Boswell, James. *Life of Johnson*. Edited by R. W. Chapman. Oxford: Oxford University Press, 1980.

Bourdier, Jean-Paul, and Trinh T. Minh-Ha. *African Spaces: Designs for Living in Upper Volta*. New York: Africana, 1985.

Bourdieu, Pierre. *The Logic of Practice*. Translated by Richard Nice. Stanford, CA: Stanford University Press, 1992.

Boxer, C. R. *The Portuguese Seaborne Empire, 1415–1825*. London: Hutchinson, 1969.

Brathwaite, [Edward] Kamau. *The Arrivants: A New World Trilogy*. Oxford: Oxford University Press, 1978.

———.*Contradictory Omens: Cultural Diversity and Integration in the Caribbean*. Mona, Jamaica: Savacou Publications, 1974.

———. *The Development of Creole Society in Jamaica, 1770–1820*. Oxford: Oxford University Press, 1971.

———. *Folk Culture of the Slaves in Jamaica*. London: Beacon Books, 1981.

Brewer, John. "'The Most Polite Age and the Most Vicious'": Attitudes towards Culture as a Commodity, 1660–1800." In Bermingham and Brewer, *Consumption of Culture*, 341–61.

———. *The Pleasures of the Imagination: English Culture in the Eighteenth Century*. London: HarperCollins, 1997.

———. *Sinews of Power: War, Money, and the English State, 1688–1783*. Cambridge, MA: Harvard University Press, 1988.

British Museum. "Akan Drum." http://www.britishmuseum.org/explore/highlights/highlight_objects/aoa/a/asante-style_drum.aspx (accessed on August 19, 2010).

Brodber, Erna. *Myal*. London: New Beacon Books, 1985.

Brontë, Charlotte. *Jane Eyre*. 1847. London: Penguin Books, 2006.

Brookhiser, Richard. *Gentleman Revolutionary: Gouverneur Morris, the Rake Who Wrote the Constitution*. New York: Free Press, 2003.

Brown, Jonathan. *Kings and Connoisseurs: Collecting Art in Seventeenth-Century Europe*. Princeton, NJ: Princeton University Press, 1994.

Brown, Kathleen M. *Good Wives, Nasty Wenches, and Anxious Patriarchs: Gender, Race, and Power in Colonial Virginia*. Chapel Hill: University of North Carolina Press, 1996.

Brown, Laura. *Ends of Empire: Women and Ideology in Early Eighteenth-Century English Literature*. Ithaca, NY: Cornell University Press, 1993.

———. *Fables of Modernity: Literature and Culture in the English Eighteenth Century*. Ithaca, NY: Cornell University Press, 2001.

Brown, Vincent. *The Reaper's Garden: Death and Power in the World of Atlantic Slavery*. Cambridge, MA: Harvard University Press, 2008.

Bryson, Anna. *From Courtesy to Civility: Changing Codes of Conduct in Early Modern England*. Oxford: Clarendon Press, 1998.

Buckridge, Steve O. *The Language of Dress: Resistance and Accommodation in Jamaica, 1760–1890*. Kingston, Jamaica: University of the West Indies Press, 2004.

Buisseret, David. *Historic Architecture of the Caribbean*. London: Heinemann. 1980.

Burck-Morss, Susan. *The Dialectics of Seeing: Walter Benjamin and the Arcades Project*. Cambridge: MIT Press, 1991.

———. "Hegel and Haiti." *Critical Inquiry* 26, no. 4 (2000): 821–65.

Burnside, Madeleine. *Spirits of the Passage: The Transatlantic Slave Trade in the Seventeenth Century*. Edited by Rosemarie Robotham. New York: Simon & Schuster, 1997.

Burke, Edmund. *Letters on a Regicide Peace, Selected Works of Edmund Burke*. Vol. 3. 1796. Indianapolis: Liberty Fund, 1999.

———. *A Philosophical Enquiry into the Sublime and Beautiful*. Edited by Adam Phillips. Oxford: Oxford University Press, 1990.

Burke, Joseph. *English Art, 1714–1800*. Oxford: Oxford University Press, 1976.

Burke, Peter. *Popular Culture in Early Modern Europe*. New York: Harper and Row, 1978.

Burton, Richard D. E. *Afro-Creole: Power, Opposition, and Play in the Caribbean*. Ithaca, NY: Cornell University Press, 1997.

Byron, Lord George. "Childe Harold's Pilgrimage." In *The Poetical Works of Lord Byron*. London: John Murray, 1859.

Calder, Angus. *Revolutionary Empire: The Rise of the English-Speaking Empires from the Fifteenth Century to the 1780s*. London: Jonathan Cape, 1981.

Calhoun, Craig, ed. *Habermas and the Public Sphere*. Cambridge: MIT Press, 1996.

Callahan, Allen Dwight. *The Talking Book: African Americans and the Bible*. New Haven, CT: Yale University Press, 2008. 1–19.

Cameron, Gail, and Stan Crooke. *Liverpool: Capital of the Slave Trade*. Liverpool: Picton Press, 1992.

Canny, Nicholas. *The Oxford History of the British Empire*. Vol. 1, *The Origins of Empire*. Oxford: Oxford University Press, 2001.

Canny, Nicholas, and Anthony Pagden, eds. *Colonial Identity in the Atlantic World, 1500–1800*. Princeton, NJ: Princeton University Press, 1987.

Carmichael, Mrs. A. C. *Domestic Manners and Social Conditions of the White, Coloured, and Negro Population of the West Indies*. London: Whittaker, Treacher, 1833.

Carney, Judith. *Black Rice: The African Origins of Rice Cultivation in the Americas*. Cambridge: Harvard University Press, 2002.

Carretta, Vincent. *Equiano the African: Biography of a Self-made Man*. Athens: University of Georgia Press, 2005.

———. "Property of Author: Olaudah Equiano's Place in the History of the Book." In Carretta and Gould, *Genius in Bondage*, 130–50.

Carretta, Vincent, and Philip Gould, eds. *Genius in Bondage: Literature of the Early Black Atlantic*. Lexington: University Press of Kentucky, 2000.

Carrithers, Michael, Steven Collins, and Steven Lukes, eds. *The Category of the Person: Anthropology, Philosophy, History*. Cambridge: Cambridge University Press, 1985. 1–26.

Cascardi, Anthony. *Consequences of Enlightenment*. Cambridge: Cambridge University Press, 1999.

Casid, Jill H. *Sowing Empire: Landscape and Colonization*. Minneapolis: University of Minnesota Press, 2005.

Cassidy, Frederic G. *Jamaica Talk: Three Hundred Years of the English Language in Jamaica*. London: Macmillan, 1961.

Cassirer, Ernest. *The Philosophy of the Enlightenment*. Princeton, NJ: Princeton University Press, 1951.

Castle, Terry. *The Female Thermometer: Eighteenth-Century Culture and the Invention of the Uncanny*. New York: Oxford University Press, 1995.

————. *Masquerade and Civilization: The Carnivalesque in Eighteenth-Century English Culture and Fiction*. Stanford, CA: Stanford University Press, 1986.

Castronovo, David. *The English Gentleman: Images and Ideals in Literature and Society*. New York: Ungar, 1987.

Cavazzi de Montecúccolo, António. *Descrição histórica dos três reinos do Congo, Matamba e Angola, pelo P.e João*. 2 vols. 1660. Lisbon: Junta de Investigações do Ultramar, 1965.

Caygill, Howard. *Art of Judgement*. Oxford: Blackwell, 1989.

Certeau, Michel de. *The Practice of Everyday Life*. Translated by Steven Rendall. Berkeley: University of California Press, 1984.

————. *The Writing of History*. Translated by Tom Conley. New York: Columbia University Press, 1988.

Chambers, Ross. *Room for Maneuver: Reading Oppositional Narrative*. Chicago: University of Chicago Press, 1991.

Cheng, Anne Anlin. *The Melancholy of Race: Psychoanalysis, Assimilation, and Hidden Grief*. Oxford: Oxford University Press, 2001.

Clarkson, Thomas. *The History of the Rise, Progress, and Accomplishment of the Abolition of the African Slave Trade by the British Parliament*. London: Longman, 1808.

Cohen, William B. *The French Encounter with Africans: White Responses to Blacks, 1530–1880*. Bloomington: Indiana University Press, 1980.

Colley, Linda. *Britons: Forging the Nation, 1707–1837*. New Haven, CT: Yale University Press, 1992.

————. *Captives: Britain, Empire, and the World, 1600–1850*. New York: Anchor Books, 2004.

Colombo, Claire Miller. "This Pen of Mine Will Say Too Much: Public Performance in the Journals of Anna Larpent." *Texas Studies in Literature and Language* 38 (1996): 285–301.

Cone, James H. *The Spirituals and the Blues: An Interpretation*. New York: Seabury Press, 1972.

Conrad, David. *Status and Identity in West Africa: Nyamakalaw of Mande*. Bloomington: Indiana University Press, 1995.

Crary, Jonathan. *Techniques of the Observer: On Vision and Modernity in the Nineteenth Century*. Cambridge: MIT Press, 1992.

Craton, Michael. *Searching for the Invisible Man: Slaves and Plantation Life in Jamaica*. Cambridge, MA: Harvard University Press, 1978.

Craven, Wayne. *American Art: History and Culture*. New York: McGraw-Hill Professional, 2003.

Crowe, Eyre. *With Thackeray in America*. London: Cassell, 1893.

Cugoano, Quobna Ottobah. *Thoughts and Sentiments on the Evil of Slavery and Other Writings*. Edited by Vincent Carretta. 1787. New York: Penguin Books, 1999.

Culler, Jonathan. *The Pursuit of Signs*. Ithaca, NY: Cornell University Press, 1983.

Curtin, Phillip. *The Image of Africa: British Ideas and Action, 1780–1850*. 2 vols. Madison: University of Wisconsin Press, 1964.

Dalzel, Archibald. *The History of Dahomy, an Inland Kingdom of Africa*. 1793. London: Cass, 1967.

Daniels, Stephen. *Fields of Vision: Landscape, Imagery, and National Identity in England and the United States*. Princeton, NJ: Princeton University Press, 1993.

Danto, A. C. *The Philosophical Disenfranchisement of Art*. New York: Columbia University Press, 1986.

Dapper, Olfert. *Description de l'Afrique, contenant les noms, la situation & les confins de toutes ses parties, leurs rivières, leurs villes & leurs habitations, leurs plantes & leurs animaux, les moeurs, les coûtumes, la langue, les richesses, la religion & le gouvernement de ses peoples*. 1666. Reprint, New York: Johnson, 1970.

Daston, Loraine. "Historical Epistemology." In *Questions of Evidence: Proof, Practice and Persuasion Across the Disciplines*, edited by James Chandler, Arnold I. Davidson, and Harry D. Harootunian, 243–74. Chicago: University of Chicago Press, 1994.

Davies, K. G. *The Royal African Company*. London: Holiday House, 1970.

Davies, Natalie Zemon. "Women on Top: Symbolic Sexual Inversion and Political Disorder in Early Modern Europe." In Babcock, *Reversible World,* 147–92.

Davis, David Brion. *The Problem of Slavery in Western Culture*. Ithaca, NY: Cornell University Press, 1966.

Dawes, Kwame. *Requiem*. Leeds, UK: Peepal Tree, 1996.

Dayan, Joan. *Haiti, History, and the Gods*. Berkeley: University of California Press, 1995.

D'Costa, Jean, and Barbara Lalla, eds. *Voices in Exile: Jamaican Texts of the 18th and 19th Centuries*. Tuscaloosa: University of Alabama Press, 1989.

Debord, Guy. *The Society of the Spectacle*. Translated by Donald Nicholson-Smith. New York: Zone Books, 1995.

Decorse, Christopher R. *An Archeology of Elmina: Africans and Europeans on the Gold Coast, 1400–1900*. Washington, DC: Smithsonian Institution Press, 2001.

Delbourgo, James. "Slavery in the Cabinet of Curiosities: Hans Sloane's Atlantic World." British Museum. http://www.britishmuseum.org/the_museum/news_and_press_releases/latest_news/hans_sloanes_atlantic_world.aspx (accessed June 26, 2010).

Denyer, Susan. *African Traditional Architecture*. New York: Africana Publishing, 1978.

Derrida, Jacques. *Archive Fever: A Freudian Impression*. Translated by Eric Prenowitz. Chicago: University of Chicago Press, 1996.

———. *Of Grammatology*. Translated by Gayatri Chakravorty Spivak. Baltimore: Johns Hopkins University Press, 1976.

———. "Plato's Pharmacy." In *Dissemination,* edited by Barbara Johnson, 63–171. Chicago: University of Chicago Press, 1981.

———. *Specters of Marx: The State of the Debt, the Work of Mourning, and the New International.* Translated by Peggy Kamuf. New York: Routledge, 1994.

———. *Speech and Phenomena: And Other Essays on Husserl's Theory of Signs.* Evanston, IL: Northwestern University Press, 1973.

———. *Truth in Painting.* Translated by Geoffrey Bennington and Ian McLeod. Chicago: University of Chicago Press, 1987.

Dirks, Robert. *The Black Saturnalia: Conflict and Its Ritual Expression on British West Indian Slave Plantations.* Gainesville: University of Florida Press, 1987.

Docherty, Thomas. *Criticism and Modernity: Aesthetics, Literature, and Nations in Europe and Its Academies.* Oxford: Oxford University Press, 1999.

Donnan, Elizabeth. *Documents Illustrative of the History of the Slave Trade to America.* 4 vols. 1930–1935. Buffalo, NY: William S. Hein, 2002.

Douglas, Mary. *In the Wilderness: The Doctrine of Defilement in the Book of Numbers.* Oxford: Oxford University Press, 2001.

———. *Purity and Danger: An Analysis of Concepts of Pollution and Taboo.* London: Routledge, 1966.

Douglass, Frederick. *Life and Times of Frederick Douglass.* In *Autobiographies: Narrative of the Life of Frederick Douglass, an American Slave; My Bondage and Freedom; Life and Times of Frederick Douglass.* New York: Library of America, 1994.

Dow, George Francis. *Slave Ships and Slaving.* Salem, MA: Marine Research Institute, 1927.

Dresser, Madge, and Sue Giles, eds. *Bristol and Transatlantic Slavery: Catalogue of the Exhibition "'A Respectable Trade?' Bristol & Transatlantic Slavery."* Bristol, UK: Bristol Museums and Art Gallery, 2000.

Dubois, Laurent. *Avengers of the New World: The Story of the Haitian Revolution.* Cambridge, MA: Harvard University Press, 2005.

DuBois, Page. *Slaves and Other Objects.* Chicago: University of Chicago Press, 2003.

Du Bois, W.E.B. *Dusk of Dawn: An Essay Toward an Autobiography of a Race Concept.* 1940. New Brunswick, NJ: Transaction Publishers, 1994.

———. *The Souls of Black Folk.* New York: Vintage Books, 1990.

Duchet, Michel. *Anthropologie et historie au siecle des lumieres.* Paris: Albin Michel, 1971.

Dunn, Richard S. "The English Sugar Islands and the Founding of South Carolina." In *Shaping Southern Society: The Colonial Experience,* edited by T. H. Breen. New York: Oxford University Press, 1976.

———. *Sugar and Slaves: The Rise of the Planter Class in the English West Indies, 1624–1713.* New York: W. W. Norton, 1973.

Dupré, Louis. *Passage to Modernity: An Essay in the Hermeneutics of Nature and Culture.* New Haven, CT: Yale University Press, 1993.

Dwyer, John, and Richard B. Sher, ed. *Sociability and Society in Eighteenth-Century Scotland.* Edinburgh: Mercat Press, 1993.

Dykes, Eva Beatrice. *The Negro in English Romantic Thought; or, A Study of Sympathy for the Oppressed.* Washington, DC: Associated Publishers, 1942.

Eagleton, Terry. *The Ideology of the Aesthetic*. Cambridge, MA: Blackwell, 1990.

Earle, William. *Obi; or, The History of Three-Fingered Jack*. Worcester, UK: Isaiah Thomas, 1804.

Earler, T. F., and K.J.P. Lowe, eds. *Black Africans in Renaissance Europe*. Cambridge: Cambridge University Press, 2005.

Edelstein, T. J. "Vauxhall Gardens." In Ford, *Cambridge Cultural History*, 203–15.

Edwardes, Michael. *The Nabobs at Home*. London: Constable, 1991.

Edwards, Bryan. Preface to *An Historical Survey of the French Colony in the Island of St. Domingo*. London: Printed for John Stockdale, Piccadilly, 1797.

———. The *History, Civil and Commercial, of the British Colonies in the West Indies*. Vol. 2. London: Printed for John Stockdale, 1801.

———. *Poems, Written Chiefly in the West-Indies*. Kingston, Jamaica: Printed for the author, by Alexander Aikman, 1792.

Edwards, Paul, and James Walvin. *Black Personalities in the Era of the Slave Trade*. Baton Rouge: Louisiana State University Press, 1983.

Elam, Harry J., Jr., and David Krasner, eds. *African America Performance and Theater History: A Critical Reader*. Oxford: Oxford University Press, 2001.

Elias, Norbert. *The Civilizing Process*. Rev. ed. Translated by Edmund Jephcott. Edited by Eric Dunning, Johan Goudsholm, and Stephen Mennell. Oxford: Blackwell, 2004.

Elkins, Stanley. *Slavery: A Problem in American Institutional and Intellectual Life*. Chicago: University of Chicago Press, 1959.

Elleh, Nnamdi. *African Architecture: Evolution and Transition*. New York: McGraw Hill, 1997.

Ellis, Markman. "Ignatius Sancho's Letters: Sentimental Libertinism and the Politics of Form." In Carretta and Gould, *Genius in Bondage*, 199–217.

———. *The Politics of Sensibility: Race, Gender, and Commerce in the Sentimental Novel*. Cambridge: Cambridge University Press, 1996.

Elsner, John, and Roger Cardinal. Introduction to *The Cultures of Collecting*, 1–6.

———. "A Collector's Model of Desire: The House and Museum of Sir John Soane." In *The Cultures of Collecting*, edited by John Elsner and Roger Cardinal, 155–76. Cambridge, MA: Harvard University Press, 1994.

Eltis, David. *The Rise of African Slavery in the Americas*. Cambridge: Cambridge University Press, 2000.

Emery, Lynne Fauley. *Black Dance: From 1619 to Today*. 2nd rev. ed. Hightstown, NJ: Princeton Book Company, 1988.

Equiano, Olaudah. *The Interesting Narrative and Other Writings*. Edited by Vincent Carretta. 1789. New York: Penguin Books, 2003.

Erickson, Peter. "The Moment of Race in Renaissance Studies." *Shakespeare Studies* 26 (1998): 27–36.

———. "Representations of Blacks and Blackness in the Renaissance." *Criticism* 35 (1993): 499–527.

Erickson, Peter, and Clark Hulse, eds. *Early Modern Visual Culture: Representation, Race, and Empire in Renaissance England*. Philadelphia: University of Pennsylvania Press, 2000.

Eze, Emmanuel Chukwudi, ed. "The Color of Reason: The Idea of 'Race' in Kant's Anthropology." In *Anthropology and the German Enlightenment: Perspectives on Humanity*, edited by Katherine M. Faull, 200–41. Lewisburg, PA: Bucknell University Press, 1995.

———. *Race and the Enlightenment: A Reader*. Cambridge, MA: Blackwell, 1997.

Fabre, Genevieve, and Robert O'Meally. *History and Memory in African-American Culture*. New York: Oxford University Press, 1994.

Fagan, Jean Yellin, and John C. Van Horne. "Graphic Discord: Abolitionist and Antiabolitionist Images." In *The Abolitionist Sisterhood: Women's Political Culture in Antebellum America*, 201–30. Ithaca, NY: Cornell University Press, 1994.

Falconbridge, Alexander. *An Account of the Slave Trade on the Coast of Africa*. London: J. Phillips, 1788.

Falola, Toyin, and Matt D. Childs, eds. *The Yoruba Diaspora in the Atlantic World*. Bloomington: Indiana University Press, 2004.

Fanon, Frantz. *Black Skin, White Masks*. Translated by Charles Lam Markham. New York: Grove Press, 1967.

———. *The Wretched of the Earth*. Translated by Constance Farrington. New York: Grove Press, 1953.

Faulkner, William. *Absalom Absalom*. New York: Random House, 1936.

Faust, Drew Gilpin, ed. *The Ideology of Slavery: Proslavery Thought in the Antebellum South, 1830–1860*. Baton Rouge: Louisiana State University Press, 1981.

Feelings, Tom. *The Middle Passage*. New York: Dial, 1995.

Feinberg, Harvey. *Africans and Europeans in West Africa: Elminans and Dutchmen on the Gold Coast during the Eighteenth Century*. Philadelphia: American Philosophical Society, 1989.

Feischner, Jennifer. *Mastering Slavery: Memory, Family, and Identity in Women's Slave Narratives*. New York: New York University Press, 1996.

Ferguson, Leland. *Uncommon Ground: Archeology and Early African America, 1650–1800*. Washington, DC: Smithsonian Books, 1992.

Ferguson, Moira. *Subject to Others: British Women Writers and Colonial Slavery, 1670–1834*. London: Routledge, 1992.

Fink, Eugen, Ute Saine, and Thomas Saine, "The Oasis of Happiness: Toward an Ontology of Play." *Yale French Studies* 41 (1968): 19–30.

Finley, Cheryl. "Committed to Memory: The Slave-Ship Icon and the Black-Atlantic Imagination." *Chicago Art Journal* (1999): 2–21.

Finley, Moses. *Ancient Slavery and Modern Ideology*. New York: Viking, 1960.

Fischer, Sibylle. *Modernity Disavowed: Haiti and the Cultures of Slavery in the Age of Revolution*. Durham, NC: Duke University Press, 2004.

Fitzhugh, George. *Sociology for the South; or, The Failure of Free Society*. Richmond, VA: A. Morris, 1854. Samuel J. May Anti-Slavery Collection. Cornell University Library Digital Collection. http://digital.library.cornell.edu/m/mayantislavery (accessed August 28, 2010).

Floyd Samuel A., Jr. *The Power of Black Music: Interpreting Its History from Africa to the United States*. Oxford: Oxford University Press, 1995.

Forbes, Robert Pierce. *The Missouri Compromise and Its Aftermath: Slavery and the Meaning of America*. Chapel Hill: University of North Carolina Press, 2007.

Ford, Boris, ed. *The Cambridge Cultural History of Britain.* Vol. 5. Cambridge: Cambridge University Press, 1992.

Foster, Helen Bradley. *"New Rainments of Self": African American Clothing in the Antebellum South.* Oxford: Berg, 1997.

Fothergill, Brian. *Beckford of Fonthill.* London: Faber, 1979.

Foucault, Michel. Afterword to *Michel Foucault, Beyond Structuralism and Hermeneutics,* 2nd ed., edited by Hubert L. Dreyfus and Paul Rabinow, 229–52. Chicago: University of Chicago Press, 1983.

———. *Discipline and Punish: The Birth of the Prison.* Translated by Alan Sheridan. New York: Vintage Books, 1979.

———. *The History of Sexuality.* Translated by Robert Hurley. New York: Vintage Books, 1988.

———. Introduction to *On the Normal and the Pathological,* by Georges Canguilhem. Translated by Carolyn R. Fawcett, 7–24. Boston: MIT Press, 1991.

Freud, Sigmund. *Civilization and Its Discontents.* Translated and edited by James Strachey. 1926. New York: W. W. Norton, 1961.

———. "Negation." In *Collected Papers.* Vol. 5. Edited by James Strachey. Translated by Joan Riviere. London: Hogarth, 1950.

Fryer, Peter. *Staying Power: The History of Black People in Britain.* London: Pluto Press, 1984.

Gadamer, Hans-Georg. *Truth and Method.* New York: Crossroad, 1995.

Gamble, Samuel. *A Slaving Voyage to Africa and Jamaica: The Log of the Sandown, 1793–1794.* Edited by Bruce L. Mouser. Bloomington: Indiana University Press, 2002.

Garnsey, Peter. *Ideas of Slavery from Aristotle to Augustine.* Cambridge: Cambridge University Press, 1996.

Gates, Henry Louis, Jr. *The Signifying Monkey: A Theory of African-American Literary Criticism.* Oxford: Oxford University Press, 1988.

———. *The Trials of Phillis Wheatley: America's First Black Poet and Her Encounters with the Founding Fathers.* New York: Oxford University Press, 2003.

Gates, Henry Louis, Jr., and Kwame Anthony Appiah, eds. *"Race," Writing, and Difference.* Chicago: University of Chicago Press, 1992

Gates, Henry Louis, Jr., and Nellie Y. McKay. *Norton Anthology of African American Literature.* New York: Norton, 1997.

Geertz, Clifford. "Thick Description: Toward an Interpretative Theory of Culture." In *The Interpretation of Cultures,* 3–32. New York: Basic Books, 1977.

Geggus, David P. *The Impact of the Haitian Revolution in the Atlantic World.* Columbia: University of South Carolina Press, 2002.

Genovese, Eugene D. *Roll, Jordan, Roll: The World the Slaves Made.* New York: Vintage, 1976.

Georgiana, Duchess of Cavendish. "Anonymous." In *Amazing Grace: An Anthology of Poems about Slavery,* edited by James G. Basker. New Haven, CT: Yale University Press, 2002.

Gerzina, Gretchen. *Black England: Life before Emancipation.* London: John Murray, 1995.

———. *Black London: Life before Emancipation.* New Brunswick, NJ: Rutgers University Press, 1995.

Gikandi, Simon. *Maps of Englishnesss: Writing Identity in the Culture of Colonialism*. New York: Columbia University Press, 1996.

Gilman, Sander. "The Figure of the Black in German Aesthetic Theory." *Eighteenth-Century Studies* 8, no. 4 (1975): 373–91.

Gilroy, Paul. *The Black Atlantic: Modernity and Double-Consciousness*. Cambridge, MA: Harvard University Press, 1993.

———. *Postcolonial Melancholia*. New York: Columbia University Press, 2005.

Glissant, Édouard. *Caribbean Discourse: Selected Essays*. Translated by J. Michael Dash. Charlottesville: University Press of Virginia, 1989.

———. "Free and Forced Poetics." In *Ethno-Poetics: A First International Symposium*, edited by Michel Benamou and Jerome Rothenberg, 95–101. Boston: Boston University Scholarly Press, 1976.

Gluckman, Max. *Rituals of Rebellion in South-East Africa*. Frazer Lecture 1952. Manchester: Manchester University Press, 1954.

Goldsmith, Oliver. *A History of the Earth, and Animated Nature*. 1778. London: William Sprent, 1854.

Gomez, Michael A. "A Quality of Anguish: The Igbo Response to Enslavement in North America." In Lovejoy and Trotman, *Trans-Atlantic Dimensions*, 82–95.

———. *Reversing Sail: A History of the African Diaspora*. Cambridge: Cambridge University Press, 2005.

Goveia, E. V. *A Study on the Historiography of the British West Indies to the End of the Nineteenth Century*. 1956. Washington, DC: Howard University Press, 1980.

———. *The West Indian Slave Laws of the 18th Century*, with C. J. Bartlett, *A New Balance of Power: The 19th Century*. Barbados: Caribbean Universities Press, 1970.

Grégoire, Henri. *An Enquiry Concerning the Intellectual and Moral Faculties, and Literature of Negroes*. New ed. Translated by David Bailie Warden. Armonk, NY: M. E. Sharpe, 1997.

Guyer, Paul. *Kant and the Claims of Taste*. Cambridge: Cambridge University Press, 1997.

Gwilliam, Tassie. "'Scenes of Horror,' Scenes of Sensibility: Sentimentality and Slavery in John Gabriel Stedman's *Narrative of a Five Years' Expedition against the Revolted Negroes of Surinam*," *ELH* 65, no. 3 (1998): 653–73.

Habermas, Jürgen. "Modernity—An Incomplete Project." In *The Anti-aesthetic: Essays on Postmodern Culture*, edited by Hal Foster, 3–15. Port Townsend, WA: Bay Press, 1983.

———. *The Philosophical Discourse of Modernity: Twelve Lectures*. Translated by Frederick G. Lawrence. Cambridge: MIT Press, 1987.

———. *The Structural Transformation of the Public Sphere: An Inquiry into a Category of Bourgeois Society*. Translated by Thomas Burger. 1961. Cambridge: MIT Press, 1991.

Hair, P.E.H., Adam Jones, and Robin Law, eds. *Barbot on Guinea: The Writings of Jean Barbot on West Africa, 1678–1712*. London: Hakluyt Society, 1992.

Hall, Catherine. *Civilising Subjects: Metropole and Colony in the English Imagination, 1830–1867*. Oxford: Polity Press, 2002.

Hall, Douglas. *In Miserable Slavery: Thomas Thistlewood in Jamaica, 1750–1786*. Kingston, Jamaica: University of the West Indies Press, 1999.

Hall, Edith. *Inventing the Barbarian: Greek Self-definition through Tragedy*. Oxford: Oxford University Press, 1989.

Hall, Gwendolyn Midlo. *Africans in Colonial Louisiana: The Development of Afro-Creole Culture in the Eighteenth Century*. Baton Rouge: Louisiana State University Press, 1992.

———. *Slavery and African Ethnicities in the Americas: Restoring the Links*. Chapel Hill: University of North Carolina Press, 2005.

Hall, Kim F. "Object into Object? Some Thoughts on the Presence of Black Women in Early Modern Culture." In Erickson and Hulse, *Early Modern Visual Culture*, 346–79.

———. *Things of Darkness: Economies of Race and Gender in Early Modern England*. Ithaca, NY: Cornell University Press, 1995.

Hallett, Mark, and Christine Riding. *Hogarth*. London: Tate, 2006.

Hammermeister, Kai. *The German Aesthetic Tradition*. Cambridge: Cambridge University Press, 2002.

Hammond, Dorothy, and Alta Jablow. *The Africa That Never Was: Four Centuries of British Writing about Africa*. New York: Twayne, 1970.

Hansen, Thorkild. *Coast of Slaves*. Translated by Kari Dako. Accra, Ghana: Sub-Saharan Publishers, 2002.

Harlow, Vincent. *Christopher Codrington, 1668–1710*. Oxford: Clarendon Press, 1928.

Hartman, Saidiya V. *Lose Your Mother: A Journey along the Atlantic Slave Route*. New York: Farrar, Straus and Giroux, 2007.

———. *Scenes of Subjection: Terror, Slavery, and Self-making in Nineteenth-Century America*. New York: Oxford University Press, 1997.

———. "The Time of Slavery." *South Atlantic Quarterly* 101, no. 4 (2002): 757–77.

Hartog, Francois. *The Mirror of Herodotus: The Representation of the Other in the Writing of History*. Translated by Janet Lloyd. Berkeley: University of California Press, 1988.

Harvey, David. *The Condition of Postmodernity*. Oxford: Blackwell, 1989.

Hauptman, William. "Clinging Fast: 'To My Tutelary Mountains': Beckford in Helvetia." In Ostergard, *William Beckford*, 73–88.

Hayden, Robert. "Middle Passage." In *Collected Poems*, edited by Frederick Glaysher, 48–54. New York: Liverlight, 1985.

Hazlewood, Nick. *The Queen's Slave Trader: John Hawkyns, Elizabeth I, and the Trafficking in Human Souls*. New York: HarperCollins, 2005.

Hazlitt, William. "Fonthill Abbey." In *Criticisms on Art and Sketches on the Picture Galleries of England*, 2nd ed., 284–99. London: C. Templeman, 1824.

Hegel, G.W.F. Preface to *Phenomenology of the Mind*. In *Hegel: Texts and Commentary*, translated and edited by Walter Kaufmann. Garden City, NY: Anchor Books, 1966.

Heidegger, Martin. "The Age of the World Picture." In *Technology and Other Essays*, translated by William Lovitt, 3–35. New York: Harper and Row, 1977.

———. "Building Dwelling Thinking." In Martin Heidegger, *Basic Writings*, edited by David Farrell Krell, 323–39. New York: Harper and Row, 1977.

Hendricks, Margo, and Patricia Parker, eds. *Women, "Race," and Writing in the Early Modern Period*. London: Routledge, 1994.

Hewat-Jaboor, Philip. "Fonthill House: One of the Most Princely Edifices in the Kingdom." In Ostergard, *William Beckford*, 51–71.

Higman, B. W. *Slave Populations of the British Caribbean*. Baltimore: Johns Hopkins University Press, 1984.

Higman, B. W., with contributions by George A. Aarons, Karlis Karklins, and Elizabeth J. Reitz. *Montpelier, Jamaica: A Plantation Community in Slavery and Freedom, 1739–1912*. Kingston, Jamaica: University of the West Indies Press, 1998.

———. *Plantation Jamaica, 1750–1850: Capital and Control in a Colonial Economy*. Kingston, Jamaica: University of the West Indies Press, 2005.

Hill, Errol. *The Jamaican Stage, 1655–1900: Profile of a Colonial Theatre*. Amherst: University of Massachusetts Press, 1992.

Hill, Thomas, and Bernard Boxill. "Kant and Race." In *Race and Racism*, edited by Bernard Boxill, 448–72. Oxford: Oxford University Press, 2001.

Hochschild, Adam. *Bury the Chains: Prophets and Rebels in the Fight to Free an Empire's Slaves*. Boston: Houghton Mifflin, 2005.

Hodgen, Margaret T. *Early Anthropology in the Sixteenth and Seventeenth Centuries*. Philadelphia: University of Pennsylvania Press, 1964.

Hogarth, William. *The Analysis of Beauty: Written with a View of Fixing the Fluctuating Ideas of Taste*. London: J. Reeves, 1753.

Holt, Thomas. *The Problem of Freedom: Race, Labor, and Politics in Jamaica and Britain, 1832–1938*. Baltimore: Johns Hopkins University Press, 1991.

Honour, Hugh. *The Image of the Black in Western Art*. Vol. 4. *From the American Revolution to World War I, Section 1: Slaves and Liberators*. Cambridge, MA: Harvard University Press, 1989.

Hont, Istvan, and Michael Ignatieff, eds. *Wealth and Virtue: The Shaping of Political Economy in the Scottish Enlightenment*. Cambridge: Cambridge University Press, 1983.

Horkheimer, Max, and Theodor W. Adorno. *Dialectic of Enlightenment*. Translated by John Cumming. New York: Continuum, 1998.

Huggins, Nathaniel Irvin. *Black Odyssey: The African-American Ordeal in Slavery*. 1977. New York: Vintage, 1990.

Hulme, Peter, and Ludmilla Jordanova, eds. *The Enlightenment and Its Shadows*. London: Routledge, 1990.

Hume, David. "Of National Characters." In *Essays: Moral, Political, and Literary*, 202–22. New York: Cosmo Classics, 2006.

———. "Of Refinements in the Arts." In *Essays: Moral, Political, and Literary*, 275–88. New York: Cosmo Classics, 2006.

———. "Of the Standard of Taste." In *Essays: Moral, Political, and Literary*, 231–58. New York: Cosmo Classics, 2006.

———. "On the Dignity or Meanness of Human Nature." In *Essays and Treatises on Several Subjects in Two Volumes*, 1:83–92. Edinburgh: Bell and Bradflute, 1804.

Hume, David. *A Treatise on Human Nature*. Edited by P. H. Nidditch. 1739–1740. Oxford: Oxford University Press, 1981.

Humphreys, Arthur. "The Arts in Eighteenth-Century Britain." In Ford, *Cambridge Cultural History*, 5:2–47.

Hutcheson, Francis. *An Inquiry into the Original of Our Ideas of Beauty and Virtue in Two Treatises*. Edited by Wolfgang Leidhold. 1729. Indianapolis: Liberty Fund, 2004.

Impey, Oliver, and John Whitehead. "Observations on Japanese Lacquer in the Collection of William Beckford." In Ostergard, *William Beckford*, 217–28.

International Slavery Museum. "Liverpool and the Slave Trade." http://www.liverpoolmuseums.org.uk/maritime/slavery/liverpool.asp (accessed August 27, 2010).

Jacobs, Harriet. *Incidents in the Life of a Slave Girl*. Edited by Nellie Y. McKay and Francis Smith Forster. 1860. New York: Norton, 2001.

James, C.L.R. *The Black Jacobins: Toussaint L'Ouverture and the San Domingo Revolution*. 2nd ed. New York: Vintage, 1989.

Jameson, Fredric. *The Political Unconscious: Narrative as a Socially Symbolic Act*. Ithaca, NY: Cornell University Press, 1981.

Jay, Martin. "'The Aesthetic Ideology' as Ideology; or, What Does It Mean to Aestheticize Politics?" *Cultural Critique* 21 (Spring 1992): 41–61.

———. "Scopic Regimes of Modernity." In *Vision and Visuality*, edited by Hal Foster, 3–28. New York: New Press, 1999.

Jefferson, Thomas. *Notes on the State of Virginia*. Edited by William Peden. Chapel Hill: University of North Carolina Press, 1995.

Jeffery, Sally. "Architecture." In Ford, *Cambridge Cultural History*, 216–59.

Jobson, Richard. *The Golden Trade; or, a Discovery of the River Gambra, and the Golden Trade of the Aethiopians*. 1623. London: Dawsons, 1968.

Johnson, Charles. *Middle Passage*. New York: Scribner, 1998.

Johnson, Samuel. *The Rambler*, no. 92 (February 2, 1751). In *The Rambler*, vol. 2, 18th ed. London: Rivington and Others, 1823.

Johnson, Walter. "Time and Revolution in African America: Temporality and the History of Atlantic Slavery." In K. Wilson, *New Imperial History*, 197–215.

Jones, Ann Rosalind, and Peter Stallybrass. *Renaissance Clothing and the Materials of Memory*. Cambridge: Cambridge University Press, 2000.

Jones, Eldred D. *The Elizabethan Image of Africa*. Charlottesville: University Press of Virginia, 1971.

———. *Othello's Countrymen: The African in English Renaissance Drama*. London: Oxford University Press, 1965.

Jones, Robert W. *Gender and the Formation of Taste in Eighteenth-Century Britain: The Analysis of Beauty*. Cambridge: Cambridge University Press, 1998.

Jordan, Winthrop. *White over Black: American Attitudes toward the Negro, 1550–1812*. Chapel Hill: University of North Carolina Press, 1968.

Judy, Raymond A. T. "Kant and the Negro." *Sapina* 10, no. 2 (1997): 319–77.

Juster, Susan. "Virginian Luxuries: Sex and Power in a Slave Society." *Reviews in American History* 25, no. 3 (1997): 379–85.

Kames, Lord (Henry Home). *Essays on the Principles of Morality and Natural Religion*. Edited by Mary Catherine Moran. Indianapolis: Liberty Fund, 2005.

Kant, Immanuel. "An Answer to the Question: What is Enlightenment?" In *Kant: Political Writings*, 2nd ed., edited by Hans Reiss, translated by H. B. Nisbet, 54–60. Cambridge: Cambridge University Press, 1991.

———. *Critique of the Power of Judgment*. Edited and translated by Paul Guyer and Eric Matthews. Cambridge: Cambridge University Press, 2001.

———. *Observations on the Feeling of the Beautiful and the Sublime*. Translated by John T. Goldthwaite. Berkeley: University of California Press, 1960.

Kaplan, Sidney, and Emma Nogrady Kaplan. *The Black Presence in the Era of the American Revolution*. Rev. ed. Amherst: University of Massachusetts Press, 1989.

Karasch, Mary C. *Slave Life in Rio de Janeiro, 1808–1850*. Princeton, NJ: Princeton University Press, 1987.

Kaye, Anthony E. *Joining Places: Slave Neighborhoods in the Old South*. Chapel Hill: University of North Carolina Press, 2007.

Kidd, Colin. *British Identities before Nationalism: Ethnicity and Nationhood in the Atlantic World, 1600–1800*. Cambridge: Cambridge University Press, 1999.

———. "Ethnicity in the British Atlantic World, 1688–1830." In K. Wilson, *New Imperial History*, 260–77.

Kilbride, Daniel. *An American Aristocracy: Southern Planters in Antebellum Philadelphia*. Columbia: University of South Carolina Press, 2006.

King, J.C.H. *First Peoples, First Contacts*. London: British Museum Press, 1999.

King, Reyahn, et al. *Ignatius Sancho: An African Man of Letters*. London: National Portrait Gallery, 1997.

Klein, Lawrence E. "Politeness for Plebes: Consumption and Social Identity in Early Eighteenth-Century England." In Bermingham and Brewer, *Consumption of Culture*, 364–82.

———. *Shaftesbury and the Culture of Politeness: Moral Discourse and Cultural Politics in Early Eighteenth-Century England*. Cambridge: Cambridge University Press, 1994.

———. "The Third Earl of Shaftesbury and the Progress of Politeness." *Eighteenth-Century Studies* 18, no. 2 (1984–1985): 186–214.

Kramnick, Isaac. ed. *The Portable Enlightenment Reader*. New York: Penguin, 1995.

Kranish, Michael. "At Capitol, slavery's story turns full circle; Historians hope significance comes to light as Obama takes office." *Boston Globe*, December 28, 2008. http://www.boston.com/news/nation/articles/2008/12/28/at_capitol_slaverys_story_turns_full_circle (accessed June 26, 2010).

Kristeller, Paul Oskar. *Renaissance Thought and the Arts: Collected Essays*. Exp. ed. Princeton, NJ: Princeton University Press, 1990.

Kristeva, Julia. *Black Sun: Depression and Melancholia*. Translated by Leon S. Roudiez. New York: Columbia University Press, 1989.

———. *Powers of Horror: An Essay on Abjection*. Translated by Leon S. Roudiez. New York: Columbia University Press, 1941.

Kriz, Kay Dian. "Marketing Mulatresses in Paintings and Prints of Agostino Brunias." In Nussbaum, *Global Eighteenth Century*, 195–210.

Kriz, Kay Dian. *Slavery, Sugar, and the Culture of Refinement: Picturing the British West Indies, 1700–1840*. New Haven, CT: Yale University Press, 2008.

Kunst, Hans-Joachim. *The African in European Art*. Bonn-Bad Godesberg: Inter Nationes, 1967.

Lacan, Jacques. *The Four Fundamental Concepts of Psychoanalysis*. Translated by Alan Sheridan. London: Hogarth Press, 1977.

Ladurie, Emmanuel Le Roy. *Carnival in Romans*. Translated by Mary Feeney. New York: George Braziller, 1979.

Lambert, David. *White Creole Culture, Politics, and Identity during the Age of Abolition*. Cambridge: Cambridge University Press, 2005.

Lamont, Michèle, and Marcel Fournier, eds. *Cultivating Differences: Symbolic Boundaries and the Making of Inequality*. Chicago: University of Chicago Press, 1992.

Langford, Paul. *A Polite and Commercial People: England, 1727–1783*. Oxford: Clarendon Press, 1989.

Laplanche, J., and J.-B. Pontalis. *The Language of Psycho-Analysis*. Translated by Donald Nicholson-Smith. New York: Norton, 1974.

Lapsansky, Phillip. "Graphic Discord: Abolitionist and Antiabolitionist Images." In *The Abolitionist Sisterhood: Women's Political Culture in Antebellum America,* edited by Jean Yellin Fagan and John C. Van Horne, 201–30. Ithaca, NY: Cornell University Press, 1994.

Larpent. Anna Margaretta. *A Woman's View of Drama, 1790–1830: The Diaries of Anna Margaretta Larpent from the Huntington Library*. Microfilm. Marlborough, Wiltshire, Eng.: Adam Matthew, 1995.

Latrobe, Benjamin Henry. *The Journals of Benjamin Henry Latrobe, 1799–1820: From Philadelphia to New Orleans*. Vol. 3. Edited by Edward C. Carter II, John C. Van Horne, and Lee W. Formwalt. New Haven, CT: Yale University Press, 1980.

Lawal, Babatunde. "Reclaiming the African Past: Yoruba Elements in African American Arts." In *The Yoruba Diaspora in the Atlantic World,* edited by Toyin Falola and Matt D. Childs, 291–325. Bloomington: Indiana University Press, 2004.

Lawrence, A. W. *Fortified Trade-Posts: The English in West Africa, 1645–1822*. London: Jonathan Cape, 1963.

Lawson, Bill E. "Locke and the Legal Obligations of Black Americans." In *Subjugation and Bondage: Critical Essays on Slavery and Social Philosophy,* edited by Tommy Lott, 131–50. Lanham, MD: Rowman and Littlefield, 1998.

Lees-Milne, James. *William Beckford*. Tisbury, Wiltshire, Eng.: Compton Russell, 1976.

Leslie, Charles. *A New and Exact Account of Jamaica*. 3rd ed. Edinburgh: R. Fleming, 1740.

Levine, Lawrence. *Black Culture and Black Consciousness*. Oxford: Oxford University Press, 1977.

Lewis, Matthew Gregory. *Journal of a West Indian Proprietor*. Edited by Judith Terry. Oxford: Oxford University Press, 1999.

Library of Congress. "The Largest Slave Auction, March 3, 1859." America's Library, http://www.americaslibrary.gov/jb/reform/jb_reform_slaveauc_1.html (accessed August 27, 2010).

Ligon, Richard. *A True and Exact History of the Island of Barbadoes*. 1657. London: Frank Cass, 1970.

Lipking, Lawrence. *The Ordering of the Arts in Eighteenth-Century England*. Princeton, NJ: Princeton University Press, 1970.

Little, K. L. *Negroes in Britain: A Study of Racial Relations in English Society*. London: Kegan Paul, Trench and Trubner, 1947.

Littlefield, Daniel C. *Rice and Slaves: Ethnicity and the Slave Trade in Colonial South Carolina*. Baton Rouge: Louisiana State University Press, 1981.

Lloyd, G.E.R. *Polarity and Analogy: Two Types of Argumentation in Early Greek Thought*. Cambridge: Cambridge University Press, 1966.

Locke, John. *Second Treatise of Government*. Edited by C. B. Macpherson. Indianapolis: Hackett, 1980. 8.

Lockridge, Kenneth A. *The Diary and Life of William Byrd II of Virginia, 1674–1744*. Chapel Hill: University of North Carolina Press, 1987.

———. *On the Sources of Patriarchal Rage: The Commonplace Books of William Byrd and Thomas Jefferson and the Gendering of Power in the Eighteenth Century*. New York: New York University Press, 1992.

Long, Edward. *Candid Reflections upon the Judgment Lately Awarded by the Court of King's Bench, in Westminster-Hall, on What Is Commonly Called the Negroe-Cause*. London: Printed for T. Lowndes, 1772.

———. *The History of Jamaica*. 3 vols. 1774. London: Frank Cass, 1979.

Loomba, Ania. *Shakespeare, Race, and Colonialism*. Oxford: Oxford University Press, 2002.

Lott, Tommy, ed. *Subjugation and Bondage: Critical Essays on Slavery and Social Philosophy*. Lanham, MD: Rowman and Littlefield, 1998.

Lovejoy, Paul E. "Ethnic Designations of the Slave Trade and the Reconstruction of the History of Trans-Atlantic Slavery." In Lovejoy and Trotman, *Trans-Atlantic Dimensions*, 9–42.

Lovejoy, Paul E., and Robin Law, eds. *The Biography of Mahommah Gardo Baquaqua: His Passage from Slavery to Freedom in Africa and America*. Princeton, NJ: Markus Wiener, 2001.

Lovejoy, Paul E., and David V. Trotman, eds. *Trans-Atlantic Dimensions of Ethnicity in the African Diaspora*. London: Continuum, 2004.

Lufman, John. *A Brief Account of the Island of Antigua*. London: Printed for T. Cadell, 1789.

Lupton, Kenneth. *Mungo Park, the African Traveler*. Oxford: Oxford University Press, 1979.

Lyotard, Jean-François. *The Postmodern Condition: A Report on Knowledge*. Translated by Geoff Bennington and Brian Massumi. Minneapolis: University of Minnesota Press, 1984.

MacGregor, A. *Sir Hans Sloane*. London: British Museum Press, 1994.

Madden, Richard Robert. *A Twelvemonth's Residence in the West Indies, During the Transition from Slavery to Apprenticeship*. Philadelphia: Carey, Lea, and Blanchard, 1835.

Man, Paul de. *Aesthetic Ideology*. Edited by Andrzej Warminski. Minneapolis: University of Minnesota Press, 1996.

Man, Paul de. *Allegories of Reading: Figural Language in Rousseau, Nietzsche, Rilke, and Proust.* New Haven, CT: Yale University Press, 1979.

Mannings, David. "The Visual Arts." In Ford, *Cambridge Cultural History,* 106–47.

Marambaud, Pierre. *William Byrd of Westover, 1674–1744.* Charlottesville: University Press of Virginia, 1971.

Markley, Robert. "Sentimentality as Performance: Shaftesbury, Sterne, and the Theatrics of Virtue." In Nussbaum and Brown, *New Eighteenth Century,* 210–30.

Markman, Ellis. "Ignatius Sancho's Letters: Sentimental Libertinism and the Politics of Form." In Caretta and Gould, *Genius in Bondage,* 199–217.

Marshall, P. J. *The Oxford History of the British Empire.* Vol. 2. *The Eighteenth Century.* Oxford: Oxford University Press, 2001.

Marsters, Kate Ferguson. Introduction to *Travels in the Interior Districts of Africa.* Durham, NC: Duke University Press, 2000. 1–38.

Marx, Karl. *Capital.* Vol. 1. *A Critique of Political Economy.* Translated by Ben Fowkes. London: Penguin Classics, 1990.

———. *A Contribution to the Critique of Political Economy.* Translated by N. I. Stone. Chicago: Charles H. Kerr, 1904.

———. *Economic and Philosophic Manuscripts of 1844.* Edited by Dirk J. Struik. New York: International Publishers, 1964.

———. *The German Ideology, Part I.* In *The Marx-Engels Reader,* 2nd ed., edited by Robert C. Tucker, 146–200. New York: W. W. Norton, 1978.

Mattick, Paul, Jr., ed. *Eighteenth-Century Aesthetics and the Reconstruction of Art.* Cambridge: Cambridge University Press, 1993.

Mauss, Marcel. "The Category of the Human Mind: The Notion of the Person; the Notion of the Self." In Carrithers, Collins, and Lukes, *Category of the Person,* 1–26.

McCloy, Shelby T. *The Negro in France.* Lexington: University of Kentucky Press, 1961.

McDonald, Roderick A. *Goods and Chattels on the Sugar Plantations of Jamaica and Louisiana.* Baton Rouge: Louisiana State University Press, 1993.

McInnis, Maurice D. *The Politics of Taste in Antebellum Charleston.* Chapel Hill: University of North Carolina Press, 2005.

McKendrick, Neil, John Brewer, and J. H. Plumb. *The Birth of a Consumer Society: The Commercialization of Eighteenth-Century England.* Bloomington: Indiana University Press, 1982.

———. "Josiah Wedgwood and the Commercialization of the Potteries." In McKendrick, Brewer, and Plumb, *Birth of a Consumer Society,* 100–45.

McLaughlin, Fiona. "Senegal: The Emergence of a National Lingua Franca." In Andrew Simpson, *Language and National Identity in Africa.* New York: Oxford University Press, 2008.

McLeod, Bet. "A Celebrated Collector." In Ostergard, *William Beckford,* 155–76.

McMillan, Beverly C., ed. *Captive Passage: The Transatlantic Slave Trade and the Making of the Americas.* Washington, DC: Smithsonian Institution Press, 2002.

Melville, Lewis. *The Life and Letters of William Beckford of Fronthill.* New York: Duffield, 1910.

Mendelssohn, Moses. "On the Question: What is Enlightenment?" [1784]. In *What is Enlightenment? Eighteenth-Century Answers and Twentieth-Century Questions,* ed. James Schmidt, 53–57. Berkeley: University of California Press, 1996.

Menke, Christoph. "Modernity, Subjectivity and Aesthetic Reflection." In *From an Aesthetic Point of View,* edited by Peter Osborne, 35–56. London: Serpent's Tail, 2000.

Metz, Christian. *The Imaginary Signifier: Psychoanalysis and the Cinema.* Translated by Ben Brewster, Alfred Guzzetti, Celia Britton, and Annwyl Williams. Bloomington: Indiana University Press, 1982.

Miers, Suzanne, and Igor Kopytoff, eds. *Slavery in Africa: Historical and Anthropological Perspectives.* Madison: University of Wisconsin Press, 1977.

Mill, Gary B. *The Forgotten People: Cane River's Creoles of Color.* Baton Rouge: Louisiana State University Press, 1977.

Miller, Christopher L. *The French Atlantic Triangle: Literature and Culture of the Slave Trade.* Durham, NC: Duke University Press, 2008.

Miller, John Chester. *The Wolf by the Ears: Thomas Jefferson and Slavery.* New York: Free Press, 1977.

Miller, Joseph Calder. *Way of Death: Merchant Capitalism and the Angolan Slave Trade, 1730–1830.* Madison: University of Wisconsin Press, 1996.

Mintz, Sidney. *Sweetness and Power: The Place of Sugar in Modern History.* New York: Penguin, 1985.

Montgomery, Charles J. "Survivors from the Cargo of the Negro Slave Yacht *Wanderer.*" *American Anthropologist,* n.s., 10, no. 4. (1908): 611–23.

Moreton, J. B. *West India Customs and Manners.* London: J. Parsons et al., 1793.

Morgan, Edmund. *American Slavery, American Freedom: The Ordeal of Colonial Virginia.* New York: W. W. Norton, 1975.

Morgan, Kenneth. "Bristol West India Merchants in the Eighteenth Century." *Transactions of the Royal Historical Society* 6, Vol. 3 (1993): 185–208.

Morgan, Philip D. *Slave Counterpoint: Black Culture in the Eighteenth-Century Chesapeake and Lowcountry.* Chapel Hill: University of North Carolina Press, 1998.

———. "Work and Culture: The Task Systems and the World of Lowcountry Blacks, 1700–1880." In *Material Life in America, 1600–1860,* edited by Robert Blair St. George, 203–32. Boston: Northeastern University Press, 1988.

Morrison, Toni. *Playing in the Dark: Whiteness and the Literary Imagination.* New York: Vintage, 1992.

Mortensen, Preben. *Art in the Social Order.* Albany: State University of New York Press, 1997.

Mowl, Timothy. "William Beckford: A Biographical Perspective." In Ostergard, *William Beckford,* 17–31.

Mudimbe-Boyi, Elisabeth. *Essais sur les Cultures en Contact: Afrique, Amériques, Europe.* Paris: Karthala, 2006.

Nash, Andy. "John Pinney." Bristol Slavery. http://www.bristolandslavery.4t.com/pinney.htm (accessed August 28, 2010).

National Archives. "The Somerset Case, Howell's State Trials," vol. 20, cols. 1–6, 79–82. Transcript. National Archive, UK. http://www.nationalarchives.gov.uk/pathways/blackhistory/rights/transcripts/somerset_case.htm (accessed August 28, 2010).

Nettleford, Rex. *Caribbean Cultural Identity: The Case of Jamaica: An Essay in Cultural Dynamics.* Los Angeles: Center for Afro-American Studies and UCLA Latin American Center, 1979.

———. *Dance Jamaica: Renewal and Continuity: The National Dance Theatre Company of Jamaica, 1962–1983.* New York: Grove Press, 1985.

Neugerbauer, Christian M. "The Racism of Hegel and Kant." In *Sage Philosophy: Indigenous Thinkers and Modern Debate on African Philosophy,* edited by H. Odera Oruka, 259–73. Leiden: E. J. Brill, 1990.

Newton, John. *The Journal of a Slave Trader, 1750–1754.* Edited by Bernard Martin and Mark Sourrell. London: Epworth Press, 1962.

Nora, Pierre. "Between Memory and History: *Les Lieux de Memoire.*" In *History and Memory in African-American Culture,* edited by Genevieve Fabre and Robert O'Meally, 284–300. New York: Oxford University Press, 1994.

Norris, Robert. *Memoirs of the Reign of Bossa Ahádee, King of Dahomy, an Inland country of Guiney, to which are added the author's journey to Abomey, the capital, and a short account of the African slave trade.* 1789. London, Cass, 1968.

Nugent, Lady Maria. *Lady Nugent's Journal of Her Residence in Jamaica from 1801 to 1805.* Edited by Philip Wright. 1839. Kingston, Jamaica: University of the West Indies Press, 2002.

Nussbaum, Felicity A. *The Autobiographical Subject: Gender and Ideology in Eighteenth-Century England.* Baltimore: Johns Hopkins University Press, 1989.

———. "Being a Man: Olaudah Equiano and Ignatius Sancho." In Caretta and Gould, *Genius in Bondage,* 54–71.

———. *The Global Eighteenth Century.* Baltimore: Johns Hopkins University Press, 2003.

———. *Limits of the Human: Fictions of Anomaly, Race, and Gender in the Long Eighteenth Century.* Cambridge: Cambridge University Press, 2003.

———. *Torrid Zones: Maternity, Sexuality, and Empire in Eighteenth-Century English Narratives.* Baltimore: Johns Hopkins University Press, 1995.

Nussbaum, Felicity A., and Laura Brown. *The New Eighteenth Century: Theory, Politics, English Literature.* New York: Routledge, 1987.

Oakes, James. *The Ruling Race: A History of American Slaveholders.* London: W. W. Norton, 1998.

Ogude, S. E. *Genius in Bondage: A Study of the Origins of African Literature in English.* Ile-Ife, Nigeria: University of Ife Press, 1983.

Olmstead, Frederick Law. *Journeys in the Seaboard Negro Slave States.* New York: Mason Brothers, 1861.

Onuf, Peter S. *The Mind of Thomas Jefferson.* Charlottesville: University of Virginia Press, 2007.

———. "'To Declare Them a Free and Independent People': Race, Slavery, and National Identity in Jefferson's Thought." *Journal of the Early Republic* 18, no. 1 (1998): 1–46.

Osborne, Peter, ed. *From an Aesthetic Point of View: Philosophy, Art and the Senses*. London: Serpent's Tail, 2000.

Ostergard, Derek E., ed. *William Beckford, 1760–1844: An Eye for the Magnificent*. New Haven, CT: Yale University Press, 2001.

Outram, Dorinda. *The Enlightenment*. Cambridge: Cambridge University Press, 1995.

———. *Panorama of the Enlightenment*. Los Angeles: J. Paul Getty Museum, 2006.

Ownby, Ted, ed. *Black and White Cultural Interaction in the Antebellum South*. Jackson: University of Mississippi Press, 1993.

Pares, Richard. *Merchants and Planters*. Cambridge: Cambridge University Press, 1960.

Paravisini-Gebert, Lizabeth, and Margarite Fernandez-Olmos, eds. *Sacred Possessions: Vodoun, Santeria, Obeah, and the Caribbean*. New Brunswick, NJ: Rutgers University Press, 1997.

———. *Creole Religions of the Caribbean: An Introduction from Vodou and Santeria to Obeah and Espiritismo*. New York: New York University Press, 2003.

Park, Mungo. *Travels in the Interior Districts of Africa Performed under the Direction and Patronage of the African Association, in the Years 1795, 1796, and 1797*. 4th ed. London: Printed by W. Bulmer and Company, 1800.

Parry, Ellwood. *The Image of the Indian and the Black Man in American Art, 1590–1900*. New York: G. Braziller, 1974.

Paton, Diana. *No Bond but the Law: Punishment, Race, and Gender in Jamaican State Formation, 1780–1870*. Durham, NC: Duke University Press, 2004.

Patterson, Orlando. *Rituals of Blood: Consequences of Slavery in Two American Centuries*. Washington, DC: Civitas/CounterPoint, 1998.

———. *Slavery and Social Death*. Cambridge, MA: Harvard University Press, 1982.

———. *The Sociology of Slavery: An Analysis of the Origins, Development, and Structure of Negro Slave Society in Jamaica*. Rutherford, NJ: Fairleigh Dickinson University Press, 1969.

Patton, Sharon F. *African-American Art*. Oxford: Oxford University Press, 1998.

Paulson, Ronald. *Breaking and Remaking: Aesthetic Practice in England, 1700–1820*. New Brunswick: Rutgers University Press, 1989.

———. "Burke's Sublime and the Representation of Revolution." In *Culture and Politics from Puritanism to Enlightenment*, edited by Perez Zagorin, 241–69. Berkeley: University of California Press, 1980.

Pawlowicz, Peter H. "Reading Women: Text and Image in Eighteenth-Century England." In Bermingham and Brewer, *Consumption of Culture*, 42-53.

Peabody, Sue. *There Are No Slaves in France: The Political Culture of Race and Slavery in the Ancien Regime*. New York: Oxford University Press, 1996.

Perbi, Akosua Adoma. *A History of Indigenous Slavery in Ghana from the 15th to the 19th Century*. Accra, Ghana: Sub-Saharan Publishers, 2004.

Perinbam, B. Marie. *Family Identity and the State in the Bamako Kafu*. Boulder, CO: West View Press, 1998.

Phillips, Wendell. *The Constitution a Pro-Slavery Compact; or, Extracts from the Madison Papers*, 3rd ed. New York: Anti-Slavery Society, 1856.

Pietz, William. "Fetishism and Materialism: The Limits of Theory in Marx." In Apter and Pietz, *Fetishism as Cultural Discourse*, 119–51.

———. "The Problem of the Fetish, I." *Res* 9 (1985): 5–17.

———. "The Problem of the Fetish, II." *Res* 13 (1987): 23–45.

———. "The Problem of the Fetish, IIIa." *Res* 16 (1988): 105–23.

Pifagetta, P. *Report of the Kingdom of Congo and of the Surrounding Countries Drawn Out of the Writing of the Portuguese Duarte Lopez*. 1591. London: Frank Cass, 1970.

Pinckard, George. *Notes on the West Indies*. London: Printed for Longman, Hurst, Rees and Orme, 1806.

Plumb, J. H. *The Commercialization of Leisure in Eighteenth-Century England*. Reading, UK: University of Reading, 1973.

Pocock, J.G.A. *Virtue, Commerce, and History: Essays on Political Thought and History, Chiefly in the Eighteenth Century*. Cambridge: Cambridge University Press, 1985.

Pollitt, Ronald. "John Hawkins's Troublesome Voyages: Merchants, Bureaucrats, and the Origins of the Slave Trade." *Journal of British Studies* 12, no. 2 (1973): 26–40.

Popkin, Richard H. "Hume's Racism." In *The High Road to Pyrrhonism*, edited by Richard A. Watson and James E. Force, 251–66. San Diego: Austin Hill Press, 1980.

———. "Hume's Racism Reconsidered." In *The Third Force in Seventh-Century Thought*. Leiden: Brill, 1992. 64–75.

———. "The Philosophical Basis of Eighteenth-Century Racism." In *Racism in the Eighteenth Century*, edited by Harold E. Pagliaro, 245–62. Cleveland: Case Western Reserve University, 1973.

Porter, Roy. *English Society in the Eighteenth Century*. London: Allen Lane, 1982.

———. *Enlightenment: Britain and the Creation of the Modern World*. London: Allen Lane, 2000.

———. "The Enlightenment in England." In *The Enlightenment in National Context*, edited by Roy Porter and Mikulas Teich, 1–18. Cambridge: Cambridge University Press, 1981.

Potkay, Adam. *The Passion for Happiness: Samuel Johnson and David Hume*. Ithaca, NY: Cornell University Press, 2000.

Pratt, Mary Louise. *Imperial Eyes*. New York: Routledge, 1992.

Price, Richard. *First Time: The Historical Vision of an Afro-American People*. Baltimore: Johns Hopkins University Press, 1983.

Price, Richard, and Sally Price. *Stedman's Surinam: Life in an Eighteenth-Century Slave Society*. Baltimore: Johns Hopkins University Press, 1992.

———. *Two Evenings in Saramaka*. Chicago: Chicago University Press, 1991.

Prince, Mary. *The History of Mary Prince*. Edited by Sarah Salih. 1831. London: Penguin Books, 2001.

Prussin, Labelle. "An Introduction to Indigenous African Architecture." *Journal of the Society of Architectural Historians* 33, no. 3. (1974): 182–205.

Puckrein, Gary A. *Little England: Plantation Society and Anglo-Barbadian Politics, 1627–1700.* New York: New York University Press, 1984.

Quilley, Geoff, and Kay Dian Kriz, eds. *Economy of Colour: Visual Culture and the Atlantic World, 1660–1830.* Manchester: Manchester University Press, 2003.

Rafael, Vicente. *Contracting Colonialism: Translation and Christian Conversion in Tagalog Society under Spanish Rule.* Durham, NC: Duke University Press, 1988.

Ragatz, Lowell Joseph. *The Fall of the Planter Class in the British Caribbean, 1763–1833: A Study in Social and Economic History.* New York: Century Company, 1928.

Rediker, Marcus. *The Slave Ship: A Human History.* New York: Viking, 2007.

Reid, Ira De A. "The John Canoe Festival: A New World Africanism." *Phylon* 3, no. 4 (1942): 345–70.

Reilly, Kevin. "Race and Racism." In *Racism: A Global Reader,* edited by Kevin Reilly, Stephen Kaufman, and Angela Bodino, 119–41. Armonk, NY: M.E. Sharpe, 2003.

Reiss, Hans. Introduction to *Kant: Political Writings,* 2nd ed., edited by Hans Reiss, translated by H. B. Nisbet, 54–60. Cambridge: Cambridge University Press, 1991.

Richardson, Alan. "Romantic Voodoo: Obeah and British Culture, 1797–1807." *Studies in Romanticism* 32 (1993): 3–28.

Richardson, David. "Liverpool and the English Slave Trade." In *Transatlantic Slavery: Against Human Dignity,* edited by Anthony Tibbles, 70–76. London: HMSO, 1994.

Ricoeur, Paul. *Freud and Philosophy: An Essay on Interpretation.* Translated by Denis Savage. New Haven, CT: Yale University Press, 1970.

———. *The Symbolism of Evil.* Translated from the French by Emerson Buchanan. Boston: Beacon Press, 1969.

Roach, Joseph. *Cities of the Dead: Circum-Atlantic Performance.* New York: Columbia University Press, 1996.

———. "Deep Skin: Reconstructing Congo Square." In *African American Performance and Theater History: A Critical Reader,* edited by Harry J. Elam Jr. and David Krasner. Oxford: Oxford University Press, 2001.

Roberts, Bruce. *Plantation Homes of the James River.* Chapel Hill: University of North Carolina Press, 1990.

Ronnick, Michele Valerie. "Francis Williams: An Eighteenth-Century Tertium Quid." *Negro History Bulletin* 61 (April–June 1998). FindArticles.com. January 8, 2009. http://findarticles.com/p/articles/mi_m1157/is_2_61/ai_55411637, p. 2.

Rubert de Ventós, Xavier. *The Hispanic Labyrinth: Tradition and Modernity in the Colonization of the Americas.* New Brunswick, NJ: Transaction, 1991.

Said, Edward W. *Culture and Imperialism.* New York: Vintage, 1994.

Salih, Sarah. Introduction to *The History of Mary Prince.* 1831. London: Penguin Books, 2001. vii–xxxiv.

———. "Putting Down Rebellion: Witnessing the Body of the Condemned in Abolition-Era Narratives." In *Slavery and the Cultures of Abolition: Essays*

Marking the Bicentennial of the British Abolition Act of 1807, edited by Bryc-chan Carey and Peter J. Kitson, 87–109. Woodbridge, UK: D. S. Brewer, 2007.

Sancho, Ignatius. *Letters of the Late Ignatius Sancho, an African.* Edited by Vincent Carretta. 1782. New York: Penguin, 1998.

———. *New Light on the Life of Ignatius Sancho: Some Unpublished Letters.* Microform. Princeton, NJ: Photographic Services, Princeton University Library, 1989.

Sandiford, Keith A. *The Cultural Politics of Sugar: Caribbean Slavery and Narratives of Colonialism.* Cambridge: Cambridge University Press, 2000.

———. *Measuring the Moment: Strategies of Protest in Eighteenth-Century Afro-English Writing.* Selinsgrove, PA: Susquehanna University Press, 1988.

Scarborough, William Kauffman. *Masters of the Big House: Elite Slaveholders of the Mid-Nineteenth-Century South.* Baton Rouge: Louisiana State University Press, 2003.

Sartre, Jean-Paul. *Being and Nothingness.* Translated by Hazel E. Barnes. New York: Pocket Books, 1966.

Scarry, Elaine. *The Body in Pain: The Making and Unmaking of the World.* New York: Oxford University Press, 1985.

———. *On Beauty and Being Just.* Princeton, NJ: Princeton University Press, 1999.

Schama, Simon. *The Embarrassment of Riches*: *An Interpretation of Dutch Culture in the Golden Age.* New York: Knopf, 1987.

———. *Rembrandt's Eyes.* New York: Knopf, 2001.

———. *Rough Crossings: Britain, the Slaves and the American Revolution.* London: BBC, 2005.

Schaw, Janet. *Journal of a Lady of Quality: Being the Narrative of a Journey from Scotland to the West Indies, North Carolina, and Portugal in the Years 1774 to 1776.* New Haven, CT: Yale University Press, 1934.

Schiller, Friedrich. *On the Aesthetic Education of Man.* Edited and translated by Elizabeth M. Wilkinson and L. A. Willoughby. Oxford: Clarendon Press, 1967.

Schlereth, Thomas J. *The Cosmopolitan Ideal in Enlightenment Thought: Its Form and Function in the Ideas of Franklin, Hume, and Voltaire, 1694–1790.* Terre Haute, IN: University of Notre Dame Press, 1977.

Schuler, Monica. *Alas, Alas, Kongo: A Social History of Indentured African Immigration into Jamaica, 1841–1865.* Baltimore: Johns Hopkins University Press, 1980.

Scott, David. *Conscripts of Modernity: The Tragedy of Colonial Enlightenment.* Durham, NC: Duke University Press, 2004.

———. *Refashioning Futures: Criticism after Postcoloniality.* Princeton, NJ: Princeton University Press, 1999.

Scott, Michael. *Tom Cringle's Log.* Philadelphia: Carey and Hart, 1833.

Scott, Rebecca J. *Degrees of Freedom: Louisiana and Cuba after Slavery.* Cambridge, MA: Harvard University Press, 2005.

Searing, James F. "'No Kings, No Lords, No Slaves'": Ethnicity and Religion among the Sereer-Safén of Western Bawol." *Journal of African History* 43, no. 3 (2002): 407–29.

————. *West African Slavery and Atlantic Commerce: The Senegal River Valley, 1700–1860*. Cambridge: Cambridge University Press, 1993.

Seed, Patricia. *Ceremonies of Possession in Europe's Conquest of the New World, 1492–1640*. Cambridge: Cambridge University Press, 1995.

Segal, Charles. *Solo in the New Order*. Princeton, NJ: Princeton University Press, 1993.

Sekora, John. *Luxury: The Concept in Western Thought, Eden to Smollett*. Baltimore: Johns Hopkins University Press, 1977.

Shaffer, E. S. "'To Remind Us of China': William Beckford, Mental Traveler on the Grand Tour." In *Transports: Travel, Pleasure, and Imaginative Geography, 1600–1830*, edited by Chloe Chard and Helen Langdon, 207–42. London: Paul Mellon Center, 1996.

Shaftesbury [Anthony Ashley Cooper]. *Characteristics of Men, Manners, Opinions, Times*. Edited by Lawrence E. Klein. Cambridge: Cambridge University Press, 2000.

————. "Sensus Communis: An Essay on the Freedom of Wit and Humour in a Letter to a Friend." In Shaftesbury, *Characteristics of Men*, 29–69.

Sharpe, Jenny. *Ghosts of Slavery: A Literary Archaeology of Black Women's Lives*. Minneapolis: University of Minnesota Press, 2003.

Shyllon, F. O. *Black Britannia: A History of Blacks in Britain*. Chicago: Johnson Publishing, 1972.

————. *Black Slaves in Britain*. London: Oxford University Press, 1974.

Sidbury, James. *Becoming African in America: Race and Nation in the Early Black Atlantic*. Oxford: Oxford University Press, 2007.

Sloan, K., ed. *Discovering the Enlightenment*. London: British Museum Press, 2003.

Sloane, Sir Hans. *A Voyage to the Islands Madera, Barbados, Nieves, S. Christophers and Jamaica*. Vol. 1. London: Printed by B. M. for the author, 1707.

Smallwood, Stephanie. *Saltwater Slavery: A Middle Passage from Africa to America*. Cambridge, MA: Harvard University Press, 2007.

Smith, Adam. *An Inquiry into the Nature and Causes of the Wealth of Nations: A Selected Edition*, ed. Kathryn Sutherland. New York: Oxford University Press, 2008.

————. *The Theory of Moral Sentiments*. Edited by Knud Haakonssen. 1759. Cambridge: Cambridge University Press, 2002.

Smith, Mark M. *How Race Is Made: Slavery, Segregation, and the Senses*. Chapel Hill: University of North Carolina Press, 2006.

Snelgrave, William. *A New Account of Guinea and the Slave Trade*. London: Printed for James, John, and Paul Knapton, 1734.

Sobel, Mechal. *The World They Made Together*. Princeton, NJ: Princeton University Press, 1987.

Solkin, David H. *Painting for Money: The Visual Arts and the Public Sphere in Eighteenth-Century England*. New Haven, CT: Yale University Press, 1992.

Southern, Eileen. *The Music of Black Americans: A History*. 2nd ed. New York: W. W. Norton, 1983.

Spillers, Hortense J. "Mama's Baby, Papa's Maybe: An American Grammar Book." *Diacritics* 17, no. 2, special issue, Culture and Countermemory: The "American" Connection (1987): 64–81.

Spivak, Gayatri Chakravorty. Translator's preface to Derrida, *Of Grammatology,* translated by Gayatri Chakravorty Spivak, ix-lxxxvii. Baltimore: Johns Hopkins University Press, 1976.

Stallybrass, Peter, and Allon White. *The Politics and Poetics of Transgression.* Ithaca, NY: Cornell University Press, 1986.

Stanton, Lucia. *Free Some Day: The African-American Families of Monticello.* Monticello, VA: Thomas Jefferson Foundation, 2000.

Starobinski, Jean. *1789: The Emblems of Reason.* Translated by Barbara Bray. Charlottesville: University Press of Virginia, 1982.

Stauffer, John. *The Black Hearts of Men: Radical Abolitionists and the Transformation of Race.* Harvard University Press, 2002.

———. "Creating an Image in Black: The Power of Abolition Pictures." Paper presented at the Working Group on "Slavery in the Artistic, Literary, and Historical Imagination." Gilder Lehrman Center for the Study of Slavery, Resistance, and Abolition, Yale University, New Haven, Connecticut, February 2005.

Stedman, John Gabriel. *Narrative of a Five Years' Expedition against the Revolted Negroes of Surinam.* 1796. London: Folio Society, 1963.

———. *Narrative of a Five Years' Expedition against the Revolted Negroes of Surinam,* by John Gabriel Stedman. Edited by Richard Price and Sally Price. Baltimore: Johns Hopkins University Press, 1988.

Steiner, George. Introduction to *The Origin of German Tragic Drama,* by Walter Benjamin. Translated by John Osborne. London: Verso, 1998. 7–24.

Stewart, Dianne M. *Three Eyes for the Journey: African Dimensions of the Jamaican Religious Experience.* New York: Oxford University Press, 2005.

Stewart, Garrett. *The Look of Reading: Book, Painting, Text.* Chicago: University of Chicago Press, 2006.

Stewart, J. *View of the Past and Present State of the Island of Jamaica.* Edinburgh: Oliver & Boyd, 1823.

Stuckey, Sterling. *Going through the Storm: The Influence of African American Art in History.* New York: Oxford University Press, 1994.

———. *Slave Culture: Nationalist Theory and the Foundations of Black America.* Oxford: Oxford University Press, 1988.

Styles, John. *The Dress of the People: Everyday Fashion in Eighteenth-Century England.* New Haven, CT: Yale University Press, 2007.

Sugrue, Michael. "South Carolina College: The Education of an Antebellum Elite." PhD thesis, Department of History, Columbia University, 1992.

Summerson, John. *Architecture in Britain, 1530–1830.* New Haven, CT: Yale University Press, 1993.

Symes, Michael. "The English Taste in Gardening." In Ford, *Cambridge Cultural History,* 5:26–73.

Tallmadge, James, Jr.. "Speech of the Hon. James Tallmadge, of Duchess County, New York, in the House of Representatives of the United States, on Slavery." Internet Archive. http://www.archive.org/stream/speechofhonjames00tall/speech ofhonjames00tall_djvu.txt (accessed June 26, 2010).

Taussig, Michael T. *Shamanism, Colonialism, and the Wild Man: A Study in Terror and Healing.* Chicago: University of Chicago Press, 1980.

Taylor, Charles. "The Person." In Carrithers, Collins, and Lukes, *Category of the Person*, 257–81.

———. *A Secular Age*. Cambridge, MA: Harvard University Press, 2007.

———. *Sources of the Self: The Making of the Modern Identity*. Cambridge, MA: Harvard University Press, 1989.

Taylor, Diana. *The Archive and the Repertoire: Performing Cultural Memories in the Americas*. Durham, NC: Duke University Press, 2003.

Thomas, Hugh. *The Slave Trade: The Story of the Atlantic Slave Trade, 1440–1870*. New York: Simon and Schuster, 1997.

Thompson, E. P. "The Moral Economy of the English Crowd in the Eighteenth Century." *Past and Present* 50 (February 1971): 76–136.

Thompson, Richard Farris. "African Art in Motion." In *Art from Africa: Long Steps Never Broke a Back*, edited by Pamela McClusky, 17–60. Princeton, NJ: Princeton University Press, 2002.

———. *Faces of the Gods: Art and Atlas of Africa and the African Americans*. New York: Museum of African Art, 1983.

———. "Recapturing Heaven's Glamour: Afro-Caribbean Festivalizing Arts." In *Caribbean Festival Arts*, edited by John W. Nunley and Judith Bettelheim, 17–30. Seattle: University of Washington Press, 1988.

Thornton, John. *Africa and Africans in the Making of the Atlantic World, 1400–1680*, 2nd ed. Cambridge: Cambridge University Press, 1998.

———. "Africa: The Source." In *Captive Passage: The Transatlantic Slave Trade and the Making of the Americas*. Washington, DC: Smithsonian Institution Press, 2002.

Tibbles, Anthony, ed. *Transatlantic Slavery: Against Human Dignity*. London: HMSO, 1994.

Tise, Larry E. *Proslavery: A History of the Defense of Slavery in America, 1701–1840*. Athens: University of Georgia Press, 1987.

Tobin, Beth. "'And there raise yams': Slaves' Gardens in the Writings of West Indian Plantocrats." *Eighteenth-Century Life* 23, no. 23 (1999): 164–76.

———. *Picturing Imperial Power: Colonial Subjects in Eighteenth-Century British Painting*. Durham, NC: Duke University Press, 1999.

Todd, Janet. *Sensibility: An Introduction*. London: Methuen, 1986.

Trouillot, Michel-Rolph. "Anthropology and the Savage Slot: The Poetic and Politics of Otherness." In *Recapturing Anthropology*, edited by Richard Fox, 18–44. Santa Fe: School of American Research, 1991.

———. *Silencing the Past: Power and the Production of History*. Boston: Beacon Press, 1997.

Tucker, Josiah. *A Treatise Concerning Civil Government*. London: T. Cadell, 1781.

Turner, Mary. *Slaves and Missionaries: The Disintegration of Jamaican Slave Society, 1787–1834*. Kingston, Jamaica: University Press of the West Indies, 2000.

Van Dantzig, Albert. *Forts and Castles of Ghana*. Accra, Ghana: Sedco Publishing, 1980.

Vaughan, Alden T. *The Roots of American Racism: Essays on the Colonial Experience*. New York: Oxford University Press, 1995.

Villeneuve, René Claude Geoffroy de. *L'Afrique, ou histoire, moeurs, usages et coutumes des africains: le Sénégal*. Paris, 1814.

Vlach, John Michael. *The Afro-American Tradition in Decorative Arts*. Athens: University of Georgia Press, 1990.

———. *Back of the Big House: The Architecture of Plantation Slavery*. Chapel Hill: University of North Carolina Press, 1993.

———. *The Planter's Prospect: Privilege and Slavery in Plantation Paintings*. Chapel Hill: University of North Carolina Press, 2002.

Venturi, Franco. *Italy and the Enlightenment: Studies in a Cosmopolitan Century*. Edited by Stuart Woolf. Translated by Susan Corsi. New York: New York University Press, 1972.

Vickery, Amanda. *The Gentleman's Daughter: Women's Lives in Georgian England*. New Haven, CT: Yale University Press, 1998.

Wahrman, Dror. *The Making of the Modern Self: Identity and Culture in Eighteenth-Century England*. New Haven, CT: Yale University Press, 2007.

Walcott, Derek. *Collected Poems, 1948–1984*. New York: Farrar, Straus and Giroux, 1986.

———. "Forty Acres: A Poem for Barack Obama from Nobel winner Derek Walcott." Times Online. http://www.timesonline.co.uk/tol/news/world/us_and_americas/us_elections/article5088429.ece (accessed June 26, 2010).

Walvin, James. *Black and White: The Negro and English Society, 1555–1945*. London: Allen Lane, 1973.

———. *Black Ivory: A History of British Slavery*. London: HarperCollins, 1992.

———. *The Black Presence: A Documentary History of the Negro in England, 1555–1860*. London: Orbach and Chambers, 1971.

———. *England, Slaves, and Freedom, 1776–1838*. Houndmills, Basingstoke: Macmillan, 1986.

———. *Fruits of Empire: Exotic Produce and British Taste, 1660–1800*. Basingstoke, UK: Macmillan, 1997.

Warner, Michael B. "Staging Readers Reading." http://www.english.ucsb.edu/faculty/warner/courses/w00/engl30/StagingReaders.ecf.8.99.htm (accessed June 26, 2010).

Warner-Lewis, Maureen. *Central Africa in the Caribbean: Transcending Time, Transforming Cultures*. Kingston, Jamaica: University of the West Indies Press, 2002.

Warren, Anne. "The Building of Dodington Park." *Architectural History* 34 (1991): 171–95.

Waterhouse, Ellis. *Painting in Britain, 1530–1790*. New Haven, CT: Yale University Press, 1994.

Watkin, David. "Beckford, Soane, and Hope: The Psychology of the Collector." In Ostergard, *William Beckford*, 33–50.

Wheatley, Phillis. *Complete Writings*. Edited by Vincent Carretta. 1773. New York: Penguin, 2001.

Wheeler, Roxanne. *The Complexion of Race: Categories of Difference in -Century British Culture*. Philadelphia: University of Pennsylvania Press, 2000.

White, Deborah Gray. *Ar'n't I a Woman? Female Slaves in the Plantation South*. New York: W. W. Norton, 1999.

White, John, and Ralph Willett. *Slavery in the American South*. Harlow: Longmans, 1970.

White, Shane, and Graham White. *The Sounds of Slavery: Discovering African American History through Songs, Sermons, and Speech*. Boston: Beacon Press, 2006.

———. *Stylin': African American Expressive Culture from its Beginnings to the Zoot Suit*. Ithaca, NY: Cornell University Press, 1998.

Williams, Bernard. *Moral Luck*. Cambridge: Cambridge University Press, 1982.

Williams, Cynric. *A Tour through the Island of Jamaica*. London: Thomas Hurst, 1827.

Williams, Eric. *Capitalism and Slavery*. 1944. Chapel Hill: University of North Carolina Press, 1994.

Williams, Raymond. *The Country and the City*. New York: Oxford University Press, 1973.

———. "Forms of Fiction in 1848." In Baker, et al., *Literature, Politics, and Theory*, 1–16.

———. *Keywords*. Oxford: Oxford University Press, 1976.

Wilson, Kathleen. Introduction to *A New Imperial History: Culture, Identity, and Modernity in Britain and the Empire, 1660–1840*. Cambridge: Cambridge University Press, 2004.

———. *The Island Race: Englishness, Empire, and Gender in the Eighteenth Century*. London: Routledge, 2003.

———. *The Sense of the People: Politics, Culture, and Imperialism in England, 1715–1785*. Cambridge: Cambridge University Press, 1995.

Wish, Harvey. "Aristotle, Plato, and the Mason-Dixon Line." In *Race, Class, and Gender in Nineteenth-Century Culture*. Edited by Maryanne Cline Horowitz, 77–89. Rochester, NY: University of Rochester Press, 1991.

Wood, Marcus. *Blind Memory: Visual Representations of Slavery in England and America, 1780–1865*. Manchester: Manchester University Press, 2000.

———. *Slavery, Empathy, and Pornography*. Oxford: Oxford University Press, 2002.

Woodmansee, Martha. *The Author, Art, and the Market: Rereading the History of Aesthetics*. New York: Columbia University Press, 1994.

Wordsworth, William. "Preface to *Lyrical Ballads*." *Wordsworth and Coleridge: Lyrical Ballads and Other Poems*. Ware, Hertfordshire, Eng.: Wordsworth Editions, 2003.

Work Projects Administration. *Drums and Shadows: Survival Studies among the Georgia Coastal Negroes*. Athens: University of Georgia Press, 1940.

Wright, Josephine R. B., ed. *Ignatius Sancho: An Early African Composer in England: The Collected Editions of His Music in Facsimile*. New York: Garland, 1981.

Wright, Louis B. *The First Gentlemen of Virginia: Intellectual Qualities of the Early Colonial Ruling Class*. San Marino, CA: Huntington Library, 1940.

———. *Teach Me Dreams: The Search for Self in the Revolutionary Era*. Princeton, NJ: Princeton University Press, 2000.

Wright, Louis B., et al. "From Wilderness to Republic, 1607–1787." In *The Arts in America: The Colonial Period*. New York: Scribner's, 1966.

Wright, Richardson. *Revels in Jamaica, 1682–1838: Plays and Players of a Century.* New York: Dodd, Mead, 1937.

Wyatt-Brown, Bertram. *Honor and Violence in the Old South.* New York: Oxford University Press, 1986.

Wynter, Sylvia. "Jonkonnu in Jamaica: Towards the Interpretation of Folk Dances as Cultural Process." *Jamaica Journal* 4, no.2 (1970): 34–48.

Young, William the Second. *Observations Respecting the Conduct, the Accounts and the Claims of the Late Sir William Young.* London: W. Bulmer, 1793.

Index

Illustrations are indicated by italic page numbers.